NAPOLI
⋙⋙⋙ GUIDE TO ⋘⋘⋘
NAPLES

by

Bonnie Alberts, Barbara Zaragoza,
Penny Ewles-Bergeron and Erin Romano

DEDICATED TO NAPLES

NAPOLI UNPLUGGED GUIDE TO NAPLES

Dedicated to
La più bella città del mondo

An honest to God, living, breathing, working city, Naples is an ever evolving mosaic. Alive with colours, patterns and textures, it's a myriad of disparate pieces where ancient, old and new create surprising harmony from seemingly random chaos.

Hence the fascination. Hence the fear.

A fear, though while unfounded, nevertheless keeps tourists away. After all, with a reputation for being gritty, dirty, chaotic, overcrowded and dangerous, it's easy to look down your nose at Naples. Many Italians do. But ask a Neapolitan about his city and his face will light up with pride and he'll tell you that it is the most beautiful city in the world.

Rising up from the Tyrrhenian Sea, Naples boasts some of the most spectacular panoramas imaginable. A veritable feast for the eyes. The view towards the Bay and Vesuvius is unrivalled. But the view looking back at the city, that one will take your breath away. Like a field of wildflowers in the springtime, an intricate patchwork of every colour of the rainbow climbs along Naples terraced hills while its ancient alleys weave in and out, the threads that tie it together.

And it's in the alleys where Naples' true beauty lives. A city with precious little private space and so full of passion, it is literally bursting at the seams. Stores, markets and cafés spill out into the streets as cars and motos weave in and out of throngs of strolling pedestrians. Laundry flaps in the breeze and the smell of classic Neapolitan caffè and the sounds of a thousand conversations fill the air. Some might call it chaos but it is in fact, a perfectly choreographed ballet.

Wander down Naples streets for a while and you will find its rhythm and charm hidden between the chaotic notes - the loving embrace of two friends meeting on the street, tiny fingers finding comfort in the chiselled hand of their grandfather, fathers and sons, mothers and daughters working side by side, or four generations of family gathering in tiny apartments to share a Sunday meal.

Patrick Brydone said it best some two hundred plus years ago. "It is hard to say, whether the view is more pleasing from the singularity of many of the objects, or from the incredible variety of the whole." Naples is a mosaic. Each piece plays its part, and together it creates a beautiful harmony. And that is the fascination. That is Napoli.

TABLE OF CONTENTS

WELCOME TO NAPLES, ITALY
THE CITY, THE BAY... AND A BIT BEYOND!

The Bay of Naples holds within its curving arms the history and the legends of two thousand years. Few spots on earth awaken such absorbing interest. Not one surpasses it in beauty.

JOHN L. STODDARD, 1898

Surrender to the lure of the Greek sirens, journey to Hades along the river Styx, let Dante be your guide through Purgatory. Wander around gracious villas once inhabited by Roman emperors and see where gladiators lived, fought and died. Seek out Virgil's divine inspiration or visit the town where Pliny took his last breath, or find the rock upon which San Gennaro was beheaded. Traverse bubbling lava fields and ascend 1,000 metres above ground to the top of a live volcano; burrow far, far below into ancient catacombs and cisterns. Explore medieval castles haunted by the ghosts of kings and queens past. Witness miracles and devotion or the chiaroscuro of Caravaggio's Baroque and amble through royal parks and gardens, each more spectacular than the next. And then... have lunch!

From its humble beginnings as the city of the siren Parthenope - Naples was founded by the Greeks as early as the 8th century BC and is one of the oldest cities in the Western world - to as recently as the 19th century AD, colonisers and conquerors have vied for control. Operating as both blessing and curse, Naples' strategic position with its mild climate and abundance of natural resources branded it prime real estate worth fighting for. The battle scars from its tumultuous history and reminders of its former occupiers survive today in the urban fabric of the entire region, while the spirit of the Neapolitans remains, as ever, unwavering.

Just a few hundred years ago, Naples was the capital of the Kingdom of the Two Sicilies and one of the largest and most important cities in Europe, rivalling London and Paris. It was a centre for the arts and sciences and the musical capital of Europe, an obligatory stop on the Grand Tour. It was only after Italian unification that Naples spiralled into decline when most of its wealth disappeared into the coffers of the new Italian treasury. The Two Sicilies held more than four times the gold reserves and circulating currency of any other pre-unification Italian state, including the Papal one. The local economy collapsed and Neapolitans fled to foreign shores in vast numbers. Estimates are in the millions; the 1884 cholera epidemic wiped out even more of the population. The ensuing widespread poverty acted as an embossed invitation to the Camorra. They had had a stronghold in the region since the mid 18th century and by the end of the 19th century widespread corruption had latched onto the city like a grim parasite. Naples fared no better in the 20th century, becoming the most bombed city in Italy during WWII. Scars from that war haunt the city still.

Yet just 40 years later, the city was once again on an upward trajectory, driven in equal measure by economic, cultural and environmental initiatives and large scale projects to improve the city's ageing infrastructure. Naples' annual celebration of its cultural heritage, *Maggio dei Monumenti*, premiered in 1992 as *Napoli porte aperte* (Naples Open Doors) and the arrival of the G7 in 1994 sparked a sudden rush of cultural initiatives that heralded a cultural renaissance. It was Mimmo Paladino's *Salt Mountain* installation in Piazza Plebiscito in 1995 for the inauguration of the Art in Piazza programme that led the charge and within ten years Naples' Metro Art station project was in full swing and two major contemporary art museums had opened their doors in refurbished ancient *palazzi*. The last decade has seen the renovation and reopening of numerous churches and cultural sites thanks to both public initiatives and private endeavours.

Meanwhile, the construction of metro lines 1 and 6 that has been stop - start for decades is back on track; three stunning stations have opened since 2011 and the long awaited station at Piazza Municipio is expected to open in early 2015. More recently, the Mayor of Naples, Luigi de Magistris, has pushed a pro-environmental agenda that has not only cleaned up many of the trash problems that have plagued the city for years but has brought recycling, electric car and bike sharing, bike paths, limited traffic zones (ZTL's) and pedestrian zones to the forefront. Half the city's prime waterfront – the Lungomare - has been car-free since the first visit of the Americas Cup to Naples in 2012, yet another catalyst for change. Social media-savvy and forward thinking, the Mayor said:

> *I wanted these regattas very much because I felt that they have extraordinary potential as a means to show to the world the image of the Neapolitan Renaissance we are building, via television, the press, the Internet and social networks.*

ANSA, APRIL 14, 2012

For the mayor, and, of course, for so many in Naples, both the "livability" and the reputation of the city matter enormously. On the various search engines, typing in "Naples" no longer yields up only images of those difficult days when rubbish lined the streets. The positive is overtaking the negative. Though Naples, like the whole of southern Italy still tends to be less explored (not necessarily a bad thing in these authors' opinions), its future looks bright. Until recently, the mere mention of Naples, or the Mezzogiorno (the Italian South) for that matter, would send the would-be visitor running for the (northern) hills. Little by little however, the tourists are returning and the conversations in the media have gone from being about trash to being about treasures.

So... welcome to Naples, Italy, rich in culture and panoramic views, romantic, restless, invigorating and yes, every bit as chaotic, confusing and frustrating as you've heard. A thoroughly modern city wrapped up in ancient accommodations, Naples is a place of vast extremes where the past, present and future co-habit both in harmony and in radical, striking contrast. There is simply no other place like it on earth. And if you let it, it will steal your heart.

THE CITY OF NAPLES (COMUNE DI NAPOLI)

Population:	952,052 (2012)*
Area:	117.27 km²
Density:	8,118 people per km²**
Families:	377,487
Median Age:	41
Median Income:	€9,273 (Natl - €11,787)
Municipalities:	10
Quartieri:	30
Languages:	Italian and Neapolitan
Patron Saint:	San Gennaro (19 Sept)
Mayor:	Luigi de Magistris
Highest point:	470 metres
Green space:	5,239,600 m²

THE CAMPANIA REGION (REGIONE CAMPANIA)

Population:	5,769,750
Area:	13,589.90 km²
Density:	424 people per km²
Provinces:	5
Capital:	Napoli
Zone:	Italia Meridionale***
Coastline:	Stretches from the mouth of the Garigliano River to the Gulf of Policastro.

*Naples is the 3rd largest city in Italy after Rome and Milan; the population has been steadily decreasing since 2001 (1,004,500) and is 98.5% Italian.

**Naples is the 5th most densely populated city in Italy. Portici, which is in the Province of Naples is the most densely populated city in Italy (12,236.7 people per km²).

***The Italian South comprises 6 of Italy's 20 regions: Abruzzo, Basilicata, Calabria, Campania, Molise, Puglia

THE PROVINCES OF CAMPANIA

	Population	Area	Density
Avellino	428,523	2,791.64 km²	153.5 per km²
Benevento	137.753	2,070.63 km²	137.0 per km²
Caserta	908,784	2,639.38 km²	344.3 per km²
Napoli	3,055,339	1,170.78 km²	2,609.7 per km²
Salerno	1,093,453	4,917.47 km²	222.4 per km²

There are more than 90 comuni in the Province of Naples, among which is the Comune di Napoli – the City of Naples, which is both the capital of the Province of Naples and of the Campania Region.

GETTING ORIENTED

EMERGENCY NUMBERS

Ambulance	118
Carabinieri	112
City Police	113
Fire	115

EMBASSIES AND CONSULATES

AUSTRALIAN EMBASSY ROME
Via Antonio Bosio, 5, Rome
Open Mon - Fri 09.00 – 17.00
+ 39 06 852721
italy.embassy.gov.au/rome/home

BRITISH EMBASSY ROME
Via XX Settembre, 80/a, Rome
By appointment only
+39 06 42200001
gov.uk/government/world/organisations/
british-embassy-rome

CANADIAN EMBASSY ROME
Via Zara, 30, Rome
Open Mon - Fri 09.00 – 12.00
+39 06 854442911
canadainternational.gc.ca/italy-italie/
offices-bureaux/contact_consular-
contactez_consulaire.aspx?lang=eng

FRENCH CONSULATE GENERAL NAPLES
Via Crispi, 86, Naples
+39 081 598071
ambafrance-it.org/-Consulat-de-Naples-

GERMAN HONORARY CONSULATE NAPLES
Via Medina, 40, Naples
Open Mon – Fri 8.30 – 12.00
+39 081 2488511
consolongermanianapoli.it

SOUTH AFRICAN EMBASSY ROME
Via Tanaro, 14, Rome
Open Mon - Fri 08.30 – 12.00
+39 06 85254262
lnx.sudafrica.it/en/
page.html?Id=32

US CONSULATE GENERAL NAPLES
Piazza Della Repubblica, Naples
Walk-in service for emergency services Mon
- Fri 08.00 – 12.00. Non-emergency services
by appointment scheduled through the
website.
+39 081 5838111
naples.usconsulate.gov

TOURIST INFO POINTS

CASTEL NUOVO
Open Mon - Fri 09.00 – 17.30
+39 081 7957778

CAPODICHINO AIRPORT
Ground floor arrivals concourse
Open weekdays 09.00 – 19.00, weekend
09.00 – 17.00

CENTRAL TRAIN STATION
+39 081 268779

PIAZZA DEL GESÙ
Open Mon - Sat 09.00 – 17.00 & Sun 09.00
– 13.00
+39 081 5512701
inaples.it/eng/home.asp

PIAZZA DEI MARTIRI, 58
+39 081 4107211

PIAZZA DEL PLEBISCITO COLONNADE
Open Mon - Fri 09.00 – 18.00
+39 081 7956160

VIA SAN CARLO, 9
Open daily 09.00 - 17.00 & Sun 09.00 –
13.00
+39 081 402394

DISCOUNT CARDS

CAMPANIA ARTE CARD

Adults €21.00 - €43.00 - includes Campania's best museums, archaeological sites, castles and more. From 3 day passes to an annual card, there are several options to choose from. Available at any of the major venues on the circuit, the Campania>artecard information point at Naples Central Station, online or by phone +39 800600601 or from mobiles and abroad +39 063 9967650. Also available at the Viaggi Dusila travel agency in the Arrivals Concourse at the Capodichino Airport. campaniartecard.it

CAMPI FLEGREI COMBINED TICKET

Adults €4.00 - includes Flavian Amphitheatre, Cuma Archaeological Park, Baia Archaeological Park and Castle and the Archaeological Museum of Campi Flegrei. Ticket is valid for two days, and can be purchased at any of the participating locations.

CAPUA COMBINED TICKET

Adults €2.50 - includes Capua Amphitheatre, Gladiator Museum, Mithraeum, Archaeological Museum of Capua Antica. Available at either the Capua Amphitheatre or Archaeological Museum of Capua Antica.

POMPEII 5 SITES/3 DAYS TICKET

Adults €20.00 - includes Pompeii, Herculaneum, Stabia, Oplontis & Boscoreale (a saving of €7.50 on all 5 sites and of €2.00 if you are visiting just Pompeii and Herculaneum). Available at any of the participating locations.

POMPEII 3 SITES/1 DAY TICKET

Adults €5.50 - includes Stabia, Oplontis & Boscoreale. Available at any of the participating locations.

CLOSING DAYS

Unlike other Italian cities where closing days are often Mondays, museum and archaeological sites closing days vary widely in Naples and Campania. Check the listings carefully before setting off.

USEFUL WEBSITES

napoliunplugged.com - the website that inspired the book
enit.it - Italian Tourist Board
incampania.com - Campania Tourist Board
naples.it - Naples Tourist Board
comune.napoli.it - City of Naples official website

GETTING IN, OUT & AROUND

Planes, boats and trains; funiculars and buses; electric bikes and cars; and moving sidewalks and street elevators - Naples is a public transport mecca. Of course, explaining this rather complex set of moving parts is like trying to explain abstract art. Individually, the parts seem disconnected, yet somehow the compilation works. Despite that, Naples' transport system is extremely economical and it is easier to use and more reliable than ever before thanks to major initiatives in recent years that have expanded, improved and upgraded the network. A seemingly disparate conglomerate of bus, rail, sea and air transportation agencies, the system nevertheless moves millions of passengers in, out and around the city every year.

ARRIVALS & DEPARTURES

BY AIR

Naples' **Capodichino Airport** services nearly 3 million arrivals and the same number of departures a year. There are direct connections to 11 national and 49 international destinations including Spain, Greece, Germany, Hungary, Turkey, France and the UK. Meridiana runs a direct flight between Naples and New York's JFK a few times a week during the summer. An additional 50 charter routes transport passengers to destinations such as Cairo, Djerba, Ibiza, Monastir, Palma De Mallorca, Rhodes, Sharm el Sheikh, Tel Aviv and Tenerife. The airport is located just 6km north-east of the city centre. Ample short, medium, long term and valet parking is available at the airport, as well as car rental. The taxi rank is situated in front of the arrivals concourse and bus connections include the Naples Alibus Airport Shuttle to the city centre, the Curreri Viaggi bus to Sorrento and buses to Benevento, Caserta and Avellino. portal.gesac.it

BY RAIL

Trenitalia operates the national railway system and provides service to/from Naples on Regional, InterCity (IC) and the High-Speed Frecciarossa, Frecciargento and Frecciabianca trains. The main train station in Naples, Stazione Centrale, is located at Piazza Garibaldi. Travelling on high speed trains is not only super quick - 1 hour 10 minutes to Rome, 4 hours 15 minutes to Milan - and comfortable, but when purchased in advance, tickets on high-speed trains can be super economical as well. Book a few months in advance and you might find a ticket to Rome (€19.00) for less than the price of a 2 hour ride on an Intercity train (€24.50). Tickets to Milan can cost as little as €39.00. The website can be viewed and consulted in English. trenitalia.com

Italotreno by contrast is a private company formed by four businessmen to compete directly with Trenitalia's high-speed Freccia trains. The maiden voyages set off in April 2012 and today, Italotreno serves all of Italy's major cities - Naples, Rome, Florence, Bologna, Milan and Venice, as well as a number of smaller cities. Though the company was formed to compete with Trenitalia, prices are comparable depending on the specials either company is offering, so it is best to check both before booking. italotreno.it

❧ CONNECTIONS ☙

TAXI

Contrary to what you might have heard, Naples' taxis won't necessarily "take you for a ride"! Naples' taxis are clean, comfortable, well regulated and fairly economical. The Naples taxi tariff system offers both **meter rates** and **fixed tariffs**. All taxis are required to display the Tariff Card (in Italian and English) on the back of the front seat of the taxi to allow the rider to choose either a metered journey or fixed price. If you want a fixed tariff rate you **must inform the driver** of that before proceeding. Some of the 2014 published fixed tariff rates from the airport are: Chiaia - €23.00; Porto Molo Beverello - €19.00; Central Train Station and Centro Storico - €16.00.

Hailing taxis on the street is frowned upon, but there are more than 100 taxi ranks throughout the city. Find them at all major train stations, the airport, the passenger ports and at most major tourist attractions. Getting a taxi at a rank is also a good way of ensuring you are getting into an official taxi. Politely ignore other offers you receive, for example, while crossing the airport concourse on your way to the rank. You can also book a taxi by phone or online with several of Naples' taxi companies and some accept credit cards. Handy numbers: +39 081 202020 (Consortaxi), +39 081 8888 (Consorzio Taxi), +39 081 5564444 (Radio Taxi) and +39 081 0101 (Radio Taxi La Partenope).

ALIBUS AIRPORT SHUTTLE

The **Naples Alibus Airport Shuttle** connects passengers with the Naples Central Train Station and main passenger port, Porto Molo Beverello. The bus runs daily, every 20 to 30 minutes from 06.00 - midnight and stops only at the airport, train station and passenger port. anm.it/Upload/RES/PDF/LINEE/Alibus_2014.pdf

CAR HIRE

Most of the major European car hire companies have offices at the Capodichino Airport: AVIS, Dollar, Europcar, Hertz and Maggiore. However, if you've never driven in Italy, especially Naples, we suggest you reconsider. The heart of the city is riddled with limited traffic zones, one-way streets and a general lack of parking not to mention drive-free ecological days. Outside the city a car might be more practical but most tourist sites can be reached by public transport. But if you do decide to drive, here are a few simple things to keep in mind:

• Almost all rental cars in Italy have manual transmission. You have to know how to use a gear lever/drive a stick. If you do find an automatic, you pay almost double the regular daily rate.

- Insurance. Definitely and absolutely - accident coverage and theft.
- Petrol/Gas. It is very expensive. The current price per gallon is about 4.7 pounds sterling/6 dollars.
- Know the rules. The Carabinieri (Italian National Police) can pull you over at any time to check your documents. They do this by flagging you down with what English speakers (un)affectionately call a lollipop, a round red reflector on a 2 foot stick. If you get flagged down, pull over immediately and have your documentation (i.e. passport, rental agreement, licence and insurance) at the ready.

PROVINCIAL, REGIONAL, NATIONAL BUSES

CLP - Caserta urban buses: service within the Province of Caserta which includes connections between Caserta, Santa Maria Capua Vetere and Capua and national service to Foggia from Napoli, Benevento and Avellino. clpbus.it

Curreri Viaggi: service between Capodichino Airport and Sorrento (€10.00) with ten departures daily and stops at Castellammare, Pompeii and several other towns along the Sorrento coast. curreriviaggi.it

EAVCampania: operates service between Naples and the western suburbs (Campi Flegrei), eastern suburbs (Vesuvian) and on the island of Ischia. The Napoli - Vesuvius bus runs two morning departures to Vesuvius and two afternoon returns. eavcampania.it

Marino Autolinee: national and international routes including the Naples - Bari route. marinobus.it

Marozzi: direct service between Rome and Sorrento that continues on to Positano and beyond to Amalfi. marozzivt.it

Miccolis: service between Naples and Lecce with stops at Salerno, Potenza, Matera, Taranto, Brindisi and Lecce. miccolis-spa.it

Positano Shuttle: direct service from Naples Capodichino Airport, the Central Train Station and the Molo Beverello Port to Positano. positanoshuttle.com

La Reggia Shuttle Bus: service between Naples and La Reggia Designer Outlet Mall in Caserta. Departs daily at 09.30 and 15.30 from Piazza Municipio and returns at 14.00 and 19.30 from the mall (intermediate stops at Porto Molo Beverello and the Central Station in front of the Terminus Hotel). Adults €10.00 mcarthurglen. com/it/la-reggia-designer-outlet/en/plan-your-visit/getting-here/

SITASud: service in and between the southern regions of Puglia, Basilicata and Campania. Popular routes include: Sorrento - Positano - Amalfi; Amalfi - Maiori - Salerno; Amalfi - Scala- Ravello. sitasudtrasporti.it

REGIONAL RAILWAY/METRO LINES

Circumflegrea and Cumana lines connect the city centre to the western suburbs in the Phlegraean Fields. eavcampania.it

The five **Circumvesuviana** railway lines connect the city centre with the eastern suburbs around Mount Vesuvius. The **Naples - Sorrento** line stops at all the major Vesuvian archaeological sites: Herculaneum, Oplontis, Pompeii and Stabia and continues on to Sorrento. Though the trains may feel as old as the ancient ruins they transport you to and as crowded as a brothel in Pompeii, they are an economical means of transportation. Tickets from Naples range from €2.20 to Herculaneum to €4.10 for Sorrento. The Napoli - Sorrento train runs about every half hour during peak hours and the entire journey takes just a little over an hour. The Circumvesuviana station is easily reached from Naples Central Train Station, Stazione Centrale via an underground walkway. However, you will have better luck finding a seat if you get on at the start of the line at the Porta Nolana Station on Corso Garibaldi. The Supporto Bus Linee Circumvesuviana runs after hour buses between Naples and Sorrento. eavcampania.it

MetroCampania NordEst: service to Benevento, Piedimonte Matese and Giugliano Averso. eavcampania.it

SEA CONNECTIONS

Six million passengers and one million cruisers pass through the Naples port system every year. High speed hydrofoils (*aliscafi*) run in and out of Naples' Molo Beverello and Mergellina ports. The Porta di Massa and Pozzuoli ports service passenger and car ferries (*traghetti*). Destinations in the Bay of Naples include Sorrento, Procida, Capri and Ischia's Porto, Casamicciola and Forio ports. While there are no longer any direct connections between Naples and the ports in the Bay of Salerno (i.e. Positano and Amalfi), connections can be made via Capri and Sorrento (or Salerno). Other destinations include the Aeolian Islands of Lipari, Panarea, Salina, Stromboli and Vulcano; Catania and Palermo (Sicily); Cagliari (Sardinia). Routes, schedules and prices vary widely from carrier to carrier and season to season. The daily schedule can be found in the *Il Mattino* newspaper ilmattino.it/docs/parte.pdf Major carriers include:

Alilauro: services around the Gulf of Naples and to the Aeolian Islands. alilauro.it

Caremar: ferries around the Gulf of Naples from Naples and Pozzuoli. caremar.it

Gescab: services around the Gulf of Naples with connections to Positano and Seiano via Capri and Mini Amalfi Coast Cruises. gescab.it

Lucibello: Positano based ferry and private boat rental company with service between Positano and both Amalfi and Capri. lucibello.it

Medmar: ferry services to Ischia and Procida from Naples and Pozzuoli. medmar-group.it

Navigazione Libera del Golfo (NLG): services around the Amalfi Coast, connections to Castellammare di Stabia, Sorrento, Positano, Amalfi and Salerno from Capri. navlib.it

Siremar: services to the Aeolian Islands. siremar.it

SNAV: services to Ischia and Procida, Sorrento and Capri, the Aeolian Islands and Palermo. snav.it

Tirrenia: ferries to Palermo, Sicily and Cagliari, Sardinia. tirrenia.it

TravelMar: connects Salerno with the towns along the Amalfi Coast – Maiori, Minori, Almalfi and Positano. travelmar.it

TTTLines: ferries to Catania, Sicily. tttlines.it

Ustica Lines: service to Trapani, Favignana and Ustica. usticalines.it

LEFT LUGGAGE

Capodichino Airport at the Quick car parking lot (outside arrivals), open daily 24 hours a day. €5.00 per bag. +39 081 7896366

Central Station on the main level near Track 1. Open daily 07.00 - 20.00. Starting at €6.00 per bag, max weight 25 kg.

Molo Beverello Port in the parking lot in front of the Stazione Marittima. Open daily 06.00 - 21.00 €2.00 per bag.

Pompeii - left luggage is available at the Porta Marina and Amphitheatre gates and the Villa dei Misteri station.

TRAVELLING AROUND THE CITY

METRO

Intercity Metro Line M2 is operated by **Trenitalia** (trenitalia.it) and M1 and M6 are operated by **ANM** (anm.it) and are part of the Metro Art Stations project.

Metro Line 1 (M1) Piazza Dante ←→ Piscinola

Metro Line 2 (M2) Pozzuoli ←→ Napoli Gianturco

Metro Line 6 (M6) Fuorigrotta ←→ Mergellina

FUNICULAR

Four funicular lines - *i funiculari* - connect the city centre with the Vomero and Posillipo hill districts.

Centrale: Augusteo ←→ Corso Vittorio Emanuele ←→ Petraio ←→ Piazza Fuga (Vomero)

Chiaia: Parco Margherita ←→ Corso Vittorio Emanuele ←→ Palazzolo ←→ Cimarosa (Vomero)

Montesanto: Montesanto ←→ Corso Vittorio Emanuele ←→ Morghen (Vomero)

Mergellina: Mergellina ←→ Sant'Antonio ←→ S. Gioacchino ←→ Parco Angelina ←→ Manzoni (Posillipo)

NAPLES BUSES

Naples buses are an economical way to get around the city and are a fun way to sightsee. Operated by **ANM** (anm.it), their fleet of vehicles includes diesel, electric, cabled, methane and hybrid buses. Some of the more useful lines include:

#1 Tram: catch it just east of the Molo Beverello port for transport to the Porta Nolana Station (Porta Nolana Market and the Circumvesuviana), the Central Train Station and beyond to the Poggioreale Market.

151: connects the Central Train Station to Piazza Vittoria in Chiaia and beyond to Piazzale Tecchio in Fuorigrotta.

178: catch the 178 at Piazza Museo to go to the Capodimonte Museum.

R2: connects the Central Train Station at Piazza Garibaldi and Galleria Umberto at Piazza Trieste e Trento. If you stay on the bus at Galleria Umberto it will circle back around and stop in front of Castel Nuovo. From there it is a quick walk to the Molo Beverello Port.

C55: runs around the perimeter of Centro Storico. Catch it at the Metro Line 2 stop at Piazza Cavour or the Metro Line 1 stop at Museo or Piazza Bovio.

V1: catch it just outside the Chiaia or Montesanto funicular stations in the Vomero for transportation to Castel Sant'Elmo and the San Martino Charterhouse.

SCENIC BUS ROUTES

C16: from Mergellina, it runs along the length of Corso Vittorio Emanuele to Via Salvator Rosa.

C21: runs from Mergellina to Capo Posillipo along the über panoramic Via Petrarca with a stop at Parco Virgiliano a Posillipo (and the Posillipo Market).

C27: from Capo Posillipo to Piazza Amedeo, it takes you along the scenic Via Manzoni, Via Tasso and Corso Vittorio Emanuele.

140: from Piazza Municipio to Capo Posillipo; the scenic route is along Via Posillipo. Get off the bus at Via Santo Strato to reach Parco Virgiliano a Posillipo (and the Posillipo Market).

City Sightseeing Napoli: hop-on hop-off service 365 days a year. City Sightseeing Napoli operates three sightseeing bus routes: Line A, the art route around the Centro Storico with stops at the Archaeological Museum, Capodimonte and Madre; Line B, the Views of the Gulf along Via Posillipo and Via Petrarca and Line C, the San Martino route to Castel Sant'Elmo and the San Martino Charterhouse in the Vomero. Buses leave from the large parking lot in front of Castel Nuovo. Adults €22.00 napoli.city-sightseeing.it

ANM INFODRIN SYSTEM

Introduced in October 2012, the ANM Infodrin System provides real-time arrival times based on satellite tracking and the actual location of vehicles on the road. To use the Infodrin system, send a text message (SMS) with the 4 digit code of the bus stop (the 4 digit number shown on the yellow stripe at the top of the bus stop sign) to +39 339 9941326 or TIM clients can use 41326. Estimated arrival times will be sent via text messaging. Text messages sent to ANM are charged according to your carrier's rate plan; return messages from ANM are free.

STREET ELEVATORS

ANM (anm.it) maintains Naples' 3 street elevators that connect different levels of the city. The elevators are free and run weekdays 07.00 – 21.30, Sundays and Holidays 08.00 – 14.30.

Acton Elevator: connects Piazza del Plebiscito and Via Acton just a short walk from Molo Beverello.

Chiaia Elevator: connects Via Chiaia with Pizzofalcone hill. Find the elevator tucked inside the 17th-century Ponte (bridge) di Chiaia.

Rione Sanità Elevator: located inside the Ponte della Sanità (or Ponte Maddalena Cerasuolo) bridge, it connects Rione Sanità to the city.

❧ TICKETS & FARES ❧

The ticketing agency for Naples and the Campania region is the Unico Campania consortium - unicocampania.it. In general, all riders need a ticket to use public transportation within the city, the province and the region and there are no discounts for age except children under 6, who generally don't need a ticket.

Urbano Napoli tickets are required for travel within the City of Naples (Comune di Napoli). Urbano Napoli TIC type (integrated) tickets are valid on: all city (ANM) buses; the four funicular lines; regional buses, Metro Lines 1, 2 and 6, and the Circumvesuviana, Circumflegrei and Cumana lines within the confines of the city. (Agency issued, single transport mode tickets are also available) Urbano Napoli TIC type (integrated) tickets include:

> **Biglietto Orario** (hourly): €1.50 (valid for 90 minutes from the time the ticket is validated)

> **Biglietto Giornaliero** (daily): €4.50 (valid until midnight on the day the ticket is validated)

> **Biglietto Settimanale** (weekly): €15.80 (valid until midnight on the last day of the week of validity)

> **Abbonamento Mensile** (monthly): €42.00 (valid until midnight on the last day of the month of validity)

> **Annuale Ordinario** (annual): €294.00 (valid for 12 months from the first month of validity)

Unico Alibus tickets are required for travel via Naples Alibus. Tickets are €3.00 at an authorised agent, €4.00 if purchased on board the bus. Tickets are valid for 90 minutes from the time of validation. They CANNOT be used for a round trip on the Alibus but can be used on a combination trip (Alibus followed by any other mode of transport that normally would be valid with a Urbano Napoli TIC ticket, or vice versa).

TIC NA tickets are used for transport to/from Naples and the towns in the Province of Naples. These tickets are organised into 16 fare bands - NA1 through NA16 and tickets are available as a single journey, monthly and annual and require the same validation as Urbano Napoli TIC tickets. (Agency issued, single transport mode tickets are also available) The examples below are for single journey fares:

> **NA1**: Portici €2.00 (valid for 100 minutes)

> **NA2**: Pozzuoli and Herculaneum €2.50 (valid for 120 minutes)

> **NA3**: Pompeii €3.20 (valid for 140 minutes)

> **NA5**: Sorrento €4.50 (valid for 180 minutes)

TIC AC tickets are used for travel between towns in the Province of Naples without connecting with the city of Naples. These tickets are organised into 16 fare bands - AC1 through AC16. Tickets are available as a single journey, monthly and annual and require the same validation as Urbano Napoli TIC tickets. (Agency issued, single transport mode tickets are also available) The examples below are for single journey fares:

AC1: Sorrento to Piano di Sorrento €1.60

AC2: Sorrento to Castellammare di Stabia €2.20

AC3: Sorrento to Pompeii €2.80

AC4: Sorrento to Herculaneum €3.40

Hourly tickets **must** be validated in the electronic ticket machines on the buses or inside the train/metro stations prior to boarding. Daily, weekend daily and monthly tickets **must** be validated at first use and you must also fill out your name and date of birth on the back of the ticket and be able to provide identification on request. If a ticket machine is out of order you **must** validate your ticket by writing the day, month and hour on the back of the ticket in the space provided. If you do not do this and a ticket inspector checks your ticket, on the spot fines may be levied; being a foreign visitor to the city is unlikely to excuse you.

Hourly, daily, weekend and monthly tickets can be purchased at any tobacco shop (*tabaccheria*) and many newspaper stands. There are also ticket machines at many of the railway, metro and cable railway stations as well as at selected bus stops throughout the city. Monthly tickets can be purchased only between the last four days of the month preceding the month of validity and the first two days of the month of validity. They are available at most tobacco shops.

WHAT'S YOUR PASSION?

POP CULTURE & CURIOSITIES

- From the original king of pop culture... Andy Warhol's *Vesuvius* at Capodimonte. p. 119
- Cosplay your heroes at Comicon/Gamecon - Naples' annual pop-culture fan convention (Apr - May). comicon.it
- Body art at Tattoo Expo Napoli (May - June). tattooexponapoli.com
- Rock music legacy at the annual Mostra ROCK! exhibition at PAN Palazzo delle Arti (Jan - Feb). facebook.com/MostraRockNapoli

- Get on down with Disco Days (Apr – Oct). discodays.it
- Ride the rails - explore 150 years of Italy's train history at the National Railway Museum of Petrarsa, site of the Royal Workshop for Mechanical Works (1842). Italy's first railway, Naples-Portici, opened in 1839. museodipietrarsa.it
- Visit these film locations: 4 movies include scenes filmed at the Royal Palace of Caserta: *Star Wars Episode I and II, Mission Impossible III* and *Angels and Demons*. Naples has been the gritty or glorious setting for numerous Italian films, of course. *Gomorrah* brought Roberto Saviano's disturbing study of the Camorra to the screen. By way of radical contrast, John Turturro produced a love song for Naples and its music in *Passione*. Foreign film and television series with scenes filmed here include *Eat Pray Love* and a major episode of *The Sopranos*. Villa Volpicelli in Posillipo is home to the Italian soap opera *Un Posto al Sole*.
- Sleep under the stars in a smouldering lava field. solfatara.it
- Slumber at the top of a mysterious tower. latorrediro.com

LANGUAGE & LITERATURE

- Learn a language: Italian (and a bit of Neapolitan too) at Centro Italiano; Spanish at the Cervantes Institute; German at the Goethe Institute. centroitaliano.it or napoles.cervantes.es or goethe.de
- Scavenge for old books at Port'Alba. p. 61
- Join the English language book club at the Biblioteca Nazionale American Section. bnnonline.it/index.php?it/126/americana&pag=1
- Scrawl your wishes on a scrap of paper and leave them for Virgil in a tripod burner at his tomb. p. 190
- Meet a local author at Naples' best known bookstore La Feltrinelli. lafeltrinelli.it
- Visit the library of the oldest public university (1224) in the world. p. 75
- See ancient Papyri scrolls at Naples Biblioteca Nazionale. p. 44, 45

SPORTS & RECREATION

- Root for the home team... Napoli Serie A Football. sscnapoli.it
- Search for underwater treasures in the Bay of Naples... dive, snorkelling and glass bottom boat tours. napolidivingcenter.it or baiasommersa.it
- Kayak the Posillipo coast to discover its hidden coves and historic villas. kayaknapoli.com

- Compete in the Naples Marathon (Feb). napolimarathon.it
- Celebrate 2 wheels in Naples' Bike Festival (Sep). napolibikefestival.it
- Trek to Vesuvius on horseback. hostelnapoli.com
- Watch the spectacular midnight departure from Castel dell'Ovo of yachts competing in the Settimana dei Tre Golfi race (Jul). crvitalia.it

THE SACRED & PROFANE

- Witness the liquefaction of a saint's blood... San Gennaro or Santa Patrizia, take your pick. p. 99 and p. 70, 318
- Seek a favour from or cherish one of the Lost Souls of Purgatory, Anime Pezzentelle, at the Fontanelle Cemetery. p. 303, 304
- Behold the burning of a bell tower. p .105
- Join nature-minded Neapolitans at a Solstice or Equinox festival at the Temple of Apollo in Lago Averno. p. 216
- Contemplate the highly controversial work of Austrian artist Hermann Nitsch - warning, subject matter is extremely graphic. museonitsch.org

TOURS WORTH TAKING

- Capture cityscapes, seascapes, landscapes and breathtaking vistas on a Naples Photo Walk with Giorgio Cossu. walkandphoto.com
- Crawl through ancient aqueducts, raft along a tunnel, fly around a cistern on a zip-line on a spelunking tour of underground caves at the Bourbon Tunnel. p. 299
- Bask in the beauty of the Posillipo coastline on a Bateau Mouche coastal boat tour (May – Sep). alilauro.it
- Take a private, one-of-kind tour with Daniela. naplesprivatetours.com
- "Segway" your way through the streets of Napoli. segwayofnaples.com
- Get your "shop" on with a personalised bespoke shopping tour. discovernapolidestinations.com
- Go underground to see Naples' largest public museum of contemporary art. p. 306 - 307
- Explore Naples' parallel city. Napoli Sotteranea p. 294 and Napoli Sotteranea L.A.E.S p. 297
- Go behind the scenes at the San Carlo Opera House. teatrosancarlo.it
- Discover the many facets of Naples' Rione Sanità district. Join Carlo Leggiere for a stroll through the Sanità and peek at the Hellenistic Necrop-

olis of Neapolis or take the Holy Mile or Valley of the Dead tours with the Catacombs of Naples. celanapoli.it and catacombedinapoli.it

- Delve deep into Naples' cultural history during the city's month-long celebration Maggio dei Monumenti - May of the Monuments. It features hundreds of guided tours, special events and access to sites not normally open to the public.

MAY WE SUGGEST?

Eat gelato before dinner. Neapolitan meal hours and offerings might be very different from what you are accustomed to. It's all sweet treats and caffè for breakfast, a large meal around 2.00 p.m. and a light dinner - often a pizza around 9.00 or 10.00 at night. That makes late afternoon the best time for a gelato - winter, spring, summer and fall.

Take your caffè at the bar. Lingering at an outdoor table is the cosmopolitan way to take your caffè, but for about €2.00 less (a caffè at the bar goes for about €.90), not only is it much cheaper, but barista-watching is completely **free**. Do remember to leave them a €.10 or €.20 tip on the counter.

Pay it forward. Naples invented the charitable tradition known as *caffè sospeso* (pending coffee) - that is to pay for an extra coffee so that one could be served free to someone less fortunate. The tradition fell out of favour for a while, but it is making a comeback and inspiring others - even the Starbucks chain - to follow suit.

Remember your greetings and salutations. Salute the store owner, the bus driver, the waiter, the barista, the thin air! Not the hand to the head kind of salute, but a warm salutation - *buon giorno* (good day) until mid afternoon, *buona sera* (good evening) for the remainder of the day. Whenever entering someone's personal space, the use of *posso?* (may I?) is a respectful gesture and a simple *grazie* (thank you) will go a long way to endearing you to the locals.

Mind your manners. When travelling on public transport in Naples, it is expected that you will offer your seat to anyone who is elderly, pregnant or disabled.

Don't mind the queue. Neapolitans are notorious for gathering in a horde rather than lining up. Just when you think you're next in line, three people will step in front of you. Diminutive grandmas are perhaps the worst offenders; they give you friction burns as they pass under your arm. Don't take it to heart; it's not because you are a tourist. Either be patient or learn to be pushy.

Don't touch the produce. While you can (and you must) bag your own produce in the supermarket - don't try that at a market in Naples. Tell the grocer what you want (or point to it) and they will bag and weigh it for you.

Live like a local. For a more authentic experience, skip the hotel and try a B&B or holiday flat. Choose a small *trattoria* over a large restaurant and skip the chain stores and supermarkets in favour of the small local businesses and open air markets.

Dress to (un)impress. Though *la bella figura* is still alive and well, dress codes in Naples have relaxed a lot in the last decade or so. The once taboo sneakers/ trainers are now second in evidence only to the all-important boots and short shorts - especially jean cut-off shorts have become a staple - but they are worn in a style only a Neapolitan could pull off. Baseball caps, fanny packs/bumbags and jeans below the waist are rarely seen. If you want to blend in, save the beachwear for the islands, Sorrento and the Amalfi Coast and opt instead for jeans or trousers, polo shirts and comfortable walking shoes for those thousands of cobbles. Remember also, dress modestly if you will be visiting any churches. If you are in shorts or sleeveless/skimpy tee-shirts you might be asked to leave.

If you've got two good feet - use them. Naples is a walking city and there is no better way to see it than by foot. Having said that, however, there is a lot of ground to cover and Naples is a city of hills. Opt for public transportation whenever your feet can't go the distance. A UnicoNapoli daily ticket (€3.70) will get you around all day, anywhere in the city, be it by bus, metro, rail, or funicular.

Be cautious, NOT afraid. Naples is a city and all that that entails but it doesn't live up to the reputation with which it is plagued. Though petty theft and pick pocketing beset Naples - as they do Rome, Florence and other tourist destinations all over Europe, violent crime in Naples and Italy for that matter is almost unheard of. Use the same precautions you would in any other major city. Don't flaunt expensive watches or jewellery. A tip from insiders; carry a folded copy of an Italian newspaper, even if you don't plan to read it.

ONE FINAL NOTE...

Slow down and breathe in the culture. Naples wasn't built in a day and you surely won't see it in a day either (or a week, month, year or lifetime for that matter). Choose just a few key sites to visit during your stay and spend the rest of your time relaxing at local cafés, wandering the hidden streets and alleys, lingering over a long lunch, or taking in the sun and panoramas along the Lungomare.

RAMBLES

❧ THROUGH ❧

THE CITY

NAPLES

❧ BY THE ❧

NEIGHBOURHOOD

SEAT OF POWER
MUNICIPIO
AND
THE CITY
CENTRE

Cover Photo: Courtyard of Castel Nuovo
with Mimmo Paladino helmet

MUNICIPIO
AND
THE CITY CENTRE

TOLEDO

11

SANTA MARIA INCORONATA

VIA MEDINA

RUA CATALANA

VIA SAN GIACOMO

PALAZZO SAN GIACOMO

SPANISH QUARTER

VIA TOLEDO

2

3

AUGUSTEO

VIA SAN CARLO

4

GIARDINO ROMANTICO

9

10

VIA CHIAIA

7

8

6

5

RSITÀ

CORSO UMBERTO

VIA ALCIDE de GASPERI

VIA CRISTOFORO COLOMBO

VIA ACTON

PORTA di MASSA

STAZIONE MARITTIMA

BAY of NAPLES

Creative Cartography by Kelly Medford 2014

Surely the ghosts of sovereigns past keep watch over this area of the city, the **epicentre of Neapolitan power** and politics for more than 700 years.

The Angevins and Aragonese held court at Castel Nuovo. The Spanish, Bourbons and Austrians reigned supreme from Palazzo Reale. And today the mayor and his team administer city government from Palazzo San Giacomo. Not more than 500 metres separates these monumental civic edifices.

The streets are a bit wider and the piazzas somewhat larger in the Municipal centre of the city, which is also its cultural capital. Here Charles VII (III of Spain) built the San Carlo Theatre, setting the stage for Naples to become

the musical capital of Europe. Several of Naples' most important theatres are located in and around Piazza Municipio, including the historic 18th-century Teatro Mercadante.

Centuries before, Robert the Wise had filled his court with the intellects and artists of the day, chatting with Giotto while he toiled away on the Castel Nuovo's frescoes. In 1341 he put Petrarch through his paces in a 3-day formal oral examination a few days before his coronation as Poet Laureate in Rome. During the Belle Époque, that "beautiful era", Salone Margherita was the most famous café-chantant in Italy and Caffè Gambrinus opened the doors to the city's first literary coffee house. The Savoys turned over much of Palazzo Reale to a museum in 1919 and the philosopher and politician Benedetto Croce lobbied to have the Biblioteca Nazionale moved to the palace in 1922.

With its bustling civic life, rich café culture, grand architectural sweep and an abundance of shops and theatres, Municipio is one of the most dynamic and beautiful districts in Naples.

Piazza del Plebiscito

Plan Your Visit

Transport

METRO/RAILWAYS
M1: Dante & Toledo
M2 & Cumana: Montesanto
FUNICULAR: Montesanto & Centrale

BUSES
Naples Alibus Airport Shuttle, 140, 151, 154, R1, R2, R4, #1 Tram

ACTON ELEVATOR
Open weekdays 07.00 – 21.30, Sun 08.00 – 14.30; connects Piazza Plebiscito with Via Acton

Tourist Info

CAMPANIA ARTECARD
ArteCard 365, Napoli & Tutta la Regione

AZIENDA AUTONOMA DI SOGGIORNO CURA E TURISMO DI NAPOLI
Via San Carlo, 9
Open daily 09.00 - 17.00 & Sun 09.00 - 13.00
+39 081 402394
inaples.it

TOURIST INFO POINT AT CASTEL NUOVO
Via Vittorio Emanuele III
Open Mon - Fri 09.00 - 17.30
+39 081 7957778

OSSERVATORIO TURISTICO
Piazza del Plebiscito Colonnato S. Francesco di Paolo, 14
Open Mon - Fri 09.00 - 18.00
+39 081 7956160

Sights & Attractions

BIBLIOTECA NAZIONALE
Piazza del Plebiscito, 1
Open Mon - Fri 08.30 – 19.30, Sat 08.30 – 13.30 (last admission 13.00)
Free
Children under 16 must be accompanied by an adult. With the exception of laptops, notebooks, and pens/pencils, all personal belongings must be stowed in the lockers (free) near the entrance. Only residents of Campania can check out books, but you can peruse any of the library's materials in the reading rooms.
For tours contact the Public Relations Department by email bn-na.urp@beniculturali.it or call +39 081 781 9231
bnnonline.it

CASTEL NUOVO
Piazza Municipio
Open Mon - Sat 09.00 – 19.00 (ticket office closes at 18.00), Sun 09.00 - 14.00
Adults €5.00, free on Sun
+39 081 7955877
De Mura Library is open Mon – Fri 09.30 - 13.30
La Società Napoletana di Storia Patria is open Tues & Wed 10.00 – 18.00
storiapatrianapoli.it

GALLERIA DEL MARE
Piazzale Stazione Marittima
Open daily 10.00 - 21.00 (some shops open/close depending on when ships are in)
+39 081 551 4448
terminalnapoli.it

MEMUS
Piazza del Plebiscito, 1
Open Mon - Sat 09.00 - 17.00 **except Wed**
Sun 09.00 – 14.00
Adults €6.00
+39 081 404064
memus.squarespace.com

NAPOLI SOTTERANEA L.A.E.S.
Caffè Gambrinus at Piazza Trieste e Trento
Guided tours Thurs 21.00, Sat 10.00, 12.00
& 18.00, Sun and Holidays 10.00, 11.00,
12.00 & 18.00
Adults €10.00
+39 081 400256
lanapolisotterranea.it

PALAZZO REALE
Piazza del Plebiscito, 1
Open daily except Wed 09.00 – 19.00 (ticket
office closes 1 hour before)
Adults €4.00, including audio guide
There is also a QR Code guide available via
your mobile, both in English and Italian
+39 081 400547

PALAZZO ZEVALLOS STIGLIANO
Via Toledo, 185
Open Tues - Fri & Sun 10.00 - 18.00,
Saturday 10.00 - 20.00
Adults €4.00
+39 800 454229
gallerieditalia.com/en/palazzi/palazzo-
zevallos-stigliano

PORTO MOLO BEVERELLO
+39 081 5523968
porto.napoli.it

S. FRANCESCO DI PAOLA
Piazza del Plebiscito
Open daily 08.30 – 12.00 & 16.00 – 19.30
Free
+39 081 7645133
santuariopaola.it

S. MARIA DELL'INCORONATA
Via Medina, 19
Open Mon - Sat 09.30 - 14.30
Free

TEATRO SAN CARLO
Via San Carlo, 98
Guided Tours €6.00
Mon - Sat 10.30, 11.30, 12.30, 14.30, 15.30,
1630; Sun 10.30, 11.30 &12.30
Duration approximately 45 minutes,
includes the main hall, boxes, Royal Box &
2 foyers.
+39 081 7972111
teatrosancarlo.it

TOLEDO METRO ART STATION
Via Toledo
Open daily, according to the train schedule,
approximately 06.30 – 22.30
Metro ticket is required beyond the turnstiles
+39 081 7631111
anm.it

FERRIES TO THE ISLANDS

To savour the views, take a ferry instead of a hydrofoil, which are typically enclosed. It might take longer but you can sit or stand outside on most ferries and enjoy the sea air and the seascape. The ferries (*traghetti*) leave from Calata Porta Massa, just a few kms east of Beverello. Tickets can be purchased at Beverello or at the Calata Porta Massa port building. A free shuttle bus runs daily from 06.00 - midnight between the two ports.

APPROACH FROM THE SEA: PORTO MOLO BEVERELLO ⟨MAP 1⟩

From the middle of the bay, Sorrento behind us, Vesuvius at our right, Naples is alone now before our eyes, lying along the beach. How pure it is in its beauty, heightened by the green scarf of the Villa Nazionale [Villa Comunale] lying lightly across it! In its radiance it is smiling with a thousand dimples, playing with the foam that caresses it and with the branches that fan it.

ANDRÉ MAUREL, A FORTNIGHT IN NAPLES, ENGLISH EDITION 1921

In the days before planes, trains and automobiles, most visitors to Naples arrived by sea. If you get the chance to do this, you absolutely should. **This view is THE view.** And while it changes with the hour, the season, the centuries, it always shows visitors some version of its spectacular self and remains today one of the most beautiful vistas of the city you will ever see.

Porto Molo Beverello sits at the eastern end of Piazza Municipio in the centre of the city. From here, the *aliscafi*, high speed, foot passenger hydrofoils whisk eager voyagers away to Sorrento, Capri, Ischia and Procida and ultimately beyond

Port of Naples from the Sea

to Amalfi and Positano. Hard to imagine now, but this bustling tourist port was once lined with war ships from the U.S. Navy's Sixth Fleet and was known as Fleet Landing. Nearby, in Palazzo Reale, the Naples United Seamen's Service Club operated for more than 53 years, bringing a bit of Americana to sailors far from home.

These days Beverello is one of 29 commercial and passenger ports situated along the coast of the Province of Naples. Millions of passengers and vast quantities of cargo pass through the Port of Naples every year. Vast cruise ships dock at Molo Angioino, just behind Molo Beverello. They deposit passengers into Stazione Marittima, an early 20th-century terminal building whose 2011 remodelling included the addition of the **Galleria del Mare** shopping mall and a congress centre.

GATEWAY TO THE CITY: PIAZZA MUNICIPIO ⟨MAP 2⟩

From Porto Molo Beverello to the Castel Nuovo entrance on the northern side of the castle, you'll walk along a (temporary) ramp that straddles a huge chasm. Currently both construction site and archaeological excavation, you might not realise it at first, but this area is part of one of Naples' largest and most important squares, Piazza Municipio. Once known as Largo Castello, this half-kilometre long piazza extends from city hall - the early 19th-century Palazzo San Giacomo, all the way down to Porto Molo Beverello.

For years, construction of the Municipio Metro Station has obscured any sign of this piazza behind a haze of traffic, construction equipment and temporary barriers. Meanwhile the landmark buildings on the piazza's northern side have lost some of their cohesion – and their appeal - to the fray: they include the 20th-century Palazzo of the Bank of Italy, the 19th-century Art Nouveau Grand Hotel de Londres (now the Administrative Courts of the Campania Region) and the 18th-century Teatro Mercadante. The statue of Vittorio Emanuele II that once graced the centre of Piazza Municipio now stands at the centre of Piazza Borsa and the bust of Giuseppe Mazzini (a major player in the Unification of Italy) in front of Castel Nuovo remains concealed by a protective barrier.

At the same time, however, the metro project has brought to light some amazing archaeological finds, including the hulls of three Roman ships. (See a photographic display of them in the Armoury Hall in Castel Nuovo.) Many of these finds will be fused into the station's design, which at its completion will be a major transportation hub connecting Metro Lines 1 and 6 and the port to the metro. Other finds were installed at Neapolis Station. Eventually the piazza, we are promised, **will be a stunning new gateway to the city**, ushering pedestrians from the port to the city centre along a tree-lined archaeological path overlooking the ancient Port of Neapolis.

■ ■

EXPLORE SOME MORE

Just off Piazza Municipio on Via Medina is the 14th-century **Santa Maria dell'Incoronata** church built by Queen Joanna I to safeguard a precious fragment from Christ's Crown of Thorns.

■ ■

THE NEW CASTLE: CASTEL NUOVO ⟨MAP 3⟩

What's the first thing you do when you lose the Kingdom of Sicily to the Aragonese in the War of the Sicilian Vespers? **Hold on to the rest of your kingdom and your title as the King of Sicily, move your court from Palermo to Naples, hire a French architect and build yourself a brand new castle.** Charles I (Anjou) ordered its construction, which began in 1279, but unfortunately he died before he settled in. He called it the "New Castle", lest it be confused with the older castles, Castel Capuano and Castel dell'Ovo. Throughout the centuries, the castle underwent many renovations. Today it has a trapezoidal plan made up of tuff stone walls with five cylindrical towers.

The Angevins, for whom locals call the castle the Maschio Angioino, would rule until the mid 1400s. Castel Nuovo stands as a powerful reminder of the complex political forces at play that led to the transition of power from Angevin to Aragonese, and then to Spanish rule. The Triumphal Arch at the entrance to the castle was added in 1470 to commemorate the victory of Alfonso I (V of Aragon) (1442). To see Belisario Corenzio's 1630 fresco depicting his victorious entry into the city, visit the Palazzo Reale (Room IV).

Entering the castle courtyard you can't miss the Mimmo Paladino bronze helmet that is set over the entrance to the Municipal Museum. Of special interest are: Guillem Sagrera's 28 metre high star-shaped vaulted ceiling in the Barons' Hall; the ancient ruins and skeletons lurking below a glass floor in Armoury Hall; and the Giotto fragments in the Palatine Chapel. The castle offers two vantage points from which to see the city: the top of Beverello Tower and the large terrace overlooking the bay on the second floor of the Municipal Museum.

There are also two important archives preserved in Castel Nuovo. The **De Mura Library** houses some 4,000 volumes of the personal collection of the Neapolitan poet, journalist and writer of *canzoni napoletane* (Neapolitan songs), Ettore De

Castel Nuovo

Mura. By contrast the voluminous library maintained by **La Società Napoletana di Storia Patria**, the Neapolitan Society of National History, is one of the most important repositories of antique books and manuscripts, the majority relating to Naples and the Mezzogiorno, (southern Italy).

CROWNED HEADS OF NAPLES

To understand the history of Naples is to know that after the fall of the Roman Empire, the region had no national identity, but rather was occupied and owned by many external powers, including the Normans, the Swabians, the Angevins, the Aragonese, the Austrian Hapsburgs and the Bourbons, both Spanish and French. The two most notable influences on Naples' structure and architecture today continue to be Angevin and Bourbon. The Angevins ruled from roughly 1266 until 1442 and memorable monarchs include Charles II (of Naples); Robert the Wise - King of Naples and his wife Sancha of Majorca; Joanna I (of Naples) - Robert's granddaughter; Ladislaus - King of Naples; and his sister, Joanna II (of Naples).

Once Naples fell under Spanish control after the battle of Garigliano (1503), the city was ruled by a series of viceroys, regal representatives. Of these the most significant in terms of political reform and change to the physical appearance of Naples was Pedro Álvarez de Toledo who governed 1532–1552. Austrian Hapsburgs also ruled through their viceroys from 1714. The reign of the so-called Bourbons began with Charles VII of Naples to whom we owe much gratitude for his building projects, among which is the San Carlo Theatre. His son and successor ruled as Ferdinand the IV of Naples, the III of Sicily and as I of the Two Sicilies, his reigns interrupted by the short lived Parthenopean Republic (1799) and the Neapolitan War of 1815. The Bourbons remained in power until Naples united with Italy in 1861. Unification brought about the collapse of the Southern economy and about 4 million people emigrated from the Naples area between 1876 and 1913.

IRON & GLASS: GALLERIA UMBERTO I (MAP 4)

There's an arcade in Naples that they call the Galleria Umberto Primo. It's a cross between a railroad station and a church. Once this Galleria had a dome of glass, but the bombing of Naples shattered this skylight, and tinkling glass fell like cruel snow to the pavement. But life went on in the Galleria. In August 1944, it was the unofficial heart of Naples.

JOHN HORNE BURNS, THE GALLERY, 1947

Galleria Umberto I (1885 – 1892) is the title character in John Horne Burns' WWII novel, *The Gallery*. It emulated Giuseppe Mengoni's Galleria Vittorio Emanuele II in Milan (1863 – 1875) and was designed by Emanuele Rocco and Francesco Paolo Boubée as a covered passageway to connect the San Carlo Theatre to Via Toledo, ensuring wealthy theatre patrons would not be bothered by adverse weather conditions or undesirable street urchins. The gallery was a key element in Naples' Urban Renewal - the Risanamento di Napoli; its construction cleared away the urban decay that for centuries had infested the area known as Santa Brigida. A smaller version with three entries, the Galleria Principe, was also built during the Risanamento, near the Archaeological Museum.

■ ■

EXPLORE SOME MORE

Palazzo della Borghesia at Via San Carlo,16 was once the headquarters of the Belle Époque fashion and luxury goods department store chain, I Grandi Magazzini Mele. Owned by the Mele Brothers, Emiddio and Alfonso, their Paris-inspired stores operated from 1889 to 1932. They even opened their own post office in Galleria Umberto I to support the company's thriving mail order business. You can see a collection of 32 of their large scale advertising posters at Capodimonte Museum.

■ ■

Opposite page: Galleria Umberto I

The glass in the dome at the centre has long since been replaced and Galleria Umberto I is once again a bustling hub of Neapolitan life. This upmarket shopping centre, home to a posh art hotel and the Ascione Coral Museum and Showroom, is most definitely one of those places you just don't want to miss. It's a convenient place to grab a caffè or a bit of pastry - a Caffè Nocciola from Bar Brasiliano or a *sfogliatella* from Sfogliatella Mary – this is a people watcher's paradise. On any given day, you might catch a flashmob, a tango show or a group of rapping or break-dancing teenagers. During the holidays you'll find the Galleria decked out in its Christmas best, the centrepiece the Naples Giving Tree that has been erected here for the last thirty years.

Photographers love **the Galleria's glass and iron construction and its enigmatic details**; the gallery is always an eager model. See if you can spot the masonic symbology fused into the Galleria's skeleton (hint - look for the hexagrams in the semi-circular windows below the dome at each of the Galleria's four entrances). Below the Galleria is a hidden reminder of Belle Époque Naples, the Salone Margherita. This most famous of *cafés-chantants* in Italy was inspired by the Parisian models Les Folies Bergère and Le Moulin Rouge and hosted internationally renowned artists and variety acts.

RAGS TO RICHES: PIAZZA DEL PLEBISCITO ⟨MAP 5⟩

In the centre of the Piazza Plebiscite stands the great fountain opened by Humbert in 1885, which may be looked upon as the crowning monument of modern Naples. If the ghosts of past generations were to revisit their native town, they would surely pause before this simple marble basin. It marks the boundary between the night and the dawn of its history—between the days of epidemic and disease, of terrible and enforced squalor, of fetid water supply, and today, when the water of Naples can hold its own with the classic springs of Rome.

SYBIL FITZGERALD, NAPLES, 1904

Once upon a time, there was a huge fountain in the centre of this mammoth piazza, built in honour of the city's new water supply - the Serino aqueduct. The fountain is long gone, but from the centre of the piazza you can catch a glimpse of the glass and steel dome of Galleria Umberto I to one side, and Vesuvius towering over the bay to the other. In the evening golden hour (about one hour before dusk), the views of Vesuvius can be spectacular. In the morning, the vistas of Castel Sant'Elmo and the San Martino Charterhouse peering down from Vomero

Hill are equally as stunning.

After taking in the views, cross the piazza to Palazzo Reale, the Royal Palace of Naples. The palace was built by the Spanish Viceroys. Eight statues of eight rulers of Naples from eight different monarchies peer down at you from marble niches that were added to the palace by Umberto I (King of Italy) almost 300 years after the Spaniards laid the palace's first cornerstone. Find the centre of the Palazzo (hint - look for the huge arched centre portal with the iron gate) and 'turn yourself around'. Facing the Basilica of San Francesco di Paola on the other side, align yourself with the centre of the two bronze equestrian statues that sit in front of the church, Ferdinand IV (I of the Two Sicilies) to the left, his father Charles VII (III of Spain) on the right. Now close your eyes, and try your hand at a local game known as *passare bendati tra i due cavalli di Piazza Plebiscito* - walk between the two horses of Piazza Plebiscito blindfolded.

It's still very much in search of its own identity, this civic space. One might say: "so goes the piazza, so goes the city". **In a rags to riches and back again story, the area was once a modest fairground of the people and had the name Largo di Palazzo**. Claimed by the Spanish for their palace, the French and Bourbons who came after redesigned the piazza in their own image. Later, it took on the name Piazza del Plebiscito in honour of the 1860 plebiscite (vote) that annexed the Kingdom of the Two Sicilies to Sardinia, part of the process that led to the unification of the Kingdom of Italy in 1861.

The 1950s relegated the piazza to a bus depot, the 1960s to a car park, which remained until the G7 came to town in 1994. A year later, Mimmo Paladino's

Piazza del Plebiscito

enormous installation piece *Salt Mountain* was erected in the piazza, triggering a cultural renaissance that has been revitalising the city ever since. Today, Piazza Plebiscito is a pedestrian area, a pass-through and a playground - code for watch out for flying soccer balls - and it's a 25,000 square metre open air arena set between the city and the sea. In recent years it has hosted some of the city's biggest events, and has served as the stage for some of the best names in music – Elton John, Bruce Springsteen, Andrea Bocelli, Sting, and Pino Danielle, to name just a few.

NAPLES PANTHEON: SAN FRANCESCO DI PAOLA ‹MAP 6›

Though his debut and only performance at the San Carlo Theatre was panned, Enrico Caruso (1873-1921) - Errico in Neapolitan, was a hometown hero.

> *...he sang at New York's Metropolitan Opera no fewer than 607 times. His sudden death in his beloved Naples was marked by the entire city with 'the sorrow of hundreds of thousands of the dead man's fellow citizens... shared by millions all over the world', and with King Victor Emmanuel, granting the use of his royal basilica of San Francisco di Paola for the ceremony.*
> ABBY DAY (ED) RELIGION AND THE INDIVIDUAL: BELIEF, PRACTICE AND IDENTITY, 2008

The Bourbon ruler Ferdinand had a long and tumultuous reign over Naples and Sicily. This third son of Charles VII (III of Spain) was born in the Royal Palace of Naples and ruled on again and off again from 1759 to 1825, bearing a different title with each reign. While King of Naples, he bore the title Ferdinand IV and while King of Sicily, he reigned as Ferdinand III. In 1816 he returned to the throne as Ferdinand I, King of the Two Sicilies. In gratitude for his reinstatement as King, Ferdinand erected this larger-than-life ex-voto, the Basilica of San Francesco di Paola, dedicated to the saint of the same name. His offering must have worked, because he remained King until his death in 1825 at the ripe old age of 73.

This is Naples' own version of the Roman Pantheon - without the crowds. San Francesco di Paola was completed in 1824 and inaugurated by Pope Gregory XVI in 1836. The work of Swiss architect Pietro Bianchi, it sits at the centre of a hemicycle of 38 Doric columns commissioned by Napoleon's brother-in-law, Joachim Murat some years earlier. This is a rare example of the Neo-Classical style in Naples, the basilica's pristine and unembellished interior being a welcome contrast to the highly 'Baroquised' churches typically seen in the city. The only exception to this perhaps, is the ornate polychrome altar that was the work of Ferdinando Fuga (1751) and moved to San Francesco di Paola from the church of Santi Apostoli.

The circular church is topped by a 53 metre-high coffered dome with an ocular centre. Its weight is supported by 34 corinthian columns faced in Mondragone marble, a particular type of marble mined in the Campania region that was also used in Palazzo Reale, Teatro San Carlo, Capodimonte and Caserta Royal Palace.

THREE REIGNS UNDER ONE ROOF: PALAZZO REALE (MAP 7)

As a stark contrast to the royal digs of the Angevins and Aragonese just down the street at Castel Nuovo, **the Royal Palace of Naples, Palazzo Reale, touts all of the glitz and glitter befitting a monarchy, or even three**. This is a labyrinth of public and private chambers, adorned in the most opulent furnishings, paintings, tapestries and decorative art objects of the day. It's a veritable who's-who and what's-what of Baroque, Neo-Classical and Neapolitan arts and architecture.

The first iteration of the palace we owe to the Spaniards, who built it to host King Philip III of Spain. They were unceremoniously stood up by the King, but the palace built by Domenico Fontana in 1600 remained, serving as the Royal residence of the monarchies who followed. Much of the palace's current design and decor is owed to Bourbon renovations; their first monarch, Charles VII (III of Spain), added the San Carlo Theatre in 1737 at the back of the palace.

After the Unification of Italy, Naples lost its status as a capital city, and the palace became redundant. The Savoy Kings, whose heir to the throne bore the title of Prince of Naples, used the palace from time to time for official events. In 1919, the *piano nobile* was converted into a museum, the 30-room Appartamento Storico, Historic Apartment. Just a few years later the Savoys gave over an entire wing to the National library, the Biblioteca Nazionale Vittorio Emanuele III.

Entrance to the Historic Apartment is via Francesco Antonio Picchiatti's Monumental Staircase, the Scalone d'Onore (1651). Of special interest are: the whimsical Court Theatre with its 12 papier-mâché and plaster statues - Apollo, Mercury, Minerva and the nine muses; Belisario Corenzio's ceiling fresco in the 2nd Antechamber depicting Alfonso I's (V of Aragon) victorious entry into the city; Vincenzo Camuccini 's Portrait of Ferdinand IV (I of the Two Sicilies) portraying the King pointing out of the window of the throne room to his ex-voto, San Francesco di Paola, across the piazza; Christopher Columbus discovering the new world - one of the 14 ceiling panels of *The Magnificence of the House of Spain* in Ambassadors' Hall; two restored works by the female Baroque painter Artemisia Gentileschi: *San Gennaro in the Pozzuoli Amphitheatre* (1636-37) and *Saints Procolus and Nicea* (1635-37) in the Queen's Room; one of two revolving lecterns made for Queen Maria Caroline (the other is in Biblioteca Nazionale).

An upstairs roof garden is currently closed to the public while it undergoes a 35-million euro renovation. The Giardino Romantico on the ground level boasts

FINDING MIMMO PALADINO IN NAPLES

Mimmo Paladino is one of Italy's most prolific and imaginative contemporary artists, a sculptor, print and film-maker, photographer, painter and theatre designer. Born in 1948 in Paduli, near Benevento, his talent was encouraged by an uncle who was an artist. Mimmo enrolled at his local art school, graduating in 1968 and in that same year saw two gallery exhibitions of his work in Portici and Caserta.

His focus at the time was on drawing and photography as routes into exploring the ancient Mediterranean world of Etruscan, Egyptian, classical and religious imagery. Little by little his own rich eclectic language of images formed and while throughout his life Paladino has remained open to new impressions and ideas, his personal iconography is manifest in every piece of art he produces. This is so much the case that if you see a modern Italian drawing or sculpture that includes a mask-like helmet, (as at Castel Sant'Elmo or Castel Nuovo), a sword or horse (see his mosaic near the elevator doors at Castel dell'Ovo), or a figure studded with birds, Paladino will come to mind. In addition his sculptures often have worked surfaces that suggest the effects of ageing, inviting the viewer to invest them with a sacred, mythic or antique quality.

In 1980 he was invited by Achille Bonito Oliva to exhibit at the Venice Biennale, along with artists Francesco Clemente, Enzo Cucchi, Sandro Chia and Nicola de Maria. This assembly of work is acknowledged as the beginning of the Transavanguardia movement, marking a return to figurative painting after recent experiments in conceptualism and minimalism. Paladino's participation in the Biennale led to his inclusion in important exhibitions at the Royal Academy and Tate Gallery in London and MOMA in New York. Such successes, coupled with an increasing self-assurance in employing his language of forms and colours, allowed him to gravitate towards ever larger scale public works. Theatre designs and large sculptural installations cross-pollinate each other so that Paladino's ideas travel between the visual and dramatic arts.

Today his projects embellish public spaces, theatres and churches in many parts of Italy while his work is included in many collections world-wide. Meanwhile the myths he explores have broadened to include Pinocchio and Don Quijote. There are visual connections between Paladino's art and that of two British-based artists, Anish Kapoor and Anthony Gormley. La Montagna di Sale, Mountain of Salt, a vast hill of salt sealed with resin in which horses seem to be sinking, is on the large scale of public works by Kapoor, while Gormley's metal casts of his own body arranged in buildings, public spaces and landscapes, inhabit the same mythic atmosphere evoked by Paladino.

La Montagna di Sale was first installed in Gibellina in 1990, then in Piazza del Plebiscito in Naples in 1995. The mound of salt seemed to echo the shape of the volcano well in view from the square. The concept was revived in Milan in 2011 to celebrate the 150th anniversary of the Unification of Italy. Though these installations were temporary, it's still possible to see a smaller version of Paladino's mountain in a courtyard of the Palazzo Reale. Here the horses have been immersed not in salt but in concrete but the effect is still striking, their heads raised as if surveying the ramparts of some ancient city – Troy? This inspired structure caps the new practice room of the San Carlo opera company.

Where else can you find Mimmo in Naples? Apart from those instances cited above, his work is integral to the Salvator Rosa metro station and the colourful walls of several buildings in the Materdei district of the city. Naples, an ancient city itself, has embraced the modern not just in Mimmo Paladino but in numerous other contemporary artists, recognising their shared profound roots in Mediterranean culture.

Mimmo Paladino's Horses at Palazzo Reale

beautiful views of Castel Nuovo and is home to Mimmo Paladino's controversial work, a series of large stone horses that were erected above the San Carlo Theatre's practice room, the Prova d'Orchestra. The east door of the San Carlo Theatre's grand lobby also leads to the garden.

HISTORY OF THE PRINTED WORD: BIBLIOTECA NAZIONALE VITTORIO EMANUELE III ⟨MAP 8⟩

There was a time when an olfactory sensation went hand in hand with the visual pleasure of reading. Yes, books and libraries had smells, whether of paper or of leather, that cannot be replicated in the online world.

A free tour of the National Library in Naples, the **Biblioteca Nazionale**, is a trek back into the past. It's a walk through high ceilinged hallways and past rooms bursting with materials collected to preserve the art, history and culture of Italy. Here in room after room is **an extraordinary collection that is nearly as old as the printed word**. Treasures include an original handwritten book by St. Thomas Aquinas (who spent time in Naples), a 5th-century AD manuscript on purple vellum with fragments of the Gospels by Luke and Mark, a 6th-century AD Greek manuscript on pharmacology and the precious collection of 1,800 **Papyri scrolls from Herculaneum**, not to mention more than 1.8 million printed volumes, 19,000 manuscripts, over 8,300 periodicals and more than 4,500 incunabula (books printed before 1501).

This is the 3rd largest library in Italy; its humble beginnings come from the Farnese collection. Charles VII (III of Spain) moved the collection to the Meridiana room at Capodimonte in 1750 and his son Ferdinand IV (I of the Two Sicilies) moved it to the Palazzo degli Studi, now the Archaeological Museum. When the Jesuits were expelled from the reign, their library was absorbed and thus began a centuries-long tradition of growth through acquisitions from dissolved religious orders, defunct institutions and donations from private collections.

There were so many acquisitions in the 1800s that by the turn of the century the library had outgrown its space at Palazzo degli Studi. Thanks to the tireless efforts of Benedetto Croce, it was moved to Palazzo Reale in 1922.

If you make an appointment, the library most hospitably offers free tours. They will take you through a number of these collections, or you can request a tour of a specific collection: the Brancaccio collection - over 50,000 volumes collected by Cardinal Francesco Maria Brancaccio, the collection of the marquis Taccone, the musical and furniture collection of Count Lucchesi Palli, the volumes of German works collected by that avid reader, Queen Maria Caroline with another of her revolving lecterns on display, the Neapolitan collection and the rare manuscripts, just to name a few.

The library also has an American section formed from 5,000 volumes donated by the United States Information Service of the American Consulate in 1963. The American Section - J.F. Kennedy was instituted with the "aim of spreading the knowledge of America in postwar Italy." It was inaugurated in June, 1964 and its holdings include English language works relating to American history, civics, literature and art, as well as magazines from the 1950s through the 1980s (*Time*, *Life*, *Newsweek*).

While the vast majority of the library's holdings belong to the past, the library has its eyes towards the future, as a contributing member of the Google project, dubbed the "digital renaissance". This partnership between Google and the Italian Ministry of Cultural Heritage foresees the digitalisation of some 1 million out-of-copyright books from Italian libraries. In the maze of back rooms, like Santa's elves, young employees hired specifically for the task are filling carts with tons of books destined for digitalisation.

THE PAPYRUS SCROLLS

The same eruption which destroyed Pompeii in 79 AD also destroyed Herculaneum, but there, extremely hot ash travelling at high speed turned a private library into charcoal, paradoxically preserving it. The documents were found in a gigantic luxurious villa, called "the villa of the papyri," which may have belonged to Julius Caesar's father-in-law and which served as the model for the Getty Villa in Los Angeles. (Papyrus, made from an Egyptian reed-like plant served as paper in the ancient world, and scrolls made from it were used as books.) A monk named Antonio Piaggio developed a machine which unrolled many of the rolls at a snail's pace, but left them intact and legible. Work on the papyri has accelerated with the introduction of electric light, microscopes and most recently, infrared photography, which allows scholars to read even faded and damaged papyri.

The vast majority of the papyri contain philosophical texts from the Epicurean school, most of them by a relatively unknown philosopher named Philodemus of Gadara. But other texts were written by Epicurus himself and by Chrysippus, an extremely important, early Stoic philosopher. There are even some papyri in Latin, including an epic poem about the victory of Augustus over Mark Antony. So far, none of the texts in the Herculaneum library is known from other sources: this makes the library extremely important for scholars of antiquity. But beyond their interest for philosophers, several Roman poets, including Virgil, studied Epicurean philosophy in Naples. One text, a treatise on ethics, is even dedicated to Virgil and some of his friends and co-students.

A THEATRE BUILT FOR A KING: TEATRO SAN CARLO ⟨MAP 9⟩

A performance at Teatro San Carlo is **absolutely magical**. The first opera house of its kind (1737) in Europe, the San Carlo was built 41 years before La Scala, Milan. Its design was the model which many, and if you ask a Neapolitan, all other opera houses would emulate. When you step into its hallowed halls, you'll be transported to a bygone era - a time when women donned furs to go to the theatre, opera reigned supreme, and Naples was the musical capital of Europe, if not the world.

With pitch-perfect acoustics, this royal opera house was the venue of the masters, the dream of the hopefuls, and only the *crème de la crème* graced its stage: Rossini, Verdi, Bellini, Händel and Haydn, Cimarosa and Paisiello. Even Mozart, who played here at the age of 14, couldn't secure a permanent position. A few centuries later, Enrico Caruso's performance at the San Carlo met with a chilly reception and he never returned (though a monumental sculpture was erected at the theatre in his honour).

Teatro San Carlo

A veritable institution, the San Carlo has been a Neapolitan fixture for nearly 300 years, giving life to the Neapolitan School of opera and to four music conservatories. Like the city itself, the opera house has experienced its own peaks and valleys. After a two-year, 76-million euro renovation in 2009, the San Carlo seems poised to reclaim its title as one of the most important opera houses in the world.

Before the house lights dim, take a moment to breathe in the theatre's ambiance. Built for a king - Bourbon Charles VII (III of Spain) - nearly 300 hundred theatre boxes climb six storeys above the main floor. They wrap left to right around the theatre's horseshoe design with the three-storey royal box commanding centre stage rear. Each box is adorned with a large mirror; opinion is divided as to why. Some say these alllowed the king to see who was in the theatre, especially the young ladies, though some contend it was entirely the other way around.

The theatre's sumptuous red and gold decor was formerly the colours of the Bourbon Monarchy - blue, silver and gold - and was changed only after a severe fire in 1816. Upon the frescoed ceiling Apollo, God of music, presents the greatest poets of the world to Minerva, Goddess of wisdom and sponsor of the arts in a painting that was also part of the restoration following the fire. Verdi's orchestra pit was added in the 1870s, the theatre got electricity in 1890 and air-conditioning was finally installed during the most recent renovation in 2009.

Today, the San Carlo boasts its own orchestra, ballet company, choir and children's choir. Tuscan-born Maestro Nicola Luisotti has served as the musical director since 2012. He is also the musical director of the San Francisco Opera. In October 2013, the orchestras and choruses of both houses were united at the War Memorial Opera House in San Francisco to perform Giuseppe Verdi's *Messa da Requiem* as part of the Year of Italian Culture in the US and the Unite the Two Bays initiative.

EXPLORE SOME MORE

If your visit to Naples doesn't happen to coincide with a performance at the San Carlo, make sure to take a guided tour of the theatre. Über fans should visit **MeMus**, the Museum and Historical Archives of the San Carlo Theatre. This opened in 2011 next to the opera house; the museum uses state-of-the-art exhibition methods such as interactive touch screens, 3D video and iPads to preserve and promote the history of the San Carlo Theatre.

CULTURAL CAROUSEL: PIAZZA TRIESTE E TRENTO ‹MAP 10›

To the casual observer, Piazza Plebiscito would seem to be fused onto the southern end of Via Toledo. There is, however, a piazza between the two, Piazza Trieste e Trento. The fountain in the centre of the piazza should be a dead give-away, but because it's a roundabout for screeching buses, cars and motos rather than a centrepiece, you might not notice it at first.

The fountain is a relatively new addition to a centuries-old piazza. If you know a little Italian and look closely at the fountain, you might be able to guess its name. It's the **Fontana del Carciofo or Carcioffola** as it is affectionately known, the Artichoke Fountain. Donated by Naples' famed Mayor Achille Lauro in the 1950s, it is said to be based on the 17th-century fountain of the same name located between the Pitti Palace and the Amphitheatre of the Boboli Gardens in Florence.

As for the piazza itself, **it was known as Piazza San Ferdinando (and to many it still is) until the Savoys changed its name in the early 20th century**. Its new name refers to the annexation of two Austrian cities to Italy: Trieste and Trento, following the WWI Battle of Piave River (1918).

The famed *café-chantant* and literary café, Caffè Gambrinus, resides on the ground floor of Palazzo della Prefettura on the southwest corner of Piazza Trieste e Trento. It is a Neapolitan landmark and enduring reminder of the Belle Époque. The **Napoli Sotteranea L.A.E.S Tour** departs from in front of Caffè Gambrinus.

At the northeast corner of the piazza is the 17th-century San Ferdinando Church. Lucia Migliaccio, the Duchess of Floridia and second wife of Ferdinand IV (I of the Two Sicilies) is buried here. Her funeral monument, the work of Tito Angelini, has a beautiful relief sculpture on the front, which makes a peek inside this church more than worthwhile. Her tomb sits inconspicuously enough in the left transept, just a few steps away from Domenico Vaccaro's major altar. The Duchess' estate on Vomero hill, Villa Floridiana, is home to the Duca di Martina Ceramics Museum.

A ROAD BY ANY OTHER NAME: VIA TOLEDO ‹MAP 11›

It's only 1.2 kms long, stem to stern, but along the way you'll find more than enough retail therapy to while away an afternoon, plenty of sights to savour and a ton of tasty treats to tantalise your tastebuds. At the southern end of Via Toledo find Caravaggio's final work, the *Martyrdom of Saint Ursula* at Banca Commerciale Italiana's Galleria d'Italia in the 17th-century **Palazzo Zevallos Stigliano**. At the northern end, find one of the most beautiful presepe in the city on display at Christmas in the San Nicola alla Carità Church. In between, noble *palazzi*, historic piazzas and ancient churches mix and mingle with retail stores and pastry, chocolate and ice cream shops while a band of street vendors hawk all manner of knock-off goods.

For nearly five hundred years, the road that the Spanish built along the western limits of the walled Aragonese city has connected Piazza Trieste e Trento to Piazza Dante. A major artery, it has pumped the lifeblood of the city up and down its corridor, and in this regard resembles Rome's Via del Corso, Paris' Avenue des Champs-Élysées, or London's Bond Street. The name records its creator, Viceroy Pedro Álvarez de Toledo, Spanish Viceroy of Naples (1532 – 1552). Spanish expansion of the city can be seen all along the western side of Via Toledo. Here are the crowded and characteristic alleys of the Quartieri Spagnoli, Naples' Spanish Quarter, which was built in the 16th century to house Spanish troops. In an interesting juxtaposition to upmarket Via Toledo, the Spanish quarter is one of the city's most densely populated and "toughest" neighbourhoods. Tourists are typically cautioned to avoid this area, but if you want to experience an authentic neighbourhood, there is much to explore: narrow cobblestoned alleyways, incomparable street art and authentic trattorias - the most well known being the famed Trattoria da Nennella.

The Quartieri Spagnoli also offers a fine pedigree of churches. Luca Giordano was baptised in Chiesa di Sant'Anna di Palazzo and the revolutionary Eleonora Pimentel Fonseca married in this church and buried her son here. The 19th-century Chiesa di Santa Maria Francesca delle Cinque Piaghe was built into the ground and first floors of an ancient palazzo in honour of the first woman from Naples to be canonised. Ana Maria Rosa Gallo (1715 – 1791) was venerated as Santa Maria Francesca delle Cinque Piaghe (Saint Mary Francis of the Five Wounds), patron Saint of the Quartieri Spagnoli and of the pregnant and infertile. In a nod to this piece of Naples history, the Spanish firm Oscar Tusquets Blanca designed the **Toledo Metro Station**. MetroNapoli's 16th station on Metro Line 1, and 13th Metro Art Station, this urban masterpiece opened on Via Toledo in September 2012. One year later, a second portal was opened into the Spanish Quarter.

Beyond the metro station a monumental bronze sculpture on the east side of Piazza Carità honours WWII hero, Salvo D'Acquisto. On the west side of the piazza, narrow alleys fan out like spider veins into the Pignasecca and Montesanto. Meanwhile, the road we know as Via Toledo took a hundred-year detour following the Presa di Roma, the Capture of Rome (September 1870). It was renamed Via Roma già via Toledo, in celebration of a Unified Italy and as a symbolic way of washing off centuries of foreign control of Naples. The "già via Toledo" was a compromise between proponents of the old name and new. Gradually it became just Via Roma, which you will still hear from time to time, but in the 1980s, it reclaimed its former name - Via Toledo.

ANCIENT NEAPOLIS
CENTRO STORICO

Cover Photo: Detail of San Lorenzo Maggiore

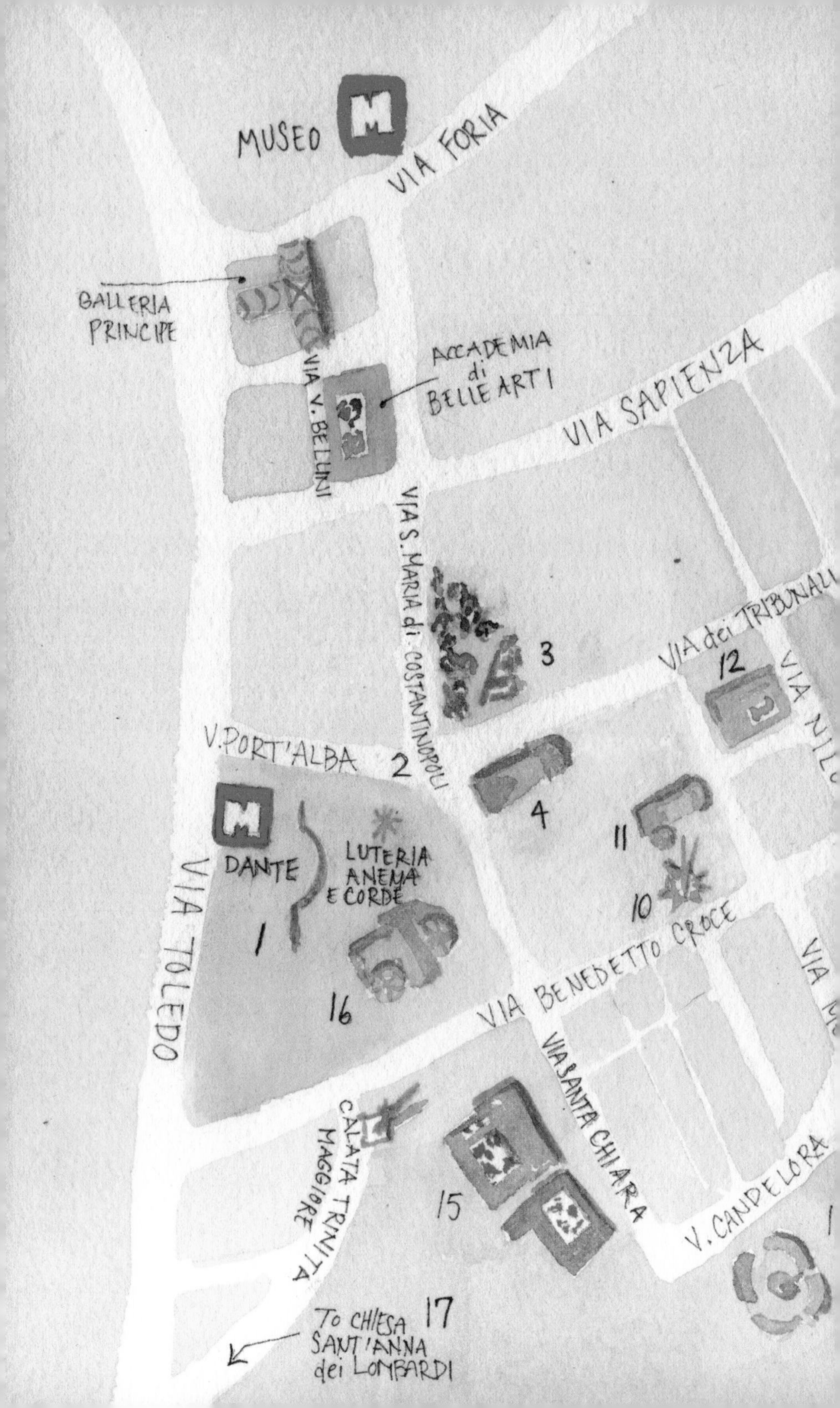

MUSEO **M**

VIA FORIA

GALLERIA
PRINCIPE

ACCADEMIA
di
BELLE ARTI

VIA SAPIENZA

VIA V. BELLINI

VIA S. MARIA di COSTANTINOPOLI

VIA dei TRIBUNALI

3

12

2

VIA NILO

V. PORT'ALBA

2

4

11

10

M

DANTE

LUTERIA
ANEMA
E CORDE

1

16

VIA BENEDETTO CROCE

VIA M

VIA TOLEDO

CALATA TRINITA MAGGIORE

VIA SANTA CHIARA

V. CANDELORA

15

17

To CHIESA
SANT'ANNA
dei LOMBARDI

IL DUOMO

VIA DUOMO

CENTRO STORICO

5

VIA S. GREGORIO ARMENO

7

9

OSPEDALE delle BAMBOLE

VIA S. BIAGIO dei LIBRAI

ATORIO

13

CORSO UMBERTO

Creative Cartography by Kelly Medford 2014

A stroll through the cobbled alleys of Naples' Historic District, the Centro Storico, is filled with "Oh my God" moments that, like your first kiss, you never forget.

Ancient Greco-Roman ruins lurk below the surface of Gothic, Renaissance and Baroque churches; statues and obelisks reach towards the heavens and modern-day life plays out in a tapestry woven from every fibre of Naples' past. When this district was designated a UNESCO World Heritage Site in 1995 the ICOMOS recommendation said: "Naples is one of the most ancient cities in Europe, whose contemporary urban fabric preserves the elements of its long and eventful history."

Centro Storico is the original walled city of Neapolis founded by the Greeks

in the 5th century BC, not far from the older city of Parthenope. As a wealthy maritime centre, Neapolis was an important nexus of Hellenistic culture, the Greek language and institutions surviving well into the Roman era. For the next 20 centuries or so, the Byzantines and Goths, Normans and Swabians, Angevins, Aragonese and Bourbons, one line of monarchs after another, vied for control of Naples, each leaving their imprint on the city.

Today, past, present and future collide within Naples' ancient skeleton. Defunct churches find new uses as centres of culture, castle halls become administrative offices, and residences, businesses, offices and schools are carved into the ancient *palazzi* of the metropolis.

As part of the city's continued efforts towards sustainable mobility, Centro Storico was designated a limited traffic zone, ZTL - *zona traffico limitato* - in 2013. The alleyways that were once described as chaotic and buzzing with cars and motos are very nearly pedestrianised most of the day making a stroll through Centro Storico an even more pleasant endeavour.

Piazza San Gaetano, Lorenzo Dotti, 2009

Plan Your Visit

You can't explore this enormous span of history in a lifetime, let alone a day, but a morning stroll through Centro's cobbled alleys will give you a taste of each moment of Naples' history. Start early in the morning as most churches close around 1 p.m. and remember to dress appropriately - if you are in shorts or sleeveless/skimpy tee-shirts you might be asked to leave.

Transport

METRO/RAILWAYS
M1: Museo or Università
M2: Cavour or Montesanto
FUNICULAR: Montesanto & Centrale
CUMANA: Montesanto

BUSES
C55

Tourist Info

AZIENDA AUTONOMA DI SOGGIORNO CURA E TURISMO DI NAPOLI
Piazza del Gesù Nuovo
Open Mon - Sat 09.00 – 17.00 & Sun 09.00 – 13.00
+39 081 5512701
inaples.it/eng/home.asp

CAMPANIA ARTECARD
ArteCard 365, Napoli and Tutta la Regione

Sights & Attractions

ACCADEMIA DI BELLE ARTI
Via Santa Maria di Constantinopoli, 107 but entrance is at Via Bellini, 36
Open daily 10.00 – 13.30
Free

+39 081 441887
accademiadinapoli.it

GESÙ NUOVO CHURCH
Piazza del Gesù Nuovo, 1
Church open Mon – Sat 07.00 – 12.45 & 16.00 – 19.45; Sun 07.00 – 12.45 & 16.00 – 20.45
Sala San Guiseppe Moscati open daily 09.30 – 12.45 & 16.30 – 19.15
Free
+39 081 5578111
gesunuovo.it

LIUTERIA ANEMA E CORDE
Via Port'Alba, 30
Open daily **except Sun** 09.30 – 13.30 & 16.00 – 20.30
+39 3895141352
anemaecorde.weebly.com

OSPEDALE DELLE BAMBOLE
Via San Biagio dei Librai, 81 (shop)
Via San Biagio dei Librai, 46 (hospital)
Hospital open Mon - Fri 10.00 – 15.00, Sat by appointment only
Shop open upon request
+39 081 203067 or +39 3395872274
ospedaledellebambole.it

PAPPACODA CHAPEL
Largo S. Giovanni Maggiore, 30
Part of the Orientale University, rarely open to the public but the church is visible from outside
+39 081 6909403

PLAN YOUR
VISIT

unior.it/ateneo/130/1/palazzo-giusso-e-cappella-pappacoda.html

S. ANNA DEI LOMBARDI
Piazza Monteoliveto, 4
Open Mon – Thurs 10.00 – 13.30 & 14.00 – 16.00; Fri & Sat 10.00 – 13.30 & 14.00 – 18.00; Sun 09.00 – 10.30
Free
+39 081 5513333

S. CHIARA
Via Santa Chiara, 49
The church is open daily 07.30 – 13.00 & 16.30 – 20.00
The Neapolitan Presepe room, museum (Museo dell'Opera) and Archaeological Courtyard are accessed via the Majolica Cloister which is open Mon - Sat 09.30 – 17.30, Sun & holidays 10.00 – 14.30
Adults €6.00 includes Cloister, Museum and Archaeology area; Church is free
+39 081 5516673
monasterodisantachiara.com

S. DOMENICO MAGGIORE
Piazza San Domenico Maggiore
Church open daily 08.30 – 12.00 & 16.30 - 19.00 except during services   Treasure Room Tues - Thu & Sun 09.30 - 12.00, Fri & Sat 09.30 - 12.00 & 16.30 – 19.00
Cloister open daily 10.00 – 22.00
Entrance to the church is free; guided tour of the Treasure Room €3.00, audio guide €1.00 (available from the Treasure Room); entrance to the cloister €5.00
+39 081 459188

S. GIOVANNI MAGGIORE
Vico S. Maria dell'Aiuto
Open daily 10.00 – 13.30 & 15.30 – 19.00
Touring Club of Italy runs free guided tours (also in English) on Thurs & Fri from 10.00 – 17.00
Free
+39 081 5528155

S. GREGORIO ARMENO
The Cloister: Piazzetta San Gregorio Armeno, 1
The Church: Via San Gregorio Armeno, 44
Church is open Mon - Fri 09.00 - 12.00, Sun & Tues 09.00 - 13.00, Cloister daily 09.30 – 12.00
Blood liquefaction ceremony (Santa Patrizia) every Tues 09.30
+39 081 5520186

S. LORENZO MAGGIORE
Via Tribunali, 316
Open Mon - Sat 09.30 – 17.30, Sun 09.30 – 13.30
Adults €9.00 for the underground and museum; entry to the church is free
+39 081 2110860
sanlorenzomaggiorenapoli.it

S. PAOLO MAGGIORE
Piazza San Gaetano, 76
Church open daily, **except Sun** 09.00 - 12.00 & 17.00 – 18.00
San Gaetano Sanctuary open daily 09.00 – 12.00 & 17.00 – 18.00
Free
+39 081 454048

S. PIETRO A MAJELLA CONSERVATORY
Via San Pietro a Majella, 35
Visits only upon request by e-mailing diretore@sanpietroamajella.it or sending a fax to +39 081 564415
+39 08 15644411
sanpietroamajella.it

SANSEVERO CHAPEL
Via Francesco De Sanctis, 19
Open Mon & Wed - Sat 09.30 – 18.30, Sun & holidays 09.30 – 14.00
Adults €7.00
+39 081 5518470
museosansevero.it

San Paolo Maggiore and Piazza San Gaetano

UNIVERSITY OF NAPLES MUSEUMS

Adults 1 museum €2.50, 2 museums €3.50, 4 museums €4.50

- MUSEUMS OF ANTHROPOLOGY, MINERALOGY AND ZOOLOGY

Via Mezzocannone, 8 in the Collegio massimo dei Gesuiti (College of the Jesuits)
Open Mon - Fri 09.00 – 13.30, Tues & Thu 14.30 – 16.50

- MUSEUM OF PALEONTOLOGY

Largo San Marcellino, 10, in the 17th-century complex of Saints Marcellino and Festo at the west end of the cloister
Open Mon - Fri 09.00 – 13.30, Tues & Thu 14.30 – 16.50
+39 081 2535162
musei.unina.it

- MUSEUM OF PHYSICS

Via Mezzocannone, 8
Open Mon - Fri 09.00 – 13.30, also Mon & Thu 14.30 – 16.30
+39 081.2536256
museodifisica.unina.it

- BIBLIOTECA UNIVERSITARIA DI NAPOLI

Via Mezzocannone, 8
Open Mon - Fri 08.00 – 18.30, Sat 09.00 – 13.30
Entry is free, but ID is required.
+39 081 5517025
bibliotecauniversitarianapoli.beniculturali.it

LARGER THAN LIFE EX-VOTOS :
THE THREE OBELISKS OF CENTRO STORICO

Catholic devotion and miracles go hand in hand in Naples. The liquefaction of the blood of San Gennaro and Santa Patrizia are just two instances of this, while another is the tradition of votive offerings - offerings of an object made to a divinity in return for granting a wish or prayer. Ex-votos of all shapes and sizes are found throughout the city. Bourbon King Ferdinand IV (I of the Two Sicilies) built San Francesco di Paola as an ex-voto and the Chapel of San Gennaro fits the same bill. In Gesù Nuovo the walls and ceilings of two side chapels overflow with silver ex-votos representing body parts. They are most numerous in the side chapel housing the remains of San Giuseppe Moscati, a physician canonised in 1987. These tokens are placed there by worshippers either asking for healing or in gratitude for healing received. Walk along these streets, especially along Via Tribunali and Via San Biagio dei Librai and you'll find numerous religious shops like Statuaria Sacra with an abundance of silver and faux-silver body parts with which to make your own offering.

Neapolitans erected larger than life ex-votos outside three churches in Centro. The tallest of the three sits in the centre of Piazza Gesù Nuovo. The copper sculpture on the top is that of the *Immacolata*, the Immaculate One, the Virgin Mary. Each year on December 8th (Immaculate Conception) Naples honours the Virgin Mary by placing a wreath in her hands. At Piazza San Domenico Maggiore the Spire of San Domenico was begun by Cosimo Fanzago after the plague of 1656. It was built in honour of the founder of the Domini-can Order, Domenico Guzman, who is immortalised in the statue on top. Construction was halted for a time, and the spire wasn't completed until 1737.

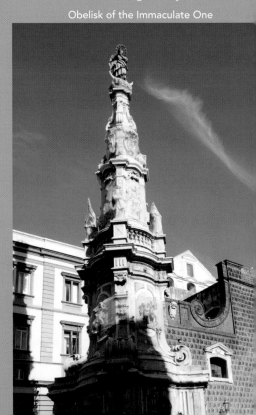

Obelisk of the Immaculate One

The oldest of the three, the Spire of San Gennaro, sits just around the corner from the Duomo. Designed by Cosimo Fanzango, it was erected at the south entrance to the Cathedral in Piazza Riario Sforza as an ex-voto to San Gennaro in gratitude for protect-ing the city from the 1631 eruption of Mount Vesuvius.

Statue of Dante at Piazza Dante

OF WRITERS AND POETS: PIAZZA DANTE (MAP 1)

Built on a grand scale, **Piazza Dante is dedicated to Italy's *Sommo Poeta* - Supreme Poet - Dante Alighieri of *The Divine Comedy* fame**. His imposing statue surveys the piazza, while the metro station that bears his name rumbles below in the not-so-infernal depths of Naples. The statue is the work of Neapolitan sculptor Tito Angelini (1806 - 1878), sculptor of the tomb of the Duchess of Floridia, second wife of Ferdinand IV (I of the Two Sicilies), Lucia Migliaccio. Two smaller marble examples of his work - *Eva* and *Nude Woman* – are in the Gallery of Naples Academy of Fine Arts just a few hundred metres north of here. The statue, which was installed in 1871, sits well with the piazza's 18th-century design and the mammoth hemicyclic structure that dominates the rear of it, the work of Luigi Vanvitelli for Charles VII (III of Spain). This dates from the phase when the former marketplace became the *Foro Carolino* - the Caroline Forum. The 26 statues at the top of the hemicycle represent the King's virtues; evidently he had an above average number of these. A few of the statues are the work of Giuseppe Sanmartino, the sculptor of the celebrated Veiled Christ.

With the opening of the Dante metro station in 2002, one of the earliest Metro Art Stations, the piazza was redesigned and pedestrianised. To ensure continued visibility of Vanvitelli's hemicircle, now the Convitto Nazionale Vittorio Emanuele boarding school, the station's designer Gae Aulenti had the entrances to the station constructed in glass and steel. Inside the station are works by Jannis Kounellis and Carlo Alfano as well as Joseph Kosuth's neon installation that pays tribute to Dante with a passage from the poet's *Convivio* – The Banquet.

> *These visible things, the proper as well as the common,*
> *insofar as they are visible, enter into the eye - I do not*

mean the things themselves but their forms - through the diaphanous medium, not as matter but as an image, just as through transparent glass. The passage that the visible form makes through this medium is completed in the water within the pupil of the eye, because that water has a boundary - almost like a mirror, which is glass backed by lead - so that it cannot pass beyond but is arrested there like a ball that is stopped when struck, so that the form, which cannot be seen in the transparent medium, here appears lucid where it is arrested.

TRANSLATED BY RICHARD LANSING, 1998 DANTE.ILT.COLUMBIA.EDU/BOOKS/CONVIVI/CONVIVIO03.HTML

This piazza of slightly crumbling glory is rarely deserted. It's a meeting and market place by day, with room for an impromptu football game or a political demonstration. By night, it's a place to linger with family and friends, and there is plenty of space to set up the occasional bandstand for outdoor concerts.

A TUG AT THE HEARTSTRINGS: PORT'ALBA ⟨MAP 2⟩

San Gaetano is perched atop Port'Alba beckoning all those who come near to pass through this ancient gate. This was one of two gates the Spanish bored in the Angevin walls in the 17th century. It was also one of the gates that was frescoed by Mattia Preti after the 1656 plague, though that fresco has unfortunately been lost. Behind Port'Alba, the street of the same name connects Piazza Dante to Piazza Bellini and along its length, rusty green bins are filled to the brim with books: new, used and antiquarian. Via Port'Alba's indoor/outdoor book market is a book lover's dream.

Wedged into the side of a palazzo courtyard on Via Port'Alba is a small studio. **Wood shavings drop tendril-like from work benches to the floor**; there are interesting smells – is that glue or rosin? Intriguingly curved cut outs cover the table awaiting their moment in the creative process. This is **Liuteria Anema e Corde**, the master-lutemakers of Naples. The four young musicians and crafts-people who founded this studio were inspired by Neapolitan maestri of the past – but while they work in traditional ways their work is informed by careful research and performance practice. Their instruments, whether violins, mandolins or guitars, may appear in the hands of eminent musicians at the San Carlo opera house, or on exhibition stands from Cremona to Frankfurt. But whatever their considerable wider reputation, Naples remains their heartland; they have given younger musicians the opportunity to play in their concert series and have taught at the 'Obiettivo Napoli' Institute which works with at-risk youth in the city. Best of all, there's always a warm welcome in the studio. And the name? Well, there's a popular Neapolitan song by Salvatore d'Esposito from the 50s called *Anema e Core* – we would say Heart and Soul. Add a 'd' to *core* (heart) and you get the word for strings. Need we say more?

Opposite page: Pulcinella, Vico Fico al Purgatorio

EXPLORE SOME MORE

If you are keen on works by 19th-century Neapolitan painters or sculptors, stop by the **Gallery of the Accademia di Belle Arti - Naples Academy of Fine Arts**. This massive structure runs along Via Santa Maria di Costantinopoli but the entrance sits arouhd the corner on the small pedestrian street, Via Vincenzo Bellini. The second-floor gallery features works by 19th-century masters such as Vincenzo Gemito, Tito Angelini, Achille D'Orsi, Domenico Morelli and Filippo Palizzi, a former president of the academy.

Back in the square you can see the **Galleria Principe**, a covered passageway connecting the Archaeological Museum and the Academy of Fine Arts. The three sided big brother of Galleria Umberto I, it was completed in 1883 (before Galleria Umberto I) and like its little brother, it was built during Naples' Urban Renewal - the **Risanamento di Napoli**. The Galleria has faced several periods of degradation over the years and was most recently renovated in 2009.

GENERATION NEXT: PIAZZA BELLINI ⟨MAP 3⟩

Tucked between Via Port'Alba, several university buildings, the Academy of Fine Arts and the Music Conservatory of San Pietro a Majella, Piazza Bellini has a vibe unlike any other in the city. **This lively square has a young, funky, left of centre, intellectual and gay ethos**. A spritz in one hand and a hand-rolled cigarette in the other, Naples' next generation of artists, writers, politicians and thinkers debate the burning questions of the day under the watchful eye of the statue for which the piazza is named, the 19th-century Sicilian operatic composer Vincenzo

On your way to Piazza San Gaetano you will pass two curiosities: a Pulcinella statue at the corner of Via dei Tribunali and Vico Fico al Purgatorio and just beyond, a church whose entrance is framed by skulls and femurs. The latter is the Santa Maria delle Anime del Purgatorio ad Arco Church where you can visit a small crypt in an ancient underground chamber. The former is the work of Neapolitan artist Lello Esposito, who perched his Pulcinella statue atop a pedestal made of the same weathered stone as the *vicolo*. The aim was to make it look as if Pulcinella had always been part of the alleyway. And indeed, to the majority of Neapolitans, Pulcinella has always seemed part of the city itself. In fact, this cheeky, beaky-nosed anti-establishment figure originated in the 16th-century masked theatre genre, *Commedia dell'Arte* and morphed into a standard character in Neapolitan puppetry. He stands for every Neapolitan who has ever wanted or tried to put one over on the powers that be. And frankly there have been quite a few of those. He is woven into art, theatre and both low and high culture; his image is for sale in the hundreds on Via San Gregorio Armeno while the eminent Italian Institute for Studies in Philosophy considers him a fit subject for debate. At the unveiling of Esposito's work in November 2012, Mayor Luigi de Magistris summed him up thus: "Pulcinella is the history of our city, the energy, the philosophy, culture, folk art, revolution."

Bellini. The 4th-century Greco-Roman ruins of the city's western wall lie just a few feet away, a mute reminder of the piazza's place in history.

In this favoured meeting place among university students which is also a great place for travelling writers to get their thoughts on the page, most of the cafés offer free WiFi. There is also free coverage as part of Naples' WiFi in the City, which launched in Piazza Bellini in 2011. On most evenings, you're liable to stumble upon live jazz, a concert or a poetry reading here. Favourite hangouts include the Caffè Intra Moenia "literary caffè", with its large collection of books to peruse while you take a caffè or sip an aperitivo. Nearby, the new Nea Art Gallery's Bistro Caffè opens onto the courtyard of the University Library.

MUSIC TO YOUR EARS: SAN PIETRO A MAJELLA ⟨MAP 4⟩

While enjoying your aperitivo at one of Piazza Bellini's delightful bars, you might become aware of **a cascade of notes from the nearby music conservatory, San Pietro a Majella**. Its origins can be traced to four orphanages active in the 16th and 17th centuries whose programmes came to include musical training in response to an ever rising demand for fine singers and musicians. After a period of decline, however, only the Pietà dei Turchini orphanage survived and this was moved to the Convento delle Dame di San Sebastiano in 1808. In 1826 the organisation became the Royal Conservatory of Music at its current location in a former Celestine monastery. Close by, Via San Sebastiano is lined on both sides with music shops, making this one of the most melodious streets in the city.

The word 'conservatory' originally meant a place where orphans and young women were sheltered and educated but semantic drift has given the term its musical sense, precisely because of the history of places like San Pietro a Majella. Today you will find here all the teaching, concert and research activity expected of a fine international school, plus a museum of rare antique instruments and an extensive manuscript library relating to the lives and music of composers associated with Naples. These include Alessandro Scarlatti, Giovanni Battista Pergolesi, Domenico Cimarosa, Vincenzo Bellini and Gaetano Donizetti. The composer of *Csárdás*, Neapolitan Vittorio Monti, studied violin and composition at this conservatory.

THE FORUM OF NEAPOLIS: PIAZZA SAN GAETANO ⟨MAP 5⟩

The meeting and market place of the ancient Greco-Roman city of Neapolis - **the Greek Agora and later the Roman Forum - lies just below the surface of Piazza San Gaetano**, the bustling intersection of Via dei Tribunali (the ancient Decumano Maggiore) and Via San Gregorio Armeno. A quick look around the piazza today and one might surmise things haven't changed that much in the last few millennia.

Shops, cafés and eateries line this "T" shaped piazza, while the ruins of their ancient predecessors lie beneath. There are two underground tours at Piazza San Gaetano: Napoli Sotterranea and Naples' Ancient Marketplace at San Lorenzo Maggiore. Some of the best pizza in Naples can be had here at I Decumani or try the *panini napoletani* at Pasticceria Rosticceria San Gaetano di Ippolito Nunzio whose selection of savoury street foods is only outdone by their sweet pastries, especially their *babà*. Meanwhile, Limonè serves up *limoncello* and a variety of other spirits while duelling cafés sit diagonally across from each other on Via dei Tribunali. And on any given day you might hear the sweet sounds of Neapolitan music coming from the direction of San Lorenzo Maggiore. That is most likely Alfredo Imparato, one of a small number of *posteggiatori* remaining in Naples, keeping the centuries old tradition of public singing alive.

Alfredo Imparato in Piazza San Gaetano

The most important example of ancient Neapolis by far is the urban layout of the city, which is clearly visible today: a grid pattern plan of the type developed by the Greek Hippodamus of Miletos, the father of urban planning. A 70 hectare area, it is bound by Via Foria and Corso Umberto to the north and south and Via Carbonara and Via Costantinopoli to the east and west.

There are three major arteries (15 metres wide) that run east to west. The Greeks called these the *platelai* (singular - *plateia*) and Romans called them the *decumani* (singular - *decumano*). They correspond to today's Via Anticaglia, Via dei Tribunali and Via San Biagio ai Librai/Via Benedetto Croce/Via Giudecca Vecchia, the Decumano Superiore, Maggiore and Inferiore respectively. Very narrow (3 metres wide) *stenopoi* (singular - *stenopos*) or Roman *cardini* (singular - *cardine*) alleys like Via San Gregorio Armeno and Via Nilo, intersect the *decumani* at right angles.

TEMPLE OF THE DIOSCURI: SAN PAOLO MAGGIORE (MAP 6)

To get a sense of the history of this church, you need look no further than the grand porch that sits atop its monumental double staircase. Here you'll see two Corinthian columns braced against the façade. They are the only reminder we have of its ancient beginnings as **the pagan Temple of the Dioscuri** which sat on the north side of the ancient *Foro di Neapolis*, today's Piazza San Gaetano. The Dioscuri, aka the twins Castor and Pollux, were two of the founding gods of the Greek city of Neapolis. The statues in the two niches embedded into the principal façade, those of Peter and Paul, recall the erection of the first church on this temple site in the late 8th/early 9th century AD. As Acts 28:13-14 tells us, Saint Paul, to whom the church is dedicated, landed on the shores of Pozzuoli on his way to Rome to stand trial. This scene was immortalised by Giovanni Lanfranco in his *Lo Sbarco di San Paolo a Pozzuoli*, which is now in the Naples Diocesan Museum, where you'll also find a Caravaggioesque portrait of the saint, a reliquary statue of him and a painting of him with Saint Peter.

The entrance below the staircase and the statue in the piazza tell of the church's medieval history. The statue, arms outstretched, head raised towards the heavens, depicts San Gaetano, one of the patron saints of Naples and a founding member of the religious order known as the Congregation of the Clerks Regular of the Divine Providence, the Theatines. After a long period of neglect, the church was given to this order in 1538. Some ten years later San Gaetano died in Naples and his remains were interred in a crypt below the stairs. His tomb is now the centrepiece of a beautiful little chapel here.

Inside the main church we find its more recent past. Like most churches in Naples it was subject to a complete restyling during the Baroque era, and like many it suffered grave damage during WWII. The frescoed ceiling in the central nave, *Stories of the Lives of Saint Peter and Saint Paul* by Massimo Stanzione (1585 - 1656) was among the casualties. However, much of San Paolo's rich artistic heritage escaped unscathed, for example Francesco Solimena's (1657 - 1747) frescoes in the sacristy and Ferdinando Fuga's (1699 - 1782) altar.

GOTHIC GLORY: SAN LORENZO MAGGIORE (MAP 7)

As another instance of those "don't judge a book by its cover" moments in Naples, this church's weathered Sanfelice (Ferdinando Sanfelice 1675 - 1748) façade hides one of the most important Gothic monuments in the city. We have the Angevins to thank (a French dynasty who ruled from 1266 - 1442) for many of Naples' monumental religious structures - the Duomo, Santa Chiara, San Domenico Maggiore, San Martino... and San Lorenzo Maggiore, one of their earliest triumphs. Charles I (1226 - 1285), the first monarch of the Angevin Dynasty, replaced the ageing 6th-century basilica dedicated to the same saint with this French Gothic complex he commissioned for the Franciscans. Both basilicas were built on top of the *macellum*, the ancient marketplace of Neapolis. The church retains a prominent place in Naples' history: Charles of Calabria's first wife Catherine of Austria is buried here, her tomb the work of Tino di Camaino; Fiammetta stole Giovanni Boccaccio's (1313 - 1375) heart in this church, Francesco Petrarca (1304 - 1374) stayed in the adjacent monastery and for centuries the complex served as a political meeting place.

Like its counterparts, San Lorenzo Maggiore was highly "Baroquised" in the 16th and 17th centuries, so much so that the weight of the embellishments threatened the structural integrity of the building. Decades of renovations stripped away most of its ornamentation, returning San Lorenzo Maggiore to some version of its original Gothic self. Two chapels were left in their Baroque state, however, the third chapel on the right - the Cacace Chapel and the Chapel of San Antonio in the transept, both the work of Cosimo Fanzago. Also in the transept a **precious section of the 6th-century mosaic floor is visible under glass**.

CHRISTMAS ALLEY: VIA SAN GREGORIO ARMENO ⟨MAP 8⟩

Christmas lives year round along Via San Gregorio Armeno. Affectionately known to English speakers as "Christmas Alley", it is home to the **artisan workshops that bring Naples' famed *presepi*, the Neapolitan nativity scenes and figurines, to life**. An ancient, narrow alley from the street plan laid down by the Greeks, it is flanked on either side by tall, dark *palazzi* that maintain an eerie dusk-like gloom. Twinkling Christmas lights add to the mystique, creating an atmosphere reminiscent of the chiaroscuro of the Neapolitan Baroque. Halfway down the street, a bell tower ominously straddles the alley, forming an archway that looks like an ancient city portal.

Via San Gregorio Armeno is best experienced during the Christmas season when things are at their frenzied peak. The crowds swell in number and the merchants, whose shops already spill out onto both sides of this tiny alley, are joined by a sea of temporary stalls tucked into every conceivable open space. Here in this delightful kaleidoscope you'll find the finest hand-crafted *presepe* pieces and cave settings, mass-produced kits made of plastic, wax or poor quality ceramic, plenty of Christmas kitsch and other traditional Neapolitan crafts like the famed Pulcinella and the *Tammorra Napoletana*, the Neapolitan Tambourine.

THE NEAPOLITAN CRÈCHE: THE ART OF THE PRESEPIO

Every piece is a masterpiece. In these spectacular miniature replicas of Neapolitan life the entire range of emotions springs from the faces, the eyes and the gestures. It's a centuries-old tradition said to date back to Saint Francis of Assisi's commissioning of a nativity scene in the 13th century. Neapolitan artists of the Baroque period elevated this craft to high art and it continues to evolve with each successive generation.

The 18th century was the Golden Age of the art of the *presepio*, thanks in part to the patronage of King Charles VII (III of Spain). By then the life-sized wooden religious nativity scenes crafted for the church had evolved into animated, detailed and expressive miniature terracotta figurines. The art form became an amalgam of sculpting, painting, fashion and tailoring. In this truly Baroque collision of sacred and profane, the Holy Family and the Magi appeared cheek by jowl with vignettes in which ordinary people went about their everyday lives: shoemakers and innkeepers, bakers and fruit vendors, fishmongers and butchers, carpenters and blacksmiths alongside the beggars, the poor and the derelict. Among these figurines were a cast of characters with symbolic meanings - figures like the Gypsy, the shepherd Benino or Bacchus, the ancient God of Wine. These intricate scenes soon found their way into the homes of royalty, nobility and the wealthy bourgeoisie and the "keeping up with the Joneses" mentality catapulted the art to new heights as patrons sought to outdo one another. Today the Neapolitan *Presepio* or *Presepe, o'Presebbio* in dialect, is probably Naples' most widely known artisan craft.

In centuries-old workshops and modern studios, master and apprentice artisans still ply their craft. The hands, feet or limbs of figures may be entrusted to an apprentice, but sculpting of faces will be the work of a master. The pieces are coloured by expert painters and attached to a body made of iron wire and a thick hemp wick, then finished with hand-blown glass eyes and costumes made of fine fabrics. The figurines are placed in and around mangers or "caves" made of natural materials such as cork or in elaborate city or country landscape settings, many with lights, mechanical and/or water features. And the remarkable part the *presepe* plays in the life of the nation is demonstrated by the fact that every time someone shoots to fame, whether actor, politician, athlete or cleric, he or she will be immortalised in a new figurine and appear on Via San Gregorio Armeno the next morning.

OF BYZANTINE & BAROQUE: SAN GREGORIO ARMENO <MAP 9>

At the top of Via San Gregorio Armeno, a large iron gate stands watch over a frescoed stairway. This is the entrance to a 16th-century cloister built by Giovanni Vincenzo Della Monica. **It is one of the most beautiful cloisters in the city**. From the back of the cloister you can look down on the altar of a tiny, ancient church, the 12th-century Chapel of the Madonna dell'Idria. Of the Byzantine mosaics on the wall behind the altar, only the heads of the Madonna and child remain, and the chapel itself is the sole reminder of the complex's eastern origins. San Gregorio Armeno, Bishop of Armenia, is credited with having converted Armenia from Paganism to Christianity in the 4th century. Four centuries later, Byzantine iconoclasm (the destruction of a culture's religious icons for religious/political reasons) forced a group of nuns to flee the Byzantine Empire. When they did, they absconded with the relics of Saint Gregory. The nuns landed in Naples, and it has been said by nuns in the know, that Saint Gregory's relics are still secreted away somewhere in the enormous monastic complex that bears his name. The complex spans the entire length of Via San Gregorio Armeno, is about half as wide and was founded on the pagan temple of Ceres in the 10th century. Later it was connected to the convent of the San Pantaleone church across the street by means of a footbridge, the bell tower that now straddles Via San Gregorio Armeno. It was built according to eastern conventions, but after the Council of Trent (1545 - 1563) it was completely rebuilt in western style. Today it is a magnificent example of the Neapolitan Baroque.

In bygone eras, the nuns who lived here came from wealthy families, i.e. they were daughters that couldn't be married off. These nuns were known for their cooking: they became famous for their *sfogliatelle* and have been credited with inventing Naples' traditional wheat and ricotta Easter pie, *pastiera*. Elizabeth David tells us in *Harvest of the Cold Months: The Social History of Ice and Ices*, that they were also experts "in the very specialised field of creating ices in the guise of roasted birds, joints of meat, hams and so on." The nuns that live here now, Le Suore Crocifisse Adoratrici dell'Eucaristia or Santa Patrizia are involved in more charitable pursuits. They provide food, shelter and clothing and operate a school for at-risk youth as well as feed the impoverished in the neighbourhood. They also revere another saint, Santa Patrizia whose remains, her blood and her body, were secreted away here in 1864. Every Tuesday morning the saint's blood liquifies in a ceremony that is held at the end of morning mass. Her following is so strong, that the church is also known as Santa Patrizia.

Entry to the church is at the bottom of Via San Gregorio Armeno, just a few steps from Via San Biagio dei Librai. The church is adorned with frescoes by Luca Giordano, including a *Glory of San Gregorio Armeno* in the cupola. At the entrance itself are three frescoed scenes of his depicting respectively the arrival of the Greek nuns in Naples, the nuns in white tunic and black veil bearing

San Gregorio's relics and finally the abbess Donna Giulia Caracciolo (who had conceived the idea of building the church over a century before), descending to earth to be greeted devoutly by the Neapolitans. The gilded, coffered ceiling, the work of Flemish painter Teodoro d'Errico (Dirk Hendricksz, 1544 - 1618) is nothing short of spectacular.

Cloister, San Gregorio Armeno

The bottom of Via San Gregorio Armeno meets up with Via San Biagio dei Librai, the so-called Spaccanapoli. If you go up to Castel Sant'Elmo in the Vomero and look down over Centro Storico, you'll see why. This street cuts a narrow, yet distinct swathe across the ancient city, literally splitting it in two and giving way to its name Spaccanapoli, or the "Naples-splitter". You'll also be treated to a bird's eye view of Santa Chiara, its green roof standing head and shoulders above the rest. Spaccanapoli goes by three different names across its length. East of Via Duomo it's Via Vicaria Vecchia, in the centre, Via San Biagio dei Librai and then Via Benedetto Croce from Piazzetta Nilo to Piazza del Gesù Nuovo. At Piazzetta Nilo are two "shrines" worth mentioning: the statue of Nilo, which was erected here by the people from Alexandria, Egypt who settled in Naples some 2,000 years ago and the shrine to Argentine footballer, Diego Maradona, inside Bar Nilo. Maradona played for Naples from 1984 to 1991 and led the Azzurri to their only two *Serie* A championships.

■ ■

EXPLORE SOME MORE

Just a few steps from Via San Gregorio Armeno on Spaccanapoli, Tiziana Grassi runs the **Ospedale delle Bambole**, the Doll Hospital. People from all over the world call on the hospital to repair and restore treasured dolls, sacred objects and even stuffed animals. Family-owned since it was founded in the late 19th century, this unusual trade has been passed down for four generations.

■ ■

FROM PAST TO PASTRY:
PIAZZA SAN DOMENICO MAGGIORE ⟨MAP10⟩

Piazza San Domenico Maggiore is the **centre of the Centro Storico and for some Napoletani, the epicentre of the universe, not to mention the universities**. Tourists and students alike find it irresistible as a place to linger. It is dominated by the apsidal side of San Domenico Maggiore, the church from which the Piazza takes its name, and the spire dedicated to the same saint and one of the Three Obelisks of Centro Storico. The piazza is beautifully framed by centuries-old *palazzi*.

Along Vico San Domenico Maggiore, the alley that leads to the *Veiled Christ*, is Palazzo Corigliano, seat of the Orientale University's department of Asian, African and Mediterranean studies. On the west side of the piazza is Palazzo Petrucci, home to the Michelin star restaurant, Ristorante Palazzo Petrucci. On the south side, find perhaps the piazza's greatest glory, a perfect pastry - *sfogliatelle, babà* or *zeppole San Giuseppe* at Scaturchio's.

ST. THOMAS AQUINAS: SAN DOMENICO MAGGIORE ⟨MAP11⟩

Now to savour one of the most beautiful churches in Naples, a church filled with so many treasures, no matter how many times you visit, you'll always discover something new. Royal sepulchres, fragments of 14th-century Giotto-esque frescoes, 16th-century Neapolitan sculpture, Cosimo Fanzago's high altar (1652), a Baroque era panelled ceiling (1670) and **24 side chapels, each one**

more beautiful than the next.
San Domenico Maggiore was one
of the largest convent complexes
in the city when it was built by the
Angevins (1238 – 1324); it served
as the Aragonese royal church
and was the mother church of the
Dominicans. The monastery was
the original seat of the University
of Naples and it was here that Saint
Thomas Aquinas studied and read
Aristotle's works. As the author of
Summa Theologica, this Dominican
priest remains the foremost philosopher and theologian of the Catholic
Church. If you make an appointment, you can find one of his
handwritten works in the Manuscript
Department of the National Library.
After living in many cities, including
Rome, Monte Cassino, Orvieto and
Paris, he returned to Naples in 1272
to teach and founded his University
of Theology in what is today the
San Domenico Maggiore Church.
Rumour has it that Saint Thomas'
arm still rests somewhere in the
church.

Spire of San Domenico

Don't miss the sacristy beyond his chapel in the right nave. It features Francesco
Solimena's frescoed ceiling, *The Triumph of Faith over Heresy Due to the Work of
the Dominicans* and a 3-sided double-tier gallery with 45 coffins containing the
remains of members of the Aragonese court. A mystery attaches to this sacristy:
the Treasure Room was supposed to hold the hearts of King Charles II (Anjou) as
well as those of King Alfonso I (V of Aragon) and King Ferdinand I (Don Ferrante),
but when the French occupied the Kingdom of Naples in the 19th century, the
relics disappeared forever.

At the end of the right nave is the Chapel of San Michele Arcangelo a Morfisa, a
10th-century church that was incorporated as a side chapel when the complex was
built. It is through this chapel that most visitors enter the church, but this is not the
main entrance, and explains the less than regal façade we see from the piazza. The
front of the church is set in a courtyard to the north which also leads to the ancient
convent. After a lengthy restoration, the convent was reopened to the public for
May of the Monuments 2012. A small café in the cloister there is a peaceful spot
to take a quick break. The space upstairs hosts exhibits from time to time.

THE VEILED CHRIST: SANSEVERO CHAPEL ⟨MAP12⟩

This inconspicuous chapel located in a tiny alley around the corner from Piazza San Domenico Maggiore safeguards one of the "wonders of the world". It is one of the best known attractions in Naples, yet one of the most difficult to find. The chapel sits on a side street about a block north of the piazza and the modern ticket office installed a few doors down (with a new price tag to match) has done little to help. Regardless, few visitors leave Naples without having made their pilgrimage here. Built in the 17th century, this family chapel was completely restyled in the mid-18th by Prince Raimondo di Sangro (1710 - 1771), Prince of Sansevero VII. A nobleman, freemason, inventor, alchemist, scientist and patron of the arts, the Prince commissioned the most important artists of his day to embellish the chapel. Working to his exacting standards, the result was as complex, elaborate and multifaceted as the man who designed it.

The chapel's most prized asset is *The Veiled Christ*. This marble masterpiece was conceived of by the eccentric Prince, designed by Venetian sculptor Antonio Corradini and re-imagined and executed by the Neapolitan artist and sculptor, Giuseppe Sanmartino in 1753. **Two and a half centuries later, nothing else compares**. The life-size statue of Christ lying in repose is covered in a transparent shroud (the veil) sculpted so thin, you can see every contour of Christ's body. The sculpture was carved from a single block of stone. Corradini's terracotta preliminary model for the commission is kept in the "Farmacia" at the San Martino Charterhouse.

If you walk down the steps to an underground chamber, two anatomical display pieces constructed by Doctor Giuseppe Salerno in 1763 - 64 – male and female skeletons overlaid with vein and artery structures made most likely of wire, beeswax and silk – offer a small sampling of Raimondo's scientific work. Sangro invented a long range cannon while serving in the military and created a water-proof cape for his friend King Charles VII (III of Spain). His interest in alchemy led to wild rumours that he could create blood out of nothing, that he could replicate the liquefaction of San Gennaro's blood and that he killed people to use their bodies for experiments.

We do know that Sangro was Master of the Neapolitan masonic lodge, for which the Church excommunicated him. Although the Church revoked this, thanks to Raimondo's influence in the city, upon his death in 1771 the Church threatened to excommunicate Raimondo's family if they didn't destroy his writings and the results of his scientific experiments. They acquiesced and today the man who commissioned such wonderful art is himself shrouded in mystery. The astronomer de Lalande described him not as an academic, but as an entire academy.

BONES AND MINERALS:
THE UNIVERSITY OF NAPLES MUSEUMS (MAP 13)

Turn onto the Mezzocannone and you'll immediately **feel the vibe of the University**, the Università degli Studi di Napoli Federico II. From Piazza San Domenico Maggiore all the way to Corso Umberto I, university buildings line one side of the street while print shops and coffee houses line the other. This is one of the oldest universities in the world, having been founded in 1224 by the Holy Roman Emperor, Frederick II. Nearly 100,000 students pass through its doors each year. Among its alumni: theologian Thomas Aquinas, philosopher Benedetto Croce and Naples' Mayor since 2011, Luigi De Magistris.

Within the building at Via Mezzocannone, 8 is the university's Centro Musei delle Scienze Naturali e Fisiche, Natural and Physical Science Museum. Established in 1992, it is comprised of four small collections: the museums of anthropology, mineralogy, paleontology and zoology. The university's physics museum founded ten years earlier and the University's library, the Biblioteca Universitaria di Napoli, are also here.

The **Museum of Anthropology** houses archaeological finds from Troy, including polished stone axes and milling querns from about 3000 BC.

The **Royal Museum of Mineralogy** includes a Vesuvian collection, a collection of scientific instruments and two hyaline (glassy) quartz from Madagascar given as a present to King Charles VII (III of Spain).

The **Museum of Paleontology** preserves more than 50,000 artefacts, the oldest dating back 600 million years. The first finds to be displayed were the Ittioliti deposits of Campania – fossils found by Oronzio Gabriele Costa (the founder of Italian Paleontology).

The **Museum of Physics** houses some 700 instruments, most dating to the 19th century. There is also a collection of instruments designed by physicist Macedonio Melloni (1798 - 1854) and some 17th-century instruments including a telescope lens from 1645.

The **Zoological Museum** has one thousand 18th-century skin specimens and several extinct animals are on display, including the Norfolk Island Pigeon, the Crescent Nail-Tailed Wallabi and the Berber Lion. They also have 30,000 specimens of insects and 2,000 specimens of parasitic worms, if parasitic worms are particularly your thing.

The **Biblioteca Università** contains 1.2 million volumes.

MUSICAL REBIRTH: LARGO S. GIOVANNI MAGGIORE ⟨MAP 14⟩

Not far from Santa Chiara is the newly restored Basilica of San Giovanni Maggiore, **a church with 4th-century roots which languished in the dark for 42 years after a roof collapse**. In fact, multiple post-earthquake reconstructions over the centuries gave this church a succession of architectural styles including Byzantine, Baroque and Neo-Classical. The 1978 restoration revealed a paleo-Christian altar and apse under the 17th-century choir. Today the basilica has found a new life in the sounds of chamber music; there is a lively series of concerts to enjoy in this beautiful space.

Across the square is a treat for fans of late Gothic architecture, the doorway to the **Cappella Pappacoda**. This little chapel contains the tombs of Angelo and Sigismondo Pappacoda, noble brothers who both rose to high office in the Church. It is owned by the Oriental Institute of the University of Naples and is rarely open to the public; however, there's a very visible campanile noted for its colour contrasts of yellow and dark grey tuff rock. High up on the tower you can see several decorative insertions of Roman marble fragments including a funerary relief of a man and wife.

RISING FROM THE RUINS: SANTA CHIARA ⟨MAP 15⟩

It was the most devastating twenty-four hours of the war. American and British air raids pounded the city night and day, their targets the port, the station and any military installations. And when it was over, thousands were dead or wounded, much of the city's infrastructure was destroyed and scores of buildings lay in ruins. Homes, hospitals, schools and churches, even Naples' Albergo dei Poveri (shelter for the poor) were shattered. Among the casualties was Santa Chiara.

Soaring high above the busy Piazza del Gesù Nuovo, **Santa Chiara bears no trace of the fate that beset her**. Yet had it not been for that dreadful night, we'd be looking at a completely different church now, some version of Domenico Antonio Vaccaro's (1678 - 1745) Baroque restyling. But the bombings on August 4th 1943 wiped out most of Vaccaro's work and left little more than a bare shell behind. When it reopened in 1953 on the 10th anniversary of that fateful day, the new Santa Chiara was once again the old Santa Chiara, restored to its original Gothic style. And, serendipitously, the remains of a Roman Thermal Bath Complex were uncovered during the restoration works (they sit behind the complex's museum, the Museo dell'Opera).

Like San Lorenzo Maggiore, Santa Chiara comes to us from the Angevins, in this case, the dynasty's 3rd ruler, Robert the Wise. Along with his wife Queen Sancha of Majorca (Sancia di Maiorca), Robert built Santa Chiara Church as their Royal

Chapel and burial place. They were devoted patrons of the Franciscans and thus included provisions for the unusual arrangement of a double convent to house both nuns and monks (the Order of the Poor Clares and the Order of Franciscans) which they enclosed in a citadel-like complex. Around the time it was completed (1328), Robert invited Giotto to execute a series of frescoes inside the church. Unfortunately, but for a few fragments, all of these were destroyed.

The work of Sienese Tino da Camaino can be seen in the funerary monuments. Robert's tomb stands behind the altar, flanked by the tombs of his son Charles, Duke of Calabria who preceded Robert in death and Charles' second wife Marie Valois. In the back of the church, in the first chapel on the left, is the tomb of local hero Salvo D'Acquisto. This young man of just 23 from the Vomero district was executed by the Germans in September 1943. The Santa Chiara bell tower is contemporary with the original church and was also given a Baroque restyling. It is currently undergoing a €158,000 restoration that will re-open the tower to the public after a gap of one hundred years.

ENIGMA SOLVED: GESÙ NUOVO ⟨MAP 16⟩

The church of Gesù Nuovo is **one of the most striking pieces of architecture in the city**. Its façade is not flat but covered with multiple mini-pyramid shapes in stone projecting from the surface. When the masons constructed Gesù Nuovo as a private palazzo for the Sanseverino family in 1470, they incised marks on these stones, the same seven symbols in varying order, each about 10 centimetres high. By 1547 the family had fallen out of favour, since it had taken the people's side in their revolt against the Inquisition. As a result Pedro de Toledo handed the building over to the Jesuits. The Sanseverini and their masons had known what these signs meant, but somehow the original meaning was lost over time, and as the years passed creative theories were devised to explain them. Were they simply indications of which quarry the stones had come from, or symbols added as magical protection for the building or, yet more excitingly, arcane marks relating to alchemy and the occult?

It does seem astonishing that the solution to this mystery was solved only a few years ago by art historian Vincenzo De Pasquale, a man motivated by a passion for the Renaissance in Naples. Together with Salvatore Onorato who helped him survey the building, De Pasquale recognised the signs as Aramaic letters, each of the seven marks corresponding to musical notes. He worked out that the musical score, devised for a plucked instrument and based on a Gregorian canon, would last some 45 minutes if it were played. He knew other houses constructed for the Sanseverini family had musical signs engraved upon their façades so it wasn't a unique phenomenon. At the time the palazzo was built, Renaissance thinkers were discovering the philosophy of classical writers such as Pythagoras, whose concept of the 'Harmony of the Spheres' or 'Universal Music' had enormous appeal -

mathematics, proportion, music, all intertwined and related. However, the Jesuits, as implacable proponents of the Counter-Reformation, had more rigid ideas about art and architecture. It is perhaps not so surprising that an understanding of the musical notation passed out of common knowledge in the city. By one of life's ironies, it was a modern-day Jesuit, Hungarian father Csar Dors who is an expert on Aramaic, who helped Da Pasquale to understand what he'd discovered. And yet another Hungarian, musicologist Lòrànt Réz, began to put flesh on the bones of the musical notes. The piece has been transcribed for organ, given the name 'Enigma', and may yet one day be played in the church of Gesù Nuovo. Not magic then, but still one of Naples' magical stories.

IN RENAISSANCE STYLE: SANT'ANNA DEI LOMBARDI ⟨MAP 17⟩

You might say that the architectural keynote of Naples is the Baroque, but here and there the Renaissance style sings out, one notable example being at Sant'Anna dei Lombardi. This site began in 1411 with a small church, Santa Maria di Monteoliveto, given to Olivetan monks of the Benedictine order. Their monastery grew as new chapels, cloisters and a refectory in Tuscan, Renaissance style were grafted on, before being substantially altered to suit Baroque taste in the 1600s. When an earthquake hit the *quartiere* in 1805, destroying the nearby church of Sant'Anna dei Lombardi (and, sadly, three works by Caravaggio) the name of that church was transferred to the surviving one. History had yet more challenges in store – the enclosure of the original four cloisters within a *carabinieri* (police) barracks and a WWII bomb strike. However, much remains to delight the visitor.

Take the **monks' refectory, frescoed by Giorgio Vasari** in the 1540s. He didn't even want the commission at first, dismissing the space as "Gothic, low and dark". But once the ceiling was re-stuccoed to his design, creating shapes in

Santa Chiara's famed **Majolica Cloister** looks nothing like the stark cloister envisioned by Queen Sancha. The version seen today, which miraculously survived the bombings of WWII, we owe to the vision of Domenico Antonio Vaccaro and the work of the Neapolitan ceramic artisans, Donato and Giuseppe Massa. Vaccaro left the Gothic structure intact but transformed the gardens and embellished the façade. The result is an exuberant, sunny delight of yellows, blues and greens. Two criss-crossing paths create four quadrants framed by benches and edged in columns faced in the Massa's hand-painted blue, green and yellow majolica tiles. Grape vines once dangled between the tops of these columns whose tiles were done in a floral motif with vines and wisteria winding around them. The benches feature secular scenes of everyday life in the 18th century. See if you can find the allegorical references to the four elements - earth, air, fire and water within the tiles. One or two cloister cats are usually langorously draped upon the tiles here.

Gesù Nuovo

which he could paint, he set to work. He assigned a vault each to Faith, Religion and Eternity, adding virtues and numerous zodiac and mythological images. The monks ate here in silence, but the images above them must have provided inspiration and interest. In 1688 the refectory became a sacristy and it was then that the beautiful early 16th-century marquetry panels by Fra Giovanni da Verona were installed. Then there's the Piccolomini Chapel, commissioned by Antonio Todeschini Piccolomini, Duke of Amalfi and begun by the Tuscan sculptor Antonio Rosselino in about 1475, though unfinished at his death in 1479. His protegé Benedetto da Maiano carved the upper part of the tomb of Maria of Aragon, daughter of Ferdinand I (Don Ferrante). Benedetto and brother Giuliano, the architect, worked together on the Curiale Chapel nearby, the former sculpting the remarkable Annunciation altarpiece. Here Maria and the angel are carved almost in the round. Finally there is the Tolosa Chapel, substantially damaged in WWII, but retaining its Renaissance layout and some colourful late 15th-century frescoes.

Of all the Renaissance treasures to be seen here, the most astonishing survival is a group of eight life-size figures by Guido Mazzoni. Together they form a *Compianto* or Lamentation over the body of Christ, sculpted in terracotta with great realism and drama. Six such tableaux are attributed to Mazzoni, a native of Modena; this is his last, created between 1492 and 1497. In his later career he worked to great acclaim at the court of Charles VIII of France and in this group we can see why. Originally painted in many colours, restoration attempts have given them the appearance of cast bronze and yet their power to move us endures. Sources have identified Mazzoni's Joseph as Alfonso II of Naples, and Nicodemus as Ferdinand I (Don Ferrante) of Naples. But what matters is the beauty of the group and the palpable emotional charge that seems to run between them.

THREE GATES
❧ AND A ☙
RENAISSANCE
⟫⟫⟫⟫⟫ AROUND ⟪⟪⟪⟪⟪
PORTA CAPUANA

Cover Photo:
San Giovanni Carbonara

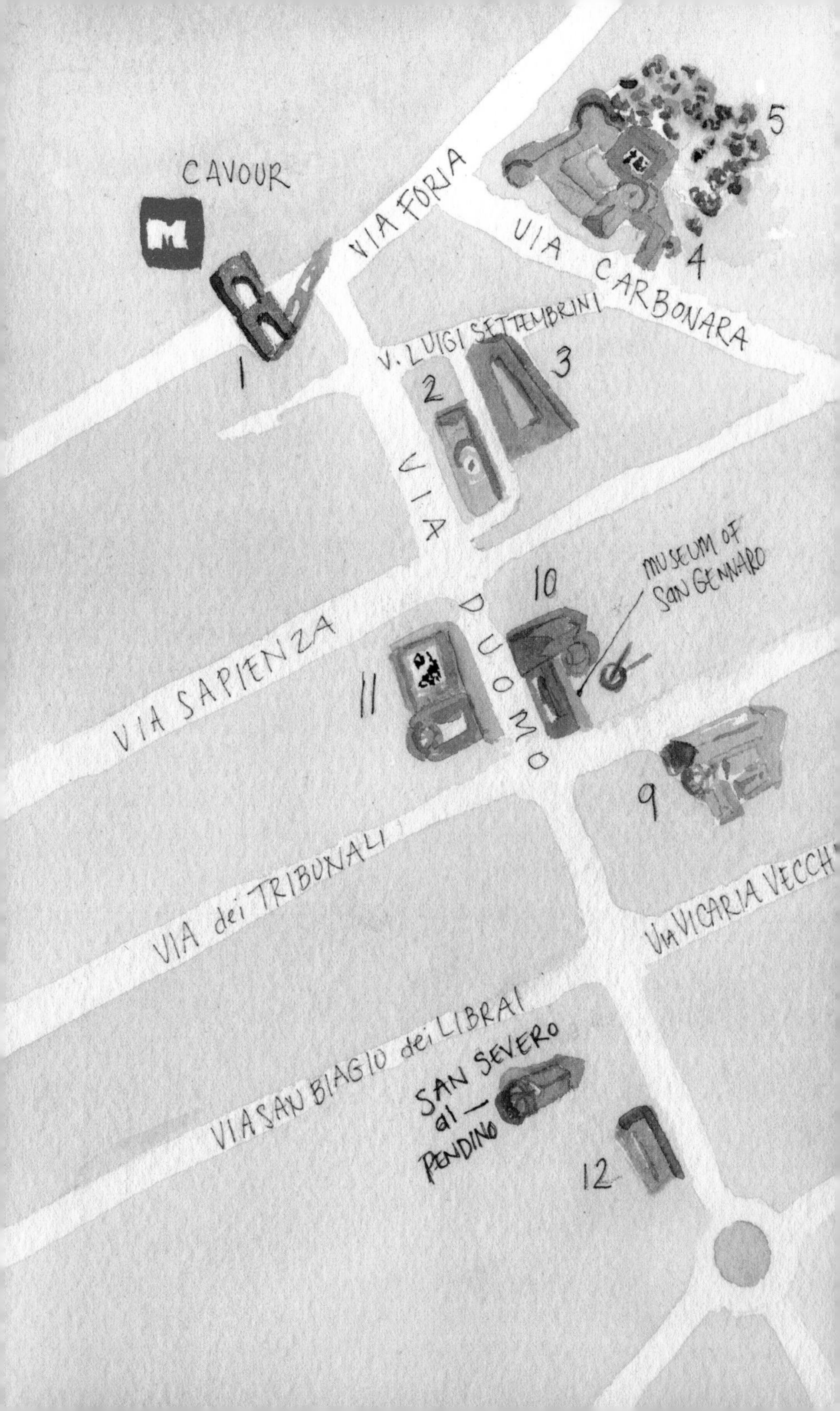

CAVOUR

VIA FORIA

VIA CARBONARA

5

4

1

v. LUIGI SETTEMBRINI

2

3

VIA

10

MUSEUM OF
SAN GENNARO

VIA SAPIENZA

VIA DUOMO

11

9

VIA dei TRIBUNALI

VIA VICARIA VECCH'

VIA SAN BIAGIO dei LIBRAI

SAN SEVERO
al —
PENDINO

12

PORTA CAPUANA

6

7

8

PIAZZA ENRICO de NICOLA

NAPOLI CENTRALE

GARIBALDI

VIA ANNUNZIATA

CIPPO A FORCELLA

VIA FORCELLA

13

CORSO UMBERTO I

V. CONFORTI
V. NOLANA

14

CORSO GARIBALDI

CIRCUMVESUVIANA

V. CESARE CARMIGNANO

PORTA NOLANA MARKET

Creative Cartography by Kelly Medford 2014

Decades in the making, the Metro Line 1 station at Stazione Centrale, Naples' Central Station opened in December 2013.

It is but one part of a larger project to modernise the station, create a transport hub connecting 5 railway stations and, after years of neglect, give a much-deserved facelift to Piazza Garibaldi. Meanwhile the entire area that stretches from Piazza Garibaldi west to Via Duomo is experiencing a similar renaissance. Since the turn of the millennium a steady stream of projects fuelled by public and private funds is breathing new life into this culturally rich neighbourhood that has historically been one of the city's poorest districts.

The first green shoots of renewal this century were seen with the restoration of a tiny park, Parco Re Ladislao a

Carbonara, which was returned to the community in 2001. The Teatro Trianon was completely refurbished between 2000 and 2002 and converted back to its original function as a theatre of *Canzone Napoletana* - Neapolitan Song. It became a public theatre in 2006 and since 2012 it has had a broader remit under new artistic direction. MADRE, the first venue in Naples' Historic District dedicated entirely to contemporary art, opened in 2005 in the renovated 19th-century Palazzo Donna Regina while the Diocesan Museum opened in the meticulously restored 17th-century Santa Maria Donnaregina Nuova church in 2007. Teatro San Ferdinando, the former theatre of Eduardo De Fillipo also

re-opened in 2007. Two years later the 4-star hotel, Hotel Palazzo Caracciolo opened in the 13th-century Caracciolo family palazzo that was also the former residence of Joachim Murat, King of Naples.

At the same time, two grassroots projects, *I Love Porta Capuana* and *Made in Cloister* are reclaiming and revitalising their neighbourhood. The *I Love Porta Capuana* project is bringing residents, business owners and social organisations together, without the aid of public funds. *Made in Cloister* is combining the "promotion and innovation of traditional craftsmanship with the preservation of architectural heritage".

Naples Central Station

Plan Your Visit

Transport

METRO/RAILWAYS
M1: Museo & Stazione Centrale
M2: Cavour & Stazione Centrale

BUSES
Naples Alibus Airport Shuttle, C55, R2, #1 Tram

Tourist Info

CAMPANIA ARTECARD
ArteCard 365, Napoli & Tutta la Regione

Combo Ticket for Museum of the Treasure of San Gennaro & Girolamini Monumental Complex – €12.00, purchase at the Museum of the Treasure of San Gennaro

Sights & Attractions

BASILICA DELL'ANNUNZIATA MAGGIORE
Via Annunziata, 34
Temporarily closed to the public, check before visiting
+39 081 283017
annunziatamaggiore.it

BASILICA SANTUARIO DEL CARMINE MAGGIORE
Via del Carmine, 2
Open daily 06.30 – 12.45 & 16.30 – 19.30
Free
+39 081 201942
santuariocarminemaggiore.it

CASTEL CAPUANO
Piazza Enrico De Nicola
Castel Capuano is not open to the general public except for special events; however, it is visible from the street. The municipal offices are open Mon - Fri 09.00 – 18.30

CIPPO A FORCELLA
Piazza Calenda
Ruins are visible any time from the street

GAETANO FILANGIERI MUNICIPAL MUSEUM
Via Duomo, 288
Open Tues - Sat 09.00 – 13.30
Adults €5.00
+39 081 203175
salviamoilmuseofilangieri.org

GIROLAMINI MONUMENTAL COMPLEX
Via Duomo, 142
Open Mon – Fri **except Wed** 09.00 – 16.30, Sat & Sun 09.00 – 13.30
Adults €5.00
Tickets must be purchased at the Museum of the Treasure of San Gennaro
+39 081 2294571
sites.google.com/site/monumentonazionalegirolamini/

LANIFICIO 25
Piazza Enrico De Nicola, 46
+39 081 6582915
lanificio25.it

MADE IN CLOISTER
The arts and crafts restoration project.
madeincloister.it

MADRE
Via Settembrini, 79
Open Mon - Sat **except Tues** 10.00 – 19.30, Sun 10.00 – 20.00; last admission one hour

PLAN YOUR
VISIT

before closing
€7.00, free entry Mon
+39 081 19313016
madrenapoli.it

MUSEUM OF THE NAPLES DIOCESE
Largo Donnaregina
Open Mon - Sat **except Tues** 09.30 – 16.30,
Sun 09.30 – 14.00
Adults €6.00
+39 081 5571365
museodiocesanonapoli.com

MUSEUM OF THE TREASURE OF SAN GENNARO
Via Duomo, 149
Open daily **except Wed** 09.00 – 17.00
Adults €5.00 (subject to change)
+39 081 294980
museosangennaro.com

NAPLES CATHEDRAL – IL DUOMO
Via Duomo, 147
Cathedral is open Mon - Sat 08.30 – 13.30
& 14.30 – 20.00, Sun 08.30 – 13.30 & 16.30
– 19.30
Baptistery is open Mon - Sat 08.30 – 12.30
& 16.30 – 19.00, Sun 08.30 – 13.30; last
entrance half an hour before closing
Cathedral - Free, Baptistery - €1.50
+39 081 449097

PARCO RE LADISLAO
Via Cardinale Seripando
Entrance at Via Cardinale Seripando and Via
Pontenuovo
The park opens at 07.00 daily, closure times
vary with the season
+39 081 7953610

PIO MONTE DELLA MISERICORDIA
Via dei Tribunali, 253
Open daily **except Wed** 09.00 – 14.30 (last
admission 14.00) Church closes at 14.00,
Picture Gallery closes at 14.30
€7.00 includes an audio guide
+39 081 446944
piomontedellamisericordia.it

PORTA NOLANA MARKET
Via Cesare Carmignano
Open daily 07.00 - 15.00

RUOTA DEGLI ESPOSTI (WHEEL OF THE ESPOSTI)
Via Annunziata, 34
Temporary entrance through Annunziata
Hospital around the corner
Open Mon – Sat 09.00 – 18.30
Free
+39 081 289032

S. CATERINA A FORMIELLO
Piazza Enrico de Nicola, 49
Open daily 08.00 – 20.00
Free
Information placards (Italian and English)
tell visitors about the church and each side
chapel and there are QR codes posted for
an audio guide in Italian courtesy of I Love
Porta Capuana.

S. GIOVANNI A CARBONARA
Via Carbonara, 5
Open daily 09.00 – 18.00
Free
+39 081 295873

S. SEVERO AL PENDINO
Via Duomo, 286
Open Mon - Sat 09.00 – 19.00
Free though there may be a charge during
special exhibitions
+39 081 7956423

THE GATE AS AN EX-VOTO: PORTA SAN GENNARO ⟨MAP 1⟩

It was probably the most disastrous century in Neapolitan history: three civil uprisings including Masaniello's revolt of 1647, three famines, three earthquakes, five eruptions of Vesuvius and three epidemics including **the great plague of 1656** which may have claimed the lives of half of Naples' citizens. Seeking protection from yet another calamity, Neapolitans frescoed the most vulnerable part of the city - their gates, as an ex-voto to their patron saint, San Gennaro. Interestingly, the only gate that still retains its fresco is the gate that bears the saint's name, the 10th-century Porta San Gennaro. This work by Mattia Preti (1613 - 1699) has been restored and features San Gennaro, Santa Rosalia and San Francesco Saverio. A bust of San Gaetano was added in 1659 and three years after the cholera epidemic of 1884 a painting of the Virgin Mary was added to a niche in the gate as an ex-voto.

Porta San Gennaro

ART AND RELIGION: DIOCESAN MUSEUM (MAP 2)

From humble wall paintings in ancient catacombs to masterpieces like Caravaggio's *Seven Acts of Mercy*, art and religion have been intertwined since the dawn of Christianity. As one of the first cities in Europe to be Christianised, Naples has long been a nexus of religious art and culture. The city's churches are replete with extraordinary works of art. According to a report published by the Naples Archdiocese, of the 203 churches in Centro Storico, 79 are still active Catholic churches. Each is a museum in its own right. From the remaining churches, some defunct, others unfortunately abandoned, many important pieces have been salvaged and have found a new home in the Museum of the Naples Diocese.

This is a collection of several hundred works **by masters such as Luca Giordano**, Massimo Stanzione and Andrea Vaccaro, as well as unknown Neapolitan artists and many artworks relate to the themes of the Virgin Mary and San Gennaro.

The museum opened in 2007 in the carefully restored 17th-century church of Santa Maria Donnaregina Nuova. This exceptional specimen of Neapolitan Baroque sits just a few steps away from the Archbishop's Palace and was once connected to its matriarch, the 13th-century Santa Maria Donnaregina Vecchia. A visit to the museum usually includes a tour of this Gothic church which is now home to the University of Naples Graduate School of Restoration.

A popular highlight of the church calendar is the presentation of *tableaux vivants* derived from the works of Michelangelo Merisi da Caravaggio. 7 actors use their bodies, appropriate props and draperies to recreate 21 of the artist's canvases, each one raked by a single light source to emulate his pioneering chiaroscuro technique. Music by Mozart, Vivaldi and Bach heighten the emotional impact upon the viewer. With its stunning collection and such innovative programming - exhibits, sacred music and staged performances like these - Donnaregina Nuova has established itself as one of the most vital cultural centres in the city.

The **Naples Diocese** has been around since the 1st century AD. It was elevated to an Archdiocese, *Archidioecesis Neapolitana*, in the 10th century. The Duomo is the see (official seat) of the Naples Diocese and has been since Constantine I, the first Holy Roman Emperor commissioned Naples' first Cathedral - Basilica Santa Restituta (now a side chapel in the Duomo). If you peek in the sacristy window there, you'll see the portraits of all of Naples' Bishops and Archbishops past. Two Archbishops became Popes - Pope Paul IV (1476 - 1559) and Innocent XII (1615 - 1700). In 2004 the Archdiocese of Naples counted some 1.6 million Catholics among its flock, 99.5% of the population. Their spiritual leader the Archbishop is Cardinal Crescenzio Sepe who was appointed in May 2006. His official residence, the Palazzo Arcivescovile, Archbishop's Palace, is on the north side of the Duomo, across the piazza from the Diocese Museum.

PALAZZO DONNAREGINA: MADRE ⟨MAP 3⟩

If you wander down the narrow Via Settembrini you'll find an old building that looks slightly newer compared to its counterparts. This is the 19th-century Palazzo Donnaregina that was re-imagined by the Portuguese architect Alvaro Siza and opened as the MADRE museum in 2005. **It was the first space entirely dedicated to contemporary art in the Centro Storico.** Inside it opens up to reveal an imaginative renovation that shows great respect for the building's architecture while at the same time, its wide open, bright and airy spaces are perfectly suited for displaying contemporary works of art. Meanwhile, the spectacular views of the city and its ancient *palazzi* glimpsed from the building's many windows provide an interesting contrast.

Launched with a Jannis Kounellis retrospective, the museum's temporary exhibits have featured the work of local, national and international artists such as Rachel Whiteread, Francesco Clemente, Johnnie Shand Kydd and Sislej Xhafa. A thriving centre of contemporary art in its first few years, of late, MADRE has had its share of ups and downs. It faced the threat of closure several times and had a long period of uncertainty, during which it lost some of its permanent collections. A new director was appointed in December 2012 and the museum's permanent collection is being rebuilt. It currently includes works by Sol Lewitt, Francesco Clemente, Mimmo Paladino, Anish Kapoor, Rebecca Horn, Jeff Koons and Jannis Kounellis. Meanwhile, MADRE strives to bring innovative programming and the work of national and international artists to the museum.

SWORDPLAY: SAN GIOVANNI CARBONARA ⟨MAP 4⟩

A monumental Sanfelice double staircase (1707) marks the entrance to this little known Gothic gem on Via Carbonara. It was built in an area outside the medieval city walls where refuse was collected and burned - hence the name Carbonara. The church could have just as easily taken the name Ladislaus for Angevin King Ladislaus the Magnanimous, *aka* Ladislaus of Durazzo (1377 - 1414). It was founded in the mid-14th century by the Augustinians, but Ladislaus made it his pet project, presumably to ensure his final resting place would be to his liking. In the end, **the sword-wielding King sits atop an enormous funerary monument** 18 metres tall which dominates the entire apse of the church.

It was Ladislaus' sister Queen Joanna II, however, who not only succeeded him on the throne, but commissioned this monumental structure immediately following his death. It would take more than a decade to complete. The circular chapel just behind it, the Caracciolo del Sole Chapel, was built for one of Joanna's lovers, a Seneschal of Naples, Giovanni Caracciolo, better known as Sergianni (1372 - 1432). In contrast to its Gothic surroundings, this chapel was executed in the

Neapolitan Renaissance style, as evidenced by the stunning Leonardo da Besozzo and Perinetto da Benevento frescoes.

MONKS' REFUGE: PARCO RE LADISLAO A CARBONARA ⟨MAP 5⟩

Just to your right as you are facing San Giovanni Carbonara is a small street, Via Cardinale Seripando. At the top of this street you'll find a staircase leading to a gate. Behind it is a **4,500 square metre historic garden** that was restored in 2001. It dates to the first half of the 14th century and was used by the Augustinian monks. Once medicinal and aromatic plants and citrus trees were cultivated here to supplement the monkish diet. This delightful green oasis in the middle of the city also affords visitors a unique view of the cupola and the back of the church.

Parco Re Ladislao a Carbonara

Santa Caterina a Formiello

RENAISSANCE ROOTS:
SANTA CATERINA A FORMIELLO ⟨MAP 6⟩

Just inside Porta Capuana stands a **church with Renaissance roots**. Originally part of a Celestine monastic complex, Santa Caterina a Formiello was dedicated to Catherine, virgin martyr of Alexandria. Dominican Fathers took charge of the monastery around 1493; the church was founded in 1510 and completed some eighty years later. Church funds were soon boosted by the sale of medicinal herbs, under the charge of Brother Donato d'Eremita whose fame spread throughout the city. Though remodelled in the Baroque period the church's floor plan remains as evidence of its original form and style. It is a simple Latin cross with five chapels on either side of a single nave. Now raise your eyes to see the Counter-Reformation exuberance and beauty of the marble work and frescoes; Luigi Garzi's paintings from the 1680s are especially fine.

Don't miss the 1718 organ by Neapolitan master Giuseppe de Martino tucked into the marble embellishments. But most of all admire the glorious dome, first of its kind in Naples. There is a quality of light in this church that emphasises steely blues and yellow ochres. The frescoes, by Paolo De Matteis, show the Madonna, Catherine and patron saints of Naples as supplicants to the Trinity on behalf of the city.

ALL THE KING'S HORSES AND ALL THE KING'S MEN: PORTA CAPUANA (MAP 7)

King Alfonso I (V of Aragon) rode into town in 1442 after snatching the Kingdom of Naples from the Angevins. He brought with him both his Catalan court from Barcelona and a Renaissance state of mind. To celebrate his victorious entry into Naples, he added a mammoth triumphal arch (1470), naturally in the Renaissance style, to the western entrance of Castel Nuovo.

Keeping the family tradition, Alfonso's illegitimate son Ferdinand I (Don Ferrante) built Porta Capuana (1484) as a triumphal arch to celebrate his coronation as King of Naples in 1458. It was also in the Renaissance style, with honour and virtue in the form of two towers flanking each side of the arch. For the next several hundred years, **Porta Capuana was the principal entrance to the city** (like Porta San Gennaro, it too was frescoed after the plague of 1656). It was the gate through which, as André Maurel said, "All the conquerors, all the kings, and all the armies have passed [...] either to take the city or to proclaim their victories". The entry into Naples of Charles IV (V, Holy Roman Emperor) was marked by the incision of his coat of arms in the gate and the reliefs of San Gennaro and San Aspreno in the frieze in 1535. When the Bourbons came to power in 1734, Charles VII (III of Spain) made his entry through Porta Capuana.

It was also the gate most probably used by visitors arriving from Rome and though it has been suggested otherwise, it would seem likely that Porta Capuana was named for its orientation towards Capua.

The monastic complex of Santa Caterina a Formiello, with its two cloisters, was altered radically in the early 19th century when a *lanificio*, a woollen mill, was installed. Under the Bourbons this industrial activity soldiered on with the production of military uniforms and in more recent years the site suffered from severe neglect. But all that is changing thanks to a group of architects and artists who have used kickstart funding techniques to raise money not only to restore the large cloister (complete with frescoes) but to create a permanent centre for contemporary and performance art, artisanal skills, craft and design. The project is called "***Made in Cloister***" and has received the support and encouragement of numerous local and international artists. It's early days, but craftsmen such as Raffaele Fiorentino, who now runs his five-generation family framing business from the Santa Caterina cloister, is confident that this initiative has a great future. Meanwhile the **Lanificio25** association offers musical events, art exhibitions and theatre and dance workshops in this extraordinary clerical/industrial space.

...travellers from Rome to Naples, having followed the Appian Way as far as Capua, would have proceeded by the straight road which ran due south through Atella and entered Naples by the Porta Capuana...
PAUSILIPON, THE IMPERIAL VILLA NEAR NAPLES, R.T. GUNTHER, 1913

The inside of Porta Capuana looks less like a gate and more like its nearby cousin, Castel Capuano. On the outside, however, the towers are done in *piperno* (grey tuff) while the arch is white marble.

THE HALLS OF JUSTICE: CASTEL CAPUANO <MAP 8>

This erstwhile royal residence of the Normans and Angevins - many kings and queens lived here including Queen Joanna I - served as the *Tribunali di Napoli*, **Naples' Courts of Justice for over 460 years** (ca. 1540 - 2007). The castle was built by William I of Sicily in the mid 12th century and its central location and proximity to the Capuana gate led Spanish Viceroy Don Pedro de Toledo to consolidate all of the territory's law courts here, both civil and criminal, in the 16th. He also added a prison to the basement and it was here that the Parthenopean revolutionaries were incarcerated for a time. It's situated at the very eastern end of the Decumano Maggiore; Via dei Tribunali "tribunals" took its name from the castle's function as a courthouse. In 2007 most of the courts and their offices were moved to the Nuovo Palazzo di Giustizia di Napoli in Centro Direzionale. Today the building serves as municipal offices and is generally closed to the public. The entrance is on the Via dei Tribunali side and bending the rules, you can peek into the courtyard.

THE 7 ACTS OF MERCY: PIO MONTE DELLA MISERICORDIA <MAP 9>

Around the corner from the Duomo is a small mid 16th-century octagonal church dedicated to Santa Maria della Misericordia. It sits just a few metres away from the Spire of San Gennaro, one of the Three Obelisks of Centro Storico. It was designed by Francesco Antonio Picchiatti, better known for his Scalone d'Onore (1651) at Palazzo Reale, and it holds **one of Naples' greatest treasures, Caravaggio's Seven Works of Mercy** (1607). This painting is without doubt one of the most important religious works of art of the 17th century. It depicts the Seven (Christian) Corporal Works of Mercy, those relating to the needs of the body.

Opposite page: Porta Capuana

For I was hungry and you gave me something to eat, I was thirsty and you gave me something to drink, I was a stranger and you invited me in, I needed clothes and you clothed me, I was sick and you looked after me, I was in prison and you came to visit me.

MATTHEW 25:35-36

The seventh work of mercy, "burying the dead", comes from the Book of Tobias 1:21. Caravaggio painted this large canvas as the mission statement, if you will, of a charitable organisation founded in 1601 by seven young Neapolitans from seven noble families. The foundation continues to this day.

The original concept for the commission was for seven separate panels; in a stroke of genius, however, Caravaggio brought all seven acts together in a single composition that has, since its completion in early 1607, hung over the high altar of the church. A museum touchscreen near the painting allows you to navigate around the work and zoom in to see it in greater detail. For a bird's eye view of the painting, head upstairs to the Quadreria, the picture gallery which features an impressive collection of 16th – 19th-century works, especially from Baroque painters active in Naples such as Giordano, Ribera and Caracciolo.

Michelangelo Merisi da Caravaggio, known for his love of prostitutes, young boys and brawling, fled to Naples from Rome in 1606 after killing a young man there. The Colonna family gave him protection and in that year Caravaggio painted *The Seven Acts of Mercy*. Some months later he left for Malta where he found wealthy patrons in the Knights of Malta, but he was soon arrested and imprisoned for another brawl that left a knight seriously wounded. Caravaggio escaped to Sicily where he received more well-paid commissions while displaying strange behaviours such as sleeping fully armed in his clothes.

After nine months, he returned to Naples to ask the Colonna family to protect him once more while he waited for a pardon from the Pope. He then painted *The Martyrdom of Saint Ursula*, his last work. In 1610 Caravaggio took a boat from Naples to Rome in order to receive the Pope's pardon, which he trusted would be granted thanks to his powerful friends. But he never made it, apparently dying of a fever during the journey. Speculation continues about lead poisoning – which might explain Caravaggio's uncontrollable violence. Only in 2010 did researchers exhume certain remains found in a church in Porto Ercole, Tuscany, and concluded, thanks to DNA and carbon dating analysis, that the remains were almost certainly those of Caravaggio.

Today at least three important Caravaggio paintings are on display in Naples: *The Seven Acts of Mercy* at Pio Monte della Misericordia, *The Martyrdom of Saint Ursula* at Galleria di Palazzo Zevallos Stigliano and *The Flagellation of Christ* at Capodimonte.

NAPLES CATHEDRAL: IL DUOMO ⟨MAP 10⟩

Though it was dedicated to Santa Maria Assunta (Our Lady of the Assumption) at its consecration in 1314 and is the seat of the Naples Archdiocese, **most visitors to Naples know the Duomo as the Cathedral of San Gennaro** (Naples' patron saint). It's true that the famed Miracle of San Gennaro Blood Liquefaction Ceremony takes place here three times a year and that a side chapel was installed at the Duomo as an ex-voto to the Saint after the plague beset the city in 1527. It's also true that just thirty years earlier, after being relocated several times, San Gennaro's remains finally came to rest in a special crypt beneath the apse. The cathedral, some historians contend, was built by the Angevins to coincide with the 1,000th anniversary of the death of San Gennaro (305 AD).

Arriving at Enrico Alvino's understated 19th-century Neo-Gothic façade, you may feel cheated at first. If you've visited a Duomo in another Italian city, say Florence or Milan for example, the first thing you'll notice is that Naples' Duomo doesn't necessarily pack the same punch. You won't see its cupola from all over the city - although you'll see the cupolas of a hundred other churches. There is no grand piazza leading to the Duomo's entrance - but there is enough parking in front for a large wedding party. And you just might walk right by the Duomo the first time without even noticing it. But don't let that fool you. The Duomo is much more than "just another Italian church".

This French Gothic masterpiece turned Baroque workshop sits on top of and around a mishmash of ancient pagan temples and early Christian structures. Some were demolished and some preserved. Each left some small trace of itself somewhere within or below the Cathedral. To understand what the Duomo looked like before it was Baroquised, take a good, long look at its form. Peel away all the Baroque ornamentation and you'll begin to see its pointed Gothic arches, the clerestory, the Latin Cross plan as it was conceived by its original designers. Head down the left aisle to the back of the church, where a failed attempt to return the Cathedral to its former glory left one vault stripped back, exposing its Gothic skeleton.

Find the ancient ruins upon which the Duomo was built - the 4th-century AD basilica commissioned by the first Holy Roman Emperor (306 - 337), Constantine I *aka* Constantine the Great. It was built on the remains of a pagan temple dedicated to Apollo and incorporated into the Angevin design as a side chapel. It was dedicated to the African virgin and martyr, Santa Restituta in the 5th century. Tucked in the back of this chapel is the Byzantine San Giovanni in Fonte Baptistery that is also attributed to Constantine. The oldest surviving baptistery in the western world, it was discovered in the 1970s, around the same time Greek, Roman and Paleo-Christian ruins were unearthed beneath the cathedral (they unfortunately closed to the public). Today you pay an extra small fee to get into this one-room vestige where a bulbous dome sparkles with Byzantine mosaics.

EXPLORE SOME MORE

Visitors short on time might want to skip the **Museum of the Treasure of San Gennaro**, but those with a deep interest in religious history, iconography or jewellery will want to set aside a few hours to soak up everything on offer here. Located next door to the Duomo you'll find one of the most important and valuable collections of jewels in the world, purportedly outshining the Crown Jewels of England or the treasures of the Russian tsarist court.

Naples Cathedral - Il Duomo

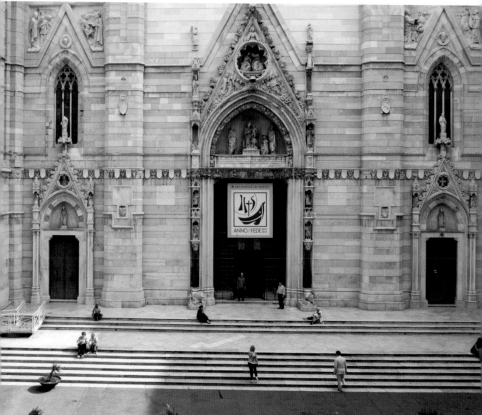

THE FESTIVAL OF SAN GENNARO

Born to a rich patrician family in the 3rd century AD, San Gennaro became a priest at fifteen years. He was sentenced to death for his beliefs during the persecution of Christians by Emperor Diocletian.

According to legend, after San Gennaro was decapitated in 305 AD at Vulcano Solfatara his blood was collected by a pious woman and conserved in two glass vials. His blood liquefies every September 19th. The event is repeated December 16th, and every Saturday before the first Sunday in May, as well as on special occasions such as for visits of prominent persons, or threats from natural disasters. The miracle is supposed to usher in a year of good fortune for Neapolitans. The blood doesn't always liquefy on command however, sometimes taking several hours or – most ominously – fails to liquefy at all.

Scientists have wanted to study the phenomenon, but are not allowed to open the ampoule as Church leaders fear they will damage or ruin the blood. Hence, scientists have used alternative methods, but have been unable to come up with an adequate explanation for the phenomenon. Many people note that during the years when San Gennaro's blood has not liquefied, bad things have happened to the city. Others maintain that when they come to mass and witness the liquefaction, in particular when they kiss the reliquary, they are healed of all sorts of ailments.

Thousands of devotees crowd into the Duomo to witness the miracle of the liquefaction. The Cardinal himself conducts the mass, then takes out the reliquary and moves to the front of the church while the congregation applauds and waves white handkerchiefs. He walks with the liquefied blood down the middle aisle for all to see. He continues his procession outside and announces to the city that the liquefaction has occurred, then he returns the blood to the altar. The people are thus reassured, as word goes out across Naples, that San Gennaro has yet again blessed the city.

BAROQUE RICHES:
GIROLAMINI MONUMENTAL COMPLEX ⟨MAP 11⟩

When you walk down Via dei Tribunali into the heart of Centro Storico, a massive church on your right commands your attention. Its principal façade, the work of Ferdinando Fuga, sits at the far end of a small piazza, Piazza dei Girolamini. You may never see the doors to this Florentine style church open and the piazza is not much to look at, but linger here a minute or two and you'll eventually notice the Banksy (British graffiti artist) work on a wall to the right of the church. The entrance to this church is actually around the corner on Via Duomo, through the Monumental Complex of Girolamini designed by the Florentine architect Giovanni Antonio Dosio. It's a vast compound built during the Spanish Vice-Royal period by the Oratorian Fathers (1592 - 1619), a secular clergy founded by San Filippo Neri in Rome. It is to him that the church is dedicated, while the complex takes its name from the order's first meeting place (1561), the San Girolamo della Carità church in Rome.

Inside the complex are two cloisters, the small *chiostro maiolicato* and the larger 17th-century cloister which is blessed with an abundance of orange and lemon trees. The former leads to the church, the latter to the picture gallery. The church, which is about as large as the Duomo, is **filled with Baroque treasures by Neapolitan masters**. Of particular interest is Luca Giordano's depiction of the Neapolitan *lazzaroni* in the fresco above the principal entrance, *Christ Expelling the Traders from the Temple*. **Giuseppe Sanmartino's Angels** are not to be missed, which along with his Veiled Christ are said to be the most famous and important works of this 18th-century Neapolitan sculptor. Very much a prized possession, they were returned to the church in June 2013 by the Capodimonte museum after a 34 year hiatus.

The Picture Gallery features a collection of 16th to 18th-century works by masters of the Neapolitan school: more works by Luca Giordano as well as those of his contemporaries like Battistello Caracciolo, Jusepe de Ribera, Francesco Solimena and Massimo Stanzione. The gallery was the first of its kind in the city and created thanks to a donation made by a Neapolitan tailor. Though it is not currently open to the public, the complex is also home to the oldest library in Naples (1586), the second oldest in Italy - the *Biblioteca dei Girolamini*. The archive of nearly 160,000 precious texts is now under the control of the Italian state after it was discovered that the library's director had been looting the library since his appointment in 2012.

Opposite page: Banksy, Piazza dei Girolamini

19TH CENTURY RELOCATION:
GAETANO FILANGIERI MUNICIPAL MUSEUM ⟨MAP 12⟩

A few hundred metres south of the Duomo is the 15th-century Florentine Renaissance palazzo, Palazzo Como. Had it not been for Prince Gaetano Filangieri (1824 - 1892), this palazzo would have been lost when Via Duomo was widened during Naples' Urban Renewal - the **Risanamento di Napoli**. **Thanks to his generosity, the palazzo was saved**, having been dismantled piece by piece, moved back 20 metres and re-erected in its current location. He filled it with an eclectic assortment of art and artefacts and presented it to the city (1888). Much of this collection was destroyed by fire during WWII, but it was rebuilt and today it includes over 3,000 objects: medieval weaponry, decorative arts furniture, paintings, especially from Neapolitan masters such as Jusepe de Ribera, Francesco Solimena and Francesco Jerace; there is also a library of 30,000 volumes dating from the 13th to 19th centuries.

A few doors down from here is the 16th-century **San Severo al Pendino** church. It was restored and reopened after 50 years during May of the Monuments in 1999 and is now the property of the city. The event and exhibition space hosts concerts, cultural events and exhibits such as the annual exhibit of *presepe* art organised by the Associazione Italiana Amici del Presepio.

Gaetano Filangieri Municipal Museum

EXPLORE SOME MORE

At the centre of Piazza Calenda is something archaeologists believe may actually be part of **one of the gates of the Greek city**. The locals call this the **Cippo a Forcella**, meaning a "marker stone in the Forcella district" or *Cipp' a' Furcella* in Neapolitan. In fact in Naples to say that something reminds you of this: "S'arricorda o' Cipp' a' Furcella", means that it is incredibly old. It is in a grave state of decay; however, the Trianon Theatre located in Piazza Calenda "adopted" this ruin in 2013, vowing to make it safe, maintain it and equip it with proper lighting.

THE WHEEL OF THE ESPOSTI: BASILICA DELL'ANNUNZIATA MAGGIORE ⟨MAP 13⟩

They were called the "**Children of the Madonna**". Abandoned babies - perhaps they were illegitimate or perhaps the family was too poor to keep them - they were given over to the protection of the Virgin and the church. From its inception in the 14th century until the state took over in the 1950s, Annunziata has always tended to these tiny souls. Today it is connected to a maternity and paediatric hospital. If you look outside to the left of the main entrance, you can still see where these babies were deposited. A plaque marks the day it was closed in 1875, though babies continued to be accepted by the orphanage till the 1980s. The child was placed into a wooden revolving wheel - **la ruota degli esposti** - and turned inward to the church. The nuns immediately washed and baptised the child in the same room, placed a medal around its neck with its registration number on one side and the image of the Virgin on the other and gave it over to a nursing mother. The nuns recorded everything they knew about each child in a book in case the parents wanted to reclaim them later. Those who weren't reclaimed often took the surname Esposito. It is a reference to the verb *esporre* (the past particle being *esposti*), which means to be exposed, put out or displayed. The name occurs in official documents for the first time in 1623 and it's the fourth most common name in Italy, though Esposito family members are especially numerous in northern Lazio and Campania. In recent years 25th March, the Feast of the Annunciation, has seen bearers of this name commemorate their origins by visiting the wheel, the focus of so much heartache and hope through the centuries.

Joachim Murat, King of Naples 1808 – 1815, attached some shame to the name Esposito, so he ordered that each day a new surname would be assigned to babies left to the church's care. This continued for some years and in 1862 a baby boy was given the name Genito, later mistranscribed as Gemito. Thus Vincenzo Gemito, that sublime sculptor, received his name.

If you visit the Annunziata Maggiore during May of the Monuments, a group of elementary school students will take you to the room where the nuns accepted the babies and they will eagerly tell you the story of this church, whose history is extremely important to this community. (Another wheel, though not in situ, is on display at the Museum of the Works at Santa Chiara.) Very little survives of the original church founded by the Angevins in the 13th century. The church we see today, whose grey and white interior is nothing short of angelic, is one of Luigi Vanvitelli's (1700 - 1773) finest works. Luigi, who was also the architect of the Royal Palace of Caserta, didn't live to finish it but his son Carlo carried out his vision.

GATEWAY TO THE SEAFOOD: PORTA NOLANA ⟨MAP 14⟩

Not far from the Circumvesuviana Station, two towers, Torre del Fede and Torre della Speranza, flank the ancient 15th-century port entrance to the city, Porta Nolana. The gate got this name because the road outside it led to Nola and, like Porta San Gennaro and Porta Capuana, it was frescoed after the plague of 1656. Behind this gate, Naples' best seafood market bustles with a chaotic hum only locals seem to understand. Rarely frequented by tourists, the Porta Nolana Market is **where Neapolitans go in search of ingredients for their daily meals that are so rich in seafood**: clams and mussels, shrimp and oysters, squid and octopus, sea bass and sword fish, anchovies and sardines, the all important *bacalà* - salted cod and *capitoni* - eels for the traditional Neapolitan Christmas Eve dinner and everything in between, plucked fresh out of the sea. Best bets are anything *veraci*, live, like *vongole veraci* or *capitoni veraci*. If you are squeamish about killing your own *capitone*, for the price of a caffè (about 90 centesimi), the expert fishmongers will take care of it for you.

Porta Nolana

MAMMA D'O CARMENE!

A useful exclamation familiar to every Neapolitan – but what are its origins? They go a long way back, possibly to the 8th century, and they are focussed on a church in the lively, chaotic, story-rich district of Naples near Piazza del Mercato. Here you'll find a church called the Basilica Santuario di Santa Maria del Carmine Maggiore, a basilica devoted to Mary of Mount Carmel. And amongst the many associated stories is that of some monks who, fleeing persecution in Palestine, arrived in Naples carrying with them a painting of a 'Brown Madonna' (dark-skinned). They were granted a chapel for the image and a strong cult of devotion developed linking the poor people of Naples to La Madonna Bruna. Experts date her image to only the 13th century and the style is definitely Tuscan; however, one shouldn't let such details get in the way of an excellent tale!

The bell tower, the tallest church tower in Naples at 75 metres high, first gets a mention in the archives in 1439 during power struggles between the Angevins and the Aragonese. What we see now outside is largely Baroque; inside are 5 bells, each named for a saint. It is the tower that draws the crowds at 10 p.m. on 15th July each year, on the eve of celebrations for Mary of Mount Carmel. To the great satisfaction of locals and the utter astonishment of visitors, Neapolitans proceed to burn down the tower. Well, that's certainly what it looks like, as all 75 metres of the structure are elaborately strung about with fireworks which explode, cascade and breathe smoke around it while flickering lights increase the Gothic horror effect in the windows.

It begins as the crowds assemble, the Mayor and VIPs in their special seating area, fire crews at the ready, band playing, sweetcorn sales in full swing. Suddenly the lights are dimmed and a line of fire shoots from a nearby building. Soon there are burning letters in front of the church Napoli devota alla Madonna Bruna. Then the tower and the sky seem to explode. After a glorious 25 minutes or so, all is darkness. And a star of lights is winched along a line to 'collect' a picture frame shape, representing La Madonna Bruna, before they climb back to the tower. Thus Mary extinguishes the fire.

No-one is sure how this tradition began, though it is known that both squares, Mercato and Del Carmine, have seen some violent times. In 1268 Conrad of Sweden was executed here by order of Charles I (Anjou) and his body buried in the church. At the time of Masaniello's revolt in 1647 there was already a practice of setting up a pretend wooden fort in Piazza Mercato and staging an attack upon it before burning it down. Certainly that revolt began in early July as preparations for church celebrations were under way. So perhaps these elements were stitched together resulting in the extraordinarily thrilling firework display we see today. However it came about we can join the locals in exclaiming Mamma d'o Carmene! with enthusiasm!

BOURBON
⚜ EXPANSION ⚜
CAPODIMONTE
⪼⪼⪼ AND ⪻⪻⪻
THE SANITÀ

Cover Photo:
Borgo dei Vergini

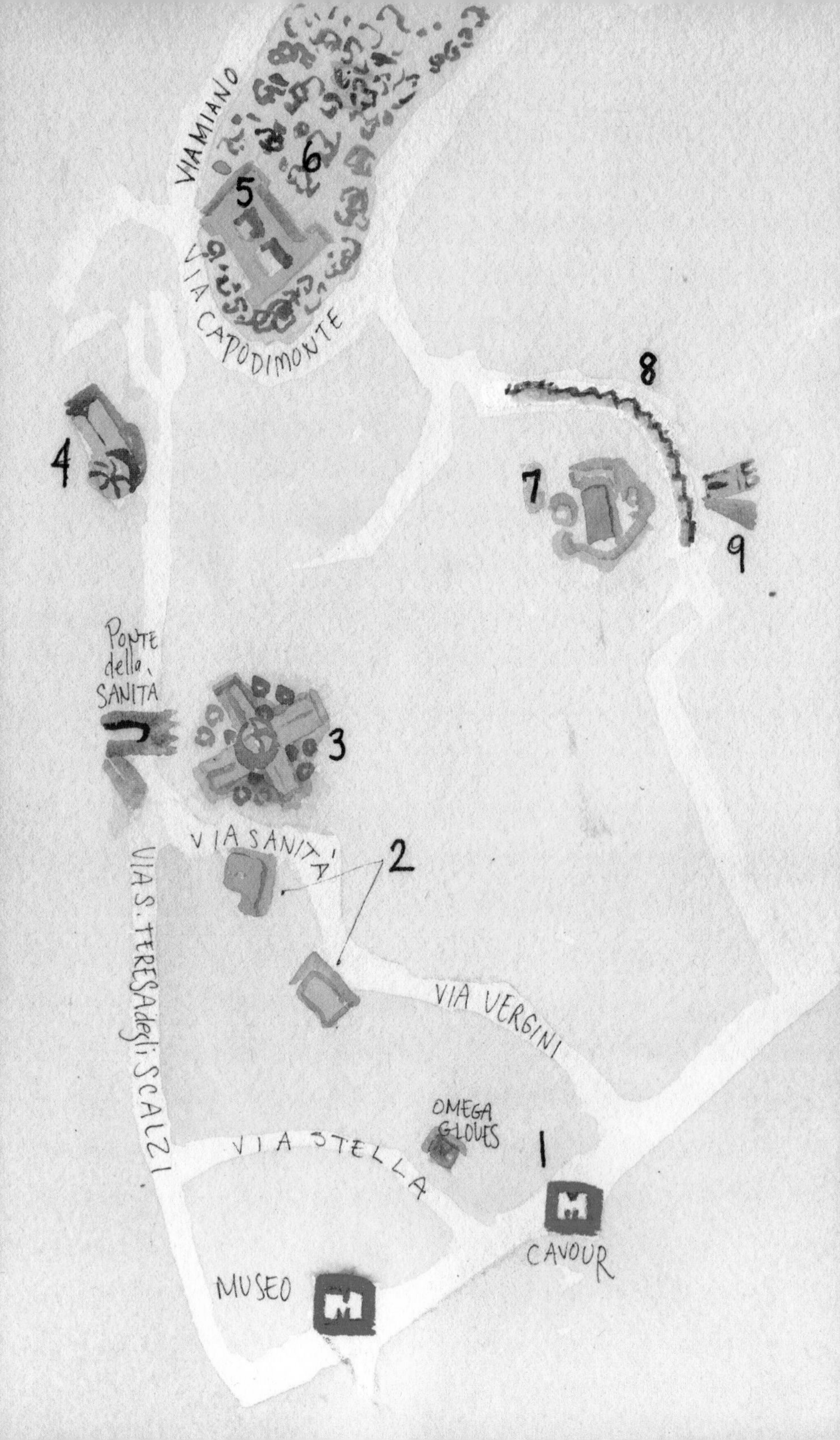

VIAMIANO

VIA CAPODIMONTE

5

6

8

4

7

9

Ponte
della
SANITA

3

VIA SANITA

2

VIA S. TERESA degli SCALZI

VIA VERGINI

OMEGA
GLOVES

VIA STELLA

1

MUSEO
Ⓜ

CAVOUR
Ⓜ

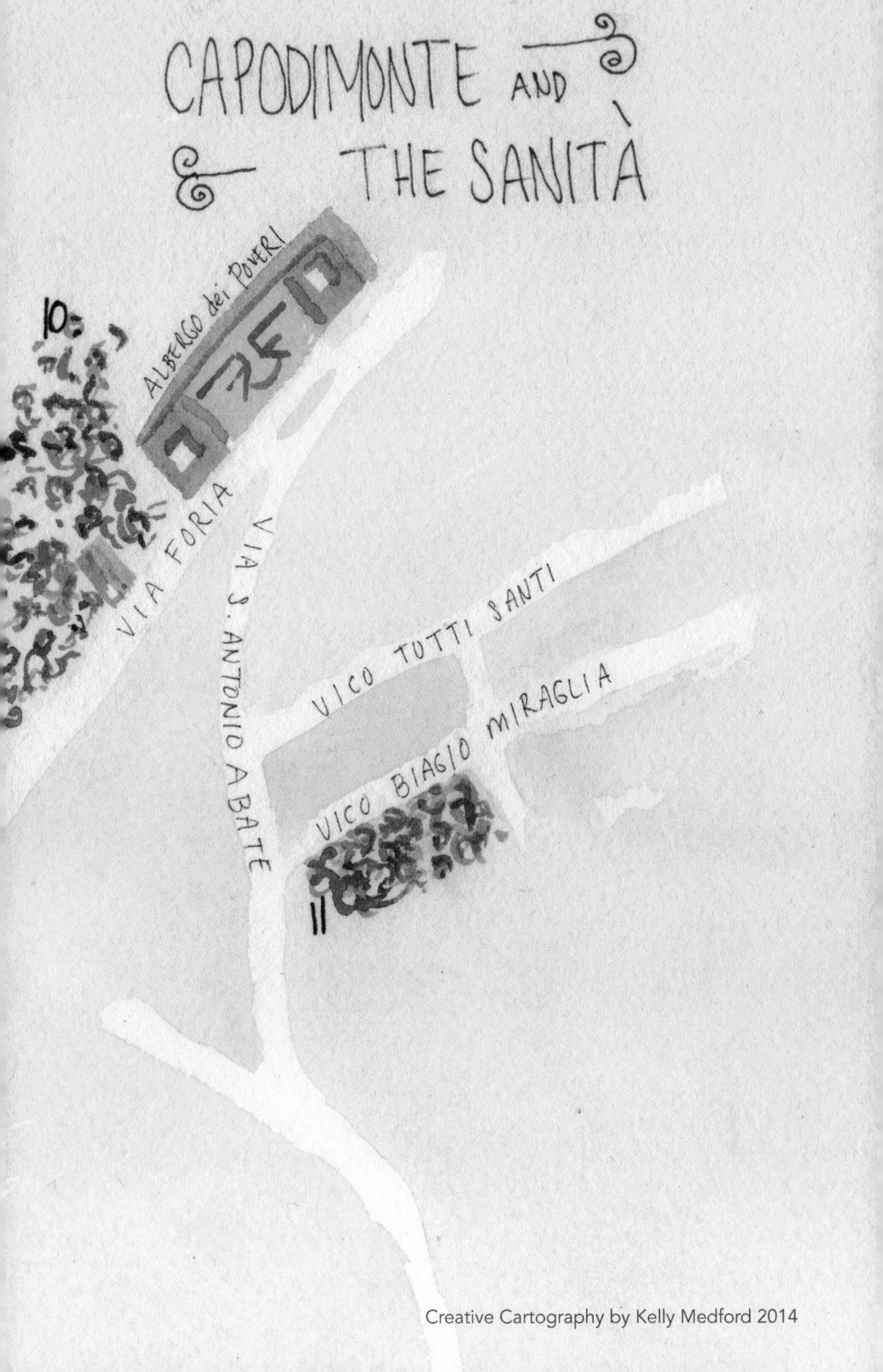
CAPODIMONTE AND THE SANITÀ
ALBERGO dei POVERI
10
VIA FORIA
VIA S. ANTONIO ABATE
VICO TUTTI SANTI
VICO BIAGIO MIRAGLIA
11

Creative Cartography by Kelly Medford 2014

When the fifth son of Philip V of Spain was crowned King Charles VII of Naples (later III of Spain) in 1735, his first stop was to pay homage to the remains of San Gennaro, the patron saint of the city, whose blood is said to have liquefied immediately.

Charles (1716 - 1788) was the first monarch of this blessed, though not turmoil-free, dynasty; the Bourbons would reign until 1861, bringing political stability and Enlightenment ideals to Naples, turning the city into a modern metropolis, and expanding the city northwards from Porta San Gennaro into today's Rione Sanità and Capodimonte districts.

His building projects constitute the most enduring mark King Charles left on the city and they continue to impress today. The Teatro San Carlo

turned Naples into a focal point for musical genius. He was 21 years old the day it opened in 1737. Charles had major upgrades done to Palazzo Reale and added three more palaces to the Bourbons' Campania collection: the Royal Palace of Caserta, the Royal Palace of Portici and Capodimonte, his hunting-lodge-turned-palace on Capodimonte hill. He brought his mother's (Elisabetta Farnese) art collection to the palace and built the Capodimonte Porcelain factory in the grounds. Charles also built the Albergo dei Poveri (Royal Hospice for the Poor).

His son and successor King Ferdinand IV (I of the Two Sicilies) brought about the Royal Astronomical Observatory and though the French decreed and laid them out, it was actually Ferdinand who conceived the "Royal" Botanical Gardens. Meanwhile, the Bourbons' expansion northward begat a flurry of building projects at the foot of Capodimonte hill. Noble families built first in the area of Borgo dei Vergini which sat along the path the Bourbon kings and their court used to make their ascent to Capodimonte Palace.

Cupola of Santa Maria della Sanità from Ponte della Sanità

PLAN YOUR VISIT

Capodimonte and the Sanità can certainly be toured on one's own with this guide. Don't forget to see the Fontanelle Cemetery, the Catacombs of Naples and the Hellenistic Necropolis (see A Tale of Two Cities: The Naples Underground). For those with a deeper interest in the neighbourhood's history, two local non-profit organisations organise excellent walking tours of the neighbourhood and the underground: Catacombe di Napoli and Celanapoli. Catacombe di Napoli (Catacombs of Naples) is a grassroots project involving a priest and the youth of the Sanità. They restored the Sanità's largest catacombs - the Catacombs of San Gennaro - and have created the infrastructure of a first rate tourist attraction complete with an excellent website and bilingual guides.

This energetic group of youths have devised two walking tours of the Rione Sanità (every Sunday by reservation): The Holy Mile and the Valley of the Dead. The group's other project is a B&B - Casa del Monacone (Big Monk) Hospitality that is housed in the convent near the Santa Maria della Sanità church. Here Neapolitan designer Riccardo Dalisi worked with the youngsters to redesign the spaces and restore the furnishings that were once used by monks. The result was six "warm and cosy" and tastefully decorated rooms. Another route through the Rione Sanità is with Carlo Leggiere and his Celanapoli Association. As a passionate advocate for his neighbourhood, Carlo Leggieri has made it his life's mission to protect, conserve, restore and promote the cultural treasures of the Sanità.

TRANSPORT

METRO/RAILWAYS
M1: Museo
M2: Cavour

BUSES
178, C52, C53, C55

PONTE DELLA SANITÀ ELEVATOR
Open weekdays 07.00 – 21.30, Sun 08.00 – 14.30

TOURIST INFO

CAMPANIA ARTECARD
ArteCard 365, Napoli & Tutta la Regione

SIGHTS & ATTRACTIONS

ASTRONOMICAL OBSERVATORY OF CAPODIMONTE
Salita Moiariello, 16
Open for special events
+39 081 5575111
na.astro.it

BASILICA MADRE DEL BUON CONSIGLIO
Tondo di Capodimonte, 13
Open daily 08.00 – 12.00 and 17.00 – 19.00
+39 081 7410006

BOSCO DI CAPODIMONTE
Via Miano, 4
The Bosco is reached through the Porta di Mezzo gate behind the Polizia di Stato building. The Porta di Miano entrance is at

the other end of the park at Discesa Bellaria.
Open daily at 07.45. Park closes 19.30 Apr -
Sept; 18.00 Oct, Feb & Mar; 17.00 Nov- Jan
Free
+39 081 7410080
boscodicapodimonte.it

CAPODIMONTE MUSEUM
Via Miano, 2
Entrances at Porta Piccola at Via Miano, 2
and Porta Grande at Via Capodimonte.
Open daily **except Wed** 08.30 – 19.30
Adults €7.50, Audio Guide €5.00
+39 081 7499111
polomusealenapoli.beniculturali.it
Due to cutbacks, some of Capodimonte's
collections are open only according to a
special schedule. Check before visiting.

ENGLISH CEMETERY
Piazza Santa Maria della Fede, entrance at
Vico Biagio Miraglia
Open daily 07.00 until 1 hour before sunset

OMEGA SRL GUANTI
Via Stella, 12
+39 081 299041
omegasrl.com
Call to visit. Purchase Omega gloves at their
shop in Stazione Marittima.

PALAZZO SANFELICE
Via Arena della Sanità, 19
Doors to the palazzo are normally open
during the day and you can peek inside.

PALAZZO DELLO SPAGNUOLO
Via dei Vergini, 19
Doors to the palazzo are normally open
during the day and you can peek inside.

S. MARIA DELLA SANITÀ
Piazza Sanità, 14
Open daily 09.30 – 13.00, Sat 09.30 – 13.00
& 17.00 – 19.00
Catacombs are open daily 10.00 – 13.00

Admission €8.00
+39 081 7443714
catacombedinapoli.it/basiliche.asp

TORRE DEL PALASCIANO
Salita Moiariello, 53
By guided tour only - contact Celanapoli
Carlo Leggieri
+39 3475597231
celanapoli.it

UNIVERSITY OF NAPLES BOTANICAL GARDENS
Via Foria, 223
Open Mon - Fri 09.00 – 14.00 with advance
notice. Call ahead, leave surname and
number of visitors. Can be done same day.
Free
+39 081 2533937
ortobotanico.unina.it

GUIDED TOURS

CATACOMBE DI NAPOLI
Sacred Mile Tour & Valley of the Dead Tour
Every Sun at 09.30 by reservation
Meeting Point is Via Capodimonte, 13
Duration circa 3 hours
€15.00
+39 081 7443714
catacombedinapoli.it

CELANAPOLI
Guided Visit of Rione Sanità
Every Sun at 10.00, duration 2 hours
Meeting Point is Porta San Gennaro
€5.00
+39 347 5597231
celanapoli.it/visite_guidate.html

THE HUB OF THE SANITÀ : BORGO DEI VERGINI ⟨MAP 1⟩

Every one of Naples' neighbourhoods tells a different part of the city's story. Centro Storico is the keeper of Naples' history while the Lungomare tells of its geography. Poets and mystics haunt Posillipo and the spirits of artists past and present linger on *le scale di Napoli*. Bellini and Dante districts are the guardians of philosophers, intellects and musicians while Kings and Queens keep watch over Municipio, the power centre of the city. And the Rione Sanità? That is the heart and soul of the city, a neighbourhood Italians would describe as *suggestivo* - "evocative". Here **wealth and poverty, ecstasy and agony, religion and superstition and life and death dance the tarantella in an animated *tableau vivant* that could have only been imagined by Caravaggio's brush**.

The Sanità starts at the foot of Capodimonte hill just behind Piazza Cavour and snakes its way up a valley cradled by the Materdei, Scudillo, Miradois and Stella hills. The name Rione Sanità derives either from the district's abundance of fresh air (in the days when it sat outside the city walls) or for the many miracles attributed to the saints and martyrs buried here in huge caverns burrowed out of the yellow tuff. The caverns gave sanctuary to the dead; the tuff was transformed into shelter for the living, the two forming an eternal symbiotic relationship. The Greeks built tombs here for their aristocrats, the Romans dug catacombs for their saints, martyrs and noblemen and starting in the 1500s, the Sanità was a depository and paupers' cemetery for every major epidemic until the cholera outbreak of 1836.

The epicentre of the Sanità is the Borgo dei Vergini (Village of the Virgins), a small area at the foot of Capodimonte hill close to the Cavour metro station. This was the point of departure for the Bourbons' northern expansion, when ornate family *palazzi* such as Palazzo Sanfelice and Palazzo dello Spagnuolo were built. Today, the Borgo dei Vergini is the busiest and liveliest part of the neighbourhood. The Sanità's daily market fans out along Via Vergini, Via Mario Pagano and Via Sanità and it was here that John Turturro staged Pietra Montecorvino and Max Casella's performance of *Dove Sta Zazà*.

WINGS OF THE HAWK: THE SANFELICE PALAZZI ⟨MAP 2⟩

The holy trinity of Bourbon architects in Naples were Luigi Vanvitelli, Ferdinando Fuga, and Ferdinando Sanfelice. Sanfelice (1675 - 1748) was a painter, nobleman, master of the Neapolitan Baroque and an architect with a very individual signature: monumental staircases, especially open ones. His double staircase dominates the entrance to San Giovanni Carbonara. He designed an unusual hexagonal double staircase at Capodimonte: one side leads to the Bourbons' apartments, the other to the servants' quarters. One of his staircases adorns Palazzo Serra di Cassano in Via Monte di Dio and there are two in the Rione Sanità, his practice piece at his

THE GLOVEMAKER: MAURO SQUILLACE

On the top floor of an 18th-century palazzo, Mauro Squillace runs the internationally renowned glove business, Omega srl Guanti. Fifty years ago, small glove shops filled the Sanità district in downtown Naples, but organised crime and large manufacturers from China and the Philippines drove most out of business. Mauro, on the other hand, took over his family enterprise, one that spans four generations. His is the third; his son is already learning the trade while his daughter designs for Omega. He's proud of his company's long heritage - a photo of his grandparents hangs on a wall of his office. Today Mauro distributes his gloves internationally, including to France, Germany and the United States. Many of his gloves have appeared in magazines and the President of Italy even visited his company, writing him a thank you letter. What's the secret of his success? Every one of his gloves is handmade by expert craftsmen and craftswomen. His employees still use the non-electric Singer treadle sewing machines from the early 1900s, they cut the leather by hand and use natural light to distinguish colour shades.

Twenty-five people play some part in each glove produced. First, the leather is stretched, being careful to make sure the stretch of the leather will be vertical rather than horizontal. The material is then cut and pounded so that the impression for the fingers becomes clear. At this point, Mauro has about fifty different (often elderly) women throughout the city who receive the cut leather and sew the gloves together. They return the gloves to Mauro, who gives them to his employees inside the palazzo. They use scraps of leather from the cutting room to fill in the gaps between the fingers. One of these women has worked in Mauro's company since she was eighteen; she is now over eighty. The gloves go on to be lined with cashmere, silk or other materials. Mauro explains that the only difference between the way he makes gloves and the way his grandfather made them is that his grandfather used one stitch to marry the lining and the leather together, whereas Mauro uses glue. The lining and leather are then sewn together at the cuff. The gloves often come and go from this palazzo twenty-four times before they are ready. At the very end of the process, each glove is put on a hot broiler that looks like a metal hand. Then it's placed between two slabs of marble for several hours in order to make its shape. Mauro checks every glove individually before it's ready to be sent out to the shops.

Palazzo Spagnuolo

family home, **Palazzo Sanfelice**, and another a few doors down at **Palazzo dello Spagnuolo**. The last of these, an awe-inspiring work of architecture and an iconic Neapolitan landmark, was the backdrop for *Comme Facette Mammeta - How Your Mama Made You* in John Turturro's *Passione*.

Though its name recalls a 19th-century Spanish resident Tommaso Atienza, Palazzo dello Spagnuolo was built in 1738 for Marquis Nicola Moscati. The palazzo is a prime example of Neapolitan Rococo; its **signature Sanfelice open staircase has been dubbed *Ali di Falco*, Wings of the Hawk**. The architect of record is Francesco Attanasio. Sanfelice's name never appeared on any documents related to the palazzo, but his hand clearly guided its design, if not directly, so that it may be considered of the Sanfelice school. Financial problems mired the palazzo in scandal and Moscati ceded it to the Marquis of Livardi after incurring high debts. In 1813 Livardi in his turn was forced to sell to the Spanish nobleman Don Tommaso Atienza. Atienza commissioned a new architect to do extension work, but he was so unhappy with the result that he went to court. The proceedings cost Atienza an exorbitant amount and he too had to sell the palazzo, apportioning several sections to three different owners; four portions, however, remained empty as no willing buyers presented themselves.

For years, and hopefully it will be again soon, this palazzo was home to the Museum of Totò, otherwise known as The Prince of Laughter - Antonio De Curtis (1898 - 1967) who was born not far from here at Via Santa Maria Antesaecula, 109. A comedic and dramatic actor, poet, writer, songwriter and singer, Totò was one of the most influential Italian artists of the 20th century. His song *Malafemmena*, a melancholy story about a man betrayed by the woman he loved, is one of the most beloved Neapolitan songs of all time.

O' MUNACONE: SANTA MARIA DELLA SANITÀ (MAP 3)

You may not know this church, but you might have seen its **striking majolica tiled cupola** from the Ponte della Sanità - the bridge the French built to connect the city proper to Capodimonte. The cupola is the signature work of its designer, the Neapolitan architect and Dominican friar, Frà Giuseppe Nuvolo. His unusual elliptical cloister was bisected by the construction of the bridge, but his early 17th-century circular-plan church survived, a shining example of counter-reformation architecture.

The double spiral staircase that leads to the main altar and presbytery was an ingenious device the friar used to incorporate the 5th-century chapel and Catacombs of San Gaudioso into the church's design. The locals know Santa Maria della Sanità as San Vincenzo (Ferreri) - the Dominican saint to whom the church is dedicated - or more commonly, as O' Munacone - the Big Monk.

The church's light-filled interior of white and grey is the setting for one of the best collections of Neapolitan art in the city. Works by Baroque masters such as Luca Giordano, Francesco Solimena and Andrea Vaccaro sit side-by-side with works by contemporary artists such as Riccardo Dalisi's *La Mensa degli Angeli* (2005) in glass and crystal and Anna Maria Bova's *San Vincenzo* as well as the frame she created for the 5th/6th-century image of the Madonna and Child that was found in the catacombs and is believed to be the oldest in Naples.

When Charles VII (III of Spain) constructed Capodimonte, his summer palace and hunting lodge on an isolated hilltop far from the city, it seemed the perfect location for a royal getaway. He forgot one pesky little detail however - to build a direct route between the city and Capodimonte. The Bourbons used to ascend to the Capodimonte Palace along a steep and winding path through the Rione Sanità. When the French took power, they embarked on a number of road projects, one of which was building a bridge, **Ponte della Sanità** or **Ponte Maddalena** over the Sanità creating a more direct route to Capodimonte Palace. While the project was a triumph for the king and his court, it not only cut Santa Maria della Sanità's cloister in half, it also effectively cut off the Rione Sanità from the city. Since it was no longer on the path of the king and his men, the Rione Sanità was eventually abandoned by nobility and it became a neighbourhood of the people. An elevator was installed in the bridge in 1937 re-connecting the residents of the Sanità with the city above. In 2011, the city honoured Maddalena Cerasuolo, (credited with saving the bridge during the Quattro Giornate of 1943), by renaming the bridge Ponte Maddalena and placing a plaque on the bridge in her honour.

THE CHURCH BUILT FOR A NUN'S PAINTING: BASILICA DELL'INCORONATA MADRE DEL BUON CONSIGLIO ⟨MAP 4⟩

A massive church not far from the Capodimonte Museum guards the entrance to the Catacombs of San Gennaro. **Designed in the likeness of St. Peter's in Rome**, Naples' youngest church (1920 – 1960) was built for the devotees of the Madonna del Buon Consiglio, Our Lady of Good Counsel and to house a painting of the same name. This painting, commissioned from Raffaele Spanò by Sister Maria di Gesù Landi in 1884, was associated with two miracles. Fervent prayer before the painting was believed to have ended the cholera epidemic of that year. In 1906, the rain of Vesuvian ash pummelling the city ceased a few days after Sister Maria displayed the artwork to the public on the balcony of her home. A ray of light shone onto the painting as the ashfall diminished. Recognition for both the painting and the cult that had developed around it came when the work was 'coronated', (formally blessed and endowed with a crown), by Pope Pius X on January 6th, 1912. Eight years later, construction started on the church that was built for the pilgrims who were pouring into the city to see the painting.

Basilica dell'Incoronata Madre del Buon Consiglio

Sister Maria di Gesù Landi did not live to see the completion of the church she longed for at the Catacombs of San Gennaro, but her miraculous painting remains, taking the place of honour on the major altar. Other works at Madre del Buon Consiglio include several rescued from abandoned and closed churches, a copy of Michelangelo's *Moses*, as well as the tombs of the Princesses of the House of Savoy, Anna and Elena d'Aosta, Archbishop of Naples Corrado Ursi and Maria di Gesù Landi herself.

The church sits just above Tondo di Capodimonte, a piazza and roundabout designed by Antonio Niccolini in the early 19th century as a stopping point on the way to the Capodimonte palace. Here there is another one of Naples' stairways - the *Scalinata di Capodimonte*, the entrance to which is framed by two Neo-Egyptian sculptures. It was built in the early 19th century to connect Corso Amedeo di Savoia to Capodimonte. The fountain outside the church - the Fontana della Duchessa - was given to the city in 1939 by the Duchess of Aosta, Hélène of Orléans.

NINE ARTFUL CENTURIES: CAPODIMONTE (MAP 5)

Overlooking gardens, courtyards, the city and the sea, Capodimonte sits atop a sun-drenched hill by the same name. Here, in this king's hunting lodge that became a palace, resides one of the finest art museums in Italy. Home to a **vast collection spanning nine centuries, it unites under one palatial roof works from the great masters to the most important artists of our time**. It's spread over three floors with much of the first floor occupied by the Farnese Gallery.

The core of the museum's original holdings was the expansive collection which King Charles VII (III of Spain) inherited from his mother Elisabetta Farnese. Today those works are split between Capodimonte and the National Archaeological Museum. Much of the second floor is devoted to the museum's most prized possession - the Galleria delle Arti a Napoli, a collection of works from the Neapolitan school spanning the 13th to the 18th century, and featuring the work of figures central to the Neapolitan Baroque movement: Jusepe de Ribera, Andrea Vaccaro, Massimo Stanzione, Artemisia Gentileschi, Luca Giordano and, of course, Caravaggio represented by his *Flagellation of Christ*, one of three Caravaggios in the city.

Overall gallery highlights include: Michelangelo's sketch for *Venus and Cupid*; Sandro Botticelli's *Madonna and Child and Two Angels*; Francisco Goya's portraits of Maria Luisa of Parma and Charles IV King of Spain: El Greco's *Portrait of Giulio Clovio* and Titian's *Annunciation*. Capodimonte was the first museum in Naples to dedicate a space entirely to contemporary art and is still the only fine art museum in Italy that has a section of modern art. This collection, housed on the third floor, features Andy Warhol's *Vesuvius* and an impressive photographic section that opened in 1996 with 50 photos by Mimmo Jodice.

THE ROYAL HUNTING GROUNDS:
REAL BOSCO DI CAPODIMONTE (MAP 6)

Robin Hood and his Merry Men might not have frolicked around the Reale Bosco di Capodimonte, but like Sherwood Forest, this royal *bosco*, (woodland), was a hunting ground fit for a king, the Bourbon Charles VII (III of Spain). Designed by Ferdinando Sanfelice to indulge the king's love of the chase, **today the gardens cover over 130 hectares** (just slightly larger than Caserta). They feature a huge variety of tree species, many of them exotic ones introduced in the 19th century, when much of the park was given a Romantic make-over. It's also one of Italy's largest urban parks, one of the largest green spaces in the city and one of Naples' best kept secrets. It's easy to see why.

Whether you enter Capodimonte through the Porta Piccola gate or the Porta Grande, the first thing you encounter are Capodimonte's English style gardens: the palm trees, grassy areas and winding paths that encircle the palace, the *belvedere*, the beautiful view once known as the *Veduta di Napoli* that overlooks the city and the bay. If you didn't know about the Bosco, you might take a quick jaunt around, perhaps even stop for a picnic in the grass, and think that was that. But go further and you'll find your way onto the king's hunting grounds, a mix of wide open grasslands and forested paths that are a peaceful and often solitary respite from the bustling city.

Not far from the Porta Piccola entrance is a building marked Polizia dello Stato. In the 19th century this was the Fabbricato Scuderie, the Royal Stables. Today it maintains much the same function, though stabling the horses of the State Police's mounted unit rather than the king's. Behind this building is the wide cobbled path that leads to the Porta di Mezzo - the gateway to Bosco Reale. Like the fingers of your hand, five major paths fan out from this gate and like spider veins, more than 100 secondary paths fan out from these.

A variety of statues, fountains and buildings pepper the park's landscape. Of special note is the Royal Porcelain Factory - the *Real Fabbrica della Porcellana* that is now the Istituto Giovanni Caselli, a secondary school (high school) with a strong artisanal programme in the tradition of porcelain making. The building was designed by Ferdinando Sanfelice, father of the winged staircases, as was the nearby Church of San Gennaro. If you follow the path by these two, you will find the Miano Gate, a secondary entrance to the park about 1½ kilometres north of the Porta Piccola gate.

ROYAL STARGAZING:
THE ASTRONOMICAL OBSERVATORY OF CAPODIMONTE ⟨MAP 7⟩

If you visit the National Archaeological Museum, you will no doubt encounter the Salone della Meridiana (meridian sundial) on the first floor. A 54 metre long room with a zodiacal sundial, this was the site of Naples' first astronomical observatory after years of pleas from scientists. In 1791 King Ferdinand IV finally decreed the founding of the Observatory and according to his wishes to create a Museum and Academy of Arts and Sciences, the north-eastern corner of the Royal Museum in Palazzo degli Studi was selected. The project was quickly abandoned, but not before the sundial was installed in the floor. Twenty years later, the observatory project found a more suitable location not far from Capodimonte and a new supporter in Joachim Murat, King of Naples who wanted to build a proper seat for the study of astronomy.

Construction started in 1812 but the king was ousted before the Observatory was completed. Ferdinand IV was returned to power as Ferdinand I, King of the Two Sicilies and he continued with the project, **calling on Giuseppe Piazzi, founder of the Palermo Astronomical Observatory and discoverer of the Ceres asteroid/ dwarf planet to complete the work**. When it was done in 1819 Ferdinand named Piazzi (1746 - 1826) director of the Naples and Sicily observatories. The Italian astronomer Annibale de Gasparis, winner of the Gold Medal of the Royal Astronomical Society (1851) and discoverer of nine asteroids was the Observatory's director from 1864 - 1889.

Had it not been for the marriage of Bourbon King Charles VII (later III of Spain) to Maria Amalia of Saxony (1738), Naples' famed **Capodimonte Porcelain Factory** might never have been born. It was Maria Amalia's family who sparked the king's interest; her grandfather Augustus II, the King of Poland, founded the first porcelain factory in Europe in Meissen, Germany. Charles and his wife brought the craft to Naples, commissioning the best scientific and artistic minds to develop a secret porcelain manufacturing technique. This was a century when courtly money and technically-minded brains across Europe were dedicated to uncovering the mysteries of porcelain production, previously monopolised and exploited by far eastern countries. The finest ceramics, as opposed to earthen or tin glazed ware, had to be imported until this period. Charles and Maria Amalia's hilltop factory opened in 1743 in a building designed by Ferdinando Sanfelice in the Real Bosco di Capodimonte. When Charles's father, King Philip V of Spain died in 1759, Charles was recalled to the Spanish throne and the factory went with him. His son and successor, King Ferdinand IV (I of the Two Sicilies) continued the tradition, opening a new factory, Real Fabbrica Ferdinandea in Portici. That factory was also short-lived but the tradition lives on outside Naples, especially in Milan and the Veneto region, where 80% of Capodimonte works are now crafted.

Salita Moiariello

DOWN THE UP STAIRCASE: SALITA MOIARIELLO ⟨MAP 8⟩

An urban trek that is not for the fainthearted (**it's a long and precipitous incline/ decline of nearly 2km**) - partly stepped and partly steep ramps - Salita Moiariello runs from Capodimonte to Via Foria. Its name is probably a nod to the area's agrarian history - a term for a measurement of grain, the Latin *modius* becoming *moggio* (Italian) or *moio* (Neapolitan). Over time the sense shifted from the grain to the amount of land you needed to plant a *moio's* worth of it and Moiariello may have been the name of some small farmstead on the spot.

The *salita* was built by the Bourbons on Miradois hill and was the site of a number of skirmishes between the Neapolitans and the Germans during the Quattro Giornate. It is said this stairway was once climbed by coaches. Perhaps that explains the short steps. Perhaps not. What is more certain is that the area near the bottom of the *salita* - on Via Giuseppe Piazzi - was the location where Sophia Loren's character, the young Neapolitan and ever pregnant Adelina, sold contraband cigarettes to support her family in director Vittorio De Sica's 1963 film, *Ieri, oggi e domani*.

LE QUATTRO GIORNATE – THE FOUR DAYS OF NAPLES

What were these 'Four Days' commemorated at the Ponte della Sanità? Naples, September 1943. A grim picture. Naples had suffered hundreds of Allied bombing raids leaving possibly as many as 25,000 dead, tens of thousands wounded, much of the city destroyed and irreplaceable cultural and artistic patrimony obliterated. What was left was in a truly desperate state. Under the terms of the Cassibile Armistice (signed 3rd September but announced on 8th) the Italians switched sides transforming the Germans overnight from allies to occupiers. By September 9th the latter had received their orders; Naples was to be reduced "to cinders and mud". This was the same day Operation Avalanche – the invasion at Salerno by U.S. & British forces – began, an operation that would cost many lives.

Meanwhile in Naples, violence against the citizenry in the ensuing days turned the place into a pressure cooker of fear and desperation. Six Germans died on 10th in a skirmish at Piazza del Plebiscito for which retaliation included the burning of the National Library. The Italian military commanders having fled, Colonel Walter Schöll assumed command of Naples on 12th September. On September 22nd a decree was issued that all males between 18 - 33 were to present themselves to be deported for forced labour. That same day resistance fighters secured some weapons from an Italian military depot, a raid repeated on 25th. Meanwhile, an order of 23rd had required the evacuation of some 240,000 citizens from buildings near the sea – a possible prelude to the destruction of the port. There was rioting and many arrests followed. On 26th resistance fighters began an armed uprising across Naples, joined by Neapolitans of all ages, all political persuasions and both genders. As impromptu barricades appeared in the alleyways, i scugnizzi, the street urchins, engaged in this new and dangerous game. On 29th Colonel Schöll was forced to begin negotiations with resistance leaders, offering to release prisoners in exchange for the safe conduct of his forces out of Naples. Fighting continued as they departed and the final German act was the destruction of port facilities and the setting of vicious booby-traps that would wreak havoc later. On the morning of 1st October, Allied forces entered Naples.

These four days in Naples, 27th - 30th September 1943, have gone down in history as a triumph of the human spirit. The city was awarded the Medaglia d'Oro al Valore Militare, the Gold Medal of Military Valour. In 1945 a film by Giacomo Gentilomo, 'O Sole Mio, recounted these events; but it was director Nanni Loy who in 1962 poured the collective emotions of Neapolitans into Le quattro giornate di Napoli. The film received two Oscar nominations. None of the actors was credited; they wanted to honour the citizens who sacrificed so much. Thanks in part to this film and to images such as Robert Capa's famous photograph (October 1943) of a Naples street child draped in an ammunition belt, the scugnizzo came to personify the ideals and courage of this time. Marino Mazzacurati's 1963 monument Allo Scugnizzo formerly in Piazza Repubblica, Riviera di Chiaia is an eloquent example of this (hopefully to be returned once metro works are competed) while numerous plaques around Naples mark places where Neapolitans fought and died. The naming of the Quattro Giornate Metro Station and the adjacent piazza also plays its part in keeping these epic four days in mind.

THE MYSTERY TOWER: TORRE DEL PALASCIANO ⟨MAP 9⟩

Riding along the tangenziale near Naples' Business District, *Centro Direzionale*, you might see the reddish-brown cap of a strange looking tower rising out of the foliage on Capodimonte hill. A unique bit of architecture, at least for Napoli, its presence here seems somewhat out of place; whereas if you were in Florence this tower would seem perfectly at home. Known as Torre del Palasciano, it's part of the 19th-century palazzo of the same name that sits on Salita Moiariello just a few hundred metres below Capodimonte. The lower structure, the part you can't see from the highway, is an eclectic mix of Neo-Gothic and Renaissance styles. The imposing central tower took on a more Romanesque look, clearly **inspired by Florence's 95 metre tall Torre d'Arnolfo atop Palazzo Vecchio** (Palazzo della Signoria). And, like its Florentine counterpart, Torre Palasciano was also adorned with a flat-faced clock near the base of the tower.

The Neapolitan architect Antonio Cipolla undertook construction of the Palazzo Palasciano for the surgeon Ferdinando Palasciano (1815 - 1891). It was completed in 1868. Palasciano bought the property from infectious disease specialist Domenico Cotugno. The estate included several structures, some of which were worked into Cipolla's design, a temple, and beautiful gardens and fruit trees. At the tippy-top, Palasciano's tower has a prospect that can only be described as a *vista mozzafiato*, a breathtaking view that sweeps across the city and the bay. Legend says the good doctor was so fond of the palazzo that his ghost continues to haunt the place, just for a glimpse of his view from the tower. If you want to tempt fate, you might try a night in the B&B La Torre di Ro located at the top of the tower.

Doctor Palasciano is better remembered for an incident that occurred while he was serving in Messina during the riots of 1848. He provided medical care to both sides, an act the king considered treasonous. The doctor, however, would not be deterred saying that:

Regardless of what army they belong to, the wounded are sacred to me and cannot be considered as enemies.
FERDINANDO PALASCIANO

Palasciano served one year in prison, but his case gained international attention and provided the basis for the Geneva Convention of 1864 that gave life to the Red Cross. His declaration became one of the guiding principles of that august humanitarian organisation.

GREEN IN THE CITY:
UNIVERSITY OF NAPLES BOTANICAL GARDEN ⟨MAP 10⟩

If you need a reprieve from the bustle of downtown Naples, the Botanical Gardens lie smack in the middle of the city, and yet cover **15 hectares of tranquil land next to Charles VII's Albergo dei Poveri** (The Royal Hospice for the Poor). It was Charles's son and successor Ferdinand IV (I of the Two Sicilies) who wanted to build a Royal Botanical Garden here, but his plans were quashed with the outbreak of the Parthenopean Revolution of 1799. The Botanical Gardens are credited to Giuseppe Bonaparte, opened in 1810 during the short lived French reign (1806 - 1815) and they are now under the purview of the University of Naples' Department of Natural Science. Among the most important botanical gardens in Italy for both the quality and the breadth of the collection exhibited, the site is more research and educational facility than a city garden, but it is nevertheless open to the public.

FOREIGNERS' FINAL RESTING PLACE:
THE (EX) ENGLISH CEMETERY ⟨MAP 11⟩

A Scottish mathematician, an Irish writer and a Dutch painter who was the founder of the Posillipo School of Painting; a Swiss industrialist, a US Navy Midshipman, and a German botanist who was a one-time director of the Botanical Gardens; an English archaeologist and a newly wed English couple that were killed on their way to Paestum by a single bullet shot that passed through the husband first and then his wife. (A plaque memorialises this tragedy at Christ Church Naples in Chiaia.) Here lie the remains of foreigners, especially Anglo Saxons, who passed away or were killed in Naples. At least they used to.

The ex-English Cemetery was built in 1826 in the Borgo of Sant'Antonio Abate in the garden of the Santa Maria della Fede complex thanks to the British Consul Sir Henry Lushington. A once elegant and serene garden, its original purpose was to give a final resting place to Protestants who passed away in Naples but it eventually served a variety of foreigners. The cemetery closed in 1893 during the Risanamento di Napoli (Naples' urban renewal program) and the burials were moved to a new English Cemetery at Doganella. The garden fell into a long period of disrepair and became the property of the Comune di Napoli. Restoration works were done to re-open it as a park in the 1990s and it has since been designated an Historic Garden. Today, **nine tombs and two sculptures by Francesco Jerace remain** including the tomb of Mary Somerville by Jerace. The adjacent church was built in 1645 and one hundred years later King Charles VII's wife, Maria Amalia of Saxony, turned it into a shelter for vagrant women. Later it became a hospital for prostitutes.

■ ■

EXPLORE SOME MORE

It was never meant to be just a hospital for the poor, but rather a self contained community for the poor where they could live, work and learn a trade. At one time several thousand people lived here. Today, it is open only for the odd exhibit or concert. This mammoth white building is on Via Foria at Piazza Carlo III; behind its recently restored façade (2006), much of the property lies dormant. It was the project of King Charles VII (III of Spain) whose building enterprises are legendary, though his altruistic activities are less so. The king commissioned Ferdinando Fuga to build his **Albergo dei Poveri, Royal Hospice for the Poor**. It is five storeys tall, 354 metres long, and possesses 100,000 square metres of usable space (1/5th of what the original plans projected). At its completion in 1751 it was one of the largest edifices in 18th-century Naples, if not Europe.

■ ■

Opposite page: Albergo dei Poveri

THE GREEN AND THE BLUE LUNGOMARE

Cover Photo:
Boats on the Bay of Naples

CORSO VITTORIO EMANUELE

AMEDEO M

CH

MERGELLINA M

VIA RIVIERA di CHIAIA

VIALE ANTONIO DOHRN

6

VIA MERGELLINA

VIALE GRAMSCI

VIA CARACCIOLO

PORT of
MERGELLINA

MERGELLINA

7

FONTANA
del
SEBETO.

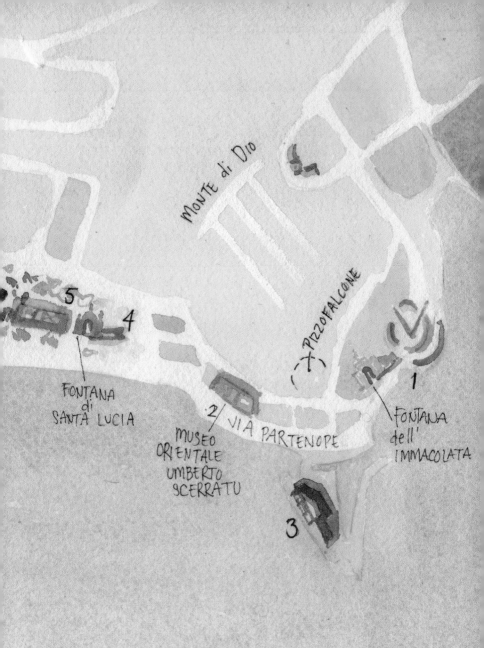

Monte di Dio

Pizzofalcone

5

4

1

FONTANA
di
SANTA LUCIA

2 VIA PARTENOPE

MUSEO
ORIENTALE
UMBERTO
SCERRATU

FONTANA
dell'
IMMACOLATA

3

LUNGOMARE

If the **Bay of Naples** is one vast amphitheatre, then the Lungomare has to be its front row seats.

The Seafront Promenade, *Lungomare*, is a **green and blue oasis in the centre of the city with some of the most sweeping, magnificent views in the world.** Towards the east you'll see Castel dell'Ovo jutting out into the bay on the tiny island of Megaride. Behind the castle Vesuvius dominates the skyline then melds into the rugged terrain of the Sorrentine Peninsula. In the middle of the bay, the unmistakable alligator shape of Capri rises out of the sea pointing towards the promontory of Posillipo, which wraps itself back around to Mergellina at the western end of Lungomare. The city behind

Castel dell'Ovo da Santa Lucia - 6 -febbraio 2008 - ore 15,42 .

Lungomare is a marvellous patchwork of reds and pinks, yellows and oranges and blues and greens climbing up the Posillipo, Pizzofalcone and Vomero hills. Castel Sant'Elmo and the San Martino Charterhouse stand guard over the city from the Vomero.

Via Nazario Sauro, Via Partenope and Via Caracciolo: three different names for this gorgeous 3.5km long stretch of road that hugs the bay. It's one of the easiest, most beautiful strolls in Naples. Piazza del Plebiscito to Mergellina is almost all flat terrain (although there might be some cobblestones along the way). Lungomare is a magnet for joggers and strollers (both the walking and the rolling kind), sunbathers and swimmers and young lovers and old married couples and it's a favoured backdrop for wedding and first holy communion pictures. Along the way you'll find boat and bike rentals, a few small free beaches, a plethora of places to stop for refreshment and plenty of Naples' famed white rocks to laze out on and take the sun. No maps, no agendas, no travel books are required (except this one of course). Let the mountain be your compass, the curve of the bay be your guide.

Castel dell' Ovo, Lorenzo Dotti, 2008

Plan Your Visit

Transport

METRO/RAILWAYS
M2: Amedeo & Mergellina
M6: Mergellina
FUNICULAR: Chiaia & Mergellina

BUSES
140, 151, 154, C12, C18, R7

Sights & Attractions

ANTON DOHRN AQUARIUM AND ZOOLOGICAL STATION
Villa Comunale

Open Mar - Oct, Tues - Sun 09.30 – 18.00,
Nov – Feb, Tues - Sun 09.30 – 16.30
Adults €1.50
+39 081 5833111
szn.it

CASTEL DELL'OVO
Via Eldorado, 1, Borgo Marinari
Open in winter Mon - Sat 09.00 – 18.30, Sun
09.00 – 14.00. In summer Mon – Sat 09.00 –
19.30, Sun 09.00 – 14.00
Free
+39 081 7954592

MUSEO ORIENTALE UMBERTO SCERRATO
Via Chiatamone, 61/62
Open Thurs & Fri 11.00 – 14.00, Mon – Wed

by appointment only
Free
museorientale.unior.it

VILLA COMUNALE PARK
Open Autumn and Winter 07.00 – 22.00,
Spring and Summer 07.00 – 24.00
Free
+39 081 7953652

Bikes, Boats & Beaches

FOX RENT
Via Partenope, 37
Tandem bikes, bikes, boats, scooters and
cars
+39 081 7645060
foxrent.it

Along Villa Comunale
on Via Caracciolo find
rentals of tandem bikes
and coin operated electric cars for kids and
skate rental near the skating rink

Boat Rentals
- Largo Nazario Sauro
- Borgo Marinari near the entrance to Castle
dell'Ovo
- Via Caracciolo near Mergellina Port

Bathing Beaches
- Largo Nazario Sauro on Via Nazario Sauro
- Spiaggia Colonna Spezzata at Piazza
Vittoria
- Spiaggia Rotonda Diaz on Via Caracciolo
- Spiaggia Largo Sermoneta on Via
Mergellina

Largo Nazario Sauro

VESUVIAN SUNRISE: LARGO NAZARIO SAURO ⟨MAP 1⟩

Via Cesario Console connects Piazza del Plebiscito with Lungomare at Via Nazario Sauro, named for the Austrian-born (now Slovenia), Italian military hero Nazario Sauro (1880 - 1916). Heading southwest from here you'll come to a bronze statue of Umberto I on the city side of the street. He sits in front of the Cervantes Institute, an organisation that teaches the Spanish language and promotes Spanish culture. At the water side is Largo Nazario Sauro, a small rotunda replete with snack kiosks and boat rentals. This is **a spectacular place to watch the sunrise behind Vesuvius** or better yet, take an award-winning shot of it. Not far from here, where

Fontana dell'Immacolata

the road takes another bend west and its name changes to Via Partenope you will find one of three 17th-century Baroque monumental fountains on Lungomare, the Fontana dell'Immacolata or del Gigante sculpted by Pietro Bernini and Michelangelo Naccherino. This is another great spot for a Vesuvian sunrise photo.

ON THE BOARDWALK: VIA PARTENOPE (MAP 2)

Via Partenope is **the most picturesque part of Lungomare**. It extends all the way to Piazza Vittoria where it becomes Via Caracciolo. Both roads were pedestrianised when the city hosted the America's Cup in April 2012 and Mayor Luigi de Magistris' battle cry of *Lungomare Liberato* kept this entire stretch of the seafront car-free. Less than a year later, however, a tragic building collapse on Riviera di Chiaia displaced scores of residents, crippled businesses and forced the city to re-open Via Caracciolo to reroute traffic away from the site. Unfortunately, Via Caracciolo remains open to traffic, but Via Partenope is still pedestrianised and is now a favourite venue for biking, jogging, power-walking, rollerblading and just plain strolling. Horsedrawn carriages and street performers - Pulcinella, local bands, breakdancers, artists - add to the atmosphere on the weekends as the crowds show up in force. For those interested in more cultural pursuits, there is the **Museo Orientale Umberto Scerrato**. It is dedicated to Umberto Scerrato, an archaeologist and professor at the Orientale University, and the museum collection includes ceramics, metals and other materials from Iran, Egyptian and Islamic funerary steles and Chinese porcelain.

At the eastern end of Via Partenope are four of Naples' most exclusive hotels: the Excelsior, the Santa Lucia, the Vesuvio - Enrico Caruso passed away here - and the Royal Continental, which sits directly across the street from Castel dell'Ovo and Borgo Marinari. From the Castle to Piazza Vittoria there is a long line of al fresco restaurants, bars and cafés serving cold drinks, fresh seafood and traditional Neapolitan Pizza - even Sorbillo opened a restaurant here in the summer of 2013. Since Via Partenope was pedestrianised these restaurants now have unimpeded views of the bay; al fresco dining means breathing in the sea breezes as opposed to car fumes and outdoor seating has doubled in size as these restaurants have expanded into former street parking.

VIRGIL'S HIDDEN EGG: CASTEL DELL'OVO (MAP 3)

Castel dell'Ovo stretches out upon a tiny island once called Megaride. Known today as Borgo Marinari for the fishermen who once plied their trade here, in recent decades this tiny village has transformed itself into a treasured spot that is popular for its seafront bars and restaurants, spectacular vistas and isolation from the din of the city. It was the famous Roman poet Virgil (70 BC - 19 BC) and

the legend of his magical, mythical egg that gave the oldest castle in the city its name. The legend goes that Virgil placed an egg into a glass jar, the jar into a metal cage and hid all three beneath the castle. As long as the egg remained intact, the city would too. One of the many flaws with this myth, of course, is that Virgil lived long before Castel dell'Ovo was actually a castle.

What stood on Megaride during Virgil's time was Castellum Lucullanum, a substantial villa built by the Roman knight and patrician Lucius Licinius Lucullus (118 – 57/56 BC). It was lavishly appointed and stretched from Megaride all the way to the top of nearby Monte Echia. Recent discoveries made during the metro project suggest the villa reached as far east as Piazza Municipio. Monte Echia is also known as Monte di Dio - "God's Mountain" - and Pizzofalcone. Erri de Luca immortalised this neighbourhood in his novel *Montedidio* and Mariano Vasi tells us:

> *This hill was formerly called Echia, perhaps from the name Hercules, and was afterwards denominated Lucullana, because it was partly occupied by the gardens and palace of Lucullus, a Roman consul; this was formerly united to the Castello dell'Uovo, but the separation of the ground was caused by an earthquake. [...] on the top of the hill, there was in Charles of Anjou's time a Royal chase of Falcons, and from this circumstance the hill derived its present name of Pizzo Falcone. The chase was afterwards cut down, and an edifice was constructed on its site for the detention of convicts, but in more recent times it was converted into military barracks...*
>
> GUIDA DI NAPOLI, DEI CONTORNI DI PROCIDA, ISCHIA E CAPRI, 1826, A NEW
> GUIDE OF NAPLES, ITS ENVIRONS, PROCIDA, ISCHIA AND CAPRI, p.184.

According to myth, Naples traces its origins back to this hill and a siren named Parthenope who washed up on the shores of Megaride. Though this colourful bit of lore has not been borne out by either the archaeological or historical record, Strabo (63/64 BC – 24 AD), the travelling Greek historian and geographer, did mention in his *Geography* (trans. H.L. Jones, 1991) that the tomb of Parthenope existed near Neapolis and that a torch race was held every year in her honour. The most plausible scenario is that Greek sailors, most likely the Euboeans who had landed first at Cuma and who were extending their settlements around the Gulf of Naples, made their way to Megaride some time between the 9th and 8th century BC. They formed a small settlement and installed commercial and military ports near Parthenope's supposed burial place at Megaride, naming it in her honour. Eventually, they expanded inland and built a walled settlement on the hilltop that corresponds to the promontory of Pizzofalcone. By the 6th century

Pizzofalcone and Caserma Nino Bixio

Look up and east from Via Caracciolo and you'll see a vast pinkish red building perched on top of Pizzofalcone hill. This is the oldest military academy in Europe which effectively seals the end of Via Monte di Dio. **La Nunziatella** was founded in 1787 to turn out officers for the kingdom of Naples. These days the boys and, in a recent innovation, girls, study strategy, topography, firearms practice, horse riding and all manner of sports within a classic Italian school programme. Twice a year the cadets parade to Piazza del Plebiscito for a grand ceremony. At other times you see them out and about, dressed either in summer white buttoned jackets and blue trousers or their winter black with dramatic cloaks and *spadini* – short dress swords – always on display. You'd think there has been a mass breakout from the opera house! But you have to dress and act the part when you live and work in a splendid red citadel like La Nunziatella. Via Monte di Dio is also the home street of Italian president Giorgio Napolitano and he remains deeply attached to this part of the city.

BC, Parthenope was thriving, yet just a century later, the Greeks built a new city a short distance away, named aptly enough, "new city" or Neapolis. Parthenope became known as Paleopolis, or the old city, eventually lost its importance and faded away. It was lost but not forgotten; even today you will hear Neapolitans refer to themselves as Parthenopeans.

Nothing of Parthenope remains at Megaride and the few modest ruins extant on the promontory of Pizzofalcone are not those of Parthenope, but those of Villa Lucullus. Evidence of the Parthenopean necropolis on Pizzofalcone, however, was found in 1949 at number 10, Via Giovanni Nicotera during the renovation of a building damaged during WWII. The artefacts found there at long last confirmed both the existence of Parthenope and its Cumaen origins. They were moved to the National Archaeological Museum and the site was covered over. By the mid 5th century Villa Lucullus had lost its allure and the structure on Megaride was converted to a fort. It was here that the so called last Roman Emperor Romulus Augustulus was exiled and lived until his death. It later found use as a monastery until the Normans turned it into a proper castle in the 12th century.

Castel dell'Ovo is open to visitors and is definitely worth a visit. You can wander through some of its echoing halls and admire the views of Vesuvius and the bay from the top. Hold your hand out over the western edge at the top (taking care not to lean out **too** far); there's an exhilarating rapid uprush of wind up the face of the castle. Nearby temporary art exhibits by local artists are often on display; the castle hosts the Vitigno Italia wine trade fair every spring, and on New Year's Eve it is illuminated by the city's fireworks display.

You can also see the promontory of Pizzofalcone from the top of the castle, peeking out from between the two buildings of the Royal Continental Hotel. The area around the promontory has been under renovation since 2009 with construction of the Santa Lucia public elevator that will eventually connect the promontory of Pizzofalcone to Santa Lucia, but it's still worth the journey. From the hilltop there is an interesting but essentially melancholy view of Lamont Young's Villa Ebe, built in late 19th-century style between 1920 - 22 but sadly now derelict following an arson attack. The Scottish (though Naples-born) architect and urban planner took a pistol to his head on the terrace here in 1929.

A ROYAL PROMENADE: VILLA COMUNALE ⟨MAP 4⟩

Nestled between Pizzofalcone and Posillipo Hills, Villa Comunale Park has the enviable position of flanking Riviera di Chiaia on one side and the bay on the other along the Via Caracciolo stretch of Lungomare. The road was named in memory of Admiral Francesco Caracciolo, a hero of the short-lived Parthenopean Republic of 1799 who was hanged for high treason by Admiral Horatio Nelson, allegedly on Queen Maria Caroline's orders.

The park extends for over 1km between Piazza Vittoria on the east and Piazza della Repubblica on the west, home to the U.S. Consulate General Naples. It was first built as a paved road between Piazza Vittoria and Piedigrotta by the Spanish viceroy Duke of Medinaceli in 1697 who adorned it with thirteen fountains and two rows of willow trees on either side. Later, it became a Royal Promenade known as Villa Reale. Sitting directly on the shore, the park provided a much needed buffer between the hustle and bustle of the city and the tranquil sea.

> ... between the street and the sea, is the villa Reale the fashionable promenade. On one side the waves kiss the wall, and if you like you may sit for hours in the seats provided and dream of coral graves and purple mullets. Or you may walk in nicely-graveled paths, beneath palms, orange trees and bowers of blooming laurestinas, even though it be March. The whole air is full of perfume, and the promenades are thronged with the flush and the fair.
>
> DICK TINTO, NEW YORK TIMES, JANUARY 22, 1858

Those were the days when women donned gowns to stroll through the park and when only the rich, the royal and the famous graced its promenade. That is except for once a year on September 9th during the Festa di Piedigrotta, when

Not far from the sea-side entrance to Dohrn's Zoological station in Villa Comunale there is a nondescript tablet inscribed with a dedication from Germany: "La Germania dedica questa lapide". At first glance, you might surmise it's a dedication to Anton Dohrn. Oddly enough, it's not. It's **in memory of another one of Germany's illustrious sons, Heinrich Schliemann** who, depending on whom you ask, was either the father of modern archaeology or the "last of the great adventurer archaeologists".

> Germany dedicates this memorial tablet to the eternal memory of one of its most illustrious sons Heinrich Schliemann
>
> Who by bringing to light the remains of Troy, Mycenae and Tiryns restored a knowledge of the Homeric culture to the world
>
> He died in Naples 26 December 1890 during one of his many journeys to Greece

Schliemann died in Naples during a brief visit to see Pompeii and the Archaeological Museum before returning to Greece in time to spend the Christmas holidays with his beloved family. He collapsed on the street on Christmas day and died the next day under the care of strangers.

Skating Rink at Villa Comunale

all citizens were welcomed into the park, provided of course that they wore shoes. **The people eventually won the rights to their park** in 1869 and it was aptly renamed Villa Comunale – the People's Park. But then between 1872 and 1883 they lost their shoreline to Via Caracciolo. Despite this the sea remains a prominent feature of Villa Comunale and is an arresting contrast to the park's alabaster statuary and the lush greens that provide much needed respite from the Mediterranean's unrelenting sun.

These tree-lined paths are adorned with Neo-Classical sculptures and fountains including the Fontana di Santa Lucia (1606). The second 17th-century Baroque memorial fountain on Lungomare, it was the work of Michelangelo Naccherino and Tommaso Montani. An interesting assortment of late 19th and early 20th-century statues and busts commemorate some of Naples' local heroes and adopted sons and commemorate tragic moments in Naples' history. Near the Piazza Vittoria entrance is a monument to victims of organised crime, installed in 1994 during the World Ministerial Conference on Organised Transnational Crime. The park is also home to the recently restored Casina Pompeiana (1870) and the historic Cassa Armonica (1877).

The Coldiretti Farmers' Market occasionally sets up its stands here and the *Fiera Antiquaria Napoletana*, Naples' Antiques Market runs along the perimeter on Viale Dohrn two weekends a month. Naples' Tennis Club sits on the other side of Viale

Dohrn near Rotonda Diaz. Villa Comunale is a great place for jogging, walking the dog or just taking the kids to run around in the sunshine. Find tandem bicycles, roller blades and pint-sized motorised vehicles for rent; pony rides, playgrounds and a rollerskating rink; and Europe's oldest aquarium, Naples' Aquarium at the Anton Dohrn Zoological Station. And when you're ready to relax, find a bit of shade and indulge in some people watching at one of the four cafés that flank Villa Comunale or grab a *gelato* and take a seat on the seawall to sigh at those views.

A 19TH-CENTURY GEM: THE NAPLES AQUARIUM AT THE ANTON DOHRN ZOOLOGICAL STATION ⟨MAP 5⟩

Aquariums may be as old as the Roman Empire, but large public aquariums didn't make their début until the mid-1800s. Of course, the term large is relative here. Today's state of the art facilities dwarf the one-room aquarium that German naturalist Anton Dohrn added to his Zoological Station in Naples Villa Comunale Park in 1874. At the time, as Clara Erskine Clement tells us, it was "the finest and most important aquarium in the world". While it is tiny compared to its modern counterparts, **this little 19th-century aquarium is an architectural, scientific and historical gem and the only one left of its kind in the world.**

Entering the aquarium hall as it was once called, you are met with Dohrn's original design. Large tanks encircle three of the room's walls and a double row down the middle bisects the room. Illuminated only by sunlight streaming in from above the tanks, this dusky space is further darkened by the volcanic rock lining the sides of the tanks. Ranging in size from 250 to 69,000 litres, the tanks are filled with fresh seawater pumped in from the bay.

The system the aquarium uses today is based on the semi-open circulation system developed for Dohrn by English aquarist William Alford Lloyd. The only inhabitants of the tanks are the fauna and marine species indigenous to the Gulf of Naples - octopus and squid, starfish and sea urchins, eels, red coral, seahorses and sea turtles large and small. The Zoological station also operates a sea turtle rescue and rehabilitation centre at Bagnoli. The aquarium was an addition to Dohrn's Zoological station that was built in 1872 on land donated at the water's edge by the city of Naples. The station was the first of what Dohrn hoped would be a network of biological research facilities, built in locations served by the railway system - hence the name *stazione*. Scientists could travel between locations without the need to transport their equipment and research materials. As a sort of "scientists without borders" concept, Dohrn's station was open to the international Scientific Community and meant to be a place scientists could freely exchange ideas and information.

CATCH OF THE DAY: ROTONDA DIAZ ⟨MAP 6⟩

One of the glories of Neapolitan cuisine is fresh fish. The fresher the better, of course, and **at Rotonda Diaz you'll find the latest catch**. This semicircular structure with its equestrian statue of the Neapolitan WWI general Armando Vittorio Diaz (1861 - 1928) has Spiaggia Rotonda Diaz, a small free beach on one side. On the other side there are dinghy moorings for the local fisherman who have been up for hours netting these beauties; now they present the fish for sale, kept lively with cold water piped across the pans.

This is not the market for bulk-buying (best leave that for Porta Nolana) – but a place where a cook who is passionate about seafood can find inspiration for lunch or supper. And on a sunny day (this is, after all, Naples) half the pleasure is the

Catch of the Day at Rotunda Diaz

walk along the seafront and the salt tang of the water and the catch as you buy. And you'll see the cats turn up too – in the hope that not all the fish is destined for a bowl of pasta.

Naples is the place to come to for a bath in the fountain of youth and to fall in love with life all over again. The sun is enamoured of the place.
GUSTAVE FLAUBERT, THE LETTERS OF GUSTAVE FLAUBERT: 1830-1857, FRANCIS STEEGMULLER (TRANSLATOR)

SUNSETS AND SEASIDE CHALETS: MERGELLINA ⟨MAP 7⟩

If the Fontana dell'Immacolata is the place to be at sunrise, **Mergellina is the place to linger at sunset**. At this hour, raked by westerly light, the views towards Vesuvius and the bay are outdone only by the views towards the city, flooding the retina with exhilarating Mediterranean colours. The best way to take in the panorama? Sipping a cocktail at one of the "Chalets of Mergellina".

A rainbow assortment of seaside cafés – a good example is the yellow Chalet Ciro renowned for its *gelato* and pastry - wrap around Mergellina port from Via Caracciolo to Largo Sermoneto. Largo Sermoneto is also where we find the third 17th-century monumental Baroque fountain on Lungomare, the Fontana del Sebeto that was designed by Cosimo Fanzago and executed by son Carlo. It takes its name from the river Sebeto that once flowed from Monte Somma (part of Mount Vesuvius) and through Neapolis on its way out to the bay.

The name Mergellina, so it is said, comes from *mergoglino - mergellus albellus* - a species of duck known as smew. True or not, you'll definitely see your fair share of aquatic birds around Mergellina, namely in the form of dive-bombing seagulls. Once a fishing village - a small component of fishermen and a few fishing shacks linger still - Mergellina is better known now for its chalet cafés, private boat and yacht mooring and a small tourist port which has seasonal connections to Ischia and the Aeolian and Pontine Islands.

In November 2012 Naples' Mayor Luigi de Magistris, city officials and dozens of citizens took the inaugural ride along **Naples' Bike Path**, *pista ciclabile*. This 10km stretch running from Piazzale Tecchio in Fuorigrotta to Lungomare is the first leg of the bike path that will eventually connect Bagnoli on the western side of the city to San Giovanni a Teduccio on the east and is expected to be the longest in southern Italy. As part of a broader plan to create a sustainable mobility network, the project will link riders with key points around the city and various modes of public transportation and will include incentives for bike riders such as free transport of bicycles on the bus, funicular and Metro Lines 1 and 6.

SHOP, STROLL, SIT
AND
SAMPLE
CHIAIA

Cover Photo:
Chiaia from Sant'Antonio a Posillipo

CHIAIA

CHIAIA

🚇 CHIAIA

AMEDEO Ⓜ

PIAZZA AMEDEO

PASS COL

VIA FRANCESCO CRISPI

VIA GIUSEPPE MARTUCCI
PLART

5

4

VIA SAN PASQUALE a CHIAIA

VIA RIVIERA di CHIAIA

VIA CARACCIOLO

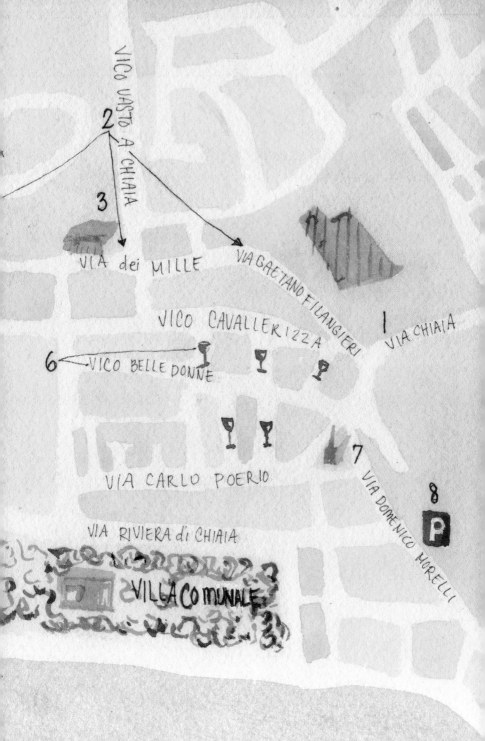

Creative Cartography by Kelly Medford 2014

Ancient and modern, shabby and chic, chaotic and... well, chaotic, Naples' Chiaia district has a vibe unlike anywhere else in the city.

Sandwiched between Pizzofalcone and Posillipo hills and stretching from the Vomero down to the sea, this neighbourhood is tailor-made for strolling, shopping, sipping and sampling... and did we mention tailoring? Neapolitan bespoke tailoring, that is.

Decked out in upmarket shops along its elegant boulevards and adorned with local boutiques and bars tucked inside the ancient *bassi* of its cobbled alleys, Chiaia is without question Naples' "hippest and happeningest" neighbourhood. Shop by day and return at night to drink in its lively wine bar scene which extends from the *vichi* to the seashore. This district's name, meaning beach, morphed from *plagia* (Late Latin) via *playa* (Castilian) or *platja* (Catalan) to become *Chiaja* and then *Chiaia* in Naples. However it got there, life's a beach.

Chiaia Alley

Plan Your Visit

Transport

METRO/RAILWAYS
M2: Amedeo
FUNICULAR: Chiaia

BUSES
128, 140, 151, 154, C12, C18, C24, C27

PONTE DI CHIAIA ELEVATOR
Open weekdays 07.00 – 21.30, Sun 08.00 – 14.30

Tourist Info

CAMPANIA ARTECARD
ArteCard 365, Napoli & Tutta la Regione

Sights & Attractions

CHRIST CHURCH NAPLES
Via San Pasquale, 15/b
English language service every Sun at 10.00
+39 081 411842
nuke.christchurchnaples.org

PAN PALAZZO DELLE ARTI
Via Dei Mille, 60
Open Mon & Wed - Sat 09.30 – 19.30, Sun 09.30 – 14.30
Free, except for special exhibitions
+39 081 7958604

PARCHEGGIO MORELLI
Via Domenico Morelli, 54
+39 081 19881166
agoramorelli.it

PLART
Via Giuseppe Martucci, 48
Open Tues - Fri 10.00 – 13.00 & 15.00 – 18.00, Sat 10.00 – 13.00
Adults €8.00 (including guided tour)
Guided tours in English available Wed – Sat
+39 081 19565703
fondazioneplart.it

VILLA PIGNATELLI
Riviera di Chiaia, 200
Open daily **except Tues** 08.30 – 14.00
Adults €2.00
+39 081 7612356
polomusealenapoli.beniculturali.it

Bespoke Tailors

(SALVATORE) ARGENIO
Suits, knitwear & accessories
Via Filangieri, 15/e
+39 081 418035
salvatoreargenio.com

(CESARE) ATTOLINI
Suits & accessories
Via Filangieri, 15D
+39 081 19506064
cesareattolini.com

CALIENDO
Suits & accessories
Vicolo S.Maria della Cappella Vecchia, 6
+39 081 7644401
sartoriacaliendo.com

(SARTORIA) CHIAIA-NAPOLI
Suits & accessories
Via Nardones, 14
+39 081 3209307549
chiaianapoli.it

FINAMORE
Shirts & accessories
Via Calabritto, 16
+39 081 477602
finamore.it

GIORGIO, NAPOLI CRAVATTE
Ties & accessories
Passeggiata Colonna, Piazza Amedeo, 16
+39 081 19574756
giorgio-napoli.com

MAGNIFIQUE
Suits, shirts, shoes, accessories including
Tombola Napoletana number cufflinks
Via Filangieri, 18
+39 081 421940
magnifiquenapoli.com

(E.) MARINELLA
Ties & accessories
Riviera di Chiaia, 287
+39 081 2451182
marinellanapoli.it

PICCOLO
Shirts & accessories
Via Chiaia, 41
+39 081 411824
camiceriapiccolo.com

RUBINACCI
Suits & accessories
Via Gaetano Filangieri, 26
+39 081 415793
Palazzo Cellamare
Via Chiaia 149/E
+39 081 403908
marianorubinacci.net

ULTURALE CRAVATTE
3, 7 and 10-fold ties
Via Carlo Poerio, 115
+39 081 2481151
ulturalecravatte.it

WINE BARS

Chiaia's wine bars are too numerous to mention and strolling around you will see one melds into the next. They are clustered primarily along the alleys of Vico Belledonne a Chiaia, Vicoletto Belledonne, Via Bisignano and Via Giuseppe Ferrigni. Here are a few of the authors' favourites:

BA-BAR KITCHEN + BAR
Via Bisignano, 20
+39 081 7643525
ba-bar.it

BARILL GARDENBAR
Via Giuseppe Fiorelli, 11
+39 3939814362

BROS
Vico Belledonne a Chiaia, 15
+39 081 416439

CHANDELIER CAFÈ
Vico Belledonne a Chiaia
+39 081 414576

ENOTECA BELLEDONNE
Vico Belledonne a Chiaia, 18
+39 081 403162
enotecabelledonne.com

The Chiaia is a long shorefront promenade, rows of live oaks arching overhead and the sea murmuring alongside. The newlyweds sitting there on moonlit nights warm their behinds on benches made of lava. The immemorial heat of the volcanos reaches their hearts by way of their buttocks: they squeeze each other's hands an choke with emotion. I envy them their sensations.

GUSTAVE FLAUBERT, THE LETTERS OF GUSTAVE FLAUBERT: 1830-1857, FRANCIS STEEGMULLER (TRANSLATOR)

PEDESTRIAN PURCHASING: VIA CHIAIA ⟨MAP 1⟩

Coming from Piazza del Plebiscito, Via Chiaia is the perfect entry point to the neighbourhood. It was once a natural water path that ran between Pizzofalcone and Mortelle hills. Today **the only thing running down it are pedestrians - mostly of the shopping persuasion** - and in fact, Via Chiaia is pedestrianised most of the day. Between Piazza del Plebiscito and Piazza dei Martiri, there's no shortage of mid-range shops along the length of Via Chiaia: clothing, shoes, handbags, sunglasses, make-up and more. Start your walk with a caffè at the ever popular Gambrinus then pick up some *taralli*, the Neapolitan version of the hard pretzel at Tarallificio Leopoldo. A few doors down find an interesting assortment of chocolate confections at Antica Cioccolateria, then look for the über photogenic Gradoni di Chiaia, one of the prettiest stairways in Naples. It is the only thing separating duelling gelato shops - Casa Infante and Fantasia Gelati.

Nearby is Ponte di Chiaia - a 17th-century bridge that connects Pizzofalcone and Mortelle hills. Built in the form of a triumphal arch, the bridge got a Neo-Classical facelift in 1834 and was adorned with marble friezes by Tito Angelini and Gennaro Calì on the Plebiscito side, and two horses on the other side, the work of Tommaso Arnoud. The Chiaia elevator which connects Via Chiaia to Via Nicotera and Pizzofalcone above is tucked inside the bridge.

Another bedecked stairway, Vicoletto S. Arpino sits behind an arch just before the massive 16th-century Palazzo Cellamare. This palace was the country estate of Giovanni Francesco Carafa, Abbot of Stigliano. It is said Goethe and Caravaggio both stayed here - though obviously not at the same time. Today, it's Rubinacci's base camp. At street level, one of their showrooms sits flanked by the Cinema Metropolitan (a converted metro station) and the new Magnum Ice Cream store.

THE STREETS OF THE ELITE:
VIA FILANGIERI TO PIAZZA AMEDEO ⟨MAP 2⟩

The smart boulevard that winds its way up from Via Chiaia to Piazza Amedeo is actually three streets in one: Via Gaetano Filangieri, Via dei Mille and Via Vittoria Colonna - the shopping streets of the elite. Along its way, **gorgeous Liberty style (Art Nouveau) palazzi play host to street level shopfronts** with names like Fendi, Hermes, Bulgari, Louis Vuitton, Burberry and Eddy Monetti. Nestled in between, Neapolitan bespoke tailors Magnifique and Cesare Attolini and local shops like Tarallificio Leopoldo, Gay Odin and Antica Libreria Regina keep Naples' artisan traditions alive.

Opposite page: Ponte di Chiaia, Kelly Medford, 2014

MADE-IN-NAPLES: NEAPOLITAN BESPOKE TAILORING

In 2014 Paolo Sorrentino's film *La Grande Bellezza – The Great Beauty –* garnered multiple awards, including an Oscar for Best Foreign Language Film of the Year. It's a film about Rome and is drenched in Roman light and culture, but its tailoring style is all about Naples. The protagonist Jeb Gambardella, played by Toni Servillo (a native of Afragola, Naples) wears classic handmade suits, jackets and shirts which embody Neapolitan style, combining exquisite craftsmanship with that studied nonchalance known as *sprezzatura*. This is a word we owe to Baldassare Castiglione's *The Book of the Courtier* (written 1508 - 28) and it's important to understand that to succeed in giving this desirable impression about yourself to others, an infinite amount of work is required to reach the point at which you appear supremely elegant and at ease. So it is with the bespoke tailoring of Naples firms such as Cesare Attolini (who made clothes for 'Jeb Gambardella'), Caliendo, Magnifique or Rubinacci; that *sprezzatura* look is the product of skilled artisan work combined with a profound dedication to tailoring traditions and a passion for quality and creativity. As happens so often with Naples, passion and craftsmanship go hand in hand.

If a piece of clothing is 'bespoke', it's commissioned by you and made to your body's exact specifications in your choice of fabric, fit and style. This might be a coat, suit, shirt or even a tie and Naples has a wealth of experts ready, for a price, to initiate you into the mysteries of style. Many of these are to be found in Chiaia, such as shirt-makers Piccolo and Finamore or tie supremos Marinella, Giorgio and Ulturale, but there are many more across the city, each with their own devoted clientèle.

For the origins of Neapolitan style in tailoring you have to go back to the Grand Tour and imagine the effect upon Naples over decades of the steady influx of English gentlemen. When all tailoring was bespoke and when the arbiters of fashion were located in London and Paris, taste was defined by the young English 'milord'. As the 19th century progressed, influences from France and Spain also came to bear on male fashions in Naples, though its tailoring remained strongly English in inspiration. This was the generation of Angelo Blasi, a tailor whose work in essence reflected London tailoring. However, things were about to change...

In the 1930s a young tailor working as a cutter at Rubinacci's 'London House' Naples workshop took a revolutionary step; anxious to produce a jacket more suited to the warm and humid southern Italian climate, Vincenzo Attolini stripped out the non-essentials. Gone were the full linings, shoulderpads and general stiffness; in came light, foldable fabric for a fundamental 'deconstruction' of the traditional garment. This seemed like a radical step, and even as late as the 1960s it was regarded as a sign of alternative thinking in fashion. And yet it exuded a certain glamour that tempted Totò and actors Marcello Mastroianni and Clark Gable to patronise Attolini. By the 1990s it could confer instant 'cool' on the wearer and today it's established as 'The Jacket' to own. This is not to say that other models influenced by Rome, Paris or London aren't still lovingly produced by master-tailors in Naples. But the Neapolitan Jacket has a cachet beyond the others.

What distinguishes a Neapolitan jacket? It's a single-breasted blazer shape in a soft cloth, half lined in silk on the body, with unlined sleeves. It fits like a second skin, but provides freedom of movement thanks to an expert cut. There are no shoulderpads and the sleevehead is constructed as though the suit were in fact a shirt, something the Italians call *spalla camicia*. When the sleeve allowance or seam is tucked (and stitched) up onto the shoulder, the sleeve can drop following the shape of the body. A slight puckering or wave can be seen at the top of the sleeve, something a fan of the jacket style loves. As for the pockets, on the breast these are styled a *barchetta* – like a little boat – and slope slightly upwards on the outer corner. The main pockets, in the *tasca a pignata* patch pocket style have the scooped corners of a brandy snifter. A further sportiness appears in quite obvious decorative hand stitching on the lapel and top pocket; it's a double backstitch - *doppia impuntura*. As for the cuff buttons, these overlap, or as Italians would say, they kiss one another and can be buttoned and unbuttoned. Buttonholes are hand-stitched. Chest buttons appear *tre buttoni su due* – three buttons over two. One button is hidden under the lapel and its corresponding button hole worked upside down. The notch, or cut in shape, on the lapel, is higher than with a classical jacket and the overall length a little shorter than the average.

There's little point in owning one of these beauties if the shirt, tie and accessories don't blazon your 'cool' as well. Luckily these items are all available in their handmade glory in Naples (and increasingly the older firms are opening shops in London, Paris, Tokyo and New York). The best known tie-maker is the firm of E. Marinella, where the long queue of shoppers seeking gifts prior to Valentine's Day or Christmas plays havoc with the traffic on Riviera di Chiaia. Maurizio Marinella is the current representative of the dynasty, grandson to Eugenio who opened the shop in 1914. The classic product is their 7 fold silk tie and such is their renown that clients have included all the presidents of Italy, various members of the Kennedy family, Aristotle Onassis, US President Bill Clinton, King Juan Carlos of Spain and French Presidents François Mitterand and Nicolas Sarkozy. When James Bond returned to cinema screens in 2012 with *Skyfall*, responsibility for dressing Daniel Craig in style was given to American designer Tom Ford; however, that much-remarked upon steel-blue tie was a Marinella handmade item. More than 20 artisans work busily at the Marinella workshop, but break from their labours each day to enjoy a lunch prepared by Maurizio's personal chef.

Such work habits and devotion to quality and design are replicated across the city of Naples with each studio or tailoring business presenting some individual twists on classic designs. Some tie-makers sell 3 and 10 fold ties as well as the classic 7. And, talking of numbers, Magnifique amongst all its other accessory options offers cufflinks in the shape of Tombola Napoletana numbers - *a' tumbulell* (the colourful local bingo game). Here's another Neapolitan passion, that of chasing good fortune, that you can interweave with the others: artisan work, beauty and the impulse to marry traditional techniques with creative thinking.

Cafés flank each end, Gran Caffè Cimmino at the "V" in the road at the Via Chiaia end, Cafè Amadeus at Piazza Amedeo. In between there's Pizzeria Mattozzi Cucina Tipica for a mouth-watering Neapolitan pizza or pasta dish or pick up a snack or daily made speciality at the gourmet *salumeria* near Piazza Amedeo. Just before the piazza find Passeggiata Colonna, a quiet cut-through from Via Vittoria Colonna to the square. Along this quaint passageway are Enoteca Mercadante Convivium, a likely place to find a great bottle and Giorgio Napoli Cravatte, a bespoke tiemaker offering up hand-sewn, three and seven fold ties. At Piazza Amedeo pause a moment to look up and admire Lamont Young's early 19th-century Castello Aselmeyer on the stunning Corso Vittorio Emanuele. The Chiaia funicular railway up to the Vomero is just steps from the Amedeo station.

A BLANK CANVAS: PALAZZO DELLE ARTI NAPOLI ⟨MAP 3⟩

Something unusual opened at PAN, Palazzo delle Arti Napoli in January 2011 – Rock! – an exhibition telling the story of rock music and presenting over 500 objects from private collections around Italy. Legendary guitars such as Fenders rubbed shoulders with signed drum-heads and vinyl discs, concert memorabilia,

PAN Palazzo delle Arti

sound equipment, original posters and artwork from the music industry. Conceived and curated by music experts Michelangelo Iossa and Carmine Aymone, who live and breathe (and teach) popular music, the show enjoyed enthusiastic support from the municipality of Naples and the US and British consulates in the city. Fast forward four years and the exhibition is now an annual date on PAN's calendar, complemented with associated musical events. Before it closed its doors in 2014, 15,000 visitors had soaked in its offerings and organisers were already planning the next edition. In April 2014, more than 14,000 people passed through PAN's doors during the first four days of the Andy Warhol retrospective, a collection of some 180 of the artist's works. It's shows like these that have made this unusual contemporary arts centre the success it is today.

Set in the 17th-century Palazzo Carafa di Roccella on Chiaia's beautiful boulevard Via dei Mille, PAN is **6,000 square metres of display space that is imagined and re-imagined for every exhibition and event it hosts.** With no permanent collections, exhibits from around the world rotate through the airy spaces spread across three floors that are open, bright, and large enough to accommodate even some of the largest works of installation art, yet intimate enough to show painting, sculpture, design, architecture, photography and cartoons. Its rooms are also used for concerts and film screenings; conferences and seminars; laboratories and workshops and literary events while a fourth-floor archive documents the history of contemporary art in the city and beyond.

EXPLORE SOME MORE

A private museum tucked at the bottom of a stairway in a pleasing palazzo along Via Giuseppe Martucci, **PLART** - Plastic + ART – is, as its name would suggest, a museum dedicated to the collection, conservation, research, education and promotion of plastic as both art medium and historical artefact. The collection has over 1,500 pieces (not all are on display at once); the items on display are elucidated by a nearby touchscreen where visitors can look up the particulars related to a specific item (Italian only). This unusual museum is worth a side-trip if your time in Naples is plentiful and offers free guided tours in English Wednesday through Saturday.

THE GOLDEN AGE OF NAPLES: VILLA PIGNATELLI ⟨MAP 4⟩

Princess Rosina Pignatelli's home and collections represent her time, yet by the time they passed to the State upon her death in 1955, **the city she once knew, Europe's fourth largest city and one of its most prosperous, was a distant memory**. What remained was the early 19th-century Pompeian style villa she shared with her husband Prince Diego Aragona Pignatelli Cortes, adorned with enough treasures to delight a King, or at least a Prince and a Princess, left in-situ for posterity.

Stepping inside Villa Pignatelli you are transported in time, to the years just after Risorgimento (the political impulse towards Italian Unification) when Naples was still an epicentre of art and culture in Europe. In those days European high society gathered at only the most fashionable venues, and under the guiding hand of the villa's mistress, Villa Pignatelli was among them. The couple inherited the property on Naples' Riviera di Chiaia from the Prince's uncle. By the time they moved there in 1897, the villa that had been designed by Pietro Valente for Ferdinando Acton in 1826 had already been enlarged and refurbished by its second owners, the Rothschild family. Rosina Pignatelli wasted no time putting her own stamp on her new home. As the wife of the Prince, the daughter of the Duke of Amalfi and lady-in-waiting to Queen Margherita, she had many social engagements to host.

Rosina's design aesthetic reflects fashionable *fin de siècle* taste and each room in the ground floor was furnished and adorned in an eclectic mix of emphatically opulent decorative styles. Wandering around it now you can picture the who's who of Europe mixing and mingling in the villa's Grand Ballroom or its three extravagant reception rooms - the lavish meals taken in the immense dining room, the gentlemen retiring to the library for an after dinner cigar. The princess filled her home with the finest art, furnishings and *objets d'art* that money could buy: an exquisite 19th-century silver collection; bronze statues including one signed by Vincenzo Gemito; French candelabras and clocks and an eclectic collection of porcelain from around the world. Rosina Pignatelli amassed a collection of 16th and 17th-century bowls and vases from Japan and China, pieces from France's Sèvres and Limoges factories, Chelsea porcelain from England and Meissen from Germany. And, of course, there are Neapolitan pieces from The Royal Works of Capodimonte and Maiolica pieces by Giustiniani and Del Vecchio.

Upstairs is the San Paolo – Banco di Napoli collection featuring works by Neapolitan artists Giuseppe Recco and Vincenzo Gemito, to whose sculptures an entire room was dedicated, plus a collection of 18th-century Neapolitan landscapes by Caspar van Wittel. Outside, a small park conceived of as an English garden wraps around the villa. In an adjoining building, the Museo delle Carrozze, the Carriage Museum - a collection of late 19th/early 20th-century Italian, French and British carriages - re-opened in June 2014 after a 20 year hiatus.

Christ Church Naples

ANGLICAN WORSHIP: CHRIST CHURCH NAPLES ⟨MAP 5⟩

The soft light streaming in from clerestory windows above Neo-Gothic arcades and onto Scots pine woodwork creates a warm glow that seems to wrap its arms around you. An immediate sense of belonging takes hold. It's like **finding your footing on an uncertain terrain**. Those who have lived or who have travelled far from home, whether by choice or by circumstance, know what it's like to seek that grounding. Though embracing a new life, new surroundings and new culture, they still feel a void, that need to connect to something familiar, something shared – be it culture, traditions or faith.

For Anglicans living in Naples 180 years ago, that was not so easy. Considered a "cult" by the Roman Catholics, Anglicans could worship only on British soil within the confines of the British Consulate. Thus, from the time the Anglicans established the Naples Legation Chaplaincy in 1831, congregants met in Palazzo Calabritto in Piazza dei Martiri, the British Ministry to the Court of the Kingdom of the Two Sicilies. Over the next 30 years the British petitioned the Bourbons for permission to build an Anglican church in Naples to no avail. It wasn't until Italy unified that they won the right. In March 1861, Giuseppe Garibaldi not only granted the Anglicans permission to build a church, but he gifted them the land as well, a show of gratitude for British support of Italian Unification.

On a small parcel of land set along Chiaia's Via San Pasquale, the British built the first Anglican Church in Southern Italy. Today, it is still one of only a handful of non-Roman Catholic churches in Naples. The cornerstone of this small, but striking neo-Gothic church was laid in 1862. It was designed by Thomas Smith &

Son of London, their plan triumphing over the designs of eleven other English architects. Constructed of red, grey, and brown tuff stones from Sorrento and adorned with white stone from Malta, its quintessentially Gothic pointed arches are one of the church's most prominent features as are the church's stunning stained glass windows. The windows underwent a €37,000 restoration in 2011 thanks to the generosity of the congregation; their intricate and jewel-like Celtic design glows anew. Christ Church was consecrated in March 1865 by the first Bishop of Gibraltar, the Right Reverend Dr. Sanford. Today, it is part of the 44th Diocese of the Church of England, the Diocese in Europe, and it serves English speaking Christians from all over the world. Whether Anglican, Episcopalian or otherwise, a diverse congregation worships every Sunday. Music plays a prominent role in these services and each week the Christ Church choir is on hand to sing to the accompaniment of one of three organists on the church's 117 year old organ.

BOUTIQUES AND WINE BARS:
ALLEYS OF THE BEAUTIFUL WOMEN ⟨MAP 6⟩

Two of Chiaia's alleys - a *vico* and a *vicoletto* - take the same name, *Belledonne* or beautiful women. The reference clearly bore an entirely different meaning in years past. Yet wander these alleys today and you'll see it is an apt description of the women ducking in and out of boutique shops and hair salons by day and sipping spritzes and cocktails by night. Of course the same could be said about the men.

Vicoletto Belledonne a Chiaia

A small area of Chiaia that sits between Via dei Mille to the north and Riviera di Chiaia to the south, this grid pattern **neighbourhood of quaint, cobbled alleys** is where ladies who lunch come to shop and where upper crust millenials pass their evenings. The local shops are plentiful for food, fashion or fun and a bite to eat might mean a quick bit of street food at La Focaccia or a leisurely meal at Umberto Ristorante or the Antica Latteria.

Another option is to stop at Enzo's Salumeria Nuovo Fiore di Greco Vincenzo and have him whip you up a made-to-order *panino*, then grab some fresh fruit at one of the *fruttivendolo* trucks that set up on virtually every corner or the nearby fruit and vegetable market along Via Achille Torre and head to the Lungomare or Villa Comunale for a picnic.

Bustling by day, Naples wine bar scene springs to life at night. Dozens of tiny wine bars carved into the ancient *bassi* swing open their doors around 7:00 pm and rustle up makeshift *al fresco* seating areas twinkling with votive candles along both sides of the narrow alleys. By decree or default, the entire area becomes largely pedestrianised as people pour in by the droves, meeting and greeting until the wee small hours of the morning.

PAY TRIBUTE TO THE FALLEN: PIAZZA DEI MARTIRI ⟨MAP 7⟩

Style and sophistication are the order of the day at one of Naples' most upmarket piazzas, **dedicated to the Neapolitans who gave their life for freedom**. The centrepiece is Enrico Alvino's 19th-century martyrs' column with a statue of the "virtues of the martyrs" on top. The monument's inscription reads:

> *The Municipality dedicates [this]*
> *to the glorious memory of those Neapolitan citizens who*
> *fell in skirmishes or died on the scaffold,*
> *who claimed for the people the right to proclaim with a*
> *solemn and eternal pact*
> *the plebiscite of 21st October 1860*

The 1860 plebiscite, or vote, annexed the Kingdom of the Two Sicilies to that of Sardinia and the following year would see the unification of the Kingdom of Italy. In the years leading up to this, there were four key Neapolitan uprisings against the Bourbon regime, each of which is represented by one of the four lions encircling the column, the choice of lions perhaps symbolising the strength of the people.

In the 1980s, the lions served a more jovial purpose, as the back drop for a quick photo-op of Andy Warhol and Joseph Beuys. Today, well-coiffed locals sip a

Lion pierced by a sword
Carbonari Revolution of 1820

Standing lion
Garibaldini Revolt of 1860

Lion in repose
Revolution of 1848

Dying lion
Parthenopean Revolution of 1799

Prosecco or a Negroni near the statue at one of Naples' smarter locales - the Gran Caffè La Caffettiera. The latest addition to the piazza is a tactile map of the city for the visually impaired; it's a 3D scale model in bronze that traces the contour and layout and the beautiful and unique shapes of the city. It was created and donated by the Rotaract Club North East and installed in front of the standing lion as part of May of the Monuments 2013.

The British Consulate was once located in Piazza dei Martiri, in the 18th-century Palazzo Calabritto. The Anglicans met here to worship for much of the 19th century until they were granted land by Garibaldi to build a church of their own, Christ Church. This huge edifice (restored by Luigi Vanvitelli) stretches all the way down to Piazza Vittoria along Via Calabritto - another high end shopping street marked by names like Louis Vuitton and Salvatore Ferragamo. When the British were in the square, W.J. Smith & Co.'s English Grocery Store sat at numbers 56 & 57 and Furchheim booksellers, who carried a "large stock of English, French, German and Italian books…" was at number 59. Today the piazza is dominated by a bookshop of the Feltrinelli chain, whose vibe one might equate with Barnes & Noble in the U.S. or Waterstones in the UK. It's a favourite place to while away a rainy afternoon and the Concerteria outlet inside is a convenient place to pick up theatre and concert tickets. Often there are book launches and small-scale concerts in the basement level here.

URBAN INNOVATION: PARCHEGGIO MORELLI ‹MAP 8›

Making a city more liveable for its residents and more accessible for its tourists is no easy task, harder still in an ancient city like Naples. Developing modern infrastructures that accommodate contemporary needs while respecting the historic fabric of the city is a balancing act. It costs much more than new development and it requires a great deal of **respect for the past and an innovative vision for the future**. Throughout Naples we find many excellent examples of this.

All four of the city's medieval castles are in contemporary use housing everything from art museums to city offices and providing spectacular backdrops for jazz concerts, theatre productions, wine tastings and more. Ancient single family *palazzi* have been subdivided into apartments, historic villas transformed into house museums and tiny single room *bassi* have been converted into shops, hair salons and wine bars. But what does one do with a huge cavernous structure burrowed into the hill of Naples earliest settlement? Turn part of it into a tourist attraction - the Bourbon Tunnel - and transform the rest into a modern parking garage at the edge of one of the city's most cosmopolitan districts, of course.

Parcheggio Morelli is a thoroughly modern structure sculpted into the bowels of Grotta del Chiatamone. The *grotta* is an ancient cave hollowed out of Monte Echia and it evokes some of the most defining periods in Naples' history: the Greco-Roman cult of Mithras, the 17th-century Carmignano Aqueduct, an escape route built for a Bourbon king, a WWII air raid shelter and a mid 20th-century impound depot.

As one of the largest cavities in the Neapolitan underground, the cave reaches 40 metres in height in some places. To take full advantage of this, the garage's architects designed a seven level structure with four levels above ground and three below, connected by a circular ramp. Within its 20,000 square metres of space there are 230 hourly parking spaces, 250 private boxes and parking for motos. Open 24 hours a day, Parcheggio Morelli also features bicycle rentals, well maintained restrooms and a state of the art video surveillance system. Also within the structure is the stunning Agorà Morelli, a cavernous multifunctional space that can be rented for private functions. A short walk to Chiaia's shopping streets and wine bars, the 2011 recipient of the European Parking Award for Innovation is also convenient for the sights around Municipio & the City Centre and the Lungomare.

THE STAIRWAYS
❧ OF ☙
NAPLES
VOMERO HILL

Cover Photo:
Rampe del Petraio

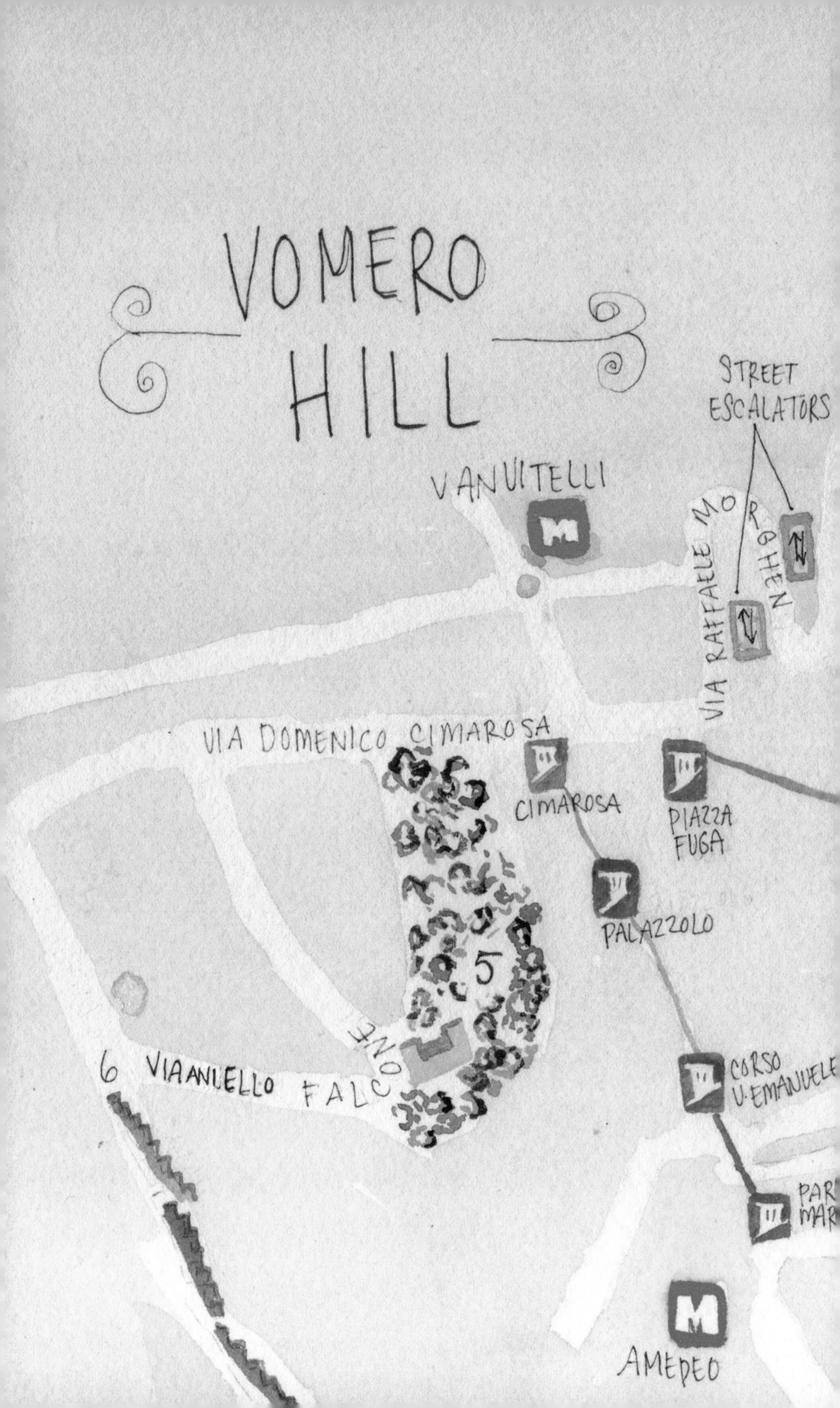

VOMERO
HILL

VANVITELLI

STREET
ESCALATORS

VIA RAFFAELE MORGHEN

VIA DOMENICO CIMAROSA

CIMAROSA

PIAZZA
FUGA

PALAZZOLO

5

CORSO
V. EMANUELE

6 VIA ANIELLO FALCONE

PARI
MAR

M
AMEDEO

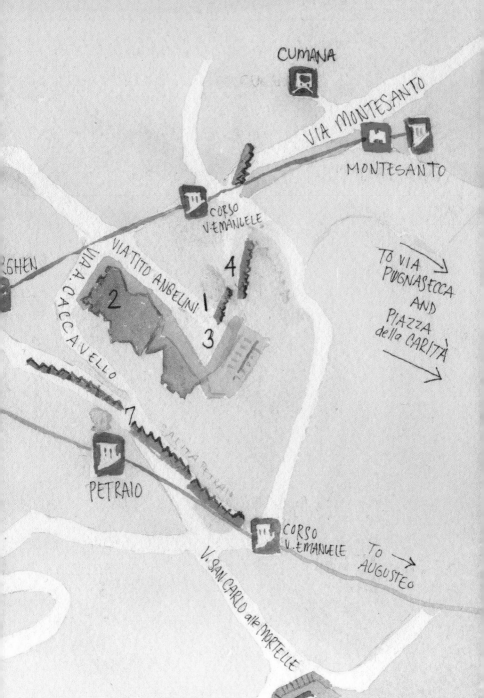

Creative Cartography by Kelly Medford 2014

The **classic postcard** of Naples has four elements – blue sea, bluer sky, the pleasing curve of the bay and the dimpled cone of Vesuvius.

That's all very well and we like it a lot, but sometimes the weather or the city mood invites us to another experience altogether. Consider then **the streets of the Vomero** district, the ones set back from the shops and traffic, the ones where discreet, bourgeois life crumbles along. Here is a place to rival those of Carlos Ruiz Zafón's old Barcelona or Peter Ackroyd's London if melancholy wandering is what you're after. Where are the cliché festooned washing, the *scugnizzi* (street kids) kicking the battered football, the droning scooters or the cheerful crash and prang of afternoon traffic? A world away from these *palazzi* with their graceful balconies and secrets obscured by palm fronds. Here the afternoon *pausa* (break) is undisturbed.

San Martino Charterhouse, Lorenzo Dotti, 2007

Here a cat has time to dream. It's never on a postcard, but it's Naples all the same, and as beguiling in its way.

The Vomero is a relatively new addition to the city it watches over. You might even say it was Naples' first suburb. Once, it was little more than farmland, the hill's agricultural tradition inspiring its name which derives from *vomere* - ploughshare and its nickname, *Collina dei Broccoli* - yes, that would be Broccoli Hill. The nobility made their way to the crest during the plague of 1656. Soon, the Vomero was all the rage. The privileged class flocked to the hill like migrating birds, building summer homes to escape the city's relentless heat, bask in the fresh air and tranquillity.

Until the Corso - Corso Vittorio Emanuele - came along in the mid 19th century and two funicular railways opened in the late 19th century, travel to the Vomero was anything but a tranquil affair. The *città alta* was connected to the *città bassa* by steep and narrow footpaths - *le Scale di Napoli*, the Stairways of Naples. Sometimes stepped, sometimes ramped, they go by many names: *calata* and *discesa*; *salita* or *scala*; the *gradini* or *gradoni* or the *rampe*. There are over 200 of these ancient footpaths across the city's hill districts, the aisles that connect the tiers of the great amphitheatre that is Naples. They too, are rarely on a postcard, but are Naples all the same; enchanting in their own way.

Plan Your Visit

Transport

METRO/RAILWAYS
M1: Vanvitelli, Medaglie d'Oro, Quattro Giornate
FUNICULARE: Chiaia, Centrale & Montesanto

BUSES
128, 181, C31, C33, C35, C36, V1

ESCALATORS
Three outdoor escalators connect Piazza Fuga and Piazza Vanvitelli up to Via Scarlatti.

Tourist Info

CAMPANIA ARTECARD
ArteCard 365, Napoli & Tutta la Regione

Sights & Attractions

CASTEL SANT'ELMO
Via Tito Angelini, 22
Open daily **except Tues** 08.30 – 19.30
Adults €5.00
+39 081 2294401
polomusealenapoli.beniculturali.it
+39 081 7958604

ELENA ALDOBRANDINI TEXTILE AND COSTUME MUSEUM
Piazzetta Mondragone, 18
Open Mon - Fri 09.00 - 13.00 & 15.00 – 17.00
Book ahead for guided visits
€5.00
+39 081 4976104
fondazionemondragone.it

MERCATINO PIGNASECCA
Piazza Pignasecca & Via Pignasecca
Open daily 07.00 – 15.00

NOVECENTO A NAPOLI MUSEUM
Via Tito Angelini, 22
Open daily **except Tues** 09.00 – 18.00
Free with paid admission to Castel Sant'Elmo
+39 081 2294401
polomusealenapoli.beniculturali.it

SAN MARTINO CHARTERHOUSE
Largo San Martino, 5
Open daily **except Wed** 08.30 – 19.30
Some sections are open only at certain times - check ahead.
Adults €6.00, Audio Guide €4.00
+39 081 2294568
polomusealenapoli.beniculturali.it

STUDIO DALISI
Calata San Francesco, 59
+39 081 681405
riccardodalisi.com

VILLA FLORIDIANA / DUCA DI MARTINA MUSEUM
Via Cimarosa, 77
Museum open daily **except Tues** 08.30 – 14.00; Park open daily 08.30 – 16.00 in winter, 08.30 – 19.00 in summer
Park free, museum €2.00
+39 081 5788418
polomusealenapoli.beniculturali.it

Opposite page: Calata San Francesco

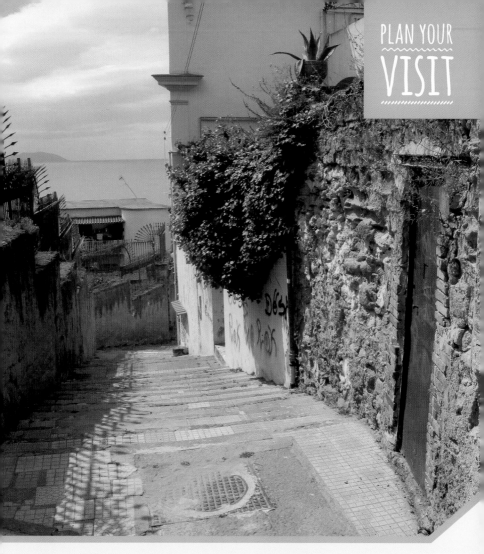

You say potato… Whether you call them *i funiculari*; funiculars or cable railways, the ingenious "funicular" is a type of "cable railway" (immortalised in the song *Funiculì, Funiculà*) in which ascending and descending vehicles are counterbalanced. The descending vehicle hoists the ascending vehicle up via a pulley system. This is not a new invention at all - the first known dates to 1515 in Salzburg, Austria - but it's worth its weight - no pun intended - in gold. This is especially true for the residents of Naples' hill districts whose ascent pre-funicular was anything but a walk in the park. Vomero hill is equipped with three such funiculars. The Chiaia funicular opened first as a steam-powered line on October 15th, 1889 (it was electrified in 1900) connecting Piazza Amedeo with Piazza Vanvitelli. Montesanto followed just two years later in 1891. Linking Montesanto and by extension, the Cumana Railway to Via Morghen, the Montesanto funicular also started as a steam-powered line that was later electrified. The Centrale, which connects Via Toledo to Piazza Fuga was a bit of a late bloomer. It didn't open until 1928. Over on Posillipo hill, the baby of Naples' four funiculars, the Mergellina funicular opened in 1931.

ROOFTOPS AND CUPOLAS: PIAZZALE SAN MARTINO ‹MAP 1›

App or map, you have to orientate yourself in an unfamiliar city. In Naples the view from Piazzale San Martino is an excellent place to begin. The last stop on the V1 bus, it is home to the San Martino Charterhouse. Castel Sant'Elmo sits just above. Be it by bus, taxi or on foot, visitors arriving here for the first time are so taken by the views, they make a beeline for the ageing balustraded railing that gives way to an unrivalled vista. The city stretches out before them, **a plethora of rooftops and cupolas in Pompeii red, white, yellow and green**.

The first thing you'll notice is the large conical object across the bay. It's often veiled in the pale blue of distance or swathed in summer haze, but we know it's there and we're keeping an eye on it. Another striking feature of this view is the cheese-cutter line across the city - Spaccanapoli. Dividing the old city in two, it draws your eye from Centro Storico all the way out to Centro Direzionale. Zooming in on Spaccanapoli you can see the unmistakable yellow tuff and green roof of Santa Chiara whose majolica cloister remains one of the many marvels of Naples; the spire of the Immacolata in Piazza del Gesù marking the western end of Centro Storico like a weather vane; the silver cupola of Chiesa Santo Spirito, the tiara on top. Turning a little, you see the Galleria Umberto with its dome and glass-vaulted wings – late 19th-century elegance newly restored. Turn the other

way and you'll see the grand Bourbon palace of Capodimonte on the crest of its hill; Naples' youngest church, Basilica dell'Incoronata Madre del Buon Consiglio hovers below.

But if you think the views from here are spectacular, wait until you see the 360° panorama from Castel Sant'Elmo's rooftop terrace and the vista from the gardens of the San Martino Charterhouse.

WRAPAROUND TERRACE: CASTEL SANT'ELMO ⟨MAP 2⟩

The youngest of Naples' four castles, this star-shaped military fortress perched atop Vomero Hill dominates the Naples skyline. Castel Sant'Elmo looms over the San Martino Charterhouse just below, the yin to Vesuvius' yang. The two create an unrivalled vista that has greeted travellers arriving from the sea for centuries. Carved into and out of Naples' famed tuff rock, the Angevins' 14th-century fortress was replaced by the six-pointed star structure we see today.

This unique example of 16th-century military architecture set like a crown on the crest of Vomero hill we owe to Viceroy Don Pedro Álvarez de Toledo and Pedro Luis Escriva, a military engineer from Valencia. Part of his design was a roof-top

Castel S. Elmo, Lorenzo Dotti, 2008

terrace that encircles the entire perimeter of the castle; this once defensive architectural device is now the castle's best feature. Though visitors often forgo visiting the castle – after all, you can't enter any of its ancient halls - **the 360° panoramic views of the city and the bay from the wraparound terrace are worth the trip**. If that isn't incentive enough, you'll find an impressive collection of 20th-century (Neapolitan) art at the Novecento a Napoli Museum that is housed in the *Carcere Alto*, the High Prison one flight below on Piazza d'Armi. Back out in Piazza d'Armi you can't miss Giancarlo Neri's large scale metal sculpture *Luna e l'Altra*. It is one of a number of contemporary art installations - one of Mimmo Paladino's helmets is perched on the castle's terrace as well - that were donated to Castel Sant'Elmo by local artists.

NEAPOLITAN MODERN ART: NOVECENTO A NAPOLI ⟨MAP 2⟩

Naples maintains a comprehensive record of Neapolitan art through the ages across its many museums, churches and local art galleries. Until the Novecento a Napoli Museum opened in March 2010, however, there was a major gap concerning works produced between the early 1900s and the 1970s - Neapolitan Modern Art. Drawing on generous contributions and long term loans by private galleries, collectors, other museums and even the artists themselves, Novecento a Napoli pieced together **an impressive collection of Neapolitan Modern Art that includes some 170 works by 90** artists, including artists like Armando de Stefano, Vincenzo Gemito and Mimmo Paladino. This collection presents a chronological record of the artists and movements at work in 20th century Naples.

Most of the works are by Neapolitans, but the collection also contains works by artists connected to the city or working in the city during that time. Organised into three major sections, the museum's collection of paintings, sculpture, design and engravings starts with the first Futurism movement in Naples (1910 – 1914) and moves through the artistic developments of the 20th century. It spans second Futurism (1920s – 1930s) to works produced between the two World Wars, the post WWII movements (1948 – 1958) – Gruppo Sud, Neorealism, Movimento Arte Concreta (MAC) to works produced in the 1970s and culminates with works produced after the tragic earthquake of November 23rd, 1980.

A CARTHUSIAN CITADEL:
SAN MARTINO CHARTERHOUSE ⟨MAP 3⟩

From just about everywhere in the city you can catch a glimpse of this beautiful white citadel stretching across Vomero Hill. It sits 251 metres above sea level with

Castel Sant'Elmo looming behind. Built as a Carthusian Monastery, this splendid piece of real estate is now the **steward of the most important repository of Neapolitan art and history**.

This is a sublime specimen of architecture rivalled only by the views of the city and the bay from its terraced gardens; its location on Vomero Hill was chosen by Charles, Duke of Calabria. Construction of his monastery started in 1325, but Charles died just a few years later. His project was finally completed in 1368 during his daughter's reign - the Queen of Dynastic Discord - Joanna I. Though it was originally conceived in the Gothic style, the complex has seen its share of modifications over the years. In fact, it became somewhat of a Baroque laboratory starting in the 17th century and is today considered one of the finest examples of Baroque art and architecture in Naples.

The Charterhouse also secrets one of the most evocative and provocative cloisters in the city, the Chiostro Grande. The cloister, which is attributed to Cosimo Fanzago (1591 - 1678), was the stage for Spakka–Neapolis 55's rendition of *Vesuvio* in John Turturro's film *Passione*. It's here that you'll find the Cistercian monks' cemetery surrounded by a beautiful balustrade topped with marble skulls. These served both as a collective memorial to departed brethren and a *memento mori* (roughly "reminder of death") to the living, especially at times when plague raged in the city below. Ah but today this is such a tranquil and pleasant spot with its fruit trees and pretty, echoing well, you'll think it worth lingering a little longer to savour what life has to offer.

San Martino Charterhouse

BUILT FOR BUILDING: SALITA DELLA PEDAMENTINA ‹MAP 4›

The unsuspecting tourist peering out from the balustraded railing of Piazzale San Martino rarely looks directly down. Hence the stairway that lies just below is often (quite literally) overlooked. Its **steep descents, zig-zag turns and 414 elongated steps** take you 650 metres down Vomero hill to Corso Vittorio Emanuele. For the Vomerese, it's a convenient if strenuous connection between the Vomero and the Corso. For the adventurous tourist, pleasing panoramas of the city and a glimpse of everyday life on the Pedamentina await. And for the Angevins who built it, it was the means by which burly young men laboured uphill with the bricks and mortar Charles, Duke of Calabria, needed to construct his charterhouse or in the case of Robert the Wise, his castle. One of Naples' oldest stairways, Salita della Pedamentina takes its name from *piedi del monte*, the foot of the mountain. It's a little rough around the edges in places and in definite need of some TLC but nevertheless a hike down the Pedamentina is rewarding.

Upon reaching Corso Vittorio Emanuele any one of a number of paths will take you down to the *città bassa*. Directly across the street you can look down onto Discesa Trinità delle Monache which continues along Via Pasquale Scura all the way to Via Toledo and beyond into Centro Storico. Though it no longer makes for a good walk, this was probably the original path of Salita della Pedamen-

Salita Pedamentina

tina. Heading west (right) onto Corso Vittorio Emanuele, several stairways lead into the Spanish Quarter. Head east about 150 metres and you'll find the **Scala Montesanto** in front of the Montesanto funicular station. The stairway, inaugurated in 1880, flanks the Montesanto Funiculare and runs from Corso Vittorio Emanuele to Piazza Montesanto where the funicular, Metro Line 2 and the Cumana railway line converge. The Montesanto Cultural Association Qi Quartiere Intelligente, a grass roots organisation dedicated to the eco-friendly urban revitalisation of the Montesanto neighbourhood, is headquartered along the stairway.

Piazza Montesanto connects to Via Pignasecca which squirrels all the way down to Piazza Carità and is a cornucopia of sights, sounds and smells. Whether it delights the senses or overloads them, the **Pignasecca Market** is one of Naples' oldest and most authentic street markets. In Matilda Serao's day it clearly occupied a much larger area but the sentiment is still very much the same:

> *The entire Pignasecca neighbourhood, from Largo Carità through the Montesanto and up to Ventaglieri is blocked by one continuous market. There are shops, but everything is sold in the street; the sidewalks have disappeared, but who has ever seen them anyway? Macaroni, greens, groceries, fruits, cold cuts and cheeses, everything, everything in the street, in the sun, in the clouds, in the rain; the crates, the counter, the scales, the display cases, everything, everything in the street; there's frying going on, because there's a famous frier lady; melons change hands because there's a melon seller famous for the street cries with which he hawks his wares; the donkeys laden with fruit come and go; the donkey is the quiet and powerful master of the Pignasecca.*
>
> THE BELLY OF NAPLES, MATILDE SERAO

KITTENS, TURTLES AND VASES: VILLA FLORIDIANA AND THE DUCA DI MARTINA CERAMICS MUSEUM ⟨MAP 5⟩

If Naples is a feast of sound and colour, the Villa Floridiana is the mint tea to follow, refreshing, green and good for your health. This is the place to stroll, jog or play tag in the cool of the morning, far from urban stresses. So we must be grateful to Ferdinand IV (I of the Two Sicilies) who acquired the property in 1816 and set about creating this Neo-Classical haven for his morganatic second wife

Lucia Migliaccio, the Duchess of Floridia. The villa was **the Duchess' summer "cottage"**, if something so grandiose could be called such. Its sea-facing southern façade is marked by a monumental staircase from which you may gaze upon the bustling city far below and out across the bay to Capri. Around the fountain green turtles navigate the waters between islands of papyrus; along the park's pathways wild cats pad gleefully after the kind but raucous signora who has fed the colony for over ten years. It's a pastoral scene you might find reflected upon some of the treasures secreted within the *palazzina* – the Duca di Martina's prodigious collection of glass, coral, enamel and ceramics. If Chinese and Japanese ceramics and porcelain are what you fancy, especially Chinese Ming (1368 - 1644) and Qing (1644 - 1911) dynasty and the Japanese Edo period (1603 - 1867), find the entrance to the villa on its northern façade and have a peek at the Duke's fine collection.

A SAINTLY STAIRCASE: CALATA SAN FRANCESCO ⟨MAP 6⟩

A back gate out of Villa Floridiana will deposit you on Via Aniello Falcone, named after the Neapolitan Baroque artist Aniello Falcone (ca. 1600 - 1665) who is known best for his battle scene painting. The view from here is anything but hostile though, as this scenic *strada* runs parallel to, albeit 100 metres or so above, the sea. About 400 metres west of Villa Floridiana, Via Aniello Falcone meets up with Calata San Francesco. To the right is a steep, yet smooth ascent to Via Belvedere - the top of the *calata*; to the left, a steep but smooth downhill stretch along which you will find the palazzo in which Riccado Dalisi has his studio and that ends at a short flight of elongated stairs. The stairs appear to be an entrance to a private *parco* but don't let that stop you. Turn the corner and the *calata* will reveal itself.

In this, the prettiest part of the journey, the *calata* zigzags down a series of precipitous stairways all the way to Via Tasso and yields **scintillating seascapes ahead and colourful cityscapes behind**. One more zigzag staircase leads to Corso Vittorio Emanuele. From there, it's a steep and slippery slope all the way down to the sea at Riviera di Chiaia and Piazza della Repubblica.

This last bit of Calata San Francesco is **not** for the faint-hearted. It's fairly narrow, has a high amount of traffic and precious little walking space. An alternative route would be to head east along Corso Vittorio Emanuele about 1½ kms to Via del Parco Margherita. Here, find the funicular station down to Piazza Amedeo or walk the 500 metres downhill. This route takes you past the Grand Hotel Parker's, a 5* hotel with a panoramic roof garden bar and restaurant; a lookout point with excellent views of the Nunziatella and Castel dell'Ovo and Lamont Young's Castello Aselmeyer (1902), an exuberant example of Gothic Revival architecture.

THE TIN SCULPTURE ARTIST: RICCARDO DALISI

Tin pot puppets with pointy noses sprout from shelves, copper birds dangle from the ceiling and painted canvases line the walls. A cross between a tinsmith workshop and an academic's experimental laboratory, this is Professor Riccardo Dalisi's art studio, tucked inside a classic Vomerese palazzo on one of the many stairways of Naples, Calata San Francesco. Born in 1931, Riccardo Dalisi grew up in Italy during the hungry years. His studies in architecture at the University of Naples led to tenured professorship, but the unconventional Dalisi wanted to experiment. In 1971 he set up workshops for children in one of the most impoverished districts of Naples, the Rione Traiano. The children were given wooden sticks and strings and told to design whatever they liked. They set to work and created complex geometrical designs that, Dalisi says, could have been signed by Paul Klee, Wassily Kandinsky or Marc Chagall.

In 1979 the household goods company Alessi asked him to create a new design for the Neapolitan Flip-Over coffee pot. From the junk dealers of Naples he sourced pot after pot for ideas, collaborating with a reclusive tinsmith, Don Vincenzo (whom he never actually met) to turn them into vestal virgins, traffic policemen or Pulcinella figures with stick legs and stick arms. More than two hundred prototypes were created and sent off to Alessi. Luckily Alessi's patience paid off in 1982 when Dalisi won the premier industrial design award in Italy, the Golden Compass, for his new rendition of the pot. MOMA, the Museum of Modern Art in New York City, exhibited Dalisi's tin pots and they soon took their place in many European and North American museum collections.

Since the 1990s Dalisi has devoted himself mostly to sculpture, using simple materials such as brass and copper and mining the city's history for his ideas. He can find inspiration in ancient Greece or Rome, but connects to other contemporary artists in Naples. Seek out the Rua Catalana (off Via Agostino Depretis) since the buildings here are peppered with sculptures and lights conceived by him and executed by master craftsmen from his and other workshops. They sell sculptures in tin, copper and bronze which bear the unmistakable junkshop-style mark of Dalisi's inspiration. One such workshop, Corrado Tamborra executed the synapse sculpture that is on the main level of the Università metro station.

As is fitting for an artist who continues to be so actively engaged in the Rione Sanità district, offering workshops for children and young people there, an important work of his, *La Mensa degli Angeli* (2005) in glass and crystal, is prominently displayed in the Santa Maria della Sanità Basilica. Accessible and friendly, Dalisi shows his studio to anyone who calls and makes an appointment.

PICTURE PERFECT: THE PETRAIO ⟨MAP 7⟩

Turning the corner from Via Annibale Caccavello onto the Gradini del Petraio is like turning back the clock. The cosmopolitan city of the Vomerese transforms into a subdued version of yesteryear where doors swing open to reveal tiny *bassi* and the air thickens with the perfume of the daily meal. Cars and motos are barred by the steep, stepped and narrow terrain and the sounds of the city fade into a soft murmur. Sun-kissed balconies are drenched in a medley of Mediterranean flowers and laundry flaps in the soft breeze. This, the zone of the washerwomen, was the inspiration for the ancient Neapolitan love song turned protest anthem *Canto delle Lavandaie del Vomero, Song of the Washerwomen of the Vomero*. **Poets and painters once made the Petraio their home. Perhaps they still do**. The Petraio is not one stairway but a tiny zone of Vomero hill that sits between the Vomero and Corso Vittorio Emanuele and the network of stairways that connects the two: Rampe del Petraio, Gradini del Petraio, Salita Petraio, Discesa Petraio, Gradoni Santa Maria Apparente and even Via Filippo Palizzi. The name Petraio derives from *pietra* or stone and carries a double meaning, both for its substance and for how it was made: cobblestone extracted from a river bed and the natural path that was formed by pebbly rocks that accumulated after heavy rains. In fact, though the Pedamentina is not among them, most of Naples' stairways follow old, natural watercourses.

Unless you have very strong legs, a stroll along the Petraio is best started at the top at Via Annibale Caccavello. Follow the path down (always veering left) to Corso Vittorio Emanuele along a series of steep and winding stairways and cobbled ramps, past tiny piazzas, buildings low and tall and a funicular (Petraio) station too. Cross Corso Vittorio Emanuele and continue on Via San Carlo alle Mortelle. The San Carlo alle Mortelle Church, a wonderful example of the Neapolitan Baroque, is located here but it is unfortunately under restoration after a terrible rain storm in 2009 rendered the church structurally unsound. The church and the road take their name from the *mirti* - myrtle trees that once flourished here. The blue/black berries of the tree are used to make a liqueur that's a cousin to *limoncello*. Via San Carlo alle Mortelle continues to Piazzetta Mondragone and the Elena Aldobrandini Textile and Costume Museum. Bear right at the piazza towards Rampe Brancaccio and Chiaia or left towards Via Nicotera Giovanni and Via Monte di Dio.

HANDIWORKS: TEXTILE AND COSTUME MUSEUM ⟨MAP 8⟩

The Elena Aldobrandini Textile and Costume Museum - La Fondazione Mondragone - traces its roots to 1655, when Elena Aldobrandini, wife of Antonio Carafa, Prince of Stigliano and Duke of Mondragone, founded a religious retreat for gentlewomen. The new institution prospered thanks to her many gifts of land, furnishings and silver treasures and her generosity was emulated by others, so much so that the community of women outgrew the small chapel provided for worship. A new church, Santa Maria delle Grazie, designed by Arcangelo Guglielmelli, was built in the early 18th century. Over time the foundation became less a convent-style retreat, and more a college, so that by 1870 orphans and widows were being educated here. The seismic shifts of war and politics brought more change; during WWI the wives of soldiers fighting at the front benefited from lessons in handiwork and craft while their children were cared for in a kindergarten on the premises. Eventually the mission altered to educating "the daughters of the people". Decades of neglect followed the disruptions of WWII, until in 1999 **a 3-year programme restored the institution to its former glory**. The foundation then became a major centre for female fashion both in terms of collections and study, and simultaneously a school teaching tailoring and lace-making, embracing above all disadvantaged women and girls from the Spanish Quarter.

Today the foundation hosts and runs the Elena Aldobrandini textile and costume museum, with its continuing emphasis on the artisans and designers of southern Italy. The Tullia Passerini Gargiula collection contains a range of textiles from late 18th-century church vestments to embroidery and lace-work from the late 1800s to early 1900s. These are beautiful enough but it is the displays from the extraordinarily rich flowering of design in Campania from the 1940s onwards that are so thrilling to see. The work of Fausto Sarli and Livia de Simone are well represented and capture their special Zeitgeist. De Simone's clients included Lana Turner, Lucia Bosè, Ingrid Bergman, Audrey Hepburn and Jacqueline Onassis. With a smile and a polite request, it may be possible to see the church.

On September 23, 2009 *Il Mattino* reported that three chasms opened up at about 4 a.m. on Vico San Carlo alle Mortelle after heavy rains. The largest was about twenty metres deep and yawned in the middle of the vico - a narrow street that carries a ton of traffic between Corso Vittorio Emanule and Chiaia. Another chasm opened up under a palazzo and the third inside the 17th-century Baroque church San Carlo alle Mortelle, putting it at risk of collapse and practically swallowing its entrance. In all, six buildings and a handful of *bassi* were evacuated and two to three hundred people had to leave their homes. In 2011, ARCUS SpA (Society for the development of arts, culture and entertainment) donated 1.5 million euro towards the restoration of the church. Those restorations are still ongoing.

PARKS, POETS ⤍ AND ⤏ PANORAMAS
POSILLIPO

Cover Photo:
Villa Carunchio

The Greeks called this area *Pausilypon* - respite from pain.

It lies between Mergellina and the promontory of Posillipo and has been a highly sought after destination since they first landed here. The Romans chose Posillipo for their extravagant seaside villas.

...this place of quiet and repose was the habitation of those ancient Romans who were free from the burdens of every care, who retreated there from the serious business of the Senate and of other occupations, of which the ancient buildings, which became rocks in the sea and give shelter to

the shellfish and sea urchins, make full testimony. *Here are some of the most beautiful palaces, with charming and delightful gardens, that are seen along the whole coast, built by the Neapolitans for comfort and the pleasures of summer and for the good and beneficial climate of the air.*

DESCRITTIONE DEL REGNO DI NAPOLI (AS TRANSLATED IN NAPLES: AN EARLY GUIDE), ENRICO BACCO

Virgil lived in Posillipo and penned *The Aeneid* here. Naples has not one, but two parks dedicated to him (with variant spellings of his name). One nestles at the foot of Posillipo hill behind the Santa Maria di Piedigrotta Church where legend says his tomb resides. The other park is perched at the top of Posillipo hill. The Spanish aristocracy found the area pleasing as well and started building their seaside retreats here in the 17th century. Many of these abodes still dot the shoreline. In the 1950s property development intensified and many claim this destroyed Posillipo's beauty. Regardless, it is still the most desirable and smartest area of Naples.

Villa Volpicelli at Riva Fiorita

Plan Your Visit

This area of the city is much more spread out. Those wanting to explore it to the fullest will want to avail themselves of a car or public transport. The C21 bus runs along Via Petrarca, the 140 along Via Posillipo. You can take the C1 bus from Parco Virgiliano a Posillipo to the back of Posillipo hill and to a stop near the entrance to Parco Pausilypon at the Seiano Grotto and beyond to the Città della Scienza.

Most of the villas along the Posillipo coast are at or near sea level. Those with strong legs who don't mind descending and ascending steep and winding roads along the way can trek down (and back up, of course). A better option is to take a boat or kayak tour of the Posillipo coast. It's a great way to see Naples and its hidden wonders from an entirely different perspective: grottoes and coves and the characteristic yellow weathered tuff cliffs that seem to rise up out of the sea; Roman ruins; the numerous seaside villas and the private, public and make-shift *bagni* and beaches that dot the Posillipo coastline.

Transport

METRO/RAILWAYS
FUNICULAR: Mergellina

BUSES
140, C1, C21

Sights & Attractions

MAUSOLEO SCHILIZZI
Via Posillipo, 157
Open daily **except Mon** 08.00 – 13.00

NAPLES SCIENCE CENTRE – CITTÀ DELLA SCIENZA
Via Coroglio, 104 & 57
Open Mon - Sat 09.00 – 15.00, Sun 10.00 – 18.00 (closed for the summer from end of Jun to end of Oct – there are special events and summer camps during that time)
Adults Sat, Sun & holidays €8.00; Mon – Fri €6.50 - includes entrance to the Science Centre, guided visits, workshops and the Science Show
+39 081 7352424
cittadellascienza.it

PARCO SOMMERSO DI GAIOLA
Discesa Gaiola, 27
+39 0812403235
areamarinaprotettagaiola.it

PARCO VERGILIANO A PIEDIGROTTA
Salita della Grotta, 20
Open daily 09.00 - 18.00
Free
+39 081 669390

PARCO VIRGILIANO A POSILLIPO
Viale Virgilio
Open 1 May – 20 Jun 07.00 – 24.00, 21 Jun – 30 Sept 07.00 – 21.00, 1 Oct - 30 Apr 07.00 – 21.00.
Free
+39 081 7953613

PAUSILYPON & THE SEIANO GROTTO
Discesa Coroglio, 36
Open Mon - Sat without a guide. Entrance at 09.00, 10.30, 11.30 but call before arriving. Guided tours are available during the week if booked in advance, guided tours on Sun are at 09.00, 10.30 & 12.00 – call +39 081 2403235 to book.
Entry is free, guided tours are €5.00
AMP Gaiola offers a variety of land and water itineraries during the warm months
+39 081 2403235
areamarinaprotettagaiola.it

POSILLIPO MARKET
Viale Virgilio
Open Thurs 09.00 – 14.00

S. ANTONIO A POSILLIPO
Via Minucio Felice, 13
From the funicular/cable railway station, head left out of the station and walk about 400 hundred metres up Via Orazio to Via Minucio Felice, which cuts off to your right. This will take you down to the church and the lookout point.

S. MARIA DI BELLAVISTA CHURCH
Via Posillipo, 112

Boats & Beaches

BAGNO ELENA
Via Posillipo, 14
+39 081 5755058
bagnoelena.it

BAGNO IDEAL
Via Posillipo, 18
+39 081 2483087
facebook.com/pages/Bagno-Ideal-Napoli/175181127527

BAGNO SIRENA
Via Posillipo, 357
+39 081 5750736

BAIA DELLA ROCCE VERDI AT VILLA FATTORUSSO
Via Posillipo, 68
+39 081 5756716
villafattorusso.com/balneazione.htm

KAYAK NAPOLI
Excursions leave from Lido Rocce Verdi, Via Posillipo, 68
+39 331 9874271
kayaknapoli.com
Kayak Napoli offers three different tours of the Posillipo coast - Wild Posillipo, Naples and its Villas and Full Moon Kayak.

LIDO IL GABBIANO
Via Marechiaro, 113/115
+39 081 5755650
ilgabbianomarechiaro.it

LIDO MARECHIARO
Calata Ponticello A Marechiaro, 33
+39 081 7691215

LIDO DELLE ROSE
Via Marechiaro, 131
+39 081 5983191

VILLA IMPERIALE
Via Marechiaro, 90
+39 081 5754344
villaimperiale.eu

PILGRIMAGE TO VIRGIL'S TOMB: PARCO VERGILIANO A PIEDIGROTTA

Naples' treasures are large and small, tucked away and hidden in plain sight. These may be original masterpieces, facsimiles thereof, or, as in this case, not what something actually is, but what it was thought to be: the tomb of Publius Vergilius Maro (70 BC – 19 BC). Known to most simply as Virgil, he is the 1st-century BC **Roman poet who left the world the *Eclogues*, the *Georgics* and the *Aeneid*** and who numbers among the most important writers of all time.

> *No other writer enjoys the unanimity of selection. When it comes to the universal choosing of the world's great literary figures we find England chooses Shakespeare and Virgil; the Germans acclaim Goethe and Virgil and Spain insists upon Cervantes and Virgil.*
> THE CHRONICLE-TELEGRAM, MAY 7TH, 1930

That this Augustan era tomb doesn't actually hold Virgil's remains seems immaterial, that he wasn't born here, inconsequential. Virgil haunts this place. The tomb was reputed to hold his ashes and it was here that Petrarch, Boccaccio and Dante came to pay their respects. An inscription quotes the master:

> *Mantua me genuit, Calabri rapuere, tenet nunc Parthenope; cecini pascua, rura, duces.*

> *Mantua gave me birth; Calabria took me away; and now Parthenope holds me: I sang of pastures, farms, leaders.*
> VIRGIL'S EPITAPH, 1ST CENTURY BC

For over 2,000 years Virgil's tomb has been a place of pilgrimage in a tradition that weaves in and out of history. The poet Martial reported that his fellow poet Silius Italicus (ca. 28 – 103 AD) owned Virgil's tomb and dedicated himself to preserving the poet's memory. It was a scene the English painter Joseph Wright depicted some sixteen centuries later in *Virgil's Tomb, with the Figure of Silius Italicus* (1779), conjuring up an air of mysticism with his use of chiaroscuro.

In the Middle Ages Virgil was considered a *magus* because he referred in Eclogues 4 to the birth of a boy and the Church was glad to paint him as a prophet predicting the birth of Christ. Dante made Virgil his guide in Hell and Purgatory in *The Divine Comedy* and so the poet was turned into a sorcerer and seer, with all manner of miracles ascribed to him. Hence the magic egg hidden in Castel dell'Ovo that protects the city from some nefarious fate and the **Crypta Neapolitana**, a tunnel near his tomb that legend tells us he conjured into existence. Is it possible that writers like Petrarch and Boccaccio, artists like Wright and the scores of other pilgrims that have visited Virgil's tomb over the millennia were seeking not inspiration but his divine intervention?

Crypta Neapolitana

For the man who buried the magical egg under Castel dell'Ovo, it would be nothing to carve a 700 metre tunnel through the volcanic rock of Posillipo ridge to connect Naples with the road to Pozzuoli. In a single night. With his intense gaze. Strong magic indeed to tunnel from the eastern entrance of the **Crypta Neapolitana** in Piedigrotta (literally, foot of the grotto), to the western one in Fuorigrotta (beyond the grotto). Actually, the tunnel was devised by the Roman architect Cocceius around 37 BC, but since nothing in Naples is so dull, let's add that he used 100,000 slaves who accomplished the work in merely 15 days.

Virgil's legend endures but his final resting place, or presumed final resting place, is not nearly as popular as it once was. It makes precious few travellers' itineraries these days. But for inspiration and not least for the atmosphere and view, it is well worth making the pilgrimage to Virgil's tomb at Parco Vergiliano a Piedigrotta. A quaint little park at the foot of Posillipo hill, it opened in 1930 on the occasion of Virgil's 2,000th birthday. On the way up the path to his tomb and set into a little niche you can see a bust of Virgil that was donated by university students from Ohio. The tomb of the 19th-century Italian poet Giacomo Leopardi (1798 - 1837) sits near the entrance and gives the park its other name, Park of the Poets. His remains were transferred to the park from the ancient church of San Vitale a Fuorigrotta in 1939.

A CHURCH WITH A VIEW: SANT'ANTONIO A POSILLIPO

If you happen to be in Mergellina after dark, look up towards Posillipo hill and you'll see the Sant'Antonio a Posillipo church glowing like a beacon in the fog. It was carved into a crag of this most picturesque of hills in the 17th century, long before anything else was built here. A journey up here is compulsory, though not to see the church, but the view.

View from Sant'Antonio a Posillipo

It's either a climb or a cable: walk up Rampe di Sant'Antonio or take the Mergellina funicular (cable railway) up one stop to the Sant'Antonio station and this picture perfect panorama: see the bay spread out before you, Mergellina in the foreground and Vesuvius straight ahead in the distance, the curve of city hugging the bay from Mergellina to Castel dell'Ovo. This is one of Naples' most iconic views and this lookout point is **an ideal spot to capture beautiful sunset pictures**.

BELVEDERE: VIA PETRARCA

So beautiful are the views from Via Petrarca that it once went by the name of **Via Panoramica**. In fact, the city installed lookout points and a panoramic terrace along this road to keep drivers distracted by the views from slowing down and causing traffic jams. One of three roads that traverse Posillipo hill, Via Petrarca is the quietest and most residential of the three. Via Posillipo sits below Via Petrarca, Via Manzoni above and at the Mergellina end, the three are connected by the zig-zagging and über-panoramic Via Orazio.

From the intersection of Via Orazio and Via Petrarca, it's a 4 km walk, much of it uphill, to the other Parco Virgiliano at the promontory of Posillipo Hill. Those who make the journey will be rewarded with unforgettable vistas of the city, the bay and Vesuvius. Of course if you get tired, you can catch a C21 bus at the bus stops that are posted every few hundred metres along the way.

A PANORAMIC PROMONTORY: PARCO VIRGILIANO A POSILLIPO

In this little piece of paradise teetering 150 metres above the sea on the promontory of Posillipo hill, one stroll around the park and its terraced gardens overlooking the gulf and you'll understand exactly why Posillipo was named thus. **The views from Parco Virgiliano are unparalleled**. They wrap around from Vesuvius and the Sorrentine Coast to the Islands of the Bay - Capri, Ischia, Procida, Nisida and Gaiola, over the Trentaremi Bay around to Bagnoli and beyond to Pozzuoli, Baia and Bacoli. There is even a lookout where you can see Pausilypon, the ancient villa of Publius Vedius Pollio.

The park first opened in the Fascist period and was known as *Parco delle Rimembranze* - Park of Remembrance in honour of the fallen of WWI. After a long period of neglect, the park was renovated and reopened in 2002 at which time it was enriched with new foliage - shrubs, rosemary, sage, strawberries and olive trees. The perfect place to watch the sunset, this lush green spot feels like it's miles away from the city. It's one of Naples' most popular parks and the perfect backdrop for wedding and first communion pictures.

Umbrella pines along Viale Virgilio frame the entrance to the park and every Thursday, the chic-est market in Naples - the **Posillipo Market** - sets up shop here from 09.00 – 14.00. Inside, playgrounds, a small amphitheatre, a large ornamental fountain at the entrance and a sports track and club round out the park's offerings. On any given day you're liable to see a game of Italian Football (soccer) and it's here where Briganti Napoli - a team of the IFL (Italian Football League) plays America's version of football.

THE CRUEL EQUESTRIAN KNIGHT: PAUSILYPON AND THE SEIANO GROTTO

Set on the promontory of Posillipo hill is **the one time villa of Publius Vedius Pollio**, friend of Emperor Augustus and a vicious and cruel eel-breeding mogul, according to both Seneca and Pliny the Elder. In the presence of Augustus, a slave of Pollio broke a crystal cup, whereupon the master insisted he be dropped into a pool of moray eels. However, the emperor ordered that the slave be spared, all Pollio's expensive drinking vessels be smashed and his pool filled in. The villa and its grounds which once covered an area of nine hectares were bequeathed to Augustus upon Pollio's death.

Though much of the site has been lost to time or submerged, ruins dating from the 1st century BC to the 4th century AD have been discovered, including part of a 2,000 seat amphitheatre. Today the amphitheatre is used to stage sunset concerts. There are also the remains of an *odeon* - a smaller theatre that would have been used for musical performances and poetry readings, as well as evidence of a thermal bath complex and a vineyard. One of the villa's ruins is a 1st-century BC *nymphaeum* (a structure dedicated to nymphs) that sits at the water's edge and is known as Palazzo degli Spiriti.

Entrance to Parco Pausilypon is through a 770 metre tunnel, the Grotta di Seiano (entrance to Grotta di Seiano is at the back of Posillipo hill on Via Discesa Coroglio). It was first built by Lucius Cocceius Auctus to connect Villa Pausilypon with the other villas in the area and to link Naples with the ports of Cuma and Pozzuoli. It takes its name from Lucius Aelius Seianus (Sejanus). A confidant of the Emperor Tiberius, he commissioned the tunnel's enlargement in the 1st century AD. The tunnel was rediscovered and restored in the mid 1800s and was used as an air raid shelter during WWII.

Pausilypon

EXPLORE SOME MORE

Capri, Procida and Ischia, the three islands that sit off the coast of Naples, are very well known. Lesser known are a number of smaller islands or islets among which are: Megaride which sits off Lungomare and is home to Castel dell'Ovo; Vivara, an islet connected to Procida by means of a bridge; the tiny island of Gaiola off the Posillipo coast: and **Nisida**, which juts out directly from the promontory of Posillipo and is connected to the mainland by a bridge. Here legend has it that the sirens perched upon these stones, luring sailors into crashing their vessels. Roman history says that Brutus had a villa here where he plotted to kill Julius Caesar in 44 BC. During the 18th century, the Bourbons turned the island into a notorious prison. Today the island serves as a juvenile detention facility where many of the youngsters learn a new trade: pizza-making.

You can see Nisida and the causeway that connects it to the mainland from Parco Virgiliano a Posillipo. A bathing beach sits to one side of the causeway while Italian yachts bob in the harbour. The causeway is monitored by a security guard who always lets people pass. There used to be a small NATO base here, but it closed in 2013. The Naples NATO Yacht Club (NNYC) is still on Nisida, though membership is limited to NATO personnel and US service members stationed in Naples. The club is affiliated with the Italian Sailing Federation, organises regattas and conducts sailing courses.

Nisida is very near to the **Naples Science Centre, *Città della Scienza*** which was built in the ex ILVA steel works plant, a former industrial area in Bagnoli being reclaimed by the city. A hands-on science museum, it was the first of its kind in Italy. It opened in 1996 and quickly became an integral part of the Naples community, serving over 350,000 visitors a year. On March 4, 2013, a tragic fire destroyed the Città della Scienza, leaving the community devastated. Within a few months however, the centre reopened its doors to a handful of exhibits. It continues to rebuild while offering rich and varied programming to the public.

THE BRIDGE TO NOWHERE: GAIOLA

A very narrow, arched bridge connects two tiny land masses about thirty metres from the shore. They are so close that one can easily swim to them. One is a blank slate, the other wears the remains of an abandoned 19th-century villa. Together, these two itsy bitsy islets are known as Gaiola and they are the star turn of a piece of local lore known as *La Maledizione della Gaiola* - the Curse of Gaiola. This lurid tale in which beauty and privilege are cursed, dovetails very neatly with a fondly held belief that the poor, excluded and dispossessed will get their just deserts in the afterlife. Apparently, from the 1920s until 1978, when its last proprietor was jailed, nefarious fates have befallen all of the island's owners. In a related calamity in 2009, Franco Ambrosio and his wife were murdered in their villa opposite Gaiola. The *Corriere della Serra* (16th April 2009) explained it thus:

> *...in the twenties two owners of La Gaiola, both German, committed suicide; in 1968 the villa was bought by Paul Getty Senior, a ·little later his grandson was kidnapped; in '78 the new owner, businessman Gianpasquale Grappone, was arrested following the collapse of the*

THE SCHOOL OF POSILLIPO

Naples had **a thriving tradition of landscape painting** – *vedute* or "views" - in the 18th century. The city was brimful with wealthy foreign visitors pursuing their Grand Tour and these mainly Protestant tourists needed portable mementoes of their visit. Today's tourists prefer to get their hands dirty in the kitchen learning the local recipes or tasting (*aka* imbibing) the local wines. In terms of overall artistic output, this meant fewer large-scale works with a religious theme would be commissioned in Naples and many hundreds more small landscapes produced to meet this demand. At the dawn of the 19th century and at the level of aristocratic patronage, the Dutch artist Jakob Philipp Hackert (1737 - 1807), court painter to Ferdinand IV (later I of the Two Sicilies), held the premier position but his star fell following French assumption of control in Naples and Ferdinand's flight to Sicily.

The arrival in the city in 1815 of another Dutchman, Anton Sminck van Pitloo (1790 - 1837), fresh from productive periods in Paris and Rome, and his choice of Posillipo as the ideal place to live and work, imported new ideas into Neapolitan landscape painting. Pitloo painted chiefly in oil on paper *en plein air*, outdoors, fixing his work onto canvas later. Whereas Hackert had assembled his compositions from a standard set of elements, a mountain, a tree, small figures, Pitloo pursued both a realistic and an emotional response to the landscape more consonant with the ideals of Romanticism. Where better than Posillipo to take in the sweep of the bay, Vesuvius, sky and water? Becoming, like Hackert before him, a professor at the Accademia di Belle Arti, he influenced many other artists including the watercolourist Giacinto Gigante (1806 - 1876) and it is the work of this next generation in addition to his own that is now known as the School of Posillipo. It's rare to see outdoor painters these days (though urban sketching has become all the rage), but American plein air painter Kelly Medford has sojourned here and has left us with some remarkable images.

Lungomare, Kelly Medford, 2014

Banca di Credito Campana and Lloyd Centauro. And to this terrible list may be added the murder of Anna Parlato Grimaldi, another member of the Neapolitan jetset, killed, again in Posillipo, in front of her villa.

It is hard to resist noting that the word *Gaiola* is related to *gabbiola*, meaning a birdcage or pen. It would seem there is a price to be paid for enjoying the gilded cage of privilege.

Gaiola sits in the **Area Marina Protetta Parco Sommerso Gaiola**, Protected Marine Area Gaiola Underwater Park, a 42 hectare area around the promontory of Posillipo that extends from Marechiaro to the Trentaremi Bay. This site is of **immense natural, historic and archaeological importance**. Under the purview of the Special Superintendent for Archaeological Heritage of Naples and Pompeii, the area includes an underwater archaeological park, archaeological remains along the coastline and the archaeological park - Parco di Pausilypon. The area is managed by the Centro Studi Interdisciplinari (CSI) Gaiola. In addition to research and educational activities, they organise a wide variety of tours in the Gaiola Underwater Park and Parco Pausilypon: glass-bottom boat tours from Marechiaro to Trentaremi; snorkelling itineraries; biological and bio-archaeological diving itineraries; tours of Parco di Pausilypon; and integrated itineraries combining a tour of Pausilypon with either snorkelling or the glass-bottom boat. They also offer courses in bird-watching, sea-watching and eco-diving (Level I "Open Water" PADI diving licence).

CLEAR SEAS: MARECHIARO

It's all clear seas - *Marechiaro* - and smooth sailing around this 13th-century seaside village immortalised in Salvatore di Giacomo's song. Arrive by boat or walk down Discesa Marechiaro to reach this fishing village turned seaside resort with **fabulous waterside dining** and a labyrinth of stairs that will lead you to hidden coves and bathing beaches: Lido Marechiaro, Villa Imperiale, Lido delle Rose and Lido Il Gabbiano. Santa Maria del Faro church – Faro being a reference to a lighthouse that once stood here – keeps watch from above. This 13th-century church was restyled in the 18th century.

VILLA FATTORUSSO: DISCESA ROCCE VERDI

It's a long way down to this renovated old mill, even longer back up. But if it's a **beach with a pool** you crave, it's worth the journey. Villa Fattorusso has four terraces and two pools that overlook the bay and at the shoreline is the bathing beach known as Le Rocce Verdi. The villa is also used for wedding receptions and private events and there is a two-story residence on the grounds that can be rented on a weekly basis.

A PRESIDENTIAL PAD: RIVA FIORITA

Riva Fiorita is reached by the long and windy descent, Via Ferdinando Russo. Lady Emma Hamilton's Pompeiian-red seaside summer home - Villa Emma - is located at Via Ferdinando Russo, 27, but it's best seen from the water. Just beyond her villa is the entrance to one of three official residences of the President of the Italian Republic, **Villa Rosebery**. It is also best seen from the sea, though occasionally it is open for tours. The Villa gets its name from the British Prime Minister Archibald Primrose, the 5th Earl of Rosebery who acquired the Villa around 1897. The Villa dates to at least the late 1700s and was purchased by the Austrian Count Giuseppe de Thurn in 1801, after which it changed hands several times. In 1932 the Villa was donated to the State and became the summer residence of the royal family.

The area around the water's edge is known as *Riva Fiorita* - flowered shore - and is where we find Villa Volpicelli. This castle-like villa is the famed face of the Italian soap opera, *Un Posto al Sole* (A Place in the Sun). Known for its characteristic towers from the fortified palace of Pietro Santacroce, the first known record of the villa dates to the early 17th century. In 1884 it was purchased by Raffaele Volpicelli. Also at Rivia Fiorita is the seaside restaurant Giuseppone a Mare and more of Naples' white rocks upon which to sunbathe.

Riva Fiorita

VILLAS AND VISTAS: VIA POSILLIPO

Via Petrarca may have its panoramas but Via Posillipo has its villas (and the vistas aren't too shabby either). The road that snakes its way down from the promontory of Posillipo to sea level at Mergellina was built (starting in 1812) on the orders of Joachim Murat. Later, a tram ran its length. It's all downhill as they say, just about 3km down to Mergellina. Here's what to look for along the way:

- The aptly named mid 19th-century **Santa Maria di Bellavista** church.

- A poet's piazza - **Piazza Salvatore di Giacomo** named for the Neapolitan poet and songwriter Salvatore di Giacomo (1860 - 1934) who gave us the tune *Marechiaro*.

- The late 19th-century **Neo-Egyptian funeral monument known as Mausoleo Schilizzi**. It was built as a family tomb - the family of Matteo Schilizzi - but the Comune di Napoli acquired it in the early 1920s and moved the remains of WWI soldiers to the mausoleum from the Poggio-reale Cemetery. It also houses the remains of another 2,000 fallen from WWII and those who died during Quattro Giornate.

- The top of a villa that is stretching out into the sea - **Villa Lauro**. Also known as Villa Peirce, it was built in the 1840s; a British engineer and naval architect, George Wightwick Rendel resided here as did a wealthy businessman of Irish descent, Guglielmo Peirce and the Italian founder of the Lauro Fleet, Achille Lauro. Today it goes by the name of Villa Rocca Matilde and can be booked for private receptions.

- A piazza that was blown out of the tuff rock by the fascists - **Piazza San Luigi**. It bustles by day and on Saturday and Sunday nights, the youth of the city and beyond come in droves. Look up and you'll see Via Petrarca above. You'll find panoramic dining here at Ristorante Reginella; the best chicken rotisserie in Naples - La Bottega del Pollo da Carlo; one of Naples' favourite gelaterias, Bilancione, and a nice lookout point as an enjoyable setting in which to eat your gelato.

- The striking pagoda of **Villa Roccaromana** at Via Posillipo, 38. It was built in 1814 for Nicola Caracciolo di Roccaromana on top of ancient caves tunnelled into the tuff rock.

- The *bagni* of Posillipo: **Bagno Elena, Bagno Sirena, Bagno Ideal**.

- **Palazzo Donn'Anna**, with its ghostly legends of Anna Carafa and Queen Joanna II. It was designed by Cosimo Fanzago for Spanish Viceroy Ramiro Guzmán and his wife princess Anna Carafa, from which it takes its name Donn'Anna. Construction was started in 1642 but it was never fully completed and it went through many periods of neglect over the years.

OUTINGS

~ IN THE ~

OUTSKIRTS

THE BAY OF

NAPLES

AND BEYOND

THE BURNING FIELDS
CAMPI FLEGREI

Cover Photo:
Vulcano Solfatara

Charon ferried souls across the river Styx and sibyls uttered their trance-induced predictions, all within an eight square mile area west of the city of Naples that today lies mostly under water.

From the Greek for "burning fields", the Phlegraean Fields or Campi Flegrei consist of twenty-four volcanic craters, many still bubbling with seismic activity today.

The Greeks first settled here on the hilltop of Cuma (also written as Cumae) and centuries later the Romans, who revered Greek culture, preserved their hilltop acropolis and built opulent getaways replete with villas, bathhouses and domed temples nearby.

Antro della Sibilla at Acropolis of Cuma
Lorenzo Dotti, 2007

The poet Virgil (70 BC - 19 BC) is the starting point within this region from which a web of myth and history spins outwards. He spent the last ten years of his life in Naples writing *The Aeneid* whose protagonist Aeneas leaves Troy and lands on these shores. Virgil roamed this region alongside the rich and famous, describing locations that can still be visited today.

Geologically the Campi Flegrei is one of the most complex volcanic configurations in the world. Today there is considerable hydrothermal activity in locations such as the Solfatara, where the ground continues to emit steam and boiling, sulphurous mud. This is the mythical home of the Roman god of fire, Vulcan. Here repeated volcanic activity gives rise to the smouldering calderas (from the Latin *caldaria*, meaning cooking pot or cauldron) which are a feature of the landscape. And ancient ruins rise from and fall into the sea due to a rare geological phenomenon known as bradyseism.

Rinolofo sp.

Vaneggia il gran fianco
dell' euboica montagna in un antro,
cui cento larghi aditi guidano,
cento gran porte;
di là cento voci precipitano:
della Sibilla i responsi.

Virgilio, Eneide, Libro VI, versi 42-44

21- febbraio 2007.

Acropoli di Cuma

Plan Your Visit

Several sites around Pozzuoli are easily reached by public transportation: the Metropolitana Line 2 Pozzuoli station sits above the Flavian Amphitheatre; the Pozzuoli Station on the Cumana line is very near to the port. The area is best visited by car or a private driver, (ask your hotel or B&B host about the options), but with a bit of planning up front and plenty of patience, many of the Campi Flegrei sights can be accessed by public transport. Exploring here without a local guide does require a spirit of adventure and a little ingenuity. Set out looking for one marvel, and you might perhaps find access is barred for any number of reasons; however, Campania is full of interest and surprises and you may well finish your day having discovered two or three other fascinating sites or people.

Transport

METRO/RAILWAYS
M2: Pozzuoli
Cumana: Pozzuoli, Arco Felice, Lucrino
Circumflegrea: Licola, Cuma

BUSES
ANM (anm.it)
CTP (ctp.na.it)
EAV Campania Bus (eavcampania.it)

Tourist Info

AZIENDA AUTONOMA DI CURA, SOGGIORNO E TURISMO DI POZZUOLI
Largo Matteoti, 1a, Pozzuoli
+39 081 5261481
infocampiflegrei.it
In the Biblioteca "Mario Manduca"
Via Marconi, 1, Pozzuoli
+39 081 5266639

CAMPI FLEGREI COMBINED TICKET
Entry to the Flavian Amphitheatre, the Cuma Archaeological Park, the Baia Archaeological Park and the Baia Castle and Archaeological Museum of Campi Flegrei is with the Campi Flegrei Combined Ticket. The ticket is €4.00, valid for two days, and can be purchased at any of the participating locations, but is generally only required on Sat, Sun and public holidays.

CAMPANIA ARTECARD
ArteCard 365 & Tutta la Regione

Sights & Attractions

BAIA ARCHAEOLOGICAL PARK
Via Sella di Baia, 22, Bacoli
The entrance across the street from the port of Baia is no longer used. Look for the small parking lot up the hill from the port marked Terme Romane (or "Roman Baths").
Open daily **except Mon** 09.00 to one hour before sunset
Free Tues - Fri, weekends and holidays - Campi Flegrei Combined €4.00 Ticket
+39 848 800288
cir.campania.beniculturali.it/luoghi-della-cultura/baia-parco-archeologico

BAIA CASTLE & ARCHAEOLOGICAL MUSEUM OF CAMPI FLEGREI
Via Castello 12, Baia
Open daily **except Mon** 09.00 - 14.20 (last entry 13.00)
Free Tues - Fri, weekends and holidays - Campi Flegrei Combined €4.00 Ticket
+39 081 5233797
cir.campania.beniculturali.it/luoghi-della-

cultura/castello-aragonese-di-baia

BAIA UNDERWATER ARCHAEOLOGICAL PARK

Centro Sub Campi Flegrei/Napoli Diving Centre offers a variety of dive itineraries at Baia and Gaiola, around the bay of Naples and to Ischia, Capri and Procida. They also offer a variety of PADI certification courses.
parcoarcheologicosommersodibaia.it
See 'Dive Resources' for more info.

CASINA VANVITELLIANA

Piazza Rossini, 2, Bacoli
Open Sat and Sun 10.00 - 12.30 & 15.00-18.00
Adults €3.00
+39 081 8687080

CRATERE DEGLI ASTRONI NATURE RESERVE

Via Agnano-Astroni, 468, Pozzuoli
Open Fri & Sat 09.30 - 14.30 in Winter, 17.00 in Summer. Sun and holidays 09.30 - 15.30 in Winter, 18.30 in Summer
Adults €6.00 or €8.00 with guided tour, which lasts around 2.5 hours (only available by pre-booking).
+39 081 5883720
wwf.it/oasi/campania/cratere_degli_astroni/

CUMA ARCHAEOLOGICAL PARK

Via Licola Cuma, 3, Pozzuoli
Open daily **except Tues** 09.00 - 20.00
Campi Flegrei Combined Ticket €4.00
+39 848 800288

FLAVIAN AMPHITHEATRE

Via Nicola Terracciano, 75, Pozzuoli
Open daily **except Tues** 09.00 - 14.00 (last entry 13.00)
There is a small parking area at the amphitheatre entrance. The site is only ten minutes' walk downhill from M2: Pozzuoli Solfatara station.
Campi Flegrei Combined Ticket €4.00
+39 848800288
cir.campania.beniculturali.it/luoghi-della-cultura/anfiteatro-flavio

GROTTA DELLA SIBILLA

Via Averno Lato Sinistro on the south side of Lago Averno, Pozzuoli
Grotta della Sibilla is privately owned
Free visits are by reservation only
Call Carlo Santillo at +39 333 6320642 - this is a personal mobile, so it's probably best to ask your hotel to call for you.

LAGO AVERNO

Via Averno Lato Sinistro, Pozzuoli
There is parking along Via Italia and the left side of the lake on Via Averno Lato Sinistro

MERCATO ITTICO A DETTAGLIO

Via Nicola Fasano, 37, Pozzuoli
Open daily 07.00 – 14.00

MONTE NUOVO NATURE OASIS

Via Virgilio, Arco Felice, Pozzuoli
Open daily 08.00 - Sunset
Free
+39 0818041462

Since most visitors opt to see Pompeii, these gems tend to remain quiet - desolate even. Before setting out, pick up a map of the Campi Flegrei at one of Naples' Information Points and purchase a copy of Massimo D'Antonio's *Campi Flegrei: A Guide of Discovery to the Lands of Fire*, a comprehensive travel guide specifically for this region. You can find it in most museum bookshops. Also, remember to bring plenty of water and wear sensible shoes, hats and sunscreen, especially during the summer when temperatures can get very high.

PISCINA MIRABILIS
Via Piscina Mirabile, 63, Bacoli
Open daily **except Mon** 09.00 - 13.30 &
14.30 - 16.00.
Call the custodian, Signora Lucci
Immacolata, ahead for an appointment.
Free
+39 333 6853278 or 333 5730225

SANCTUARY OF SAN GENNARO AT SOLFATARA
Via San Gennaro alla Solfatara 8, Pozzuoli
Open daily - it is a working church, so if mass
is in progress, you may be unable to visit
+39 081 5261114
santuariosangennaro.it

STADIO ANTONINO PIO
Via Campi Flegrei 22–30, Pozzuoli
The Stadium is rarely open to the public but
the ruins are visible from the street
+39 081 5266007

TEMPLE OF DIANA
Via delle Terme Romane, Baia
Open daily **except Mon** 09.00 - 19.00
Free Tues - Fri, weekends and holidays
Campi Flegrei Combined €4.00 Ticket
+39 081 8687592

TEMPLE OF NEPTUNE
Corso Nicola Terracciano, Pozzuoli
The Temple of Neptune is privately owned
and rarely open to the public but the ruins
are visible from the street

TEMPLE OF SERAPIS
Via Roma, 10, Pozzuoli
Ruins are visible from the street

TEMPLE OF VENUS
Via Lucullo, 98, Baia
The temple is rarely open to the public but
the ruins are visible from the street
+39 081 8687592

TOMB OF AGRIPPINA
Via Agrippina, Bacoli
From Piazza Guglielmo Marconi in Bacoli,
turn down onto Via Agrippina. Drive all the
way to the port. The tomb is off to the left
along the pedestrian walkway.
Ruins are visible from the street

VULCANO SOLFATARA
Via Solfatara, 161, Pozzuoli
Open daily Apr - Oct 08.30 – 19.00, Nov -
Mar 08.30 – 16.30
Adults €7.00
+39 081 5262341
solfatara.it
Camping at Vulcano Solfatara – campers,
trailers and tents are welcome. Tents,
caravans and bungalows can be rented
solfatara.it/camping/en/index.php

DIVE RESOURCES

NAPOLI DIVING CENTRE
Via Miliscola, 157, Lucrino, within Lido
Montenuovo directly on the shore of the
underwater Archaeology Park of Baia.
Open daily 09.00 - 17.30 - the closing day
varies, so call ahead to check
+39 081 8531563
napolidivingcenter.it

SUBMERGED BAIA, THE CYMBA GLASS BOTTOM BOAT
Port of Baia
Tours are available Sat at 12.00 and 15.00
and Sun at 10.00, 12.00 and 15.00
Booking is required at least 48 hours in
advance to prenotazioni@baiasommersa.it
Adults €10.00
+39 349 4974183
baiasommersa.it

UNDERWATER ARCHAEOLOGICAL PARK BAIA BLOG
underwaterarchaeologicalparkbaia.
blogspot.it

PLAN YOUR VISIT

Spas & Bathing Beaches

COMPLESSO TURISTICO AVERNO
Via Monte Nuovo Licola Patria, 85, Pozzuoli
+39 081 8042666
averno.it

LIDO NAPOLI
Via Miliscola, 181, Lucrino
Open daily 08.00 - 19.00 (the pool closes at 18.00) until the middle of Sept, then call to check
+39 0818664090
lidonapoli.it

LIDO RITORNO QUINTILIO
Via Spiaggia, 13, Bacoli
+39 081 5235148/5235178

(LA) SPIAGGIA DEL CASTELLO DI BAIAI – AMENA BAIA
Via Lucullo, 75, Bacoli

Open daily 08.30 - 19.00
May - Sept
Price ranges from €4.00 - €6.00, but you must take their ferry to reach the beach, which costs between €1.50 - €4.00
Ciro +39 338 1693448 or Luigi +39 333 2629253
spiaggiacastellodibaia.it

STUFE DI NERONE
Via Stufe di Nerone, 45, Bacoli
Opening times vary by day and season, check the website for complete listing
Daily ticket €30.00, 6 tickets for €120.00; 10 tickets for €190.00; 20 tickets for €350.00 which are valid all year
+39 081 8688006
termestufedinerone.it

TERME PUTEOLANE
Corso Umberto I, 195, Pozzuoli
+39 081 5261303

Casina Vanvitelliana

The next day a wind began to blow from the south, and in two days we came to the town of Puteoli. We found some believers there who asked us to stay with them a week. And so we came to Rome.

ACTS 28:13-14 ON SAINT PAUL'S JOURNEY TO ROME TO STAND TRIAL.

CHRISTIAN REST STOP: THE FISHING TOWN OF POZZUOLI

Founded as the Greek Cumaean colony Dicaearchia, this settlement thrived during Roman times as Puteoli and emerged as the modern-day bustling port town of Pozzuoli. It was named for its abundance of thermal, mineral and indeed sulphurous springs whose unmistakable odour permeated the area (it still does), mostly from the Solfatara. Whether that name derived from the Latin *putere* – to stink, or the Greek *pyteolos* meaning "little wells", however, remains a mystery.

Its history has not been uneventful. The Roman senator and writer Cicero owned a villa nearby. **St. Paul docked at Pozzuoli and stayed for seven days before making the arduous journey to Rome along the Appian way.** A few centuries later, Naples' Patron Saint San Gennaro was martyred in Pozzuoli. In the last century Sophia Loren lived in the vicinity with her grandmother when bombs rained down during World War II. Tragedy struck again in October 1983 when an earthquake damaged thousands of structures and displaced nearly 40,000 residents.

Today, contemporary blends with the ancient world and the remains of Pozzuoli's Roman past dot its landscape. Signs along Pozzuoli's roads will point you to the **Temple of Neptune** (actually the remains of a bathing complex), which overlooks the sea. Nearby is the 1st-century AD **Stadio Antonino Pio**, a Greek-style stadium that was excavated in 2008. Other signs lead through a narrow tunnel and then along a road next to the Neocropoli Romana. Hidden behind overgrown weeds, the locals walk by this ancient cemetery as though the ghosts inside are simply amicable neighbours. Further up the hill is the spectacular Flavian Amphitheatre and near the water's edge are the remains of the old Roman marketplace, better known as the Temple of Serapis.

Like their Roman forebears, fishermen still work their nets in boats and until recently, they would bring their plastic buckets filled with live fish, shellfish and octopi to the **Mercato Ittico or Mercato del Pesce a Pozzuoli**, right to the banks of the port. After much controversy, the Pozzuoli Fish market was moved to a brand new, more "hygienic" location a bit further down on Via Fasano, near the EAVBus station. Some locals still feel this move has detracted from the traditional atmosphere of the market; however, you will find the seafood is just as fresh as it ever was.

Around the port area, you'll find plenty of seafood restaurants, cafés and gelaterias. Pozzuoli is also where ferries depart to the islands of Ischia and Procida. Day trips to the islands are inexpensive and easy to take.

POZZUOLI'S ANCIENT MARKET PLACE: THE TEMPLE OF SERAPIS

Not far from the port of Pozzuoli is the Temple of Serapis. If you find yourself strolling along the waterfront, you will certainly happen upon it. **In fact it is not a temple at all, despite the name, but an important symbol of the region's Roman roots, and more significantly, of the geological forces at play in the Campi Flegrei.**

This site was first excavated in the mid 18th century, around the same time gentlemen archaeologists were unearthing Herculaneum and Pompeii. Then it was known simply as "the vineyard of the three columns". Upon finding a large statue of the God **Serapide**, archaeologists believed they had found a *serapeum*, a temple dedicated to the god of Serapis.

The god of the underworld, as well as the god of the sun, healing, and fertility, Serapis was created by Ptolemy I of Egypt as an Egyptian-Greek god to unite the two cultures. The statue of Serapis was eventually placed in the National Archaeological Museum, and it wasn't until the early 20th century that archaeologists worked

Temple of Serapis

out that the site was actually a *macellum*, the Roman marketplace of ancient Puteoli, first built in the late 1st century AD.

As you near the *macellum*, the first thing you notice is that it lies about 30 feet below sea level. The second is that its ancient granite columns seem to be suspended atop a murky pool of water, rising up from and descending into the sea at the whim of the tide. Thanks to a geological phenomenon known as bradyseism, that's exactly what is happening. Well almost.

Originally attributing this phenomenon to changes in the tide, geologists are still not sure about what causes it, though they have narrowed it down to either ebb and flow in the underlying magma chamber or to hydrothermal activity. From the Greek *bradus* = slow and *seism* = movement, bradyseism is prevalent throughout the Campi Flegrei and the *macellum* is perhaps the most important example of it in the world. In fact, scientists have been documenting the ruins' movements since the 18th century, when they found evidence of sea molluscs on some of the temple's columns, indicating they had once been submerged at least seven metres deep.

BEASTS & BISHOPS: THE FLAVIAN AMPHITHEATRE

Just up the hill from the port of Pozzuoli and the Temple of Serapis, sits the third largest amphitheatre in Italy after the Colosseum in Rome and the amphitheatre at Capua.

Like its Roman counterpart, it is known as the Flavian Amphitheatre or *Amphiteatrum Flavium*, presumably because it was constructed during the rule of the Flavian Dynasty (69 - 96 AD) and designed by the same architects who were responsible for the Colosseum. Some sources however attribute the amphitheatre to Nero (Roman Emperor 54 - 68), dating its completion to sometime around 66 AD (which, if you 'do the math', would make the Flavian amphitheatre older than the Colosseum).

It is one of two amphitheatres constructed in the ancient port town of Puteoli though little remains of the smaller amphitheatre, the *Anfiteatro Minore*. In fact, the Cumana train line runs right through the middle of what is left of its ancient ruins.

The Flavian Amphitheatre was the city's prime venue for gladiator games, chariot races, animal slayings and executions, and in its heyday it held some 20,000

spectators. One has to wonder how many spectators showed up on a fateful day in 305 AD for the "execution by wild beast" of seven men who were convicted of the crime of Christianity. These killings were carried out by local authorities during the final days of the Diocletianic Persecutions. The victims included: two laymen, two lectors, two deacons, one of which would become San Procolo (Saint Proculus), Pozzuoli's patron saint, and a bishop from Benevento, Naples' patron saint, San Gennaro (Saint Januarius).

According to legend: *All seven were cast to wild beasts; but when the animals came near the saints, they fell affectionately at their feet and refused to harm them.* Artemisia Gentileschi depicted this scene in a painting commissioned for the Cathedral of Pozzuoli, *San Gennaro nell'Anfiteatro di Pozzuoli*, which is now in Palazzo Reale.

The beasts it would seem were uncooperative, but the persecutors' thirst for blood would not go unquenched, and since the beasts didn't kill them, the men were beheaded at Solfatara. The stone on which it is believed San Gennaro was beheaded is kept in the nearby **Sanctuary of San Gennaro at Solfatara**. Local tradition has it that traces of San Gennaro's blood remain on the stone, and in the days leading up to the anniversary of his beheading, they become a ruby red colour.

The amphitheatre was excavated in the 19th century and much of its structure is still intact, the most impressive of which is the amphitheatre's well-preserved subterranean passageways. These are open to the public and you can wander the amphitheatre's underground at your leisure. Here you'll find ancient Roman arches, thick brick walls, fallen marble columns, and dark inlets which once housed the gladiators, their elaborate props, and, of course, the wild beasts in cages.

Vulcano Solfatara

SMOULDERING CRATER: VULCANO SOLFATARA

Virgil probably found his inspiration for Hades at the Solfatara crater, which continues to smoulder on endlessly today. Located a few metres from the sea, an entrance leads down a tree lined path to a sandy plain. **Curls of smoke puff on the slopes all around and the rotten egg smell is inescapable**.

Two fumaroles vent their steam at somewhere around 160 degrees Celsius and turn the rocks a shade of copper-gold. The Italians call these two vents *La Bocca Grande* or The Big Mouth. Behind their plume and hiss grows a green algae that's considered a biological rarity seen only when high temperatures and high acidity combine.

At the other end of the crater, *La Fangaia* or the boiling mud lake, sizzles at temperatures between 170-250 degrees Celsius. The mud contains a cocktail of gases and minerals that the Romans harnessed for their hydrothermal spas. A few arched bricks left by the Romans still wisp with sulphurous smoke that visitors are welcome to inhale for its healthful properties.

The Romans believed that Vulcan, the god of fire, worked beneath this ground hammering and shaping his armour for the gods. Take a stick and dig a little hole into the soil, then put your finger inside to feel the intense heat. Next, throw a large rock on the ground to hear the hollow cavities underneath you.

For those who like science, four corner reflectors dot the sandy terrain. They work with two satellites of the European Space Agency (ESA) to reflect their signals and map the volcano's ground deformations.

EXPLORE SOME MORE

After you leave Solfatara, drive up **Via Coste d'Agnano** for excellent views of the crater from above. Or better yet, spend the night breathing in Solfatara's sulphurous fumes at the park's campground. If you have time, spend a few hours at the nearby **Cratere degli Astroni Nature Reserve**, a protected oasis that was once a Bourbon hunting estate.

The Sibyl's Oracles: Cuma

One of the first stops on any tour of Naples should be the Cuma Archaeological Park to see the acropolis of Cuma (or Cumae), founded in the 8th century by Euboean Greeks. **Virgil's timeless account of the Sibyl's cave in *Book Six* of *The Aeneid* is so vivid and detailed, it leaves little doubt that the author himself once wandered these pathways.** Perhaps he strolled here with his friend Emperor Augustus who commissioned the book. Virgil left the work unfinished at his death, but Augustus insisted that it be published anyway and the epic became an instant success.

In David West's translation of the *Aeneid*, Virgil describes Aeneas' first meeting with the Cumaean Sibyl:

> *This rocky citadel had been colonised by Chalcidians from Euboea, and one side of it had been hollowed out to form a vast cavern into which led a hundred broad shafts, a hundred mouths, from which streamed as many voices giving the responses of the Sibyl.*

From the ticket office, a tree-lined path leads down to a trapezoidal shaft known as the *Antro della Sibilla*. This is where the Cumaean Sibyl may have written down her oracles on oak leaves that then blew away. When they did so, she churlishly refused to help reassemble her messages.

Archaeologists, however, ruin the mystique, claiming this was merely a Roman military tunnel and that if the Sibyl ever existed, her temple is lost to time. By Virgil's day the sibyls had already disappeared, so his own account of the woman is purely fictional.

Virgil also describes the temples at Cuma, which you can find by climbing up a flight of steps and past an overlook to the sea. Stop and take in the Bay of Naples where both the mythical Aeneas and the real-life Roman Imperial Navy could have sailed. A little further up a hill, the Temple of Apollo is nothing more than flattened stones, probably with philosopher spirits holding out their hands for a little money. While many young Roman students went to study in Athens, Greeks also came to this region to found their schools. It was the Epicurean School in Naples that first brought Virgil to the city in 48 BC.

Another path leads to a second terrace where the Temple of Jupiter has more of its structure intact. The temple's stones were later used to erect a paleo-Christian basilica, a common practice after the Roman Empire banned paganism in the 300s AD.

Every **solstice and equinox**, a group of universal-minded Italians hold a Solstice Ceremony at the Temple of Apollo in Lago Averno. The ceremony is well attended, open to everyone for free, and has a charming desire to unite all religions and all peoples. It begins at about sundown outside the temple. While everyone gathers around, an elderly gentleman gives an introduction about the coming service, urging the group to respect these silent moments. Then people file inside the temple. The ceremony begins with two circles, one inner and one outer and the first recitation is "The Invocation of the Seven Directions". Throughout the service, songs are sung and individuals read poems. Symbols of the earth, wind, fire and water are passed around: a plate of Lago Averno water, bread, incense and a torch are handed from person to person. An elderly woman gives a speech explaining that we come together with our sayings and songs from different religions in order to appreciate our unity. Once the ceremony is finished, the group makes their way from inside the temple to the lake where candles are pushed on lily pads into the water. Stones are also thrown into the water as ritual offerings. The ceremony ends with a long "OM..." just as the sun sets across the crater. Centro Nuova Era sponsors these events. Their centre is in the Vomero where they offer massages, yoga and other activities. centronuovaera.it.

Back at the ticket office, the entire ancient city of Cuma spreads out below the parking lot and an impressive amphitheatre across the street remains in situ. This area used to be a sprawling city that sat by the shore, inhabited first by the Greeks and then by the Samnites – a people who, among other things, battled the Romans and who spoke the Oscan language. The vast complex includes the Tomb of the Sibyl, a Greek *agora* (that became a Samnite forum), thermal baths, pieces of original marble strewn everywhere and a necropolis that once extended three kms.

BIRDLESS: LAGO AVERNO

Virgil's fictional character Aeneas wandered down to Lago Averno with the Sibyl, determined to travel to Hades and consult his dead father. The name of the lake, as *Book Six* of *The Aeneid* tells us, comes from the Greek word *aornos* meaning "the place without birds". **Romans believed that birds dropped like stones into the water thanks to the noxious sulphurous gases it emitted**, but this didn't prevent wealthy citizens from building villas or planting vineyards around the lake. In 37 BC it was linked by canal to Lago Lucrino and the sea and so became a secret naval training base.

Today, Lago Averno is a water-filled crater dotted with ducks and geese. Discos and restaurants line the lake, which is popular with teenagers who find this an excellent spot to display their affections in an uninhibited way. Above the lake, a lookout point along Via Montenuovo Licola Patria provides excellent views of both Lago Averno and Lago Lucrino beyond.

A footpath circles the entire lake, punctuated with signs that give descriptions of the unique animals and plants inhabiting the crater. On one end of the trail, the ancient Grotta di Cocceio once was a Roman military tunnel that connected the lake with Cuma, but it's now closed due to structural problems.

On the other side of the lake, vineyards testify to the rich volcanic soils that make everything grow abundantly here, including excellent grapes for wine. Next to the vineyards, a Temple of Apollo rises up imposingly. During the equinoxes and solstices, a group of earth lovers gathers inside the temple for a festival.

Due to bradyseism about thirty feet of earth buries the temple, actually believed to have been a bathing complex that exploited the local hot springs. Only the dome can be seen, but its massive proportions (the dome around 37 metres in diameter) show that this building once towered several stories high and probably had a technologically advanced hydraulics system.

Opposite page: Antro della Sibilla at Acropolis of Cuma

ENTRANCE TO HADES: GROTTA DELLA SIBILLA

Along the road that circles Lago Averno, an easily missed sign - Grotta della Sibilla - leads to a dirt track over-arched with trees. The path curves and ends at a cave. **Here Aeneas, with the Sibyl at his side, embarked on a journey into Hades.** Nowadays instead, a charming guide, Carlo Santillo, gives tours by reservation, handing visitors candles and oil lamps.

This, archaeologists say, was once a Roman military tunnel that connected Lago Averno to Lago Lucrino where fish used to be abundant until the 1538 volcanic eruption which not only killed them off but also created a whole new mountain nearby called Monte Nuovo. Today, you can visit the **Monte Nuovo Nature Oasis** and climb to the top for panoramic views of the lakes, the islands and the bay.

Inside the tunnel, carved out holes mark where in Roman times oil lamps perched in the crevices to light the way. This also means that the space would have been filled with noxious fumes. The cave has many corridors of what once was a sophisticated circuitry of stairs and passageways. They are no longer connected, but instead end in earth or water. One stairwell in the middle of the cave, Carlo insists, leads to the beginning of the **River Styx**. At the bottom of the stairwell lie limpid water pools, beyond which there is only blackness.

Going back down the main tunnel, at the very end a vast staircase leads to another cavern. This may have been a Roman restaurant, bathhouse, or, Carlo maintains, the cave of the Cimmerian Sibyl who uttered her oracles in Homeric times. A body of water has a wooden plank where visitors cross to see the caverns in which the Sibyl bathed and uttered her predictions. In truth, because of bradyseism it's difficult to tell exactly what existed here two thousand years ago; most of the grotto is under thirty to sixty feet of soil, but when the candles go out, the pitch blackness of the cavern will make you believe you are in a place where Hades himself still roams.

ROMAN BEACH TOWN: BAIA ARCHAEOLOGICAL PARK

Virgil pottered about in this spa town and playground for rich and debauched Romans. So did other renowned Roman writers, including Horace and Cicero. **Today the villas of Baia lie mostly under water, but the Roman ruins that remain inspire the imagination due to their vast scale**. The huge complex at the Archaeological Park encompasses three terraces of labyrinth-like structures.

Perhaps the Romans harnessed the hydrothermal activity for their baths, or wealthy patricians built summer villas, or perhaps this was the Imperial Villa for the Emperors. Layers of ancient construction spanning four centuries baffle inquiry, but we can guess that these ruins once sparkled with skyscraper-like temples and buildings faced in marble, their domes and floors tiled in mosaics and their façades splashed with deep coloured frescoes. You don't have to look too hard to find dusty mosaics, fading frescoes and partially marbled columns, enduring reminders of the ruins' former splendour.

To the uninitiated, the complex is a mere skeleton of its former self. But to those with a bit of imagination, its grandeur springs to life with the turn of every corner. And in the silence - you'll rarely find but a handful of tourists here - you can hear the whispers of a thousand Romans bubbling up from the baths.

A Statue of Hermes still stands in an alcove, framed by fading frescoes peeling away from reticulated brick. An arched corridor makes for an atmospheric photo and leads to a grassy field named after the goddess Sosandra. The Temple of Mercury (or Temple of Echoes, so named by travellers in the 18th century) has a wooden walkway over a pool of water. High-pitched yelling inside this dome makes sounds bounce in wonderful echoes. Its oculus casts a circular glow on the ancient walls and algae-green water. A fig tree grows "upside down" in a cavern nearby.

Looking out at the Baia waterfront from the ruins, the **Temple of Venus** stands overlooking the sea, now disconnected from the rest of the

Statue of Hermes at Baia

site, its dome lost to time. A few hundred metres to the north, the muddy half-shell of the **Temple of Diana** sits against a hill. As often happens with these ancient and impressive structures, successive generations assumed they were temples; in reality all three buildings were devoted not to religion but rather to bathing.

Underwater Archaeological Park of Baia

Much of the splendour and archaeological remains of Baia lie under water. The **Underwater Archaeological Park of Baia** was designated a protected marine area in 2000, along with the Underwater Park of Gaiola in Naples. Both are considered "marine environments with significant historical, archaeological, environmental and cultural value". Several organisations offer underwater archaeological excursions including diving, snorkelling and glass bottom boat trips. Just keep in mind, there won't be much to see when the water is murky.

JULIUS CAESAR'S SUMMER VILLA: BAIA CASTLE

Perched on a steep cliff, Baia Castle, as it is known, was thought to be the summer residence of Julius Caesar. **Archaeologists, however, theorise that the villa actually belonged to Emperor Nero.** Whatever the truth, by the late 15th century the Aragonese built a castle above the ancient Roman ruins and the fortress became a lookout point designed to scare pirates away from the shores.

During the 16th century Barbary Pirates seized ships throughout the Mediterranean, but even during Roman times (ca.70 BC) powerful Cicilian and Cretan pirates circled waters around Puteoli (Pozzuoli). They wanted most of all to capture slaves and bring them to the Delos market for sale. Because policing the waters proved difficult for the Romans, the owners constructed this fortress on a cliff with sheer walls that couldn't be climbed.

The outside terraces of Baia castle boast stunning views of the sea. Inside, the Archaeological Museum of Campi Flegrei has a long stretch of rooms displaying marble statues and a multitude of other ancient artefacts found in this area.

Of special interest are the Domitian-Nerva, the only equestrian bronze statue to survive from ancient times and the Nymphaeum Triclinium of Claudius which depicts a Roman dining room as it might have looked during the reign of Emperor Claudius, with marble statues in alcoves. The front niche depicts Odysseus offering black wine to a Cyclops as told in Homer's Odyssey. Baio (or Bajos) stands on the opposite side of Odysseus, squeezing a wineskin. Baio was said to have been Odysseus' navigator who died and was buried somewhere in Baia – hence how the city gets its name.

THE ROMAN CISTERN: PISCINA MIRABILIS

Piscina Mirabilis is **the largest Roman cistern still in existence today** and provides a detailed glimpse into their advanced technology. It also makes an excellent backdrop and is the setting for the *Canto delle Lavandaie del Vomero* (Song of the Washerwomen) in John Turturro's film Passione.

Here the Romans collected water brought by an aqueduct from the Serino River, but scholars disagree about who used this water tank. The cistern may have supplied water to the navy fleet stationed at Miseno about one km away or it might have provided water to the nearby villas.

Opposite page: Piscina Mirabilis

In order to visit, you must first call a number and make an appointment. Then go to the cistern at the agreed upon time, walk down a nearby block, and call out asking the locals: "*Piscina Mirabilis?*" They will point. Follow the fingers until you reach an apartment complex where someone will come out to meet you, key in hand. You might be allowed to explore on your own, trekking down steep metal steps and into the mossy cavern below, or be accompanied by the custodian.

Constructed in the Augustan period, the cistern measures 70 metres long, 25.5 metres wide, and 15 metres tall. Dug into the tuff rock, it has two entrances. The first is by way of the metal stairs. The second is on the opposite end, but the tuff stairs currently lead only to earth. A middle nave lies one metre below the rest of the structure and once served as a decantation pool for periodic cleansing and emptying of the cistern. A thick layer of waterproof *cocciopesto* or *signinum* once covered the cistern walls. They were made of broken tiles mixed with mortar. The water capacity could reach 12,600 cubic metres and the Romans created hydraulic machines on the roof terrace that pumped the water.

Added to the cistern during the first and second century AD, twelve small rooms covered by barrel vaults increased the power of the hydraulic system. These rooms can still be seen along the outside wall of the cistern.

As hollow cracks and clicks echo through this underground cavern, one wonders: if archaeologists discovered this kind of impressive knowledge, did the Romans have even more innovative technology that remains lost to us moderns?

EXPLORE SOME MORE

After a visit to the cistern, stop by **Casina Vanvitelliana**. This hunting lodge was designed by Luigi and Carlo Vanvitelli and was completed in 1782. Emperors, tsars and famous notables, including Mozart and Rossini, rested here during their visits to the Phlegraean Fields.

LIKE MOTHER, LIKE DAUGHTER: THE TOMB OF AGRIPPINA

The truth about Agrippina, her death and her remains are as difficult to find as the location itself. Signs for her tomb appear and then vanish throughout the twisting Campi Flegrei roads, but tap Piazza Guglielmo Marconi into a GPS and you'll see the "Via Agrippina" sign that leads down to a port. Park your car and make your way by crumbling buildings and a seaside walkway. Another sign marks the tomb, whose bricks today are overgrown with weeds. A fence bars visitors as though making clear that the owners haven't paid their rent in years.

It's unknown if the people who called these stones the Tomb of Agrippina meant Agrippina the Elder or Agrippina the Younger; the tales of both are full of intrigue. The former was the granddaughter of Augustus, Caligula's mother and Nero's grandmother. The latter was Agrippina the Elder's daughter, and Nero's mother. Archaeologists, however, once again ruin the myth and lore, saying that these stones were simply part of a Roman odeon (theatre). As so often with ancient sites in Campania, we nod sagely to the historians while celebrating the stories that have become entangled in these ruins.

THE ROMAN IMPERIAL NAVY: MISENUM

Capo Miseno or *Misenum* in Latin comes from Misenus, a character in Virgil's *The Aeneid* who drowned off the coast nearby after a trumpet competition with the sea-god Triton. It's a tough place to find; try some adventurous exploring by car and when the signs disappear, continue up, up, up through the steep and curvy road, trying to get to the peak of the mountain. When (or if) you come to a one-lane tunnel, you'll spill out on the other end into a beautiful Vista Point overlooking the Gulf of Pozzuoli. Vesuvius and the city of Naples glimmer through the haze.

On one side of the vista, the mountain of Miseno has a walking trail, the hike leading to a Roman Milestone. On the other side, a gate bars access to a modern military area. **The largest Roman naval base was first established here in 27 BC** during Emperor Augustus' rule. When Vesuvius erupted in 79 AD, Pliny the Elder was in charge of the naval fleet and went by ship from here toward the destruction to help rescue people, but he ended up reaching Stabia where he died. His nephew, Pliny the Younger, was a resident of Misenum at the time and much later wrote an account of the eruption as he watched from this very mountain. The Roman Caesars used Misenum as a remote place to exile their enemies, including Agrippina the Younger.

ROMAN RUINS
⤜ THE ⤛
VESUVIAN
EXCAVATIONS

Cover Photo:
Forum, Pompeii

POMPEI. L'Anfiteatro e la Palestra grande. 4. febbraio 2009

In **79 AD**, one of the most powerful volcanoes in the world erupted, destroying everything in its devastating path.

A build-up of gas below Mount Vesuvius set in motion a complex set of volcanic events lasting three days. The volcano exploded with the force of 40 atomic bombs; the entire top of the mountain was pulverised. There was no lava, but some 1.5 million tons of volcanic pumice, ash and gas was jettisoned at a speed of 3 - 5 miles per second vertically into the air. The volcano is still active today, but don't worry: central Naples is out of the *Zona Rossa* – the Red Zone. Back in the year 79 with the prevailing winds coming from the north-west and west, the falling material headed directly for Pompeii, but volcanic debris reached as far south-east as Paestum, some 100 km away. The assault raged on for three days and by the time it was done, the eruption had buried Herculaneum and Pompeii and the Roman towns of Boscoreale, Oplontis and Stabia (where Pliny the Elder took his last breath), were no more.

Pompeii Amphitheatre, Lorenzo Dotti, 2009

View of Pompeii from the Necropoli of Porta Nocera

Plan Your Visit

Pompeii is the number one tourist attraction in the Campania region. To beat the crowds, visit on a weekday in the middle of the winter – that's when you'll get the city almost all to yourself. February is the least visited month of the year and May is the most visited. While tourists flock to Pompeii by the bus load, the curious traveller will find Herculaneum much less crowded and better preserved. It is considerably smaller than Pompeii, much easier to manage and you can see the entire site in one day.

Do keep in mind that walking around these excavation sites can be exhausting, especially in the dog days of summer when temperatures and humidity levels can be high. Bring plenty of water, and wear sensible shoes, hats and sunscreen. To avoid that bitterest of disappointments - the arrival at closed gates of an historic site you've been longing to see - before you select your day and time or visit and certainly before you set out, ask your hotel, B&B staff or your tour guide to telephone ahead for you. Check that no unforeseen circumstances have led to a closure – it has been known in recent years for Pompeii to shut without warning for a morning for matters such as staff meetings.

Transport

METRO/RAILWAYS
Circumvesuviana
Napoli – Sorrento Line:
Herculaneum, Oplontis, Pompeii Villa dei Misteri (Porta Marina and Piazza Esedra entrances), Stabia

Napoli – Poggiomarino Line:
Pompei Santuario (Piazza Anfiteatro)

Travel Tip: avoid the crowds by getting the Circumvesuviana at the start of the line at the Porta Nolana station rather than at Naples Central Station.

BUSES
CurreriViaggi:
Capodichino Airport to Pompeii (no return)
8 departures daily
€10.00

EAVBus:
Napoli – Vesuvio departs from Mergellina at 09.00 and 10.15 at Piazza Piedigrotta and from Vesuvius at 12.30 and 14.00. The journey is 1.5 hours U8 (€7.30) or use a Unicocampania 3T ticket

Pompei – Vesuvio, 10 departures daily, €10.00 round trip same day ticket

SITASud:
Autolinea Salerno – Nocera – Napoli

Other Vesuvius Transport:
pompeivesuvio.info
tramvianapoli.com
vesuvioexpress.info

Tourist Info

CAMPANIA ARTECARD
ArteCard 365, Napoli & Tutta la Regione

CONSERVATION INITIATIVES
Friends of Herculaneum Society:
herculaneum.ox.ac.uk
Herculaneum Conservation Project:
herculaneum.org
Oplontis Project:
oplontisproject.org
Restoring Ancient Stabiae:
stabiae.org and vesuvianinstitute.it

POMPEII SITES COMBINED TICKETS
5 sites/3 days
(Pompeii, Herculaneum, Stabia, Oplontis,
Boscoreale)
€20.00 (a saving of €7.50 on all 5 sites and
of €2.00 if you are visiting just Pompeii and
Herculaneum)

3 sites/1 day (Stabia, Oplontis, Boscoreale)
€5.50

POMPEII WALKING TOURS
Book a private tour:
naplesprivatetours.com
Join a walking tour:
pompeiholiday.com
Book ahead:
yellowsudmarine.com

Sights & Attractions

MAV: MUSEO ARCHEOLOGICO VIRTUALE
Via IV Novembre, 44, Herculaneum
Open daily **except Mon** 09.30 - 17.00
+39 081 19806511
museomav.it

MOUNT VESUVIUS
Open Jan/Feb/Nov/Dec – 09.00 - 15.00;
March + Oct – 09.00 - 16.00; Apr/May/Jun/
Sept – 09.00 - 17.00; Jul + Aug – 09.00 -
18.00
From €10.00
+39 0812395653
epnv.it

Trails can close for inclement weather

NATIONAL ARCHAEOLOGICAL MUSEUM
Piazza Museo Nazionale, 19, Naples
Open daily **except Tues** 09.00 – 19.30
Neapolis Station is open the same days and
times, but entry is free
Adults €8.00
+39 0814422149
cir.campania.beniculturali.it/
museoarcheologiconazionale

(THE) ROMAN BATHS AROUND NAPLES
The following sites are not open to the
public, but Gruppo Archeologico Napoli
(GAN) occasionally offers tours of these
sites. Admission is typically between €3.00
and €5.00. Sign up for GAN's newsletter to
get advance notifications at ganapoletano.it

- BATHS AT TERRACINA
The corner of Via Terracina and Via Marconi
The site is only open to the public for special
events, but the ruins are visible from the
street.

- CARMINIELLO AI MANNESI ARCHAEOLOGICAL - COMPLEX
Vico Primo Carminiello ai Mannesi
The site is only open to the public for special
events, but the ruins are visible from the
street.

- DOMUS OF THE HISTORICAL ARCHIVES OF THE BANK OF NAPLES
Via Tribunale, 213 in Palazzo Ricca
Not open to the public on a regular basis
but visits can be made by request to the
Historic Archive of the Bank of Naples.

- TERME DI AGNANO
Via Agnano Agli Astroni, 12
This site is not open to the public on a
regular basis.

ROMAN BATHS AT SANTA CHIARA
Via Santa Chiara, 49/c
Open Mon - Sat 09.30 - 17.30, Sun &
Holidays 10.00 – 14.30
Adults €6.00
+39 081 5516673
monasterodisantachiara.com

THE VESUVIAN (POMPEII) SITES
Open daily 08.30 - 19.30 (last entry 18.00) 1
Apr – 31 Oct; 08.30 - 17.00 (last entry 15.30)
1 Nov – 31 Mar
Herculaneum and Pompeii - €11.00 each
Boscoreale, Oplontis and Stabia (free) - 3
sites/1day €5.50
All 5 sites/3 days €20.00
Audio guides are available at Herculaneum
and Pompeii
+39 081 8575347
pompeiisites.org

- BOSCOREALE
Via Settetermini and Viale Villa Regina,
Boscoreale
Villa closed for renovations – check ahead.

- HERCULANEUM
Corso Resina, Ercolano

- OPLONTIS VILLA OF POPPAEA
Via dei Sepolcri, Torre Annunziata

- POMPEII
Via Villa Dei Misteri, 2 - entrances and exits
at Porta Marina, Piazza Esedra and Piazza
Anfiteatro and exit at Villa dei Misteri

- STABIAN VILLAS
Villa Arianna & Villa San Marco are
situated on Via Passeggiata Archeologica,
Castellammare di Stabia, approximately 1
km from each other.

VESUVIUS OBSERVATORY
At 608 metres
+39 081 6108483
ov.ingv.it/ov/museo.html
*Vesuvius Observatory closed for renovations
– check ahead.*

VESUVIAN VILLAS
There are 122 Vesuvian Villas in total. Below
are the two major villas.
villevesuviane.net

- COMPLESSO MONUMENTALE DELLA REGGIA DI PORTICI
Via Università, 100, Portici
Guided tours of the Herculanense Museum
can be pre-booked
+39 081 2532016
segreteria@centromusa.it

- VILLA CAMPOLIETO
Corso Resina, 283, Portici
Open Tues – Sun, 10.00 – 13.00
Adult €3.00
+39 081 7322134

Opposite page: Villa San Marco, Stabia
Below: Hiking Mount Vesuvius

Copious folklore surrounds **Lacryma Christi** - wine made from grapes grown on the fertile slopes of Vesuvius. One version tells how as Christ wept over Lucifer's fall from heaven (and into the fiery pit of lava), his tears fell upon the sides of the volcano rendering the soil along the lower slopes of Mount Vesuvius extremely fertile. The problem with this story, however, (and there are a few) is that historically, volcanoes were connected to the devil and the Underworld. Who would even consider drinking a wine with sulphurous, evil connections? Bring on a second version of the tale in which during Satan's banishment from Heaven, he stole a piece of Paradise and brought it down to Earth. The piece he stole was Vesuvius! Christ's tears flowed at this outrage; they dampened the soil allowing the grapes to flourish and thus was born the wine called "Tears of Christ". This version suited the wine producers' marketing plan (members of the Medici family from Florence) because it removed the evil stigma. To further popularise the wine, the Medici, some of whom were Popes, arranged for Lacryma Christi to be the official wine of the Church. In this way, the faithful were treated to this marvellous wine at Mass and it soon became highly sought-after.

A THREATENING BEAUTY: MOUNT VESUVIUS

One of the most famous volcanoes in the world, Vesuvius began to form some 25,000 years ago, though volcanic activity predates that by some 375,000 years. Its most destructive explosion was in 79 AD, ever after to be described as a Plinian type eruption. Vesuvius last erupted in March 1944, when Allied Forces occupied much of the region. Its iconic "humpback" shape (known today as Somma-Vesuvio) is the result of the 79 AD eruption which blew the top off the mountain known as Monte Somma and created two peaks: a large volcanic cone, the **Gran Cono** at 1,281 metres high and Monte Somma at 1,149 metres. It was certainly a dramatic change. Prior to this date scientists speculate that Vesuvius might have been twice as high and records indicate its slopes were probably largely forested.

Today the lush soil that makes up the volcano's skirts favours the cultivation of various crops, especially vines. It is Vesuvius' soil that gives us San Marzano tomatoes, the Vesuvian tomatoes known as Pomodorini del Piennolo del Vesuvio or Pomodorini Vesuviani and the Catalanesca and Lacryma Christi (the famed "Tears of Christ") wines.

The summit of Vesuvius, which was declared a national park in the 1990s, is open to explore. The hike - Nature Trail (sentiero) 5, Il Gran Cono - is one of nine such trails scattered about the mountain (pick up a map of all the trails at the ticket office). On a clear day, the steep climb will be rewarded with a breathtaking view of Naples, the bay and the islands of Capri, Ischia and Procida.

A visit to the volcano means a ride (by car, bus, or 4x4 Jeep excursion) along a narrow, well-marked road that winds up the side of the volcano to about 1,000 metres. There you'll find a car park and a small hut where you can purchase tickets to hike beyond the gate. All uphill on foot from there, hiking the 800 metre or so ascent to the peak takes about thirty minutes; souvenir shops and cafés are available along the way. The pebbled path is dusty and difficult to walk on, so good walking shoes or hiking boots are a must and almost everyone will benefit from a walking stick. Pick these up for free when you start the ascent - just make sure to tip for the stick when you return it. Expect to be dusty to your knees at the end of the day.

Once at the top, the inside of the crater is filled with earth – sorry, you can't see bubbling lava. However, the experience *can* feel a bit daring because vulcanologists anticipate another eruption sometime soon. Interestingly, that doesn't prevent Neapolitans from building a sprawling metropolis all around this active volcano. In fact, it is because so many people live on/near Vesuvius, that it is considered one of the most dangerous volcanoes in the world and perhaps that's why it's also the most monitored volcano. Vesuvius won't rumble and spew lava the way Etna does; when it erupts, it will emulate a champagne cork, but

Vesuvius National Park

with much more unpleasant consequences. Experts believe they will have up to two weeks' warning of a major explosion. Communities closest to Vesuvius and therefore at highest risk, have been twinned with regions elsewhere in Italy under a contingency plan, so that in the case of an eruption they can be evacuated as fast as possible. In 2013, the Red Zone included 27 of these, some of the eastern-most suburbs of Naples featuring on the list.

Naturally the mere existence of Vesuvius makes one thoughtful; however, until the day it erupts, it will continue to evoke feelings other than a sense of danger. Its great beauty dominates the landscape, moulds our concept of the bay, appears in most of the iconography of the region. Pop artist Andy Warhol painted many images of the volcano. In 1985, thanks to his strong artistic relationship with the dynamic gallerist Lucio Amelio, Warhol created a sequence of works represent-ing the volcano, each successive depiction in different colours. Visitors can see a superb example of this at Capodimonte. This wasn't Warhol's first take on Campania's seismic landscape. His 1981 pop art silkscreen *Fate Presto – Hurry!* - based on the post-Irpinia earthquake front cover of *Il Mattino* in 1980, has an enduring power.

As a radical contrast in style, see Scipione Compagno's 1631 *L'Eruzione del Vesuvio* at the San Martino Charterhouse which features a church procession for San Giacomo (a Naples city patron from 1626). Well into the 20th century it was hoped such expressions of faith would stop the flow of fire and lava when the volcano stirred. Finally seek out online images of works by Joseph Wright of Derby and J.M.W. Turner for Vesuvius in full eruption mode.

FUNICULÌ, FUNICULÀ!

From the days when British Ambassador William Hamilton wore through his shoes (and those of his long-suffering servants) upon the hot slopes of Vesuvius, the volcano has been a magnet to visitors. Up until the 1870s the only alternative to trekking up on foot was a horseback ride or a sedan chair. But in 1878 the Hungarian entrepreneur Ernesto Emanuele Oblieght obtained permission to construct and operate a funicular railway up the slopes and in 1880 he and colleagues celebrated the new venture with a champagne reception. That year one of the song entries in the Piedigrotta Festival, *Funiculì Funiculà*, written by Peppino Turco and Luigi Denza, burst upon the scene, becoming in effect a kind of promotional jingle for Oblieght's railway.

It was not all plain sailing, or indeed, railing; from the very beginning local guides were incensed that their livelihood was under threat. Though Oblieght bought them off to some extent, subsequent owners of the line, including Thomas Cook & Son, who took over control in 1888, had to contend with sabotaged rails and carriages. As if this wasn't enough, eruptions in 1906, 1911 and 1928 wrought enormous damage to the system and the 1944 eruption put an emphatic end to this convenient method of reaching the summit. A pity, since, as the song says, you can see Procida, France and Spain from the top! ...Allegedly.

Il Vesuvio, S. Heidesheimer & Co. postcard ca.1905

KEEPING WATCH: VESUVIUS OBSERVATORY

We have Ferdinand II of the Two Sicilies to thank for the *Osservatorio Vesuviano* - the Vesuvius Observatory. Founded in 1841, it's the **oldest vulcanological monitoring station in the world**. Its first director was Italian physicist Macedonio Melloni (1798 - 1854). Historically, the observatory was located on the slopes of Vesuvius at 608 metres above sea level in the elegant Neo-Classical palazzo designed by Gaetano Fazzini. The observatory remained on Vesuvius through several eruptions until operations were moved to a new facility in Fuorigrotta in 1970.

> In the observatory of Vesuvius, situated on a spur of the mountain, scientific men are stationed to observe a delicate instrument which indicates by the vibrations of a needle the degree of the volcano's activity. It is however a position of great danger. In 1872 an awful wave of lava came rolling toward this ledge as if to overwhelm it. Happily, it divided at the base of the cliff and went on either side; but when the divisions met again at its lower extremity the director, Palmieri, and his comrades found themselves encircled by a sea of fire.
> STODDARD'S LECTURES, JOHN L. STODDARD, VOL.8, FLORENCE, NAPLES, ROME, p.161

Under the aegis of the National Institute of Geophysics and Vulcanology (INGV) (since 2001), the Vesuvius Observatory monitors the region's volcanoes: Vesuvius, the Campi Flegrei, Ischia and Stromboli, 24 hours a day. Additionally the centre is involved in scientific research in the areas of geophysics, geochemistry and vulcanology as well as educational activities. The building on Vesuvius remains and is just a short detour from the road that leads to the crater of Vesuvius. Today it houses a museum, a library and a few laboratories.

COCOON: HERCULANEUM

Herculaneum, as the myth goes, was founded by Hercules, and as its name would suggest, by the Greeks. In reality however, the Oscans, Etruscans and Samnites vied with the Greeks for control of the city from some time in the 6th century BC until it joined the Social War, the "War of the Allies" against the victorious Romans, who assumed full control in 89 BC. Soon after, the city became **a high-class resort with many wealthy Roman residences** (in contrast to Pompeii, a busy port city). The eruption of Mount Vesuvius, however, plunged the city into a huge river of boiling mud and debris. The population, four or five thousand strong, probably had time to reach the sea, but they perished in the first of a series of pyroclastic surges of ash and hot gases, as evidenced by the three hundred human skeletons found at the seafront, possibly in boathouses awaiting rescue.

In 1709 an Austrian General, Prince d'Elboeuf, hearing of treasures being unearthed near his estate at Portici, bought the land and engaged workers to dig. They discovered part of Herculaneum's theatre and in 1738 the Villa of the Papyri – an area still not open to the public – was found with a library consisting of hundreds of papyrus scrolls. Today, the scrolls are housed in Naples' National Library - Biblioteca Nazionale - and the artefacts found in the villa are located at the National Archaeological Museum. Excavations of Herculaneum were abandoned in 1780 in favour of Pompeii, which is much easier to dig since it was covered by ash instead of mud hardened into rock. Excavations have not been undertaken continuously since; the most recent campaign was 2002 - 2006 at the Villa dei Papiri.

To date, only 4.5 hectares of Herculaneum's 20 hectares have been unearthed and thus it is typically overshadowed by Pompeii, its much larger and much more famous neighbour. Entombed in a 16 – 25 metre deep cocoon of solidified mud, Herculaneum has been extremely difficult to excavate, but because of that, what has been brought to light is much more intact. Impressively, that includes original wood materials that would have decayed under normal conditions and the second storeys of many of Herculaneum's structures, which are without equal at Pompeii. Additionally, since 2001, ongoing conservation and restoration efforts

Herculaneum Conservation Project

DON'T MISS!

- THE TEMPLE (OR HALL) OF THE AUGUSTALES (24) – housed the cult of the Emperor Augustus, whose members were mostly *liberti,* freed men.

- HOUSE OF THE BLACK HALL (18) - belonged to I. Venidius Ennychius, as the wax-tablets (an ancient, informal means for writing) show. The show-piece is a large room in black frescoes. There is a similar room in the Villa of the Mysteries in Pompeii.

- HOUSE OF NEPTUNE AND AMPHITRITE (29) - it has a nymphaeum (water garden) and its recently restored mosaics sparkle in blues, reds and coral pinks.

- THE WOMEN'S BATHS (27) - several nice mosaics and some ancient glass *in situ*, not much, but an archaeological rarity none the less.

- SAMNITE HOUSE (31) – textbook example of first style painting, though it also contains second and fourth styles. Test your knowledge! (See Decorating Pompeii: The Four Pompeian Painting Styles)

- HOUSE OF THE WOOD PARTITION (36) - this house has a large wooden privacy partition between the atrium and the tablinium - the only example of its kind to survive from Greco-Roman antiquity.

- THE BOAT HOUSES AND BEACH FRONT (1) - the ancient coastline where nearly three hundred skeletons were found (victims of the eruption trying to escape) in 12 small structures archaeologists believe were boathouses.

CLOSED BUILDINGS OF HERCULANEUM

- SUBURBAN BATHS (3) are well worth a visit, but unfortunately they have been closed for conservation. The complex itself is spectacularly well preserved and also is remarkable for some details of the eruption: inside is a ball of volcanic material with glass and indentations which was created when the eruption blew through a window and then threw a gigantic basin across the room. They are the subject of a test of 3D laser scanning, conducted by the HCP in collaboration with the University of North Carolina.

- VILLA OF THE PAPYRI (44) where the most spectacular finds were made – the villa possessed at least 80 fine statues, including two celebrated athletes known as "the runners" and a set of 5 "dancers', actually female figures posing. Copies of this last group are on site in Herculaneum while the originals of both runners and dancers reside in the Archaeological Museum in Naples. The villa was never actually fully excavated: 20 metres of volcanic material still cover it and so access to all but a few rooms is through the original tunnels by which the Bourbon era excavators did their work.

- Also closed is the Theatre, due to poisonous gas which seeps in. This was the first part of the city to be found, first by well-diggers in 1709, and it is still completely underground, underneath the modern city of Ercolano.

have been aided by the Packard Humanities Institute's Herculaneum Conservation Project. Founded and run by David Packard, a classicist and son of the co-founder of Hewlett-Packard, the project bankrolls and organises conservation efforts, the most serious of which (roofing, stabilisation and drainage of the site) have been completed.

Entrance to Herculaneum is marked by a long bridge that curves above the entire ancient city, giving a bird's eye view of its streets and buildings. This is an excellent starting point to orient yourself to the site's layout. The ticket office is situated at the opposite end of the bridge, so if you are very short on time, you can steal a glance and a few pictures of Herculaneum without actually entering the ruins. To explore Herculaneum to its fullest, however, allow at least a half a day. A map and booklet are included in the ticket price. The numbers used here relate to the map and booklet. Combine your visit to Herculaneum with a trek up to Mount Vesuvius for a full day excursion, and if you have time, stop by MAV, the Virtual Archaeological Museum.

EXPLORE SOME MORE

You won't find any ancient artefacts at **MAV – Museo Archeologico Virtuale** – a "virtual archaeology" museum located just a few blocks from Herculaneum, but if you want a glimpse into what life was like before the fatal eruption of Mount Vesuvius, MAV is worth a visit. Thanks to modern technology, the museum's 70 multimedia, multi-sensory exhibits bring history to life, transporting visitors to the ancient Roman towns of Pompeii and Herculaneum in the years before the eruption of Vesuvius in 79 AD.

Forum, Pompeii

ROMAN FOR A DAY: POMPEII

*Stand at the bottom of the great market-place of Pompeii,
and look up the silent streets, through the ruined temples
of Jupiter and Isis, over the broken houses with their
inmost sanctuaries open to the day, away to Mount
Vesuvius, bright and snowy in the peaceful distance;
and lose all count of time, and heed of other things,
in the strange and melancholy sensation of seeing the
Destroyed and the Destroyer making this quiet picture
in the sun.*

CHARLES DICKENS, PICTURES FROM ITALY, 1845

Since excavators first took their spades to Pompeii almost 270 years ago, it has held a huge fascination, attracting visitors from far and wide. Celebrities have not been immune to its charms – Wolfgang Amadeus Mozart, Johann Wolfgang von Goethe, Charles Dickens, Mark Twain and Henry James came here. The father of archaeology, Heinrich Schliemann died trying to get here. More recently, Leonardo di Caprio strolled through the city's streets, though he was so anxious not to be photographed he kept his hoodie up throughout. Around 2.5 million less well-known visitors make the pilgrimage each year. Pompeii is the most visited site in the Campania region, the second most visited site in Italy after the Colosseum and it is perhaps **the most famous archaeological site in the world**. In 1997 its exceptional appeal was recognised when, along with the archaeological sites at Herculaneum and Torre Annunziata (the Villa of Poppaea at Oplontis), Pompeii joined the ranks of UNESCO's World Heritage Sites.

The city remains the single most remarkable example of what life was like in a Roman town. We look upon it as a way to experience the past and understand how Romans lived, even as we gaze, disturbed, upon the way that Romans died. Of course, the desire of archaeologists to unearth, study and share this archaeological marvel with mankind has turned it into a veritable Disneyland-like theme park of ancient history. Bear in mind that in order both to stabilise the ruins and to present them for visitors, archaeologists and curators have had to some extent to reconstruct extensive amounts of some buildings piece-by-piece. The level of historical knowledge of the time of digging/reconstruction combined with the artistic flair of restorers will affect how this occurs at any major site; the effect is magnified enormously with a site on the scale of Pompeii. In addition, visitors will instantly realise that the names of buildings and streets are not those that would be recognised by any inhabitant of Pompeii returning today. They are a useful convention for reference and to facilitate our understanding. For example, a label might be given based on a key discovery. However, where the name of the

DECORATING POMPEII: THE FOUR POMPEIAN PAINTING STYLES

On the walls in Pompeii and Herculaneum (and in the Archaeological Museum, for that matter), you'll see a lot of frescoes. You will impress your friends if you know the elements present in each. Dates are approximate: old styles continued to be used long after the next one was introduced. We have cause to be grateful to German archaeologist August Mau who ordered the frescoes into four phases or styles. Bear in mind that scholars continue to refine and redefine these categories even today.

FIRST STYLE

The **first style (incrustation or structural)** (ca. 200 - 80 BC) looks like blocks of marble in different colours, except this is paint on plaster. This technique known as faux marbling or marble veneer would also become all the rage in Renaissance Europe – indeed by the 17th century it was widespread in richer buildings - but we first meet it in ancient Roman dwellings like those in Pompeii. If using marble in a structure is ruled out by its cost or weight, this is an impressive alternative. In later styles it was used on floors and ceilings. Other elements in this style simulated cornices or beams and overall colours were bright, colour being an effective social indicator of wealth. Examples can be seen at the **Samnite House** (31) in Herculaneum and in the entrance of the **House of the Faun** (17) at Pompeii.

SECOND STYLE

Renaissance "still-lives" could well have taken their inspiration from the **second style (architectural or illusionism)** (ca. 80 - 0 BC). The major feature of this is *trompe l'oeil* paintings, either still-life works (like baskets of fruit and birds) or landscapes which take up the whole wall and fade off into the distance, making the room seem bigger. Earlier on, landscapes are framed by columns, giving the room a sort of veranda feel; later on, these are omitted. Another feature is fake niches with statuary. A good example can be seen at the **Villa of the Mysteries** (30).

First Style, House of the Faun, Pompeii

THIRD STYLE

The **third style (ornate)** (ca. 20 BC–20 AD) is extremely decorative. Faux-architectural details return with a vengeance, including small column bases supporting vases and pictures painted into frames that are also painted. As with the first style, some of the decorative elements used recall Ptolemaic originals, so that this style is known as "Egyptianising". Third style paintings tend to divide the wall into several vertical bands and ornate symmetry is a major organising principle. Again, the **Villa of the Mysteries** (30) at Pompeii provides a fine example.

FOURTH STYLE

The **fourth style** (20 - 79 AD) is essentially a reaction to the third: blank space that was painted to look like stone in the third style is simply filled with a colour, and the colours tend to be warmer and more vibrant. Decorative patterns are also simpler. The vertical bands remain, and are sometimes subdivided with horizontal bands: at the bottom, there will be two narrow bands flanking a thicker one which, at the top of the wall, is itself divided into three bands, so that all five bands are the same width at the top, preserving the symmetry. This simplicity contrasts, however, with striking instances of landscape and still-life painting, framed image by image into entire upper walls set above first style decorative panels and discs. There are fourth style frescoes at the **House of the Stags** (8) in Herculaneum.

The influence of Egyptian style has been mentioned, but, of course, the Romans adored Greek art and culture, absorbing and emulating Hellenistic originals as their own territories expanded in this time frame and Pompeii itself had a Greek past. If they have a means of access to them, societies assimilate elements of past or distant cultures, whether as something a little exotic to venerate (the worship of Egyptian goddess Isis) or as a rich world of myth and storytelling to celebrate (the Greek gods and goddesses portrayed and/or venerated in stone, metal and paint throughout the city).

Second Style, Villa of the Mysteries, Pompeii

owner of a building is known, that may supply the modern name of the edifice in question.

Just 70 years or so shy of its 2,000th birthday, Pompeii is immense. Undergoing near continuous excavations since its discovery, nearly 2/3 of the site - 45 of 66 hectares have been unearthed thus far, revealing 1,500 buildings, 2 million square metres of walls and 17,000 square metres of paintings. Yet what brings tourists in by the droves is not so much Pompeii's age or size, but its accessibility and extraordinary intimacy. Here, you can walk among the ruins – feel the ancient streets below your feet, touch the walls along the streets, walk in and out of ancient buildings, almost literally in the shoes of a Roman - it is a singular experience.

Of course Pompeii's über-accessibility may someday prove to be a factor in the demise of this archaeological site that has been flirting with disaster for decades. Pompeii was rocked by air raids during WWII and again by an earthquake in 1981. Deteriorating conditions caused officials to declare Pompeii in a state of emergency in 2008 and just two years later, heavy rains brought down the *Schola Armaturarum*, the House of the Gladiators. On the upside, the collapse gave rise to the Great Pompeii Project in 2012 and an influx of €75 million from the EU and €30 million from the Italian state. Yet ongoing environmental, economic and management issues continue to plague conservation efforts - officials have until 2015 to spend the EU funds - and experts are once again sounding alarm bells. Some even posit Pompeii is in such a rapid state of decline that if major steps are not taken, it is facing a second extinction.

Clearly, there is some veracity to these fears, but the truth is that the clock has been ticking on Pompeii since it first saw the light of day in 1748 and "that Pompeii" was then still rebuilding from an earthquake in 62 AD. Yet visiting Pompeii today isn't what it used to be. The number of tourists increases every year, many of whom arrive by the busload and tour the site en masse, putting further wear and tear on it by sheer footfall. Meanwhile, fewer and fewer structures are open and the unannounced closure of edifices, streets and occasionally the site in its entirety is a constant source of frustration to visitors. Some heritage experts say the future of Pompeii is in peril.

But rest assured, Pompeii remains as it ever was – a city in ruins.

Though we know Pompeii as a Roman city, the settlement was founded around the 8th - 6th century BC by Oscans. Its roots run even deeper as excavations have revealed neolithic settlements under the Roman city. Later, it was conquered by the Etruscans (ca. 7th - 6th century BC), the Greeks (ca. 500 BC) and then the Samnites (80 years or so later). Like Herculaneum, it came fully under Roman control after holding out to the bitter end of the Social War (91/90 - 88 BC). Pompeii was important as a crossroads between several nearby cities and because of its place at the mouth of the Sarno river.

By the time Mount Vesuvius erupted in 79 AD (commonly accepted to be on August 24th, but the exact date is still the subject of debate) the city already had several hundred years of history and was large and well-populated: ca. 13,000 people on about 66 hectares. The town was a bustling trading centre (if you enter along "Via Marina", you'll see the ancient docks – look for the tie-off points for ships) and filled with hotels (and bars/brothels) to serve the needs and wants of sailors and travellers: these buildings are rarely labelled as such; only the most famous one is now chastely labelled as the *lupanar* (Latin for "brothel"). Additionally, the town had significant connections with the world outside Italy. A temple to Isis with hieroglyphic inscriptions (on display in the Archaeological Museum) may indicate that in the cosmopolitan world of the Roman empire, Isis-worship was no longer confined to Egypt.

The ancient town's modern life began in 1599 when it was accidentally discovered by canal diggers. Excavations were begun in 1748 by Charles VII (III of Spain), 10 years after Herculaneum and have continued since.

BEFORE VISITING POMPEII

Professor Mary Beard's *Pompeii: The Life of a Roman Town* describes the smells, sounds, and important individuals of this city captured in time. The culture comes alive with chapters that describe how the Romans worshipped, dined and entertained themselves. The prose is accessible and reading the book before visiting will enrich your experience, not least because it offers authoritative challenges to some of the accepted lore about the site. The authors have been entertained and informed by this volume and wish to acknowledge its influence on our account of the city. For a fictional account of the last days of the city, Robert Harris's book *Pompeii* is also a gripping and fun read.

HOW TO VISIT POMPEII

The Porta Marina entrance is nearest to the Circumvesuviana train station and a short walk from the all-important forum - the most popular photo-op in the site. It is also the most crowded. On the other side of Pompeii, about 15 minutes along the perimeter of Pompeii and about 10 minutes to the other Circumvesuviana station – Pompeii Santuario - the Piazza Anfiteatro entrance leads to the area around the amphitheatre which boasts beautiful views and has far less crowds. The area around the Porta Ercolana gate and out to the Villa dei Misteri is also less crowded. A third entry is at Porta Esedra (many large tour groups enter here) and a fourth exit is at Villa dei Misteri.

For visitors short on time – Pompeii is best explored with a guide. Book ahead with one of the guides listed on the Napoli Unplugged website, or join up with one of the walking tours at the site; they are readily available and run frequently throughout the day. If you plan to explore on your own, remember that conditions at Pompeii can be quite fluid. Expect the unexpected. Some things you had your heart set on seeing might be closed while you might find another treasure has just re-opened around the corner. Also, don't try to see the entire site in one day. Pick just one area of the site to explore or make it a bit of a scavenger hunt by charting a path that includes a cross-section of structures.

A good map and the *Brief Guide to Pompeii* booklet are free with the purchase of a ticket. The numbers herein correspond to the map and booklet. Audio guides are available to rent at the Porta Marina entrance.

LIFE IN THE FORUM

The commercial heart of the city was **the Forum** (6). Look north towards Vesuvius, imagine it at its full height, and pretend to be in a bustling market place (not hard after a few days in Naples). Now imagine that day when pumice spewed from the sky. It's not a pleasant thought. On the south side of the forum towards the Porta Marina gate was the **Basilica** (5) where the courts were held and beyond, a temple to Venus (3). At the south east corner is **Eumachia's Building** (8). Eumachia was a priestess of Venus and patron of the fullers (cleaners of wool and other cloth types, an important step in processing it for use) of whom there were many in Pompeii. Her statue is in the Archaeological Museum and her tomb can be found in the **Porta Nocera Necropolis** (62).

A **Temple of Apollo** (4), (one of the oldest temples in Pompeii – 6th century BC), the **Forum Granaries** (13) and the **Official Dry Measures** (14) sit on the west side of the forum. The granary now houses an enormous number of less important finds, like all the storage amphorae (the big jugs with pointed bottoms and two handles) as well as some statuary and plaster casts of victims. On the east are the **Temple of Vespasian** (9), the **Sanctuary of Public Lares** (guardian deities) (10), and the **Market** (11). State and religion were intimately connected in the Roman world, as the deification of past emperors shows (Vespasian reigned from 69 - 79 and his son Titus was emperor when Vesuvius erupted). The lares were the honoured gods of each household; the public ones were those that watched over a city.

Towards the top of the forum is a **Temple of Jupiter** (12). Above the baths on Via del Foro, the **Temple of Fortuna Augusta** (16) was probably dedicated to Fortuna Redux, that form of the goddess Fortuna who watched over a return from a journey. This would have been in honour of the Emperor Augustus' safe return at the end of wars in Spain and France. An entire room of frescoes relating to the *lares* can be found at the Archaeological Museum.

PUBLIC BATHING

The **Stabian Baths** (40) on Via dell'Abbondanza re-opened in 2012 after a three year restoration. The oldest of Pompeii's three bath complexes, this is where Pompeians came to exercise, swim, steam and relax – both men and women. Public bathing was a common practice in Roman culture; read more in Bathe Like a Roman later in this section. In fact, the re-opening of the baths marked the first time the women's section of the Stabian Baths was ever seen by the public. Inside, see the inner workings of a Roman bath house including how they heated the rooms and the water for the hot baths. There are more plaster casts of eruption victims too. The other baths are the **Forum Baths** (15) on Vicolo Soprastanti near the Forum and the **Central Baths** (35) on Via Stabiana in the city centre.

THEATRES GREAT AND SMALL

Theatre was hugely popular in Pompeii; you will notice from mosaics and frescoes held in the Archaeological Museum that many houses were decorated with images from the stage. As to what was performed in Pompeii, Professor Beard says it would be wrong to assume that classic Greek drama was the staple diet of theatre goers. Two genres, mime and pantomime, may have occupied the stage. Mime was a scurrilous mixture of words, music and dance equally at home in a domestic or public context, in private houses or in a theatre. Pantomime was not the rumbustious comic entertainment we know today. It was a masked entertainment in which a star danced and mimed (in the modern sense) stories from Greek tragedy, backed by a chorus of singers and musicians. Both genres mattered to Pompeians. A portrait at the Temple of Isis and one at the Building of Eumachia in the Forum commemorate the mime actor Caius Norbanus Sorex.

There are two theatres located near Porta Esedra. The **Small Theatre** (45) or *odeon*, a covered theatre, would probably have been used for musical performances. The 2nd-century BC **Large Theatre** (43) was re-opened after four years in June 2014 with a performance of *The Oresteia*, Aeschylus' trilogy of Greek Tragedies. At the easternmost end of Pompeii, the earliest stone **Amphitheatre** (60) in the ancient world could hold up to 20,000 spectators. Adjacent to the amphitheatre was the **Large Gymnasium** (61) - the training space for gladiators, surrounded by porches and with a swimming pool in its centre.

POMPEII'S BOTANICAL ROOTS: VILLA DEI MISTERI WINE

Roman writers left numerous records about food preparation, agriculture and botany. Some recipes appear in *De Agri Cultura* – On Farming - by Marcus Porcius Cato (234 – 149 BC), though this is not the focus of the book. *De Re Coquinaria* – On the Subject of Cooking – a late 4th or early 5th century AD collection of Roman recipes, is associated with the name of gourmet Marcus Gavius Apicius, who lived sometime in the 1st century AD. These may be grouped with *De Re Rustica* – On Country Matters - by Lucius Junius Moderatus Columella (4 – ca. 70 AD) in which the author opines on agriculture in general and on livestock and the cultivation of fruit and vines in particular. More recently Eugenia Salza Prina Ricotti has collected many ancient Roman recipes into a book called *Ricette Della Cucina Romana A Pompei*, (or *Recipes of the Roman Kitchen in Pompeii*). The author is an archaeologist who has written extensively on the Roman Period.

Virgil named many of the plants that existed during his time and Pliny the Elder recorded the most salient of botanical details in his *Naturalis Historia*. Book XV deals specifically with trees while in Book XIV Pliny details grape varietals and viticulture. Vineyards were plentiful in Pompeii as wine consumption was an integral part of everyday life. Wine bars along the ancient Roman streets and frescoes depicting the wine culture have been discovered as have underground wine cellars replete with the remains of *dolia*, the large terracotta jars (sealed with resin to hold liquids) that were used to store Pompeiian wines. The ancient artefacts of Pompeii's wine culture are easy to spot as you wander around the site. Less obvious is evidence of Pompeii's botanical roots. Using the same plaster cast method developed by Giuseppe Fiorelli to make moulds of the victims of the 79 AD eruption, botanists are painstakingly re-creating Pompeii's natural environment. A number of the trees in the Large Gymnasium (61) for example were identified by botanical studies of the ancient stumps next to which they were planted. One such line of botanical inquiry has resulted in the cultivation of the first vineyards and the production of the first wine Pompeii has seen since the city was overtaken by disaster.

Not far from Pompeii's Amphitheatre gate, the road that traverses the Porta Nocera Necropolis leads to a lookout point. From here, you can cast your gaze upon a wide swathe of Pompeii; the crumbling remains of sweeping villas built by the Romans on the outskirts of the city; Vesuvius lingering in the background; and lush gardens, which are now green again with vines reborn from ancient varietals. They are part of a joint project launched in 1996 by the Archaeological Superintendence of Pompeii and the 200 year old family-owned and operated Campanian wine producer, Mastroberardino.

To better understand the varietals, viticulture and training systems in use at Pompeii, the early days of the project included several lines of inquiry: studies of the archaeological excavations; botanical studies of the land, the woods and pollen; casting moulds of ancient vine roots; bibliographic and iconographic studies of wine culture portrayed in Pompeii's frescoes. Based on this research,

Mastroberardino selected 8 varietals for planting: Greco (Vitis Aminea Gemina); Fiano (Vitis Apiana); Aglianico (Vitis Hellenica); Piedirosso (Columbina Purpurea); Sciascinoso o Olivella (Vitis Oleagina); Coda di Volpe (Cauda Vulpium); Caprettona (Vitis Alopecis) and Falanghina (perhaps named after the stakes that supported the vines). These were the vines, according to Pliny, that produced fine reds and whites enjoyed by the Romans. Some, for example Greco and Aglianico, were imported from Greece before the Roman period.

After the first vines reached maturity, Mastroberardino selected Piedirosso and Sciascinoso for further cultivation and study. From this, Villa dei Misteri (Villa of the Mysteries) was born – a blend of 85% Piedirosso and 15% Sciscinoso. Named in honour of one of Pompeii's best known villas as a way of celebrating the recovery, after some 2,000 years, of something tangible, and potable, from the deep past, the first bottles - a limited quantity of 1,721 in all - were introduced in 2001. Many were auctioned off to raise funds for continued viticulture research at Pompeii.

Villa dei Misteri is still being produced and today, Mastroberardino maintains about 1.5 hectares at Pompeii across several small vineyards: Oste Eusino, Casa della Nave Europa, Osteria del Gladiatore, Forum Boario, and Casa del Triclinio Estivo and two new gardens near the Garden of the Fugitives (56). Continued study and experimentation with grafting and the training system has also led to the successful cultivation of the Aglianico grape – the current focus of Mastrobe-rardino's studies. After cultivation and ageing - 12 months in new French oak barrels and then 6 years in the bottle – the new Villa dei Misteri blend of 40% Aglianico, 40% Piedirosso and 20% Sciascinoso will become available to the public in 2017.

Mastroberardino Vineyards at Pompeii

FAST FOOD

Guides in both human and book form will tell you to look out for the numerous fast food joints/bars of Pompeii, the *thermopolia*, places you could buy hot food or indeed hot wine. With waist-high masonry or marble topped counters and large terracotta jars – the *dolia* are set into the counter in the same way sinks are mounted into a kitchen counter top today. Do be aware, however, as Mary Beard points out, that *thermopolia* was not the standard term used in the city for these establishments. Also, given that the *dolia* were porous, they could not have held liquids, either wines or stews. Most would have held dry goods such as lentils and beans, so the evidence suggests many of the places long-held to be bars or fast food eateries were in fact grocery shops. Meanwhile, in the real bars, wine would have been poured from jars on the floor or wall into jugs for serving and hot food cooked on a stove and served directly. Pompeii's famous fermented fish sauce, *garum*, would have featured in some of these meals. Tour guides say the citizens of Pompeii always lunched outside the home, but oil lamps within the restaurants and bars are evidence they had customers day and night. See the **Thermopolium of Vetutius Placidus** (67) on Via dell'Abbondanza. The fresco at the end of the counter is a painted *lararium* – a shrine to household gods (though, says Beard, this is another word not in use in Pompeii) - in which the Genius (spirit) of the household makes a sacrifice upon a small altar, flanked by Mercury and Bacchus. Another food-related item to look for is a reconstructed stone olive oil press in the **House of the Ship Europa** (55) on Via dell'Abbondanza.

Thermopolium of Vetutius Placidus, Pompeii

BROTHELS

Just above the Stabian baths on "Brothel Lane", Via del Lupanare – Wolfden Street - is the **Brothel** (39). There are five rooms on the ground floor of this building, five more above that have an entrance from the side street. The second storey is jettied out over the street to increase floor space. Professor Beard describes the first two, heavily graffitied, downstairs rooms, their messages leaving no doubt as to the function of the place. If more evidence were needed, each of the five cubicles, with its built-in stone bed base, is decorated at its entrance with a painting of an erotic encounter. The originals of these explicit frescoes are in the Archaeological Museum; they may have been used to advertise services to a clientèle that spoke a variety of languages. This was the largest brothel of the city, run by a woman (known as a *leonine*), but money changing hands for sex in Pompeii was common and this was often less formally organised than in the *Lupanar*. Prices ranged from two to eight *sesterces* (a portion of wine cost one *sesterce*) and the earnings usually went to the *leonine*. Some guides will tell you that prostitutes weren't allowed to wear standard women's clothes, dressing instead in a plain woollen toga as a mark of shame, though Beard has her doubts about this. Prostitutes could be slaves or free women; many women simply added an economic activity to their roles as barmaids. Their customers would mostly have come from the less wealthy, whether Pompeiians or visiting sailors from the port. Better off citizens were more likely to find sexual gratification at home in a society where so many slaves were available.

LIFE AT HOME

As with many towns today, you will find urban houses in the city proper and larger villas on the outskirts. Few of Pompeii's houses are completely open to the public any more, but you can still peek inside. For the lavish and beautiful interior décor options in Pompeii, see Decorating Pompeii: The Four Pompeian Painting Styles. Large clusters of private houses can be seen on Via dell'Abbondanza and also to the north of the Forum. Here, on Via della Fortuna is the largest urban house in Pompeii, the **House of the Faun** (17). It was home to the spectacular 2nd-century BC bronze faun, a copy of which now sits in the centre of the *impluvium* (a depression for catching rainwater). Here too was the huge mosaic of Alexander's battle against the Persian King Darius at the Illissus river composed of an estimated 1.5 million tiny stones – *tesserae*. This, like the original faun, were relocated to the Archaeological Museum with a replica left on site. The mosaic 'HAVE' greets visitors at the entrance (a variant of *Ave*, "GREETINGS") and the eye-bending triangle floor decoration is an example of *opus sectile*, a technique in which larger stone or glass pieces are inlaid into floors.

The House of the Faun is particularly opulent; it has two atria (open courts) and two peristyles (colonnaded spaces, often with gardens). Professor Beard estimates that about 500 properties of a total of 1200-1300 possible 'habitable units' in Pompeii had an atrium of some size and so can be grouped as a type of dwelling. Pompeiians belonging to the elite class, public and political office holders and the like, would have had their homes embellished with mosaics, paintings and finer furniture in the interests of creating spaces to be seen and admired by visitors. Today's visitors, on the other hand, can be confused by the apparent emptiness of rooms in Pompeiian houses; we now have to use our imaginations to refurbish these spaces with all the movables and frescoes etc. that were taken away prior to the eruption, those salvaged or looted out soon after and those which were removed to the Archaeological Museum. At the other end of the social spectrum, and Beard emphasises the stark contrast between rich and poor inhabitants, there were the very basic living quarters next to stores and workshops that made up almost the entire other, non-atrium style, half of Pompeii's homes. Otherwise, accommodation ranged from single rooms opening directly onto a street, through what we might call terraced houses to apartment blocks with a mixture of atrium and non-atrium flats, probably for rental.

A few blocks west along Vicolo della Fullonica find the **House of the Tragic Poet** (22) named after one of its many fine wall paintings depicting scenes from Greek mythology. As Mary Beard explains, when the house was uncovered in 1824, it was believed this fresco showed a tragic poet reciting his work to a small audience. The subject has now been identified as Admetus and Alcestis listening to the reading of an oracle. As with the majority of the paintings and mosaics discovered here, originals are now in the Archaeological Museum. The handsome entrance, that once had double doors, is between two shops. As you enter this classic atrium-style house you cross the famous "Cave Canem!" - "Beware of the Dog!" mosaic - which is immortalised on tourist souvenirs and engraved on all our memories. Inside, a corridor leads into the house itself, which has two courts, firstly the atrium, (source of six almost life-sized paintings of figures from Greek myths) with an *impluvium* gathering rainwater for a well, and then a peristyle garden with a shrine for household gods.

Beyond the city walls, the **Villa of the Mysteries** (30) is another great example of Pompeiian private life. This gigantic villa contains a series of enigmatic frescoes which may show the rites of Dionysus (it gave name to the Mastroberardino wine). An alternative theory about this sequence of paintings, mentioned by Professor Beard, is that they constitute an allegory on marriage. The building is currently undergoing restoration, but enough of it is visible to get a great impression of the size and quality of the decorations. Indeed, there is plenty to restore, since the paintings were damaged both during excavation (by amateurs) in 1909, by restorers of limited technology and understanding thereafter and by the ravages of rising damp. Finally, and this is a surprising thought about images that have influenced art and interior décor so profoundly, have been reproduced in so many ways and found their way into so much merchandising... recent research at La

Sapienza University in Rome has revealed that many of the reds we see in Pompeii and Herculaneum were once yellow and turned dark red as a result of exposure to hot gases during the eruption. 'Pompeii Yellow' anyone?

Pompeii

BURIAL RITES

Close to the Piazza Anfiteatro entrance, a stairway just past the turnstiles on the left leads to the monumental tombs of the **Necropolis of Porta Nocera** (62). As was typical in Roman cities, the dead were buried outside the city limits. In Pompeii we find necropoles along the main arteries both outside the Nocera gate and the Ercolano gate – **Necropolis of Porta Ercolano** (28) along Via delle Tombe (also known as Via dei Sepolcri), the road that leads to the Villa of the Mysteries. The showy tombs lining these roads were an excellent way to advertise the power and wealth of the families to which they belonged. Marble statues of these families can still be seen above their tombs along with Latin inscriptions. Outside Porta Nocera, the priestess Eumachia's tomb is the largest. Nearby is a monument built by ex-slave Publius Vesonius Phileros; three statues, heads missing, stand side by side. One is a statue of Marcus Orfellius Faustus, his erstwhile friend. Not far from here is the **Garden of the Fugitives** (56), a grim reminder of that fateful day in 79 AD. This is where the famous casts of 13 men, women and children who died during the eruption of 79 AD sit behind a glass case. It was Giuseppe Fiorelli, director of the Pompeii digs in the late 19th century, who invented the plaster cast method. He poured liquid plaster into a cavity left in the bed of ashes by the gradual decomposition of the victim's body. As the plaster solidified, it reproduced the body's shape.

THE VILLA OF POPPAEA: OPLONTIS

An ancient map named this suburb of Pompeii "Oplontis". Today, the modern town is known as Torre Annunziata. What remains of the Roman suburb is a well-preserved villa ten metres below the modern street level where visitors can wander through **a massive residential complex that archaeologists believe once belonged to Nero's wife, Poppaea Sabina**. It is often called, somewhat tersely, "Villa A" to avoid prejudicing the issue. Nearby is the villa of Lucius Crassus Tertius which was not a luxury villa, but more of a plantation house. It is mostly undecorated and archaeological finds indicate that it was a processing centre for agricultural goods. In it were found the remains of 54 people who had gathered their valuables, perhaps hoping in vain for rescue by sea.

Villa of Poppaea, Oplontis

Buried during the eruption of Vesuvius in 79 AD, the rooms of Villa A still tell a compelling story about the luxurious daily lives of its former inhabitants. The first room at the entrance of the villa is the atrium, a grand sitting room with an opening in the roof and a corresponding depression in the centre of the floor to collect rainwater. A brick oven looks as though it could still be fired up and the adjacent *triclinium* (a dining room with three couches) boasts red frescoes. There are latrines with top slabs and a channel below. At the entrance to the bathroom, a tub once contained water used to clean out the channel. The bath complex is particularly impressive and includes a *caldarium* and *tepidarium* which once had an advanced system of hot and warm air flowing through the walls and under the floor. Roofless indoor gardens still depict lush vegetation on the walls and vast gardens are lined with marble sculptures. Archaeologists have also created casts out of the roots of tall trees they found here, which are believed to have been sycamores. The villa was heavily damaged during the earthquake of 62 AD and left abandoned thereafter, so by the time ash from the Vesuvian eruption covered the villa, nobody inhabited these fresco-filled rooms.

The Villas at Oplontis are currently being studied by a team of scholars whose goal is to create a digital E-book series about the archaeological site. Known as the Oplontis Project, it is a collaborative effort between the Soprintendenza Speciale per I Beni Archeologici di Napoli e Pompeii and the University of Texas at Austin under the direction of John R. Clarke and Michael L. Thomas.

COUNTRY MANOR: BOSCOREALE

Tucked away behind a complex of apartments, Boscoreale lies about two kms away from Pompeii on the south-eastern slopes of Vesuvius. **In Roman times, the area was part of a hunting reserve**. This particular villa burned down during the eruption of Mount Vesuvius, so there's not much to see. Only a few rooms remain, but the kitchen makes the visit worthwhile. Next to the villa, a small museum - the Antiquarium - houses frescoes, marble statues and other items, but there is no brochure and the collection is eclectic, not necessarily displaying what was found exclusively at this location.

Over a hundred pieces of gold and silver plate, along with a cache of coins were hidden in a cistern at Boscoreale just before the eruption. In large part they consti-tuted a *ministerium*, the ensemble of vessels and objects used during banquets and dinners. They were rediscovered in the late 19th century and museums throughout Europe, including the Louvre, snatched them up for their own collec-tions. Amongst these were two superb *skyphoi* (deep two-handled wine cups) with high relief panels showing Augustus and Tiberius. A number of the coins found their way to the National Archaeological Museum, but unfortunately, as of this writing the numismatic collection there is closed to the public. On the upside, there is an entire room of Boscoreale frescoes at the Archaeological Museum.

ROMAN RESORT: THE STABIAN VILLAS

While Pompeii and Herculaneum give us a glimpse of life in a Roman city, **Stabia by contrast was a popular resort for wealthy Romans, described by Pliny the Elder**. Alas, the poor man died there after setting sail from Misenum and crossing the Bay of Naples to rescue people during the 79 AD eruption. Stabia itself was buried by more than ten feet of volcanic ash. Stabia was once a resort town and lies about five kms from Pompeii on the way to Sorrento and the Amalfi Coast.

The **Villa of Arianna** (or Ariadne) lies along a walkway overlooking the Bay of Naples much like the ancient Roman villas that once stood along this ridge overlooking the bay. This huge villa was once richly decorated with deep coloured frescoes on every wall, detailed mosaics on every floor and a complicated maze of rooms. The building grew gradually over 150 years, so it is hard to get a complete picture of what functions the rooms had. The fact that the villa is located on a sloping site, some of which has crumbled down a cliff, further complicates the picture. In a service quarter there are a masonry hearth and a courtyard with a square pool, probably used as a hatchery for small fish. A thermal complex with a *caldarium, tepidarium* and *frigidarium* preserve a lead water-duct that brought the water from a pool. You can also see a bronze cauldron which was used to heat the *caldarium*. Some of the villa's best frescoes are now in the Naples Archaeological Museum.

One other villa is also open to the public, located down the road from the Villa of Arianna. This is the **Villa San Marco**, which extends over more than 11,000 square metres – Augustan in origin, though extended during the period of Claudius. On a stroll through this structure you will see a well-preserved atrium, *triclinium* and kitchen. The villa also once had an extensive bath system. The walls retain their detailed frescoes and there is also a large *palestra* (gymnasium) inside. As with the Villa Arianna, some finds were transferred to the Archaeological Museum in Naples, including the painted *lararium*, (shrine to household gods), removed from the kitchen.

There are initiatives in hand to create a 60-hectare archaeological park focused upon Villa Arianna. The Italian and US governments are promoting this cultural project, Restoring Ancient Stabiae (RAS), partnered by the University of Maryland and heritage bodies in Campania. If all goes to plan, visitors will soon be able to stroll along a new, tree-lined seaside walkway connecting the villas and find out about the site at a new visitor centre. RAS's Italian headquarters, the Vesuvian Institute, already offers opportunities for foreign youngsters to study abroad, attend summer courses and participate in archaeological digs.

Villa San Marco, Stabia

EXPLORE SOME MORE

Not far from the Stabian Villas on Castellammare di Stabia's waterfront, find a geological marvel - one of the city's (free) public fountains from which flows a natural sparkling water capable of curing whatever ails you. The source of this water? One of Castellammare di Stabia's 28 different mineral springs which have given the city the moniker - *Città delle acque*, City of the waters, each of which has its own therapeutic properties. The water in this particular fountain is called **Acqua della Madonna** - a hypotonic alkaline calcium bicarbonate known from the time of Pliny the Elder, that has excellent diuretic properties known to dissolve kidney stones and cure urinary tract infections and gout. Find the fountain in a small piazza on the waterfront on Via Caio Duilio. Kindly gentlemen with an abundant supply of water bottles are usually on hand to fill you a few bottles and carry them to your car for a few euros. Of course, you are welcome to fill whatever water bottles you have on hand.

THE GOLDEN MILE: THE VESUVIAN VILLAS

During the 1700s, in a now rather dilapidated area close to the ruins of Herculaneum, the nobility built 122 villas. They wanted to keep up not with the Joneses, but with Charles VII (III of Spain), who built one of his palaces in Portici. After the villas sprang up, **the area became known as the *Miglio d'Oro* or the Golden Mile**. The centrepiece here is Charles's **Reggia di Portici**, now the home of the Agriculture Faculty of the University of Naples Federico II; the university also runs the Botanic Gardens of Portici. The **Herculanense Museum**, which houses chiefly reproductions of finds from Herculaneum, is located here as well. Students sprawl throughout the airy courtyards at the palace during the weekday and anyone can do the same. On the weekends, however, custodians lock up the palace and the Golden Mile looks more like an abandoned and crumbling ghost town.

A few blocks away from the Reggia, the lavish **Villa Campolieto** welcomes tourists during weekdays as well. Ask at the ticket office there what other villas are open to the public at that moment; Villa Favorita, Villa Prota or Villa Ruggiero might be some options and each have their own interesting history. Sir William Hamilton owned a villa here and the famous architects Sanfelice and Vanvitelli designed some of the splendours around you.

ƆƆƆƆƆƆ KNOW YOUR ROMAN TERMINOLOGY froccell

apodyterium - dressing/changing room

balneator - keeper of the baths

caldarium - hot bath room

capsarii – slaves who took charge of clothes and belongings

cisterna - cistern

domus - the home of an upper class citizen or a wealthy freedman

frigidarium - cold bath room

hypocaust - underfloor heating system

hypogeum - underground area usually housing the systems needed for the spa to function

laconicum - dry steam/sweating room

latrina - latrine

palaestra - gymnasium

piscina or natatio - pool

strigilis – curved, handled scraper for removing oil and sweat

taberna – shop or drinking establishment

tepidarium - warm bath

vestibulum - vestibule

BATHE LIKE A ROMAN: THE THERMAL BATHS OF NEAPOLIS

To bathe or not to bathe, that was …rarely the question. Affordable, practical, and enjoyable, for most Romans, public bathing was just like another day at the office, or should we say, the local health club.

The Romans inherited a tradition of private and public bathing from the Greeks, who pioneered many of the cleansing and relaxing rituals of our modern spa both at the sites of religious springs and in bath complexes annexed to gymnasiums. As the Roman Empire spread out across the Mediterranean and into northern Europe and north Africa, so too did the culture of communal bathing.

Public bathing was a significant and integral part of Roman culture; time spent at the baths was very much part of the daily routine, prices being well within the budget of most social classes. Beyond the obvious cleansing and relaxing rituals, the *thermae* were epicentres of Roman social life. As with the commercial centres of today, you could find shops and entertainment, a barber or dentist, fast-food eateries, libraries and gyms and the baths also served as a place to do business or talk politics. These were richly decorated spaces with more marble and mosaic than you might afford at home, so a pleasant place to linger. It's easy to imagine two Roman businessmen hashing out a deal while bubbling away in the *caldarium* or sharing a meal after bathing was done.

In terms of bathing routine, depending on your preferences and your perceived therapeutic requirements, you might begin by gradually exposing the body to higher temperatures to induce sweating, then cooling yourself down again and anointing the skin with oil to finish. Soap was a luxury commodity but oil combined with sweating was effective at removing impurities from the skin. Wealthy patrons might bring along their own *strigils* (scrapers) and towels for this. Larger complexes might also provide a *laconicum*, or dry heat room like a sauna, and even an outdoor exercise area or *palaestra* where young men could exercise. Public *thermae* sometimes included a smaller set of baths for women. In the Roman Republic, bathing was always segregated; under the Empire mixed bathing was common, causing outrage amongst moralists who saw this as a sign of decadence and declining (and reclining) morals.

Campania has some remarkable examples that tell us a great deal about bath-time habits. We find them at Herculaneum, Pompeii, Oplontis, Stabia and Baia; and there are several examples on Ischia. In Naples, the remains of large public *thermae* have been found at Fuorigrotta, Agnano and in the heart of the Centro Storico, where some private baths have been found as well.

These complexes share many of the same characteristics. Most were built on two or more levels, with an underground service level or *hypogeum*. Interestingly, regardless of the abundance of thermal springs in the area, the baths at Santa Chiara, Fuorigrotta and Agnano were all fed by the Serino Aqueduct. One of the largest aqueduct systems of the Roman Empire, it was built between 33 and 12 BC.

TRAVELLER'S WAY STATIONS IN THE HINTERLANDS: THE BATHS AT TERRACINA AND AGNANO

At first glance, the Roman Thermal Bath Complexes of Via Terracina and Agnano would seem to have been located right smack in the middle of nowhere, at least what would have been nowhere during the Roman era. Even today, Naples' two westernmost *quartieri* Fuorigrotta (meaning outside the tunnel) and Bagnoli still feel a bit disconnected, isolated from the city proper by a large land mass known as Posillipo hill. Tagged with the Greek word *Pausilypon*, meaning respite from pain, this most picturesque piece of landscape stymied the Greeks and their successors the Romans for centuries. While less than 20 kms (as the crow flies) stood between Neapolis and Puteoli (Pozzuoli), the journey by land was anything but direct.

In need of transportation and trade routes between eastern and western colonies, the Greeks got around Posillipo hill by building a road to the north, through today's hilly districts of Soccavo and Pianura. It was a long and arduous journey with the road descending into Fuorigrotta in the area of today's Via Terracina, and then continuing on to Pozzuoli and Cuma beyond. The Romans found a shorter route over Vomero hill, but it too came down at the same location in Fuorigrotta. Then, thanks to the brilliant architect Lucius Cocceius Auctus, a more direct route was established when he found a way to tunnel more than 700 metres through Posillipo hill. This tunnel, known as the Crypta Neapolitana, remained in use for centuries. Thus the route was shortened to be sure, but **it was still a long and dusty trek from Naples to Pozzuoli and a place of respite was needed along the way**. The Romans had at least two rest stops that we know of: the baths at Via Terracina and those at Agnano in Bagnoli. Providing weary travellers a break in the journey, these baths were a place to stop and rest for a while, to meet, greet and perhaps conduct some business.

The 2nd-century AD bath complex at Via Terracina was discovered in 1939 during the construction of Naples' Convention Centre, Mostra d'Oltremare. Though much of its marble and frescoed façades have been lost to time, the complex's skeleton has remained largely intact. The site's position below modern-day ground level gives you multiple vantage points from which to orient yourself to its layout and to see how the complex functioned. What does remain of its decorative elements are some excellent specimens of black and white mosaics on the floors of the vestibule, *frigidarium* and latrine.

Just 2 kms west of Terracina and nestled inside the crater of one of the Phlegrean Fields' ancient volcanoes at the base of Monte Spina, a very large, seven level bath complex was found at Agnano. Though the remains are much less intact than those at Terracina, four statues dating to the 2nd century AD survived. These were a figure of Venus Felix (the goddess known as Aphrodite to the Greeks), a Ganymede with Eros, an armoured Venus with Eros and the figure of Hermes with the child Dionysus. The statues have a place of honour in the "new" Terme di Agnano, a Hotel and Day Spa adjacent to the ancient bath complex that continues the Greco-Roman bathing traditions.

Also part of this complex are remains of Greek walls dating to the 4th or 3rd century BC and the famed *Grotta del Cane*, the Dog Cave. Pliny the Elder studied this mysterious cave and it was the subject of great debate as well as somewhat of a carnival trick during the Grand Tour. In a rare phenomenon that continues to this day, carbon dioxide accumulates on the floor of the cave. When mixed with water vapour, it appears as steam, seeping out of the cave. The carbon dioxide remains fairly close to ground level, perhaps no more than 40 centimetres high, and thus it doesn't affect adults or anyone of average height. A dog, however, whose snout sits low to the ground will immediately succumb to its toxic effects, thus, in bygone eras, dogs were used to demonstrate this curiosity. Oddly enough, throwing the dog into the (then) nearby lake would revive it and it would suffer no lasting side affects. Though perhaps not as dramatic, today a torch makes a much more humane demonstration tool, quickly extinguishing when it comes in contact with the carbon dioxide.

PUBLIC OR PRIVATE: THE BATHS OF ROMAN NEAPOLIS

Public bathing was certainly part of everyday life in Roman Neapolis. **Many of the city's public baths would surely have been centred around athletic structures and competitions**. Archaeologists believe the southwestern area of Roman Neapolis was known as *Regio Thermensis*. At least that's what they have surmised based on an inscription they found on the base of an ancient statue. Few remains of those bathing facilities have been uncovered to date, but it is likely there were a high concentration of them in this area.

Other evidence supports this assumption. Ancient historical documents tell us that the Roman expansion of Naples included a hippodrome, gymnasiums and a stadium, a fact that seems to have been borne out by the discovery of a 1st-century AD Isolympic Games Building Complex during the construction of the Duomo metro station. Archaeologists and historians have also pieced together evidence that seems to indicate that the city hosted an athletic contest known as the *Sebastà* every five years. Surely these athletes would have required the use of thermal bath facilities, be it for training or simply relaxation.

Private baths were also part of daily life, at least for the wealthy Romans who could afford them. Two private baths have been discovered not far from the Duomo. In the 1970s the remains of a *hypocaust* were unearthed beneath the **Historical Archives of the Bank of Naples**, along with a few rooms that are believed to have been a Roman domus, suggesting this was a private bath. Nearby, it was the bombing of the 17th-century church of Carminiello ai Mannesi in 1943 that destroyed the church but brought to light ancient Roman ruins below. The remains include a 1st-century BC Roman domus, a 1st-century AD thermal bath complex, and two rooms that archaeologists believe were converted to a Mithraeum (a temple dedicated to the god Mithras similar to the Mithraeum at **Capua**) sometime in the 2nd century AD.

FROM THE RUBBLE: THE ROMAN BATHS AT SANTA CHIARA

Tucked in the southwest corner of Santa Chiara's serene, majolica-tiled cloister is the entrance to the complex's museum, the *Museo dell'Opera*. This is not a museum of the "Opera", as you might infer from the name, but rather a museum that documents the work done to restore the complex to its former splendour, having been reduced to near rubble on August 4, 1943 by WWII air raids. Outside the back door of the museum you'll find **the seldom-visited archaeological courtyard, a private bath complex that was brought to light after these tragic bombings** and was excavated in the 1980s.

Entering the archaeological courtyard, the bustle of Naples' *Centro Storico* falls away and you can't help but wonder - what would it be like to partake of these baths today? Unfortunately, however, all we have left are the spa's remains to spark our imaginations and the knowledge that in its heyday this bath complex wasn't inside the precincts of the city at all. On the contrary, archaeologists believe these baths were part of a private Roman villa that was constructed outside the city walls during the busy period of urban renewal between the earthquake of 62 AD and the eruption of Mount Vesuvius in 79 AD.

Fed by the Serino aqueduct, the complex was built on two levels and arranged in an "L" shaped plan. Though it is not open to the public, the *hypogeum* has been uncovered. Two *tepidaria* were found on the west side of the complex, one of which has been dubbed the *vasca con abside* – a bath with apses. Nearby, is a *laconicum*, which was most likely covered with a cupola, and had four apses, one at each corner. The remains of a pool extends along the east side of the complex. Half of it is visible from outside in the archaeological courtyard, the other half from inside the museum. The pool would have been covered, and it would have looked out onto a vestibule that archeologists believe separated it from the *palaestra*. Only a few traces of the perimeter wall of the gym are visible in the vestibule today.

CLASSICAL COLLECTIONS:
NATIONAL ARCHAEOLOGICAL MUSEUM

Boasting **one of the most important collections of classical archaeology in the world**, the National Archaeological Museum of Naples can and should be visited over and over again. The mainstays of the museum's collection are the Greek and Roman finds from the Vesuvius and Campi Flegrei areas and excavations that were amassed by Charles VII (III of Spain), the Elisabetta Farnese collection of art and Roman antiquities and, of course, the collection of Roman Erotic Art hidden away in the "Secret Cabinet" (or **Gabinetto Segreto**). Below the museum in the Museo Metro Station is Neapolis Station, a collection of Roman artefacts that were uncovered during the expansion of Naples' Metro System.

Visitors should keep that in mind when visiting the area: seeing Pompeii without the museum, or vice-versa, means missing half the picture. The architecture stayed *in situ*, while the small finds are collected at the museum. A last thought here. Funding and organisational difficulties over the past few years mean that not every section of the museum may be open on the day you visit, though personnel do endeavour to keep the key areas accessible. If you have a specific interest, check ahead about opening times for that section of the museum.

Farnese Bull, National Archaeological Museum

DON'T MISS!

Piano Terra / Ground Floor

From the Farnese Ancient Sculpture Collection:

• A group of large reliefs discovered in the mid 16th century from the Hadrianeum, the Temple of Hadrian on the Campus Martius in Rome.

• The mammoth Farnese Bull and Hercules statues that were found at the Baths of Caracalla in Rome in the 16th century.

• The Statua di Afrodite Callipige/Venus Callipyge: As the saying goes, men want to look at her and women want to look like her, the Venus Callipyge - quite literally, Venus of the Beautiful Buttocks, or Aphrodite if you happen to be Greek, casts her robe aside to take a peek at her cheeks.

Piano Ammezzato / Mezzanine Floor

• The Alexander Mosaic: The largest and oldest villa in Pompeii – the House of the Faun - once had a mammoth floor mosaic displaying Alexander the Great's victory over the Persian emperor Darius III. The bronze statue, the dancing faun that gave the villa its name sits in a room nearby along with a number of other mosaics from this house.

• The Secret Cabinet is a perennial favourite. Displaying erotic statues such as Priapus and sexually explicit frescoes from Pompeii, the area is off-limits to children.

Primo Piano / First Floor

• The result of a failed attempt to build an observatory here, the Salone della Meridiana is 54 metres long and sports a zodiacal sundial - meridiana. The observatory was eventually built at Capodimonte.

• On the other side of the Salone Meridiana find the Frescoes from Pompeii and other Vesuvian excavations including an entire room dedicated to frescoes recovered from Boscoreale.

From the Villa of the Papiri (Herculaneum):

> • Bronze sculptures - the Drunken Satyr and "the runners" and the five "dancers". These statues were the subject of a series of photographs by Mimmo Jodice which hang in the Museo Metro Station.

> • The largest part of the papyrus scroll collection can be found at the National Library, but here you'll see a few samples as well as the gadgets initially used to unroll the scrolls.

L'eruzione del Vesuvio (Aprile 1906), E. Ragozino, postcard ca.1910

AND BEYOND INTO CAMPANIA

Cover Photo:
Temples at Paestum

There is a **wealth** of treasures to explore beyond the Province of Naples.

The provinces of Avellino and Benevento are Campania's wine country. Scores of vineyards large and small dot the fertile landscape and ancient riches are secreted away in hilltop towns too numerous to mention. Caserta, Campania's northernmost province, is known for *Mozzarella di Bufala* and was home to Roman gladiators and Bourbon kings. It features the second largest amphitheatre in the

Roman world and a royal palace to rival Versailles. And, of course, the family of *The Sopranos'* (fictional) character Jennifer Melfi hailed from Caserta.

As regards the Province of Salerno, if the Amalfi Coast wasn't enough to wow you, Salerno safeguards two important Greek (7th – 8th century BC) archaeological sites. They were part of Magna Graecia (Greater Greece), the colonies the Greeks founded all over the boot of Italy having been driven from their own lands by overcrowding, famine and the harshness of their terrain. Campania was an important nexus of Hellenistic culture; the Greeks built monumental structures like the temples at Paestum and founded two schools in the region: the Pythagorean (mathematics) and the Eliatic (philosophy) in Elia (Velia).

The Carolino (Vanvitelli) Aqueduct

Plan Your Visit

Transport

METRO/RAILWAYS
Circumvesuviana
Napoli – Sorrento Line
Regional trains (Trenitalia) - S. Maria Capua
Vetere and Caserta

BUSES
CurreriViaggi
EAVCampania
Marozzi
Positano Shuttle
SITASud

SEA CONNECTIONS
Alilauro, Caremar, Gescab, Lucibello,
Medmar, Navigazione Libera del Golfo
(NLG), SNAV, TravelMar

Tourist Info

AMALFI TOURIST OFFICE
Via delle Repubbliche Marinare, Amalfi
+39 089 871107
amalfitouristoffice.it

CAMPANIA ARTECARD
ArteCard 365, Napoli & Tutta la Regione

CAPRI TOURIST OFFICE
Piazzetta I. Cerio, 11, Capri
+39 081 8370424
capritourism.com
comunedianacapri.it

CAPUA COMBINED TICKET
Adults €2.50 - includes admission to 4 sites:
Capua Amphitheatre, Gladiator Museum,
Mithraeum, Archaeological Museum of
Capua Antica

POSITANO TOURIST OFFICE
Via del Saracino, 4, Positano
+39 089 875067
aziendaturismopositano.it

Sights & Attractions

AMALFI PAPER MUSEUM (MUSEO DELLA CARTA)
Via delle Cartiere, 23, Amalfi
+39 089 8304561
museodellacarta.it

AUGUSTUS GARDENS
Via Krupp, Capri

ARCHAEOLOGICAL MUSEUM OF CAPUA ANTICA
Via Roberto d'Angio, 48, Santa Maria Capua
Vetere
Open daily **except Mon** 09.00 – 19.00
Adults €2.50
Combined Ticket
+39 082 3844206

ARSENALE MUSEUM AMALFI
Largo Cesareo Console, 3, Amalfi
+39 089 871170

BELVEDERE DI SAN LEUCIO
(ROYAL COLONY OF SILK WEAVERS)
Via Vaccheria, 13, Caserta Adults €6.00
Winter Hours: Open daily **except Tues** 09.00
– 18.00, last entry 16.30, by accompanied
visit. Summer Hours: Open daily **except Tues** 09.30 – 18.00, last entry 17.00, by
accompanied visit.
+39 082 3301817
realbelvedere.it

PLAN YOUR VISIT

BLUE GROTTO
Via Grotta Azzurra, Anacapri
+39 081 8375308

CAPUA AMPHITHEATRE (AND GLADIATOR MUSEUM)
Piazza I Ottobre, Santa Maria Capua Vetere
Open daily **except Mon** 09.00 – 19.00
Adults €2.50 Combined Ticket
+39 082 3844206

CAROLINO AQUEDUCT
Via Giulia, Valle di Maddaloni
Along SS265 in the Comune di Valle di Maddaloni about 7 kms east of Caserta

CASERTA PALACE (REGGIA DI CASERTA)
Via Douhet, 2/a, Caserta
Adults €14.00 includes: the Palace (historical apartments, painting gallery, grand staircase, decorative arts); the park; the English Garden. Adults €11.00 historical apartments ticket when the park is closed (after 18.00) Palace is open daily **except Tues** 08.30 – 19.30 (last admission 19.00) Park is open daily **except Tues** at 08.30. Last entry times vary by month: Nov – Feb 15.30; Mar 16.00; Oct 16.30; Apr 17.00; May, Aug & Sept 17.30; Jun & Jul 18.00 English Gardens: entry only with custodian at 10.00, 11.00, 12.00 open daily **except Tues**
+39 082 3448084
reggiadicaserta.beniculturali.it

CERAMIC ARTISTICA SOLIMENE
Via Madonna degli Angeli, 7, Vietri sul Mare
+39 089 210243
ceramicasolimene.it

Belvedere di San Leucio

BASILICA SAN GIOVANNI BATTISTA
Vietri sul Mare
+39 089 210219
parrocchiavietri.altervista.org

DUOMO OF AMALFI (DUOMO DI SANT'ANDREA)
Piazza del Duomo, Amalfi

DUOMO OF CASERTA VECCHIA - CATHEDRAL OF SAN MICHELE ARCANGELO
Piazza del Vescovado 1, Caserta Vecchia
Open daily 08.00 – 12.00 & 17.30 – 20.00
+39 082 3322493

DUOMO OF SALERNO (DUOMO DI SAN MATTEO)
Piazza Alfano I, Salerno

EMERALD GROTTO (GROTTA DELLO SMERALDO)
By boat from Spiaggia Grande, Positano or Strada Statale 163, Conca dei Marini

LUMINARIA DI SAN DOMENICO
luminariadisandomenico.it

MEDITERRANEAN CUP HIGH DIVING CHAMPIONSHIP
marmeeting.com

MITHRAEUM AT CAPUA
Via Pietro Morelli, Santa Maria Capua Vetere
Request access from the staff at the Capua Amphitheatre or Archaeological Museum of Capua
Adults €2.50 Combined Ticket

MONTE SOLARO CHAIR LIFT
Piazza della Vittoria, Anacapri
+39 081 8371438
capriseggiovia.it

MUSEO DEL CORALLO & CAMEO FACTORY
Piazza Duomo, 9, Ravello
+39 089 857461
museodelcorallo.com

MUSEO PROVINCIALE DELLA CERAMICA E VILLA GUARIGLIA
Via Nuova, Raito di Vietri sul Mare
+39 089 211835

PAESTUM
Via Magna Grecia, Paestum
Archaeological Museum open daily 08.30 - 19.30 (ticket office shuts at 18.45) **except 1st and 3rd Mon** of the month
Archaeological area open daily 08.45 until one hour before sunset **except 1st and 3rd Mon** of the month
Museum and site €10.00. Museum €7.00 (when site closed). Site €6.00 (when museum closed). Paestum and Velia 3 day ticket €11.00
+39 082 8722654
archeosa.beniculturali.it

PATH OF THE GODS
positano.com/en/i/il-sentiero-degli-dei

PROVINCIAL MUSEUM OF CAMPANIA IN CAPUA
Via Roma, 68, Capua
Open Tues - Sat 09.00 – 13.30, Tues & Thurs also 15.00 – 17.30, Sun 09.00 – 13.00
Adults €6.00
+39 082 3961402
provincia.caserta.it/museocampano

RAVELLO FESTIVAL
+39 089 858422 (seasonal box office)
ravellofestival.com

SANTA MARIA ASSUNTA
Piazza Flavio Gioia, 1, Positano
+39 089 875480
positanonline.it/chiesa_sm_assunta.htm

SANT'ANGELO IN FORMIS
Via Luigi Baia 120, Capua

PLAN YOUR
VISIT

SAN GENNARO
Via S. Gennaro, 1, Praiano
+39 089 874799
comune.praiano.sa.it/inglese/
chieseambiente/sangennaro.htm

VELIA
Contrada Piana di Velia, Velia
Open daily 09.00 – 18.30
Adults €3.00, Paestum and Velia 3 day ticket
€11.00
+39 097 4271016
archeosa.beniculturali.it

VILLA CIMBRONE
Via Santa Chiara, 26, Ravello
+39 089 857459
villacimbrone.com

VILLA JOVIS
Via Tiberio, Capri
+39 081 8370381

VILLA RUFOLO
Piazza Duomo, Ravello
+39 089 857621
villarufolo.it

BATHING BEACHES,
BOAT RENTALS & TOURS

(DA) ADOLFO
Via Laurito, 40, Positano
+39 089 875022
daadolfo.com
Free boat transfers from Positano

AMALFI BOAT RENTAL
+39 3383076125
amalfiboatrental.com
Rent a boat or book a sunset cruise or a
water taxi

AMALFI LEMON TOUR
+39 089 873211
cata.amalfi.it
facebook.com/
LaValleDeiMuliniLemonTourAmalfi

BAGNI TIBERIO
Via Palazzo a Mare, 41, Capri
+39 081 8370703
bagnitiberio.com

(IL) CALYPSO STABILIMENTO BALNEARE
Via Giuseppe Pellegrino, Vietri sul Mare
+39 089 211416 (Summer)
ilcalypso.it

CASTIGLIONE THERMAL PARK
Via Castiglione, 62, Casamicciola Terme,
Ischia
+39 081 983994
termecastiglione.it

DUOGLIO BEACH
Via Mauro Comite, Amalfi
Free boat transfers from Amalfi

EXCLUSIVE CRUISES
+39 3314414506
exclusivecruises.it
Charter boats and day cruises of the Amalfi
Coast and Capri

(IL) FARO
Località Punta Carena, Anacapri
+39 081 8371798
lidofaro.com

(DA) FERDINANDO BAR BAGNI
Spiaggia di Fornillo, Positano
+39 089 875365
facebook.com/barbagnidaferdinando

FRATELLI GRASSI BAR BAGNI
Via Fornillo, 70, Positano
+39 089 811620

(LA) GAVITELLA
Via Gavitella, 1, Praiano
+39 089 8131319
lagavitella.it
Free boat transfers from Positano & Praiano
Boat rentals & excursions for Capri, the
Emerald Grotto and Li Galli

LUCIBELLO
Via del Brigantino, 9, Positano
+39 089 875032
lucibello.it
Boat rentals and charters

MARINA GRANDE BEACH
Corso Repubbliche Marinare, Amalfi

NEGOMBO THERMAL GARDENS
S. Montano Bay, Ischia
+39 081 986152
negombo.it

POSEIDON THERMAL GARDENS
Via Giovanni Mazzella, 87, Forio d'Ischia
+39 081 9087111
giardiniposeidonterme.com

SANTA CROCE BEACH
+39 089 831089
ristorantesantacroce.it
Free boat transfers from Amalfi (Pier
Darsena) for restaurant customers
+39 338 7918315 (Antonio)

(LA) SCOGLIERA & L'INCANTO LIDI
Via Marnia, 4, Positano
+39 089 811177
lincanto.com/lascogliera

Sorrento - View from the Grand Hotel Excelsior Vittoria

SEASIDE DELIGHTS: THE BAY OF NAPLES & THE AMALFI COAST

If a seaside vacation is what you fancy, the Campania region offers up nature's beautiful bounty in spades: the Bay of Naples, its three major islands, Capri, Ischia and Procida bobbing in the deep blue sea and the Bay of Salerno which hugs **the celebrated Amalfi Coast, an area of such "great physical beauty and natural diversity", it was inscribed on the UNESCO World Heritage list in 1997.** Between the two lies the jagged coastline of the Sorrentine peninsula. The area is worthy of an entire volume of its own, and in fact, the *Napoli Unplugged Guide to The Bay & The Amalfi Coast* will be out in early 2016 – if the creek don't rise. Until then, here's a generous helpful of what the area has to offer and for travellers on the go, download Rome blogger, tweeter and beach girl Gillian Longworth McGuire's *Amalfi Coast Travel Essentials* iPhone app.

Travellers wishing to explore both sides of the bay will find **Sorrento** and the tiny towns along its northern coast - Vico Equense, Meta, Piano di Sorrento and Sant'Agnello - an excellent base from which to reach both bays, the city of Naples and the Vesuvian excavation sites (Pompeii, Herculaneum, et al). In recent years, Sorrento and Capri, which sits at the tip of the Sorrentine Peninsula have become the only two points connected to both bays by sea. Along the northern coast, the Circumvesuviana train links Sorrento to the Vesuvian excavations and the city of Naples. Along the southern coast, the SITA bus navigates the sheer cliffs and hairpin bends along the SS163, transporting (harried) passengers from Sorrento to the towns of Positano, Praiano and Amalfi. Both coastlines tend to be rocky rather than sandy; bathing establishments/beach clubs (*stabilimenti, lidi, bagni*) are set along pebbled beaches and wooden decks and adorned with colourful and striped sun beds and umbrellas. Many are reached by crumbling stairways; some beaches are as many as 800 steps down from the road. High above the coast, adventure seekers can take in amazing views hiking the Sentiero degli Dei - the Path of the Gods - (actually a network of trails) between the hilltop towns of Nocelle (just above Positano) and Agerola (though experts suggest hiking it in the opposite direction).

A train journey of just under two hours from Naples will take you to **Salerno**, an inexplicably underrated seaside destination with a 5 km long promenade adorned with rare palm trees. The town's architecture ranges from medieval to modern. Its Duomo – cathedral - was built on the site of a Roman temple and displays elements of Romanesque, Norman/Moorish, Baroque and Rococo styles. The startlingly beautiful marble-adorned crypt contains the tomb of one of Christ's disciples, Saint Matthew the Evangelist whose remains, we are told, arrived here in the 10th century to the great joy of the locals. Modern-day Salernitani, while enthusiastic about their colourful religious festivals and processions, are also likely to be found strolling by the sparkling sea enjoying a gelato with their friends and family.

Positano is the best known town on the Amalfi coast. A glamorous destination, it is loved by celebrities - Denzel Washington and Oprah are regular visitors as is the mysterious, 300 million dollar, Philippe Starck yacht known as *A*. Positano is a favoured wedding, honeymoon and bucket list destination, and it has inspired musicians and writers for centuries. Haunted by its charm, John Steinbeck famously wrote; "Positano bites deep. It is a dream place that isn't quite real when you are there and becomes beckoningly real after you have gone". And yet despite the stardust, this one time fishing village maintains a surprisingly quiet, laid back, "beachy" vibe. The pastel houses seem to cascade down towards the sea with a ramshackle charm and from just about every point in Positano, you can see the vibrant Vietri-tiled cupola of the 12th-century church of Santa Maria Assunta in the centre of town. Locals grab a morning caffè in bare feet and shout friendly greetings across the beach. Tourists climb the many, many steps in quintessential Positano style - flowy, white or flowery tunics from Antica Sartoria (they have two stores in Positano) paired with chic flat sandals custom made at a tiny workshop called Safari. It's stacked floor to ceiling with sandal parts; you pick your straps and soles (from flat to kitten heels) and in about an hour you'll have a new pair of Positano sandals.

Most of Positano's beaches are pay-as-you-bathe affairs although there is a small free beach near the ferry pier where you can plop down a towel on the pebbles and paddle in the clear blue sea. The ferry pier is also where you'll find a small boat with a big red fish on the mast, "Da Adolfo" painted in bright white letters. Hop on board and you'll soon find yourself in a tiny, volcanic cove – Laurito beach, home to Da Adolfo - the bagno and (more importantly) the restaurant. At Positano's main beach - Spiaggia Grande - find the lido L'Incanto on the beach and lido La Scogliera on the rocks. From Spiaggia Grande you can also get a boat to the Emerald Grotto or Grotta dello Smeraldo, a natural wonder where the play of light betwixt the water and caves creates an intense emerald colour. Spiaggia Grande's quieter cousin is Fornillo beach. Here, find the beach clubs Da Fernandino and Fratelli Grassi, plus free beaches on both ends of the cove and the medieval Torre de Fornillo that was once used as a defence against pirate invaders. Positano was once a powerful part of the Amalfi Republic; the origin of its name is rich with legends of pirates, gods and sirens. One version is that Positano was founded by the god of the sea, Poseidon, for the love of the nymph Pasitea. Another attributes it to Saracen pirates and a stolen 13th-century Byzantine icon of the Virgin Mary.

Just a few curves away along the SS163 is the sleepy village of **Praiano** with a slice of beach at the bottom. Nearby, the tiny cove and beach of Gavitella can be reached by boat transfer from Marina di Praia (they also make transfers from Positano). In ancient times it was the only landing point of the *pelagianum* - "open sea" - and that name morphed into Praiano over time. There's a medieval tower (as with Fornillo, a look-out for pirates) much loved by artist Sol LeWitt and a 16th-century church dedicated to Naples' patron saint, San Gennaro. Praiano faces the west, so you can catch the sunset here whilst sipping an *aperitivo*. It's at

sunset during the first week in August that the residents of this village decorate their town with candlelight in a tradition called the Luminaria di San Domenico. It began in the early 1600s and today includes music and dance events. A more modern festival, the Mediterranean Cup High Diving Championship, takes place here in early July. The best views are from the sea.

Just beyond Praiano on the SS163 is the coast's largest town, **Amalfi**. It was once one of the world's great maritime powers and it was the oldest of the four Maritime Republics (the others were Pisa, Venice and Genoa). The Maritime Republic of Amalfi prospered from the mid 9th century to the 1130s, developing mercantile relationships with Egypt and Byzantium. At its height, around 1000, the republic had a population of some 70,000 people. Amalfi has the only medieval shipyard to survive with some of the original structure intact; in the early Middle Ages the arsenal here – Arsenale Marinaro – built some of the largest warships in the Mediterranean. Today, this dramatic space hosts a small museum and can be booked for weddings and events. In celebration of its maritime history, every four years Amalfi hosts the Regata delle Antiche Repubbliche Marinare. Amalfi's Duomo, dedicated to the town's patron saint, Sant'Andrea, dominates the main piazza; it's in a mixture of styles, with a 19th-century façade, a Romanesque tower and bronze doors that were cast in Constantinople before 1066. Amalfi celebrates the saint's feast days on 27th June and 30th November.

Amalfi's other claims to fame? - paper-making and lemons. In fact, you can hike among the ruins of eleven 18th-century paper mills in the Valle dei Mulini – Valley of the Mills - and visit a paper museum, the Museo della Carta. Here, in what was once one of the town's more important paper mills, you can learn about ancient paper making techniques, see the machinery and even try your hand at making a sheet. Amalfi's ubiquitous lemons - *sfusati amalfitani* – are longer, thicker skinned and twice the size of average lemons and they are used to produce all manner of products, especially the ever popular *limoncello*. Find a wide range of these at Antichi Sapori d'Amalfi in Amalfi's main piazza or through the Amalfi Citrus-Fruit Processing Cooperative, who also organises the Amalfi Lemon Tour: visit scenic lemon groves, learn about these famous lemons and the enormous cedro citrus fruit grown here and most importantly, sample some *limoncello*. Marina Grande Beach is Amalfi's most popular beach. Get there early as the sun beds and umbrellas get snapped up quickly or make your way to either Santa Croce or Duoglio. Both of these small beaches are set in secluded coves and are reachable by boat or by stairs. Duoglio beach is less rocky and a good spot for windsurfing.

Hovering over the Amalfi Coast is the town of **Ravello**, a ravishing town filled with ancient villas and stunning gardens and fine and, dare we say, even Michelin-starred dining. Ravello is best known for its annual world class music festival, a vast programme of ballet, opera, orchestral, chamber and popular music performances staged throughout the summer. The Villa Rufolo, with its breathtaking views of the Amalfi coast, serves as the festival's centre stage. Built in the 11th century, this villa was mentioned in Boccaccio's *Decamerone*; extensively restored in the mid

1900s, it inspired Richard Wagner's Klingsor in the 2nd act of *Parsifal*. Another arresting villa is the 12th-century Villa Episcopio where Jacqueline Kennedy once stayed; find heart-stopping views at Villa Cimbrone, now a luxury hotel with a Michelin-starred restaurant. Follow the rose-scented pathways to the Terrace of Infinity. Cameo making is a well established craft throughout the region. Ravello's Museo Del Corallo is packed with exquisite cameos, coral carvings and paintings from the Filocamo's family collection. Giorgio Filocamo's cameo shop on Piazza Duomo is a must for first ladies, princesses and you.

At the eastern end of the Amalfi Coast coast is **Vietri sul Mare**, the most colourful locale on the coast. This town with Etruscan roots is best known for its ceramics factories and stores. Vietri sul Mare has been producing pottery since the Roman era, but the brightly coloured style that now defines the craft was developed with visiting German artists between the 1920s and the 1940s. You can see many examples from this period at the Museo Provinciale della Ceramica at the Villa Guariglia in the village of Raito a couple of kms outside Vietri itself. As exercises in bright ceramics work two important buildings stand out: the Basilica San Giovanni Battista with its 18th-century majolica-adorned cupola and belltower and the 1950s (Palazzo delle) Ceramica Artistica Solimene. Embellished with orange and green ceramic work, it was inspired by the Guggenheim Museum in New York and designed by Paolo Soleri. Inside there's an historic collection to admire as well as plenty of pieces to buy. Another great spot for ceramics shopping is Pinto Ceramica. It was founded by Vincenzo Pinto in the 1800s and is one of the oldest hand-crafted ceramic producers in Vietri. If topping up your tan is more your thing, find Il Calypso Stabilimento Balneare on Via dei Pini – there's easy access from Vietri and a large car park. The free beach area is at Marina di Vietri.

Back in the Bay of Naples, Capri, Ischia and Procida are like the mama bear, papa bear and baby bear of islands and each has its own distinct personality: sophisticated and stylish Capri; large and rugged Ischia; small and sweet Procida. Head to scintillating **Capri** if you want to rub elbows with the jet-set crowd. Capri is bewitchingly pretty: the water that sparkles peacock blue and emerald green, the whitewashed villas, the narrow streets garlanded with hibiscus and bougainvillea. You can explore Capri's ruins with their Roman ghosts; shop designer names the length of Via Roma, Via Camerelle and along its narrow alleys (don't leave without a made-to-measure pair of Capri pants from La Parisienne and a pair of Emanuela Caruso sandals); laze under an umbrella at a luxurious beach club; or toast the departure of the last ferry with a spritz or an ice-cold Martini at Piazza Umberto I, better known as the Piazzetta. First time visitors will want to see the quintessentially blue "Blue Grotto". The electric blue light is zingy, the silver reflections sparkle, the boatman sings; you'll be glad you did it.

Another panoramic spot can be found at Capri's Augustus Gardens – a delightful bit of nature we owe to German industrialist Friedrich Alfred Krupp. From the garden's geranium and dahlia bedecked terraces, you will see one of the best views of the three magnificent seastacks, I Faraglioni. These rock formations average 100 metres in height and each has a name: Stella is connected to the shore, the Mezzo stack has an archway in it big enough for a small boat to pass through, and the outer rock, Scopolo or Fuori has its very own blue lizard found nowhere else in the world. Just a short 2 km walk east of the Piazzetta find the eerie ruins of the Villa Jovis where Emperor Tiberius "suffered" his self-imposed exile, far away from the Roman forum and the threat of assassination. Today you can enjoy the views of the bay, Sorrento and the Amalfi coast from 345 metres above sea level.

Anacapri is the island's quieter side. The local bus will give you dizzying views (sit on the right side as you ascend). Here, find the Monte Solaro chair lift that takes you 600 metres above sea level to the mountain summit. The highest point in Capri, it affords an incredible 360° view over the island and the sea. There is a small café at the top and a short hike away is a sweet, tiny, 15th-century church, the Hermitage of Cetrella, where sailors used to pray for protection before setting out on perilous sea journeys. While in Anacapri you may also want to visit the Punta Carena lighthouse at the south western corner of the island. There's an elegant beach club called Il Faro with a salt-water pool, an excellent restaurant and a snack bar – such a pleasant place to see the sun go down. Your Capri seaside delight for a day trip may be the family-friendly beach club Bagni Tiberio, reached by a boat just to the left of the ferry ticket office in Marina Grande. There are two free beach areas in Marina Piccola one on either side of the Lo Scoglio delle Sirene.

Ischia, the largest of the three islands, is a spa lovers' paradise. The whole island is generously endowed with thermal spas large and small and nearly every hotel has a pool filled with thermal waters. In fact, with 103 thermal springs, 69 fumarole clusters and more than 300 separate bathing establishments, it is the European capital of thermal-based vacations. Large thermal parks and gardens pepper the island and are a favourite destination of day-trippers. They typically feature a variety of bathing pools, each of which is maintained at a different temperature and most feature spa and massage services, restaurants, and even hotels. Poseidon and Negombo are two of the largest while Castiglione is one of the best on the island. A visit to La Mortella, the ultimate romantic garden created by Susana and William Walton, is also an absolute must.

The tiniest island of the three, **Procida**, lies low in the bay like a snoozing crocodile. From the air it looks like a Scottie dog with a crescent tail looping toward Miseno, or, viewed sideways, like the Euro sign. It's connected to its uninhabited baby sister, Vivara, by a bridge. Procida's magnificent landscape offers sandy beaches, (dormant) volcanic coves and tranquil waters. Here too you'll find a village that still uses its fishing boats when so many other little towns on Capri and Ischia have surrendered entirely to ice cream, mud treatments and the delights of retail therapy. But tourists still come to Corricella to explore the alleyways because this is a positive paint-box of a town where everyday objects are drenched in colour. It must be the light. Any surprise so much of *Il Postino – The Postman,*

Massimo Troisi's poignant last role, was filmed here? White and pastel-washed homes pepper the island and locals aver that the polychrome houses look like this so that fishermen can determine which house is theirs when out at sea. Of course, they also say the boats were painted the same colour as the houses so the wives could keep tabs on their husbands while they were away. Above Corricella the Terra Murata – walled earthwork - looms, a vestige of marauding medieval times when the population retreated to the hill for safety. Even further back, this small island, only 4 kms square, was the playground for elite Romans; in the 18th century it became a royal game reserve and had a thriving shipbuilding trade. Today fishing still rules, and visitors find much fresh seafood to tempt them on the plate; something special to try here too is "Insalata di Limone" - lemon salad, made from *limoni pane* – bread lemons – with their sweet, abundant pith.

Sunbathing under Castello Aragonese, Ischia

A BOURBON VERSAILLES: CASERTA ROYAL PALACE

Think Palace of Caserta, and you think High Baroque and Rococo style, **a desire to out-Versailles Versailles in terms of scale, magnificence and power-projection**. It was an urge that in the 1750s drove Bourbon monarch Charles VII (III of Spain) to commission Luigi Vanvitelli to design his 1,200 room palace. Not only was this the ultimate gesture of prestige display with its multiple frescoed and gilded state rooms, vast library and theatre, 4 courtyards, 34 stairways and a rumoured 1,970 windows, but it was intended to provide a safe and more pleasant location for the court and government, far enough away from the heat and bustle of Naples and the very real possibility of coastal attack. As things turned out, however, Charles would never enjoy the palace as a resident; he abdicated in favour of his son Ferdinand in 1759. Such a huge building project took decades to complete. When Luigi Vanvitelli died in 1773, his role was assumed by his son Carlo.

The gardens were similarly vast; a long axis, 3km long, draws the eye to the distant horizon where cascades and fountains very nearly come into focus. The *pièce de résistance* is the fountain of Diana and Actaeon with its 75 metre high waterfall. The garden's water features were so monumental, they required the construction of their own aqueduct. Known as the **Carolino Aqueduct or Aqueduct of Vanvitelli**, its other purpose was to supply water from Monte Taburno (Benevento) to the "great city that would rise around the palace" (Caserta) and to the San Leucio complex. Designed in the likeness of Roman aqueducts, it was a triumph of hydraulic engineering. A well-preserved three storey section of sequential arches – the Ponti della Valle – survives today.

As the house and gardens neared completion, a sea-change occurred in garden style. Taste had moved on and Charles's son, Ferdinand IV (I of the Two Sicilies),

tutored by his wife Maria Caroline of Austria, now looked to English fashion for inspiration. So there really couldn't be a stronger contrast between the old and the new gardens. A 50 acre plot was prepared and on the advice of His Britannic Majesty's Envoy Extraordinary, William Hamilton, a plantsman-designer called John Andreas Graefer was engaged to create an 'English Garden'. He began work in 1786, collaborating with Carlo Vanvitelli. The result is something like an English country park with trees and grass, seeded with architectural elements to delight, surprise or thrill the beholder. But unlike its northern model, at Caserta the plants and trees that cluster around the little lake and the created false 'Roman ruins' are exotic ones to suit the southern climate. This is a magnificent example of the Picturesque taste in landscape as it settled into the Romantic style – a world where imagination and emotions are just as important as reason. This is a garden about sudden revelations and sudden surges of feeling. And nothing embodies this quite so well as 'Venus Bathing', where the nude goddess may be seen from the front across water, chastely guarding her charms. However, if you walk through a passageway cut into rock and glimpse her as if from a secret hiding place, her form is rather more thrillingly revealed.

In a distinctly grimmer bit of history, Caserta Palace was the seat of the Supreme Allied Commander at the end of WWII; it was here that the first allied war trial was held. A military tribunal found German General Anton Dostler guilty of war crimes. He was sentenced to death and executed by firing squad in Aversa. Among the palace's more frivolous duties – its credits as a film location include Star Wars I and II and Mission Impossible III.

Caserta palace was listed as a UNESCO World Heritage Site in 1997. The listing includes the palace, the park, the Carolino Aqueduct and the nearby **Belvedere San Leucio Complex**. An odd snippet of history, the complex was part of a mid-eighteenth century utopian social experiment: a self-contained community known as the Real Colonia dei Setaioli – the Royal Colony of Silk Weavers. Workers

Caserta Royal Palace

and their families had equal rights and education and a portion of the revenues went to care for the sick and elderly. The factory employed the most advanced technologies available at the time and the fame of silk production here spread around the world.

EXPLORE SOME MORE

Casertavecchia, a picturesque hilltop village some 10 kms from Caserta, has a long history punctuated with periods spent under the sway of Longobards, Normans, Swabians, Aragonese and Bourbons. As one might expect, its Duomo, the **Cathedral of San Michele Arcangelo**, displays a variety of styles, including Romanesque, Gothic and Baroque, though these last elements were substantially removed during the 1926 restoration. Architectural experts have also identified influences from Amalfi and Sicily and the cathedral shares some design features with the Duomo at Salerno. Casertavecchia boasts a tower remaining from a castle and a number of welcoming restaurants. Best of all there are some startlingly good views over the surrounding countryside.

OF GLADIATORS AND MITHRAS: SANTA MARIA CAPUA VETERE

About 40 kms north of Naples in the province of Caserta, the old city of Capua – Santa Maria Capua Vetere - dates back to at least the 7th century BC when Etruscans and Euboean Greeks settled the area. Capua, the modern city sits 5 kilometres further north. The ancient city has several claims to fame. In Roman times, Cicero said that the "fleshpots of Capua" defeated Hannibal because his Carthaginians became soft due to the high living in the city. At the time, Capuan residents were considered wealthy, well-groomed and always perfumed. An unguent produced here called *seplasium* was famous throughout the empire. The city was also called the *terra di lavoro* or "land of work" due to its cornucopia of agriculture, metal-working, pottery, ceramics and extensive trade in other goods. The ancient writer Livy referred to Capua as the granary of Rome because of its abundant cereal yield.

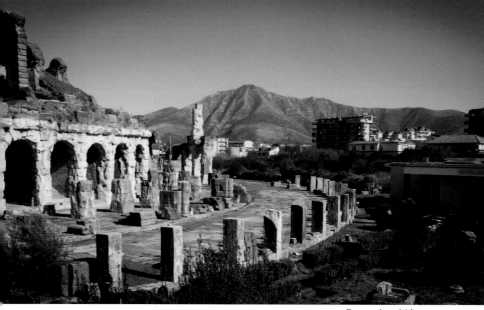

Capua Amphitheatre

The well-preserved ruins of a **2nd-century BC amphitheatre** are easy to find at the centre of Santa Maria Capua Vetere. **It was the second largest in the Roman world next to the Coliseum in Rome**, holding up to 60,000 spectators. The amphitheatre is open so visitors can roam the vaulted corridors, the gladiator field and the underground tunnels where once elaborate stage machinery as well as caged animals were kept. In Roman times the amphitheatre admitted both men and women to these popular shows for free.

The **Gladiator Museum** next to the amphitheatre contains two rooms of artefacts, a scale model of the amphitheatre and a waxwork display of fighting gladiators. At one time, Capua boasted the best gladiator schools, training both slaves and freemen. The gladiators were divided into categories according to the type of armour used and their combat speciality. The amphitheatre put on two kinds of shows: the *munera* where gladiators fought each other to the death and *venationes* where gladiators fought against wild animals, sometimes even being thrown unarmed into the arena. Professor Mary Beard, writing of the lives of gladiators in Pompeii, places them at the very bottom of the social pile. With a death rate of around one in six for each spectacle, few volunteered for this career. Most were slaves or condemned criminals; all were under the control of the *lanista* or troupe manager. He had to deliver a good show for elite sponsors, oversee training, find new recruits and buy in animals for his beast-fighters to subdue. These might include a bear or bull, but more often in provincial towns, a wild dog.

Spartacus, the leader of the slave revolt (73 BC) against Rome, first distinguished himself as a gladiator in the Capua amphitheatre. It was also here that he broke away from his training camp and, joined by slaves who broke out of their barracks en masse, Spartacus plundered towns up and down the Apennines for two years.

At the amphitheatre, make sure to ask at the ticket office to see the **Mithraeum at**

Capua – the Sanctuary of Mithras. You will follow one of the custodians by car, through the bustling streets of Capua; sparse signs for the sanctuary appear here and there. The custodian stops his car at a dead-end road, in the middle of which a red-brick building with a Latin plaque marked *Mithraevm* is squashed between apartment houses. He unlocks double iron doors and brings you down a flight of stairs to a vestibule. A rectangular vaulted room has a ceiling with vestiges of red and green stars on a yellow background. In the front niche a fresco depicts the god Mithras slaying a bull. The cult of Mithras originated in Persia during the 14th century BC. His cult travelled across Asia Minor to Greece and then to Rome where by the 1st century AD it gained popularity, especially among the common people. Scholars have written extensively about the syncretism between Mithraism and Christianity due to the many Christian churches that were formerly Mithraean and the fact that Christ's birthday coincides with the birthday of Mithras – December 25th. A few hundred metres from the Mithraeum is the **Archaeological Museum of Capua Antica**. Founded in 1995, its collections come from archaeological excavations carried out around Capua in the second half of the 20th century.

■ ■

EXPLORE SOME MORE

For those with an adventurous spirit, Santa Maria Capua Vetere holds more ancient wonders. The Etruscan Furnace remains from the Archaic period and what was believed to be a jail for gladiators, the Carceri Vecchie (old prison cells) is in fact a 1st-century AD Roman funerary monument. Meanwhile in Capua itself (the new city), the Museo Campano, the **Provincial Museum of Campania** is a must-see. Tucked halfway down a narrow street, this small museum houses mosaics, medieval paintings and funerary epigraphs of the Roman period, but the highlight has to be two rooms filled with tuff stone statues of seated mothers, the *Matres Matutae*, holding swaddled infants. More than a hundred such statues were discovered at the Santuario di Fondo Patturelli, though several were dispersed elsewhere in Italy and overseas following their discovery in 1845 on Carlo Patturelli's land. The sanctuary was active from the 2nd to 4th centuries BC and these statues, with their ancient, inscrutable gaze, were votive offerings re maternity desired or accomplished.

■ ■

A BENEDICTINE BASILICA IN CAPUA: SANT'ANGELO IN FORMIS

The Basilica Benedettina di S. Michele Arcangelo – Sant'Angelo in Formis - is located in the outskirts of Capua. It used to be an impressive Temple of Diana. The church lies at the bottom of a hilly area known as Tifata that in ancient times was densely forested. **The cult of Diana, goddess of the wood and hunt, flourished here in this land of oak trees and spring waters**. We don't know exactly when construction of this temple began. Scholars say that active building work took place at the end of the 4th century BC and the beginning of the 3rd century BC. According to an inscription still visible on the floor, the Romans rebuilt the temple in 74 BC. The date that the temple was transformed into a church is also unknown. Few manuscripts remain that detail its construction but as happened so often in the early years of Christianity, the ancient stones of the pagan temple were recycled to build it. The Lombards may have built a church consecrated to the Archangel Michael at the turn of the 6th to 7th centuries. By 1065 the Norman, Richard I of Capua, had built a monastery over the church. The Corinthian columns from the temple remain intact and the brilliant fresco colours along the walls have been well-preserved.

TIMELESS TEMPLES: PAESTUM

Doric, Ionic, Iconic... and very dramatic. That first sight of the temples of Paestum releases something potent into the bloodstream. How are these three extraordinary structures still standing in their glossy green meadow, the stone not "recycled" over the past 2,500 years?

Greek colonists built the walled city of Poseidonia, later Paestum, around the end of the 7th century (that's BC, folks). The settlement was part of Magna Graecia; a rich and sophisticated culture was transplanted into new territories. Here in Paestum two temples were raised to Hera, goddess of women and marriage and one to warrior (and wisdom) goddess Athena – a triumph, at least in number, of the domestic over the warlike. The Romans added an amphitheatre and a forum and there is much that lies hidden, yet to be explored. But no future discovery will have the visual impact of the strangely tapering columns with their capitals looking so much like squashed bagels. It's also worth bearing in mind that a springtime visit means you wander through flower-strewn meadows to see the ruins. As to why the temples are still here – step forward… the mosquito! Malarial swamps protected the site throughout the Middle Ages and explains why these stones were not robbed out. Fortunately the only thing you'll catch now is a unique aesthetic thrill. Not far away, an excellent museum displays the many finds from this site and other, nearby sites, especially Samnite tombs, including the famous diver frescoes, but also the prehistoric finds, some very fine Greek vases, discussions of the temple architecture and the Roman city. The displays are well signed and admission to the site includes the museum.

CITY OF PHILOSOPHERS: VELIA

Impecunious Greek philosophers wandered not only around the *agora* in Athens, but probably expounded their theories throughout today's Italian peninsula. Some of the earliest Greek philosophers, the Eleatics, lived in an area about three hours south of Naples. Parmenides was the founder of the Eleatic School and a citizen of Elea (today Velia). Born towards the end of the 6th century BC, at the age of sixty-five he met Socrates in Athens. He also drew up laws at Elea and his main belief was, simply stated: *All is One*.

A disciple of Parmenides, **Zeno of Elea was born in 489 BC and he created some witty arguments to prove the impossibility of motion**. His most famous argument – the paradox of the arrow in flight – explains that for any one instant in time, an arrow in flight must either move to where it is or move to where it is not. Since it can't move to where it is not, because this is a single instant and by the same token, it can't move to where it is because it's already there, logically an arrow in flight can never move in any single instant.

You can find the city of the Eleatics in the present-day Cilento and Vallo di Diano National Park. Italians call the ruins Velia, but the settlement was originally named Hyele by the Greeks who founded the city in 535 BC. These off-the-beaten-track ruins contain a complex of structures, including an old marketplace at the bottom of the hill by the entrance. You can walk up a cobblestone road, taking a small detour down an overgrown path to a crumbling villa. The pathway then becomes steep and leads first to an amphitheatre and then on to a medieval watchtower built next to an ancient temple. A one-room museum stands off to the side with sculptures that archaeologists found at the site.

VENTURES

IN A

DIFFERENT VEIN

FEED THE MIND

DELIGHT

THE SENSES

A TALE OF TWO CITIES
❧ THE ❧
NAPLES
UNDERGROUND

Cover Photo:
Catacombs of San Gaudioso

Naples, in truth, is a tale of two cities. One, the narrow streets with seemingly no logic, full of bustling traffic, the other, more than 3,000 years old that twists, collapses and burrows underground.

Sixty percent of Neapolitan inhabitants live on top of more than 700 cavities underneath the city. These subterranean passageways include ancient aqueducts and cisterns, catacombs and crypts, air raid shelters and the remains of the Greco-Roman city of Neapolis. Most of these underground cavities remain sealed or barely discovered; many are even privately owned.

Neapolitan speleologists dedicate themselves to the study of these cavities. Otherwise known as cavers, potholers or spelunkers, over time they have brought to light and painstakingly restored most of the underground cavities that are open to the public today, often at their own expense.

In Naples' Centro Storico district Enzo Albertini (Doctor of Speleology

and President of the Napoli Sotterranea Association) has been restoring and promoting the cavity known as Napoli Sotterranea since the 1980s. In the Monte di Dio district, thanks to the dedication of the Associazione Culturale Borbonica Sotterranea, the Bourbon Tunnel opened its doors to the public in 2010. In the Rione Sanità district, visitors can now tour several sites that were once part of the Ancient Necropolis of Neapolis, the city's Greek and Roman burial grounds. The Catacombs of San Gennaro and San Gaudioso have been returned to the city because of the enthusiasm of a group of young people from the Rione Sanità; meanwhile protesters are responsible for the re-opening of the Fontanelle Cemetery in 2010. And, thanks to the Celanapoli Association and its founder Carlo Leggiere,

visitors to Naples can now see one of the Greek burial sites that is part of the Hellenistic Necropolis of Neapolis.

Ancient ruins aren't the only thing lurking below the surface; MetroNapoli's Metro Art Stations project has created a huge public underground museum of contemporary art across thirteen of its stations and Neapolis Station was installed in the Museo Metro Station to display artefacts uncovered during the construction of Naples' Metro System. There are smaller underground sites at the Santa Maria Maggiore dellle Pietrasanta Church, Basilica San Pietro ad Aram, and one under a wine shop, Il Vignaiolo near Piazza Cavour. Underground tours outside the city include: the Grotta della Sibilla, Piscina Mirabilis, and the Sanctuary of Mithras in Capua.

Fontanelle Cemetery

Plan Your Visit

Tours of the underground can get claustrophobic due to narrow spaces. Wear sensible shoes and bring a jacket or sweater as it can get quite cool underground. If you have mobility issues, check ahead. With a second entrance at Parcheggio Morelli, the Bourbon Tunnel offers the only handicap-accessible underground tour in the city.

Sights & Attractions

BOURBON TUNNEL

Vico del Grottone, 4
There is a second entrance (disabled access) from Parcheggio Morelli at Via Domenico Morelli, 40
By guided tour only Fri - Sun 10.00, 12.00, 15.30 & 17.30; an Adventure Tour and Speleo Tour are also offered
Starting at €10.00 for the Standard Tour
+39 081 7645808
galleriaborbonica.com

CATACOMBS OF NAPLES

Adults €8.00 for both catacombs
Allow 4 - 5 hours to do both catacombs along with the Basilica dell'Incoronata del Buon Consiglio and Basilica Santa Maria della Sanità. If doing both, start at the Catacombs of San Gennaro. The tour ends at the 5th-century Basilica of San Gennaro dei Poveri where you can ask your guide to let you out to continue downhill to the Catacombs of San Gaudioso.
+39 081 7443714
catacombedinapoli.it

- CATACOMBS OF SAN GAUDIOSO

Piazza Sanità,14
Inside Basilica Santa Maria della Sanità
By guided tour only Mon - Sun every hour from 10.00 – 13.00

- CATACOMBS OF SAN GENNARO

Via Tondo di Capodimonte,13
On the left hand side of the Basilica dell'Incoronata del Buon Consiglio
By guided tour only, Mon - Sat every hour from 10.00 – 17.00, Sun every hour from 10.00 – 13.00

FONTANELLE CEMETERY

Via Fontanelle, 80
Open daily 10.00 - 17.00
Free
+39 081 19703197

HELLENISTIC NECROPOLIS OF NEAPOLIS

Via Santa Maria Antesaecula, 126/129
By guided tour only, every Sun 10.00 in Italian, meeting point is at Porta San Gennaro, call for tours in English.
Approximately 2 hours
Price depends on number of people
+39 347 5597231
celanapoli.it

METRO ART STATIONS

The art stations are on Metro Lines 1 and 6. Stations are open according to the train timetable.
+39 800 639525
anm.it/default.php?ids=1907&

MUSEO DEL SOTTOSUOLO

Piazza Cavour, 140
Tours by reservation by e-mailing booking@ ilmuseodelsottosuolo.com

PLAN YOUR VISIT

1 to 3 hours, depending on the tour
Adults €10.00 - €25.00
lamacchinadeltempo.info

NAPOLI SOTTERRANEA

Piazza San Gaetano, 68
By guided tour only 10.00 – 18.00, tours
every hour in Italian, every 2 hours in English
Approximately 2 hours
Adults €10.00
+39 081 296944
napolisotterranea.org

NAPOLI SOTTERRANEA LAES AT CAFFÈ GAMBRINUS

Piazza Treste e Trento outside of Caffè
Gambrinus.
By guided tour only, Thurs 21.00, Sat 10.00,
12.00 & 18.00; Sun & holidays 10.00, 11.00,
12.00 & 18.00
Adults €10.00
+39 081 400256
lanapolisotterranea.it

NEAPOLIS STATION

Piazza Museo
Open daily, **except Tues**, 09.00 – 19.30
(same hours as the National Archaeological
Museum)
Free

S. LORENZO MAGGIORE

Via Tribunali, 316
Open Mon - Sat 09.30 – 17.30, Sun 09.30
– 13.30
Adults €9.00 for the underground and
museum; entry to the church is free
+39 081 2110860
sanlorenzomaggiorenapoli.it

S. MARIA DELLE ANIME DEL PURGATORIO AD ARCO

Via Tribunali, 39
Temporarily closed, check ahead.
+39 333 3832561
purgatorioadarco.it

S. MARIA MAGGIORE DELLA PIETRASANTA

Via Tribunali, 16
The underground area below the church is
not open to the public, but if you ask the
attendant, you might gain access.

S. PIETRO AD ARAM

Via Santa Candida, 4

(IL) VIGNAIOLO WINE SHOP

Via Misericordiella, 4-5
+39 081 456561

Carlo Leggiere of the Celanapoli Association

STROLLING IN THE DEEP: NAPOLI SOTTERRANEA

Every visit to Naples should include a tour of Napoli Sotterranea. Led by passionate and knowledgeable guides, you'll **learn about the history of Naples from the bottom up**.

The entrance is located along a side-street in the Centro Storico; don't confuse this comprehensive tour with the tour given at Caffè Gambrinus by the same name, nor with the one at San Lorenzo Maggiore on the other side of Piazza San Gaetano. The tour descends down a long stairway, 40 metres below ground. At the very bottom, you emerge into a vast underground. There's a labyrinth of tunnels, hollow areas and narrow passageways.

This underground was first excavated during Greek and Roman times and dates back to the 4th century BC. Carved out of the volcanic tuff stone, the Greeks and Romans used the excavated stone to build the city's walls and temples and the excavations as a burial ground. A display of fake rocks and an electric pulley in one of the underground's cavernous rooms show how they cut the tuff stones with large axes, and hauled the pieces through holes in the ceiling. Enormous cisterns, part of the Roman aqueduct system, alternate with cramped, barely passable tunnels. The water system continued to be used until 1825 when officials shut it

Napoli Sotterranea

down because of a cholera outbreak. The underground was reopened and used as a bomb shelter.

As with other subterranean spaces in Naples, there is a grim chill to imagining how crowded this maze became during World War II, when as many as 20,000 Neapolitans sought safety from air raids here. Graffiti can still be seen on the walls, from the word *aiuto* "help" to pictures of bombs drawn by children. In several hollow areas, Napoli Sotterranea has staged World War II displays of army tanks, military uniforms, and toys left behind by children.

One section of the tour is conducted by candlelight and if you are claustrophobic (or a little thick around the waist), you might just want to wait for others to return from their inspection of the vast water cistern that lies beyond this narrow passageway. On President Clinton's visit in 1994, one of his taller, bulkier bodyguards had to sit this part out, much against his professional instincts. Down another corridor, biologists have set up a bed of plants that never need to be watered because the underground atmosphere boasts eighty percent humidity. In another cavity that sits below the San Gregorio Armeno Church, the Santa Patrizia Order of Nuns store their homemade wine.

Returning above ground, the tour takes a detour to the basement of a classic Naples *basso* (one or two-room ground-floor flat) to view a Greco-Roman odeon (theatre). Here Emperor Nero once danced and sang, and not even an earthquake could interrupt his performance. Afterwards he thanked both the audience and the Gods for their applause.

NAPLES' ANCIENT MARKET: SAN LORENZO MAGGIORE

On the south side of Piazza San Gaetano is the Monumental Complex of San Lorenzo Maggiore. A 13th-century conventual complex owed to the Angevin dynasty, **it was built on top of the *macellum*, the (Roman) city's marketplace**. It is one of only two self-guided underground tours in the Naples; here you can wander around without a guide (and without the crowds) to view crumbled archways and the remains of ancient shops.

A stairway located in the complex's cloister descends just seven metres below ground, landing on one of the narrow streets of ancient Neapolis. This 54-metre stretch of one of the *cardos* ran north-south between the Decumano Maggiore (Via dei Tribunali) and the Decumano Inferiore (Via S. Biagio di Librai). Here the centuries-old shopfronts of the *macellum* are as clearly recognisable as the structure's characteristic diamond-shaped *opus reticulatum* and its successor, *opus latericium*. And, if you look closely, you'll find a spattering of tuff stone blocks courtesy of the Greeks as well.

As we walk along this ancient street we can reanimate these plain spaces in our mind's eye into a bustling marketplace with *tabernae*, public buildings and shops. The remains of a laundry, winery, bakery, dye shop, even the public treasury, the *Erario* or *Aerarium*, have all been identified. One brick oven is so well preserved that it seems that at any moment wooden logs might flicker again with fire.

Archaeologists have found oil lamps imported from North Africa, but the lamps show no trace of usage. Hence experts hypothesise that the lamps were stock items and that this bustling marketplace must have offered international wares. The numerous amphorae discovered on the site, some with trade-names incised, attest to a lively trade in wine in exchange for Iberian garum (fish sauce), dried meat from North Africa and oil that most probably came from Greece. The amphorae as well as other ceramics are on display in the museum upstairs.

Around the corner is a cryptoportico (a subterranean covered passageway), a series of five arched and interconnected rooms which were illuminated and ventilated by a "sky-light" excavated in the wall near the ceiling. The sloped tables extant in each of these rooms give us a clue as to what was on offer in this area of the macellum. Presumed to have been the *mercato coperto del pesce*, the covered fish market, the tables here are not at all unlike those you see at any fishmonger's shop today. Another theory, however, proposes that these tables were *tricliniae* - the sort of reclining bed or chaise lounge that Romans used for dining.

A stairway at the back of the cryptoporticus leads to the most recent excavations of this site which uncovered part of the *Schola*, a meeting place of religious or commercial associations. Of interest are a slab of precious marble, parts of a mosaic floor, and fresco fragments on some of the walls.

PURGATORY: SANTA MARIA DELLE ANIME DEL PURGATORIO

According to Dante, the Mountain of Purgatory was the only land that existed in the southern hemisphere. It came into existence because of the displaced rock that resulted when Satan's fall created hell. **Today, purgatory can be found on a narrow street in the Centro Storico at the Santa Maria Church of the Souls of Purgatory** where the Baroque façade has a show of skulls and femurs adorned daily with fresh flowers and candles. Neapolitan noble families commissioned the construction of this church in the early 1600s so that they could bury their loved ones in crypts under the city.

Stairs at the back of the church descend to an underground cathedral, now only hollow tuff stone with niches on either side. Across the cathedral, a doorway leads to a hallway where rectangular holes display unburied skulls and bones. From here, the visitor enters a cavern with two long beds of dirt on either side. Looking closer, you see these are unmarked graves. Niches in the walls display a plethora of skulls and bones, overflowing onto the sides of the walkways, littered with small pictures of the deceased.

Up at the front of this cavernous room, an altar abounds with flowers, rosaries, and other memorabilia left by devotees. To the right of the altar the remains of Lucia, the virgin-bride, rest above sickly-sweet smelling flowers and handwritten cards. Legend has it – and many different versions of the legend exist – that Lucia was the only daughter of Domenico d'Amore, the prince of Ruffano. In 1789, at the age of seventeen, she died of consumption shortly before she was to wed the Marquis Giacomo Santomango. The tragedy caused a tumult of heartfelt emotion by the populace who to this day leave fresh flowers and handwritten cards underneath her skull and bones.

ANOTHER WAY INTO THE UNDERGROUND: NAPOLI SOTTERRANEA LAES

An underground tour at a café? Yes indeed. Several times every week urban speleologist, Signor Quaranta, a slender Neapolitan with lots of energy and funny stories takes groups **from Caffè Gambrinus up a narrow street and through double doors that say "Napoli Sotterranea."** From a whitewashed hallway you descend 118 stairs that spiral down past a small chapel, thence to an open space with rows of chairs, an ancient aqueduct.

It was the Greeks who first harnessed the springs from the foot of Mount Vesuvius and channelled the water into these underground cisterns, some as deep as eighty metres. Neapolitans used the cisterns as drinking water all the way up until the 1800s. Now it's your chance to experience some of the fifteen kilometres of underground made of porous tuff stone. The ceilings often drip with water due to the humidity. The moist environment is supposedly healthy for respiration, helping (and possibly curing) people with asthma.

World War II graffiti can be seen throughout this maze of narrow passageways and huge halls. Thousands hid here waiting for the war to end. Above an alcove, graffiti commemorates the day two people were married under a tuff arch in 1943. Another room has graffiti that reads: "Women are the way to true happiness."

Successive small spaces return you to the hollow space with chairs. Signor Quaranta turns off the lights for a few moments so that you can sit in the pitch black and in silence – an odd feeling when Naples bustles with frenetic activity above. This tour is especially welcome during the hot summer months, the temperate climate of the parallel city making it the most comfortable spot in Naples.

The Pozzari – Aqueduct Cleaners

At some point in the history of Naples, most *palazzi* (residential buildings) had wells in their courtyards and water-spouts in every room. The *pozzari* (or well attendants – from *pozzo* for "well") worked in these cisterns, scuttling through narrowly built holes, cleaning sinks and taps and making sure the cistern water ran clear. Palazzo owners paid the *pozzari* regularly for their services, but the *pozzari* would occasionally cheat wealthy landowners into paying them to re-clean the wells. One *pozzaro*, for example, put a dead cat in the cistern to guarantee himself more work.

There is a wealth of folklore about the *munacielli* or Neapolitan house goblins who played tricks on those who lived in their homes. It is said that one goblin was a sickly boy who was raised in a convent where nuns hid his deformity by dressing him as a monk (hence the diminutive *munaciello*). When he died under mysterious circumstances, Neapolitans began to experience sightings of him. They conferred magical powers on the dead boy and said that he carried the lucky numbers necessary to win the lottery. Other folklore maintained that the goblins were the *pozzari* themselves who would get into homes through the channels used to lower the buckets.

AN ESCAPE ROUTE BUILT FOR A KING: THE BOURBON TUNNEL

Near Piazza del Plebiscito and a little way up Via Gennaro Serra, a tiny *vicoletto* provides another route into the heart of the underground. You begin in a former veterinary clinic before descending tuff stone steps down into The Bourbon Tunnel.

The year 1848 was tough for any European monarch; riots and revolution were the order of the day in many cities. This made King Ferdinand II of the Two Sicilies more than thoughtful as he sat in his new palace in Naples. **What he needed most of all was a possible escape route**. So in 1853 he commissioned architect Enrico Alvino to construct a tunnel from the Royal Palace to a spot near the barracks at Piazza Vittoria. Officially this was to be a double tunnel, the King's and Queen's tunnels running parallel, full of stores and with an elegant interior. But in reality, the workers not only had to dig through the tuff rock to create a new passageway, but they also had to cross the existing water system that Cesare Carmignano had devised in the 17th century. This part, at least, was accomplished by bridging cisterns and carving out new spaces where once only the *pozzari* had ventured with their lanterns. Work stopped after two years and soon Ferdinand and his building projects would be overtaken by political changes that swept across Europe.

As with many other underground spaces, the tunnel was used as an air-raid shelter during the Second World War; cisterns were filled with earth to raise them to usable levels, low voltage electricity supplies were installed along with toilets and showers. One can only imagine how difficult it was to endure months of bombing in these dank spaces. Down here, as you pass along the corridors and through echoing cisterns, you can see heart-rending messages on the walls – *Noi vivi* or "We are alive" – and view the remains of beds and children's toys.

At the end of the tour comes a real surprise, the ghostly chassis and frames of cars, vans and bicycles lined up along the passageways. The tunnel was used as storage for vehicles confiscated from Neapolitans who engaged in contraband trade, chiefly that of tobacco. Just before emerging, blinking into the light of day at Via Morelli (grateful there are no stairs to climb back up) you see the broken fragments of an enormous Art Deco statue that stood throughout the war years in Piazza Santa Maria degli Angeli – a monument to Aurelio Padovani, the fascist leader of Campania in the 1920s.

It took five years for the teams of cavers and various volunteers to clear out the accumulated lumber and refuse, but now the tunnel offers a great glimpse into the history of Naples at three key points in its history.

Opposite page: Bourbon Tunnel

WRITTEN IN STONE: THE HELLENISTIC NECROPOLIS OF NEAPOLIS

Much of the human story has been written into the subsoil, though the evidence may be quite difficult to find, read and interpret. A millennium of geological, environmental and man-made changes have chipped away at it, built over it and in some cases washed away all traces of it. But if you know where to look, know what you're looking for, or as fate may have it, happen upon it after a 7.2 magnitude earthquake shakes up the city, you might just discover one monumental chapter etched into the subsoil, or quite literally, carved in the stone.

If you've been to the Colosseum or the Forum in Rome, taken a tour of Napoli Sotterranea or visited the archaeological excavations under San Lorenzo Maggiore, you might want to readjust your expectations. Uncut, uncensored, and not quite ready for prime-time public consumption, this is one site that requires keen powers of observation, elaboration and the ability to read the stones like an archaeologist. **But for those willing to venture here, their journey will be well rewarded.**

It was a structural analysis following the 1980 earthquake that led to the remarkable discovery less than 15 metres below a nondescript palazzo on a tiny alley in the city's Rione Sanità district. A work in progress, this site will have you crouching on your knees, your fingers searching for a hand-hold on walls carved some 2,400 years ago. And it will leave you with the sensation that you've crawled down Alice's rabbit hole into the bowels of ancient history and into a place so intimate, so sacred, that only the most callous observers will escape unmoved.

After descending into the basement of the palazzo you enter the Ipogeo dei Togati where you are immediately confronted with the bottom portion of a high-relief sculpture: the legs and feet of two draped figures thought to represent a funeral scene. From the Italian adjective *togato*, meaning gowned or robed, it is the draping on this sculpture that gives the *hypogeum* (underground temple or tomb) its modern name. Nearby, the Ipogeo dei Melograni is reached via an unlit staircase with only the aid of a flashlight.

SAINTS' FINAL RESTING PLACE: CATACOMBS OF SAN GENNARO

This old underground is so-named because it **once housed the remains of the patron saint of the city, San Gennaro**. It is an extensive network of tunnels, ambulatories, cubicles and chapels that constitutes the largest catacomb complex in southern Italy. Built on three underground levels (the lowest floor was only

Catacombs of San Gennaro

recently discovered and is under study), this cavernous burial chamber was burrowed into the volcanic tuff rock of Capodimonte Hill during paleo-Christian times (around the 2th century AD).

The preferred interment option of Roman noblemen, the catacombs were the first burial place of Naples' 6th Bishop and first patron saint, Agrippinus (Sant'Agrippino), though his remains were later moved. In the 5th century, the remains of San Gennaro were moved here. However, they weren't destined to 'remain' here and they were moved again in the 10th and 12th centuries before finally coming to rest in a special crypt beneath the apse of Naples' cathedral, the Duomo, in the 15th century. What was left behind in the catacombs are his (empty) tomb and the oldest known portrait of him dating to the 5th century.

A tour of the catacombs begins with a walk down many stairs and into a hollow cavern. Archaeologists think the structure, about the size of a large church, is actually the vestiges of several cemeteries and basilicas built on top of one another throughout the ages. The first area is a 5th-century cemetery. The frescoes, although faded, still have a sort of majesty. One depicts a young princess girl who died before her parents, the faces of both parents shown beside her in grief. A crown over the girl's head signifies her ascent into heaven. In an adjacent alcove, a fresco depicts San Gennaro and St. Peter at the gates of paradise.

Walking further into the belly of the catacombs, you will come to a large basilica, called *maggiore* and then pass a hollow half-dome that displays a cross and Greek lettering that says: "Christ has won." This probably was the baptismal font of the basilica. Continuing on, there is yet another basilica, called the Bishop's Church. This area is so named because frescoes – now gone – depicted a series of Bishops. Here also, a cavernous hole two stories below once held the remains of San Gennaro. Beyond the Bishop's Church, yet another basilica dates back to the second century. Here ceiling frescoes display a mix of pagan and Christian iconography, including motifs of cats alongside three women holding rocks symbolising the foundation of the Church. Most impressive of all is a massive ceiling fresco of a Christ in Byzantine style.

On the lower level, is the small Basilica of Sant'Agrippino, which is decorated with contemporary artworks and still in use today. The tour concludes in the paleo-Christian Basilica of San Gennaro **Extra Moenia** (San Gennaro Beyond the Walls). This ancient church with ties to the catacombs, became a hospital in the late 15th century and was enlarged after the plague of 1656. It is still part of the San Gennaro Hospital complex today.

THE MACABRE DOMINICANS: CATACOMBS OF SAN GAUDIOSO

Puozza scula - literally: "May you drain away" - is a Neapolitan expression that wishes death upon one's enemies. The saying derives from the macabre burial practices of the 17th century Dominicans who painted brightly coloured frescoes beside the crypts of wealthy patrons and used their skulls for decoration.

Tucked beneath the altar of the Church of Santa Maria della Sanità, **a large gate guards the entrance to an ancient chapel**. A barely noticeable passage with no door leads to the catacombs. San Gaudioso's niche comes into view first, then the blue tiles from the original basilica erected in the 5th century. Nearby there is a stunning fresco of Santa Caterina of Siena on the wall of the Nostriano niche, so called because it's believed to be the burial place of Bishop Nostriano who welcomed San Gaudioso and his other African exiles. San Gaudioso was a bishop from Abitina, a village near Carthage. He fled North Africa during the Christian persecutions and arrived in Naples on a leaky boat. Among other things, he preserved the relics of several saints, notably Santa Restituta.

The basilica eventually flooded and mud covered it entirely for hundreds of years. In the 1600s Dominican monks dug up the church and turned it into a burial place. To respect their patrons, they created frescoes of the deceased, embedding their skulls, bones and spines into the walls. Today, faded images along the walls still show the deceased as they might have looked during their lifetime, wearing skirts and capes. Explanatory notes indicate the deceased's social status.

Beyond the wealthy crypts is an array of dirt-floor rooms with carved niches. In one room, a rectangular hole at the top of the ceiling indicates that the bodies were brought down by pulley. The bones were then broken so the corpse could be put into a tight foetal position, which was believed to help bring the dead back to the Father. The body was put inside the niche and, often three holes were punctured into the stomach, particularly if a family wanted this space for more than one of their loved ones. The stomach acids and other liquids in the body ran down and into the shelled out bottom of the niche, helping it decompose more quickly. Hence, they would "drain away."

GESÙ TI AMO E CONFIDO IN TE

Fontanelle Cemetery

The Cult of the Anime Pezzentelle

Evidence of the intriguing rituals of the *Anime Pezzentelle* or "Poor Souls", can be seen at the Fontenelle Cemetery and Santa Maria delle Anime del Purgatorio ad Arco. Despite best efforts by the church to eradicate the veneration of bones, it hasn't entirely disappeared from the Neapolitan scene. The 1870s saw the development of these devotions at the cemetery. Here the ritual included the selection of a *capuzzella* (skull), which was polished carefully and placed on an embroidered handkerchief with a rosary encircling it. Later, a lace trimmed cushion was substituted, small oil lamps lit, and flowers added.

The supplicant waited for the soul to be revealed to him or her in a dream. It was thought the soul needed some kind of refreshment: "*A refrische 'e ll'anime d'o priatorio*". If the skull seemed to sweat, that meant some success. The grace or favour sought might be the finding of a son missing in war, winning lottery numbers or a much-longed for pregnancy. If these were not forthcoming, Neapolitans made no bones about putting the pampered skull back in the general mass of remains and beginning the process anew. Many stories grew up about particular skulls, devotees imposing names and personalities onto their favourite skulls and, if things worked out well, giving them special stone or wooden boxes in which to repose; even a biscuit tin would do.

At Santa Maria delle Anime del Purgatorio ad Arco, there is a more focused devotion to the bones of an 18th-century bride but other skulls also receive daily offerings of flowers and candles.

CAVERN OF THE LOST SOULS: FONTANELLE CEMETERY

In the Sanità district, *O Campusanto de Funtanelle* for many years acted as a bridge to the afterlife where the living cared for the skulls of the departed according to the cult rituals of the *Anime Pezzentelle*. It has an atmosphere shot through with Gothic imagery as fetishistic bric-a-brac is draped upon thousands of bones.

The Sanità district once lay outside the Greco-Roman city and provided a burial place for pagans before Christian interments took over. The vast cavity, which was first a tuff rock quarry, **came into use as a burial ground for the excluded – the urban poor, victims of plague (at least 300,000 died in 1656), earthquake, insurrection, executions and cholera (1836 – 7)**. When the Bourbons razed many churches, the remains of Neapolitans came up to Le Fontanelle. In the late 18th century bodies might have been bundled into a sack at the dead of night and offloaded here. It's estimated that 40,000 rest in plain sight, but at least four more metres of human remains hide under the floor level.

At some time in the late 17th century a rushing torrent of rain washed much of the contents of the cemetery out into the streets, creating a scene of apocalyptic horror. Then followed the first attempt to put some order into the charnel house, stacking the skulls and bones. Father Gaetano Barbati continued this effort until, in 1872, the cult of devotion to the *Anime Pezzentelle*, became popular.

Step into any of the three huge trapezoidal cavities and the atmosphere will begin to work on you, whether in front of the headless but winged statue of San Vincenzo Ferreri (1350 – 1419) whose cloth robe moves with the breeze, or before the three crosses set in heaped skulls laced with cobwebs. For many years the cemetery was closed to the public, but now visitors can enter thanks to an overnight occupation by locals during May of the Monuments that got the attention of the municipal authorities.

SUBTERRANEAN APÉRITIF: MUSEO DEL SOTTOSUOLO

A nondescript, half-door opens to reveal a small lobby that welcomes guests to the newest addition to the Naples Underground. Here, bottles of the museum's labelled Aglianico wine - *Museo del Sottosuolo* - are on display along the back wall. Nearby, several flights of stairs take you 25 metres below to the underground. **It's a bit smaller than its counterparts, but what Museo del Sottosuolo lacks in space it makes up for in ingenuity**. *La Macchina del Tempo*, the Time Machine, runs the association's activities - one part educational, one part adventurous, and one part entertainment.

Mildly curious visitors can take the "classic tour", a trek through the ancient

Greco-Roman cisterns turned WWII air raid shelter. To illustrate how the Naples Underground has been used over the millennia, the association has set up re-creations of Greek and Roman tombs and *cantarelle*, seats upon which bodies were placed to drain of all liquids and decompose, like those found at the Catacombs of San Gaudioso.

The more intrepid can take the "adventure tour". Outfitted in gloves, a helmet with a headlight, and disposable overalls, you'll squeeze through the narrow passages of the three most important aqueduct systems that supplied water to the city. The most adventurous cavers will want to embark on the three-hour spelunking tour into the underground's hidden cavities. And for those in search of other kinds of 'cool', the association has opened a small wine bar in the underground, complete with a stage, where they host jazz concerts a few times a month.

PROGRESS PAVES THE WAY TO NAPLES' PAST: NEAPOLIS STATION

The core of the Naples Archaeological Museum's collections came from Herculaneum and Pompeii, vast excavations that began in the golden age of archaeology. This was a time when entire civilisations could be revealed in a matter of weeks whereas today archaeologists often have just a few pottery shards to show for months of scientific study and excavation. But every once in a while fortune intervenes; on this occasion fortune's name is progress. After years of delay, the project that has torn up just about every major piazza in the city is in full swing. And **the long awaited expansion of Naples' metro system that will propel the city into the future has serendipitously given us a bird's-eye view into its past**. As engineers tunnel their way through Naples' subterranean levels, archaeologists follow right behind them piecing together the history of every layer of the city, from the Neolithic period to the present day. In the process they have uncovered much more than a few pottery shards.

The route along the coast where the new Municipio, Toledo, University and Duomo stations are being constructed have unearthed extraordinary finds that have provided new insights into the ancient cities of Parthenope and Neapolis. Three 2nd century AD ships were unearthed near Municipio station. At the Duomo station archaeologists uncovered the remains of a 1st-century AD Isolympic Games Building Complex. A 7th-century warehouse complex was discovered near the University station. And this is just the beginning. Naples' metro system will do much more for the city than just improve transportation; it will help to rewrite the city's history. In 2005, the city opened Neapolis Station to display some of the findings from the Line 1 excavations, housing it very suitably beneath the Archaeological Museum in the Museo Metro stop. Finds shown here range from the 4th millennium BC (evidence of cultivated land preserved by volcanic ash) to Spanish Naples of the 15th to 17th centuries. Greek tableware and Roman architectural elements are on display, together with 3 scale models of the ships found at Municipio.

AN UNDERGROUND ART MOVEMENT: NAPLES' METRO ART STATIONS

The construction of the art stations by internationally-re-nowned architects has brought about the transformation of vast areas of the urban landscape. The new metro stations have turned the transit areas, or "dead areas" of public transport, into the setting for an ambitious cultural project with major names in contemporary art playing a starring role.

COMUNE DI NAPOLI

When the Toledo Metro Station opened in 2012, Britain's *Daily Telegraph* immediately hailed it as **the most impressive underground station in Europe** (the Materdei station took 16th place). In 2014, it topped CNN's 12 most impressive European subway station list as well. The station is just one of Naples' *Metro dell'Arte*, Metro Art Stations (14 and counting), a project that has transformed the city's transportation centres into contemporary art museums making art accessible to the general public and revitalising the areas around these stops on the line. The project came about between 2001 and 2002 on the heels of a number of initiatives that have been sweeping the city since the mid 1990s - a cultural renaissance that seems to have been sparked by the 1994 G7 summit in Naples.

Under the artistic direction of Achille Bonto Oliva - art critic, academic and curator, it is still under way. Thus far, nearly 200 major works by some 100 important contemporary artists have been installed inside and outside MetroNapoli's Line 1 and Line 6 stations. From its inception, the Metro Art project has been a stunning example of collaboration, engaging architects, designers and craftsmen and women from all over the world. From the earliest stations featuring the works of artists like Mimmo Paladino, Mimmo Jodice and Jannis Kounellis, to the newest stations with contributions by artists like William Kentridge and Michelangelo Pistoletto, for the price of a metro ticket - €1.30 as of this printing - you can explore them all.

Toledo Metro Station

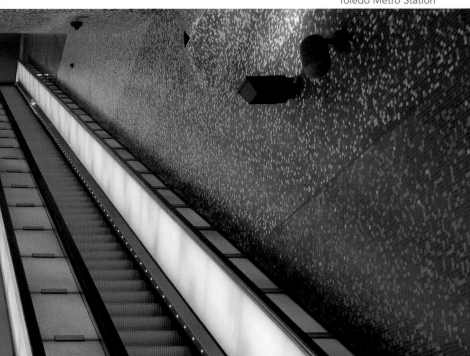

SPIRITED
SHE-APOLITANS
SIRENS, SYBILS, SAINTS & SOVEREIGNS

Cover Photo: Fountain of Parthenope
at Piazza Sannazzaro

Naples' history has been profoundly marked by **strong females**, both native Neapolitans and women who settled here.

Although the stereotype of Neapolitan women may be that they remain dedicated to domesticity and motherhood, sublimating their desires to those of a husband or family, the reality is that the public lives of Neapolitan women jump out at every corner. Back in the deep past there were the mythical women, the sirens, sibyls and goddesses and the hard-to-ignore behaviour of the only-too-real Poppaea, mistress then wife to an Emperor. At Pompeii, Eumachia was

one of the wealthiest patricians and a most generous patron. In politics and the arts, Naples has had its remarkable females, a queen who ruled in her own name in the 14th century, an artist who triumphed in the 17th, a passionate revolutionary just as the 19th began.

More recent years have seen Rosa Russo Iervolino's long tenure as mayor of Naples and conductor and choirmaster Stefania Rinaldi's remarkable career at the San Carlo opera house. Finally it is key, in this city where Catholicism is the bedrock of daily life, to acknowledge another aspect of the role of women in Neapolitan history. Naples has over fifty patron saints, at least twelve of whom are women. So many women played a role in the myth and the making of Naples; this chapter is a celebration of some of the She-apolitans who shaped the history of this region from ancient times to the modern era.

Palazzo Donn'Anna, Simonetta Capecchi

simo capecchi

THE ORIGINAL SHE-APOLITAN: PARTHENOPE

First you will come to the Sirens who enchant all who come near them. If any one unwarily draws in too close and hears the singing of the Sirens, his wife and children will never welcome him home again, for they sit in a green field and warble him to death with the sweetness of their song. There is a great heap of dead men's bones lying all around, with the flesh still rotting off them. Therefore pass these Sirens by, and stop your men's ears with wax that none of them may hear; but if you like you can listen yourself, for you may get the men to bind you as you stand upright on a cross-piece half way up the mast, and they must lash the rope's ends to the mast itself, that you may have the pleasure of listening. If you beg and pray the men to unloose you, then they must bind you faster.

HOMER, THE ODYSSEY

According to myth, Naples traces its origins back to a siren named Parthenope who lived in the Tyrrhenian Sea with her sisters Ligeia and Leucosia. She is the original She-apolitan; the legend of her beauty and seductiveness, with all its attendant drama and danger, lingers still. Her spirit lives on in the Neapolitan people.

The daughters of Melpomene, (the Muse of Tragedy), and of the River God Achelous, the sirens were portrayed on Greek vases as birds with human faces. The Roman poet Ovid tells us in his *Metamorphoses* that the sirens were companions to Zeus' daughter Persephone. When she was abducted by Hades, the sirens begged for wings to search for her. Demeter granted their wish, giving them sticks for legs and wings, yet letting them retain their female faces and human voices. Interestingly, the Italian word *sirena* does not mean siren or bird, but "mermaid" – a creature of the sea. The siren sisters haunted the shores of Campania. Perhaps they still do? Their voices, weapons of seduction, lured unsuspecting sailors to their deaths. Eventually, of course, word got around and one savvy sailor, Ulysses, devised a plan to withstand their wiles. Parthenope was so devastated by her failed attempt to lure Ulysses that she leapt into the sea and drowned. Her body washed ashore on Isolotto di Megaride, the tiny island that is now home to Castel dell'Ovo, where it is said that Greek sailors found her, buried her and named their first settlement in her honour.

♪♪♪♪♪♪ PLACES TO SEE ♪♪♪♪♪♪

- **FONTANA DI PARTENOPE** – a 19th-century fountain at Piazza Sannazzaro in Mergellina. It was originally designed for the Central Train Station.

- **FONTANA DELLA SPINACORONA** - sculpted in the 16th century for the Santa Caterina della Spina Corona church, it depicts the siren extinguishing the flames of Vesuvius with water that flows from her breast. The original was moved to the San Martino Charterhouse in the 19th century and a copy now stands in its place at the church. The original will finally be on display to the public in Fall 2014, when San Martino's new "Gothic Underground" section is scheduled to open.

- **CITY HALL, PALAZZO SAN GIOCAMO** - inside is a bust of Parthenope known as *'a capa 'e Napule'*. The provenance of this late Hellenistic style bust is unknown, but it was placed in the City Hall by Achille Lauro, Mayor of Naples from 1952 – 1957.

- **CENTRAL TRAIN STATION** - a fountain with Parthenope at its centre illuminated by a skylight greets visitors to Napoli at the Central Train Station near track 24.

- **PIAZZA MERCATO** – scene of the executions resulting from the short lived Parthenopean Republic (Jan - Jun 1799).

- **THE PARTHENOPE UNIVERSITY OF NAPLES** - main campus across the street from Porto Molo Beverello.

- **THE PARTHENOPE ASTEROID** - the siren is even commemorated in an asteroid - the Parthenope Asteroid named by Annibale de Gasparis in 1850, director of the Astronomical Observatory of Capodimonte (1864 - 1889).

Spina Corona Fountain

THE CRAZED FORTUNE TELLERS: THE SIBYLS

The sibyl of Cuma foretold wars and wrote her oracles on oak leaves which scattered in the wind, but which she refused to help her listeners re-assemble. Sibyls were known for their trance-like states and shuddering voices and were sufficiently important characters in mythology for Michelangelo to paint five of them on the Sistine Chapel ceiling. Here the Cumaean Sibyl is depicted as a dark-complexioned woman with wrinkles and a muscular build; she reads a large manuscript, perhaps the Sibylline books.

The 14th-century humanist, Giovanni Boccaccio, in his *Famous Women*, described a sibyl maiden called Almathea or Deiphebe. He claimed this virgin had a sanctuary near Lago Averno where she made many predictions. Boccaccio derived this legend from the Roman writer, Varro (116 BC – 27 BC), who composed a compendium of knowledge about the sibyls. Varro wrote that the Cumaean Sibyl journeyed to Rome with nine Sibylline books, which she wanted to sell to the Etruscan Emperor of Rome, Tarquinius Priscus. When the Emperor refused her price, she burned three in his presence. Back she came on the morrow to burn another three until he paid the full price for the remaining three books. He acquiesced because the books contained the entire destiny of Rome.

Roman writer Ovid also mentioned the Cumaean Sibyl in his *Metamorphoses*. Here she spoke in her own voice, explaining that she was not a goddess, but a mortal woman who asked Apollo that she remain a virgin and gain eternal life. Apollo granted her eternal life, but forgot to add eternal youth. As a consequence, she lived for seven hundred years, all the while shrivelling until only her voice was left. Pausanias, the Greek traveller and geographer of the 2nd century AD reinforced Ovid's myth saying that the temple guides at Cuma showed him a stone water-jug (*hydria*) of small size in which, they said, lay the bones of the sibyl. This was considered proof that before her death, the sibyl had shrunk to tiny dimensions. Petronius also told a folktale that she hung in an ampoule (a small bottle) in Cuma, longing, but unable, to die.

The highest respect to the sibyl was accorded by the Roman poet Virgil. In his fourth book of the *Eclogues* he mentioned her as having foretold the coming of Christ. Virgil also described the sibyl in *The Aeneid* when his character landed at Cuma. He wrote:

> *...her face was transfigured, her colour changed, her hair fell in disorder about her head and she stood there with heaving breast and her wild heart bursting in ecstasy. She seemed to grow in stature and speak as no mortal had ever spoken...*

Of course, whatever the source, any wise women with sibyl tendencies are so far in the past that all that remains to us is a tantalising blend of myth, fiction and history and the only place to commune with a sibyl these days is at Cuma in the Campi Flegrei.

MOTHER AND DAUGHTER: 2 AGRIPPINAS, 1 POPPAEA

Agrippina the Elder (14 BC - 33 AD) was the granddaughter of Augustus, mother of Caligula and grandmother of Nero. She had nine children but nonetheless accompanied her husband, Germanicus, on military campaigns, earning high respect from the Roman citizens who saw her as a heroic woman, wife and mother. But after the death of her husband, Emperor Tiberius banished her to an island off the coast of the Campania region. When she died, so the story goes, Caligula brought her ashes back to Rome.

Agrippina the Younger (15 or 16 - 59 AD) was the elder Agrippina's daughter and the mother of Emperor Nero. She was renowned for her sexual escapades and ruthless will to power. While her brother Caligula was still Emperor, it is said that he would hold lavish banquets and commit incest with his sisters, including Agrippina herself. Then, Agrippina, her sister Livilla and their maternal cousin Lepidus, who were all lovers, tried to kill Caligula. It's complicated. For that, Agrippina was exiled. When Caligula was murdered in 41 AD, Agrippina's uncle, the new Emperor Claudius, brought her back to Rome. She quickly married a second husband, Crispus. (Her first, Domitius, whom she had married on Tiberius' orders, was the father of Nero.) When Crispus died, rumours flew that she'd poisoned her own husband to gain his estate. And indeed, she became very wealthy. Thereafter, she became mistress to one of Emperor Claudius' advisers and through him arranged to get herself married to the Emperor himself, her motive: to put her son Nero on the throne. She succeeded. Once married to her uncle Claudius, she ordered a series of murders to rid herself of her many political rivals. Then, after Claudius had adopted Nero as his son, the Emperor died and not surprisingly it was assumed that Agrippina had poisoned him too. Nero took the throne and Agrippina tried her best to control him and indeed the Empire, but Nero had other plans, sending his mother away to Misenum. Thereafter, he tried to kill his mother several times, without success. Three poisonings failed, likewise attempts to drown and crush her. Perhaps the simplest methods work best; he finally succeeded when he sent assassins to stab her. The Roman historian Tacitus wrote that just before the assassins managed to kill her, Agrippina shouted, "Smite my womb!". Some sources, including Tacitus, claim that his murderous urge was encouraged by his lover, Poppaea Sabina.

Poppaea (30 - 65 AD) was another lady with an interesting reputation: cruel, bisexual, fond of milk baths with her female servants. She was born in Pompeii; her mother committed suicide when Poppaea was 17. At the age of 14 she married

Rufrius Crispinus, an Egyptian and leader of the Praetorian Guard (the military group that assisted emperors in their campaigns). But Poppaea divorced him and married Otho, a good friend of Nero's. It was a short path from there to becoming the emperor's favourite mistress. It was she who pressured Nero to divorce and then to execute his wife, Claudia Octavia. She bore Nero a daughter, who died at 4 months of age; 2 years later, while she was pregnant with their second child, Nero kicked her in a fit of rage, and she died. Tacitus records the fact that some thought her husband had poisoned her, for all his praise of her virtues and beauty at her funeral. The historian dismisses this idea, but slips in this barb.

> *Publicly Poppaea's death was mourned. But those who remembered her immorality and cruelty welcomed it...*
> TACITUS

PLACES TO SEE

- **TOMB OF AGRIPPINA IN BACOLI** – though tradition associates these stones with Agrippina the Younger, archaeologists do rather ruin the myth, stating that they were part of a Roman *odeon* (theatre).

- **THE ARCHAEOLOGICAL MUSEUM** - displays two statues which acquired Agrippina connections. One is a bust once thought to be a portrait of the Elder Agrippina, but which is probably just another Julio-Claudian princess. The second, the 'Seated Agrippina' – is a Roman copy of a Greek original composition that (in the original) would have represented Aphrodite. Here she bears the head of an unknown woman, but past scholars linked her to Agrippina the Younger.

- **POMPEII** – the "so-called" House of Menander where Poppaea may have lived.

Seated Agrippina

THE AFRICAN BONES: SANTA RESTITUTA

Information is sketchy about the life of Santa Restituta. She was born in North Africa near Carthage and was martyred in either 255 or 304 AD. The latter date would place her death among those of the Diocletian Persecutions. In that year a large number of Christians gathered in the city of Abitina to celebrate the Eucharist. Fifty of them were caught, arrested and dragged in chains to Carthage. There they were sentenced to death for the crime of Christianity. Although some believe that San Gaudioso brought her remains to Naples, legend has it that Santa Restituta was tortured and then placed in a blazing boat, where her body was left unharmed by the fire. Her boat landed on the shores of Ischia where a Christian woman named Lucina found the incorrupt body of Restituta, who was now dead. The Festival of Santa Restituta continues to be celebrated on the island of Ischia every May, and a sanctuary was built there in her honour. Traditionally, during the festival young women of marriageable age present young men with an egg painted in red – an Easter token. The lads respond by accompanying their young ladies to the celebrations. *Pare Santa Restituta* (she looks like Santa Restituta) is an island saying of anyone who appears overladen with jewellery – a reference to the lavish decoration heaped upon the saint's statue when it is carried in procession.

ƎƎƎƎƎƎ PLACES TO SEE ᖆᖆᖆᖆᖆᖆ

- **BASILICA SANTA RESTITUTA IN THE DUOMO**

  - It was the first cathedral built in Naples by Constantine I in the 4th century and was renamed in Santa Restituta's honour in the 5th.

  - *Madonna and Child between San Gennaro and Santa Restituta*, mosaic by Lello da Orvieto (1322), Chapel of the Madonna del Principio.

  - *Santa Restituta's body carried by angels in a boat to Ischia*, Luca Giordano, frescoed ceiling of the nave.

  - *Virgin and Archangel Michael with Santa Restituta*, Silvestro de' Buoni, behind the altar.

- **DIOCESAN MUSEUM** - reliquary bust of Santa Restituta that came from the Basilica of Santa Restituta.

- **ISCHIA** - the island where Restituta is the patron saint.

  - Santuario Santa Restituta, Lacco Ameno.

  - The Festival of Santa Restituta – 16th - 18th May, especially the procession on the saint's nameday on 17th.

A WEEKLY MIRACLE: SANTA PATRIZIA

Santa Patrizia of Constantinople (died ca. 655 AD) is one of the patroness saints of Naples. Her blood liquefies every August 25th - her feast day - and each and every Tuesday morning after the 9.30 a.m. mass at the San Gregorio Armeno Church. Santa Patrizia's waxed-coated remains as well as a tooth lie inside a coffin at a side altar. During the Tuesday mass, the vial of her blood is hung to the left of the front altar and covered with a cloth. After the Eucharist the priest lifts her blood from the hook, brings it to the middle of the altar and worshippers stand in a line to kiss the receptacle. Inside it, one opaque vial appears to contain a dark, syrupy liquid.

What little we know about Santa Patrizia comes from an oral tradition. She was born in the 7th century AD, a member of a noble Constantinople family and a descendant of Constantine the Great. Yearning for a life of celibacy, she fled to Rome to avoid an arranged marriage. When her father died, Santa Patrizia returned to Constantinople and distributed all her inherited wealth to the poor. On her way back to Rome, a furious storm drove her vessel to the Bay of Naples, and she took shelter at a small convent on the Island of Megaride. She decided to establish a prayer community in Naples with her friends and spent her life helping the needy of the city until her death around 665 AD. Legend has it that her body had already been venerated for several centuries when an over-devout knight plucked out her tooth. Out flowed blood from the empty cavity. Calling it a miracle, nuns preserved some of this blood in two bulbous vials. At San Gregorio Armeno today, the "Sisters of Santa Patrizia" help with the mass, take care of the cloister, and continue to venerate her remains. A large number of these nuns come from the Philippines.

DYNASTIC DISCORD: JOANNA I

Queen Joanna I (1326 - 1382) was the granddaughter of Robert the Wise, King of Naples. Orphaned at the age of five, married at the age of eight, crowned Queen of Naples at sixteen, her life was played out against the lively dynastic and papal conflicts of her age. She lived most of her life at the Castel Nuovo. Despite the multiple troubles that swept in upon her, Joanna's reign was marked by her close attention to government, her patronage in the fields of architecture and litera-ture and her promotion of health care provisions for the poor. Joanna married four times and had three children who died in infancy. When her first husband, Andrew, her Hungarian cousin, was killed in a conspiracy of nobles, rumours flew that she was complicit in the plot. Her next choice of husband, her Taranto cousin Louis, brought down the wrath of her Hungarian family upon her. They invaded the city. While Joanna retreated to France, Neapolitans rioted sufficiently to send the invaders packing, allowing her to return to marry Louis. Alas, the marriage was not a happy union and there may just have been some relief when Louis succumbed to the Black Death.

As with other female rulers of her age, it was easy to fling scandal at the young queen. The rumour ran, for example, that Joanna opened a brothel in Avignon for the nobility of Europe. In fact it was there that she had stood trial in the city in 1348 for the murder of Andrew and been acquitted.

Re-marriage beckoned. Husband number three was James III of Majorca, but the Queen soon realised his mind was unbalanced. In a letter to the Pope, she recounted how in front of the court James had beaten her and called her a whore. Three years later, James also died. Lastly, Joanna married Otto of Brunswick, a German warrior. The couple enjoyed some happiness, but papal intrigue brought them down. When Urban VI, a Neapolitan, became Pope his irrational behaviour so provoked the cardinals that half of them launched a "Great Schism", a split in the Church. They elected their own Pope, Clement VII (of French origin), claiming Urban VI had been unlawfully elected. Joanna found herself in a political hornet's nest. With relations with Rome in extremis, Joanna came down on the side of Clement. Pope Urban excommunicated her and declared her kingdom forfeit, naming her niece's husband, Charles of Durazzo, as king. Worse yet, when Neapolitans found out their Queen had acknowledged a French Pope, they rebelled, trapping Joanna inside the Castel Nuovo. Charles, with Hungarian support, took advantage of the situation and invaded and although her husband launched an attack, he was captured and imprisoned.

As for Joanna, she surrendered and was sent to the fortress of San Fele. The following summer, on Charles's orders, she was smothered; after public display in Naples, her body was dumped in the well within the Santa Chiara Cloister. Today it's difficult to get exact information as to where she lies.

ꙅꙅꙅꙅꙅꙅ PLACES TO SEE ꙅꙅꙅꙅꙅꙅ

- **CASTEL NUOVO** – where Joanna I grew up and lived much of her life.

- **SANTA CHIARA** - where her remains are said to lie and where her father, Charles, Duke of Calabria and grandfather, Robert the Wise are buried.

- **SANTA MARIA DELL'INCORONATA** - built by the Queen to house a spine from the thorny crown of Christ.

- **SAN MARTINO CHARTERHOUSE** - completed under Joanna I's reign in 1368.

- **THE SUMMER CASTLE IN AVERSA** - where her first husband was murdered, now a police station.

SCANDAL IN POSILLIPO: JOANNA II AND ANNA CARAFA

Queen Joanna II (1373 - 1435) lived in troubled times. Her series of court favourites and lovers was embroidered in the popular mind into a story that she sent servants onto the streets of Naples seeking the handsomest fellows for her bed. These men, having satisfied the queen's needs, were then thrown to sea monsters, or even an African crocodile, in some dark recess of the Castel Nuovo. She lived at the Castel Capuano and her amorous activities allegedly extended to the Villa Sirena in Posillipo.

Two hundred years after Joanna's death, Princess Anna Carafa (1607 – 1644) inherited this villa and ordered the architect Cosimo Fanzago to renovate it. Lavish parties ensued. Matilde Serao in her book about the legends of Naples tells how Anna Carafa competed with her niece Mercede de la Torre for the love of another man. There was a fight one night, after which Mercede was never seen again. It is said that Mercede's ghost haunts the villa, now named Palazzo Donn'Anna. Cosimo Fanzago would never complete his renovations of the palace. Instead, Anna's husband, a Spanish viceroy, returned to Spain while Anna remained in Naples taking up residence in a villa in Portici and dying a lonely woman.

۶۶۶۶۶۶ PLACES TO SEE ۶۶۶۶۶۶

- CASTEL CAPUANO – where Joanna II lived.

- CASTEL NUOVO - where Joanna II is said to have disposed of her lovers with the help of a crocodile.

- BASILICA DELL'ANNUNZIATA MAGGIORE - where Joanna II is buried.

- SAN GIOVANNI A CARBONARA - holds the tomb she commissioned for her brother, King Ladislaus the Magnanimous, as well as the tomb of one of her lovers, the Grand Seneschal Sergianni Caracciolo.

- THE ISLAND OF NISIDA - where tradition says the current young offenders' prison had its origins in her favourite villa, later converted into a fort.

- PALAZZO DONN'ANNA - where Joanna II brought her lovers and where later Anna Carafa lived.

A LIFE LIVED IN CHIAROSCURO: ARTEMISIA GENTILESCHI

Artemisia Gentileschi (1593 - ca. 1656) is regarded as one of the finest artists of the Italian Baroque, belonging to that generation that followed Caravaggio's ground-breaking work in chiaroscuro and dramatic composition. She was trained by her father Orazio and met critical success in Rome, Florence, Naples and London. Her career was coloured and informed by her rape at age 19 by her art tutor Agostino Tassi; the protagonists of her paintings were often powerful, not to mention vengeful, women. Roberto Longhi, the Italian art critic, pointed out in 1916 that 94% of her known works depicted women as protagonists or at least equals to men.

Having run up high debts with her husband in Florence and then separated from him, Gentileschi moved to Naples in about the year 1630. She hated the city "because of the fighting, and because of the hard life and the high cost of living," and yet Gentileschi would spend much of the next twenty-six years of her life there and both of her daughters would marry there. At that time, Naples was the largest city in southern Europe (three times the size of Rome) and the second largest city in Europe after Paris. Having established an excellent reputation for herself in northern Italy, Gentileschi found more abundant art commissions in the South, at a time when it was unusual and difficult for a female artist to obtain success at all.

Gentileschi's historic reputation has been enhanced by a feminist reading of her oeuvre in recent decades, but fortunately the quality and scope of her painterly output holds up under critical scrutiny on any terms.

ꙭꙭꙭꙭꙭꙭ PLACES TO SEE ꙮꙮꙮꙮꙮꙮ

- CAPODIMONTE MUSEUM – *Judith Slaying Holofernes*, *The Annunciation*, and *Lucretia* in Room 87 (when not on tour).

- PALAZZO REALE - *San Gennaro in the Pozzuoli Amphitheatre* (1636 - 37) and *The Saints Procolus and Nicea* (1635 - 37) in the Queen's Room.

SAINT OF MOTHERHOOD: MARIA FRANCESCA OF THE FIVE WOUNDS

In the heart of the Spanish Quarter is a wooden armchair revered by many Neapolitan women. You can find it in the former home of Anna Maria Gallo (1715 - 1791), the only Neapolitan woman canonised by the Catholic Church - the 'Saint of Motherhood'. She was born into an artisan family in the Spanish Quarter of Naples. Her father, a violent man, wanted her to marry well but Anna refused, asking instead to become a nun in a strict order that would allow her to pursue the religious life while living at home. Eventually her father relented and she took her vows as Sister Maria Francesca delle Cinque Piaghe "of the Five Wounds", beginning a life of charitable works and prayer, dressed in the habit of the Franciscan 3rd order. So intense was her prayer that she apparently manifested the signs of Christ's wounds, the stigmata. Her second home was shared with another sister under the protection of a priest and it is this apartment that her devoted followers visit today. Her original burial place was the church of Santa Lucia al Monte but in 2001 her remains were removed to the apartment where a shrine and a small museum had been created to receive them. She had been beatified in 1843 and canonised in 1867, when Pope Pious IX declared her to be a patroness saint of both pregnant and infertile women. So this is how her simple wooden armchair came to be a place of pilgrimage for mothers and those wishing to conceive. In this most devout of districts, this saint of motherhood continues to draw hundreds of women to her erstwhile home.

THE END OF ABSOLUTISM: MARIA CAROLINE

Maria Caroline (1752 - 1814) was born in Vienna. In 1768, age 16, she married Bourbon King Ferdinand IV of Naples (later I of the Two Sicilies) and cried all the way down to her new city, believing that Neapolitan marriages were unlucky. The first time she laid eyes on Ferdinand, she thought him very ugly; king Ferdinand, in turn, said of his new bride: "She sleeps like the dead and sweats like a pig". However, Caroline knew her dynastic duty and together they produced eighteen children, seven of whom survived to adulthood. Their court would divide its time between the Royal Palaces at Caserta and Naples.

Ferdinand spoke Neapolitan, loved nothing better than hunting, and often sold his freshly-caught fish on the streets among the *lazzaroni*. He was a practical joker and impervious to higher learning; Maria Caroline was therefore able to assume the reins of day-to-day rule with ease once the birth of an heir in 1775 confirmed her position. It was then she was admitted to the Privy Council. She built up the navy with the help of her English favourite, John Acton, nurtured the silk-weav-

Santa Maria Francesca delle Cinque Piaghe, Simonetta Capecchi

"YOUR FIRST TIME HERE? FOR YOURSELF OR YOUR FAMILY?"

A fragment of bone and lock of hair from the saint.

The saint's chair of pain. Here she received
the stigmata from Christ's passion.

ing colony of San Leucio, was instrumental in bringing the Farnese collection to Naples, patronised artists such as Angelica Kauffman and was for a time an enthusiastic supporter of the Freemasons.

As events in France took a revolutionary turn in the 1780s, fearing that the contagion would spread to Naples, Maria Caroline abandoned her policy of enlightened absolutism and turned the city into a police state. The army was kept perpetually mobilised, which caused taxes to be raised. She set up a spy network as well as a secret police force and sub-divided Naples into police wards under government-appointed commissioners, replacing the system of aldermen elected by the people. The queen, however, couldn't stem the tide of revolution. The news from Paris in 1793 was grim; her favourite sister, Marie Antoinette, queen of France, had been beheaded. The next few years would see Naples engaged in coalitions with Great Britain, Russia, Austria, Prussia, Spain, Portugal and Savoy-Sardinia ranged against their common enemy, France. Napoleon would conquer Naples and place his relatives on its throne. Maria Caroline and Ferdinand had to endure more than one exile. By 1812 Ferdinand effectively abdicated and the next year Maria Caroline, deprived of further influence over political events, travelled home to Austria where she died in 1814. Ferdinand was restored once more to the throne in 1815, merging the kingdoms of Sicily and Naples the following year; he ruled till his death in 1825.

﹌﹌﹌ PLACES TO SEE ﹌﹌﹌

- PALAZZO REALE – the Teatrino di Corte built in 1768 for Maria Caroline's wedding to Ferdinand and one of her revolving lecterns. A second lectern is at the National Library.

- CAPODIMONTE MUSEUM - Angelica Kauffman's painting of Ferdinand, Maria Caroline and their family.

- CASERTA ROYAL PALACE - the queen's apartments and a portrait of her in the art gallery.

ATTITUDES: EMMA HAMILTON

A close confidante of Queen Maria Caroline, beautiful, English-born Lady Hamilton (1765 - 1815) started out as a housemaid who tried her hand at acting and ended up having several rich lovers. Though she was tricked by one of those lovers into being the companion of his uncle, Sir William Hamilton, the British Envoy to Naples, the couple got on so well they married in 1791. Together they entertained guests from all over Europe. Emma developed a form of entertainment called Attitudes in which people had to guess the names of famous characters (such as Medea and Cleopatra) that she portrayed. For her performances, she wore Neapolitan peasant dress; she also created new styles of dance and fashion which women rushed to emulate. Many portraits were painted of her, including one by George Romney. Through her husband, Emma became a close friend of Queen Maria Caroline and she even advised the Queen during the Parthenopean Revolution. Emma began an affair with Horatio Nelson, the famous English naval hero, when he came to live in Naples, a relationship tolerated by Sir William.

Shortly after the Parthenopean Revolution in 1799, Nelson was recalled to England. Sir William and Lady Hamilton left with him, never to return to Naples. Her husband died in 1803 while her lover Nelson died at the Battle of Trafalgar in 1805, leaving instructions to the nation for the care of his mistress and his young daughter Horatia – instructions that were not honoured. Emma's life spiralled downwards. She spent a year in debtor's prison and fled to France where she eventually died a lonely alcoholic in abject poverty.

ᒫᒫᒫᒫᒫᒫ PLACES TO SEE ᕫᕫᕫᕫᕫᕫ

- PALAZZO SESSA – in the Monte di Dio district - where the couple collected paintings, ancient Greek vases, and samples of minerals. Much of the collection of ceramics formed the nucleus of the British Museum's collection and images derived from them for Josiah Wedgwood's new porcelain manufactory were soon all the rage in England.

- VILLA ANGELICA - in Portici - where Sir William conducted his extensive research in vulcanology and lived during the spring and autumn.

- VILLA EMMA - in Posillipo - was a summer home where the couple enjoyed sea-bathing and a view of Vesuvius.

THE REVOLUTIONARY: ELEONORA FONSECA PIMENTEL

On August 20th 1799 Eleonora Fonseca Pimentel was hanged in Piazza Mercato - her alleged crime was writing pamphlets denouncing the Bourbon Queen Maria Caroline for lesbianism. She calmly stepped up to the gallows and quoted Virgil: "Perhaps one day this will be worth remembering".

Eleonora was born in Rome in 1752 of a noble Portuguese family and moved with them to Naples when she was nine years old. She learned Greek and Latin and by the age of sixteen she published a nuptial hymn written for the marriage of King Ferdinand IV (I of the Two Sicilies) to Queen Maria Caroline, celebrating the accomplishments of the Bourbon dynasty. Her talents catapulted her into the intellectual circles of Naples, where she wrote sonnets, cantatas and oratorios. She married the Marquis Fonseca, but the union was a disaster as she suffered violence and mental cruelty at his hands. After they separated Eleonora thrust herself into the ideals of the French Revolution, becoming a Jacobin. The Jacobins fought against royalist forces in the city in 1799 and won. They proclaimed the Parthenopean Republic at the San Martino Charterhouse and created a government modelled along French lines, citing liberty and equality for all. The republic, however, survived a mere five months.

Eleonora fought for Jacobin ideals through her writings. She translated books and articles into the Neapolitan dialect, hoping to incite the staunchly pro-monarchist *lazzaroni* to overthrow the King. She also wrote for more than thirty issues of the newspaper *Monitore Napoletano*, the mouthpiece of the Parthenopean Republic. But the Republic had many problems and the Bourbon monarchy soon wrested back control of the city. Eleonora was one of many Jacobins who were executed at that time. The young Duke of Cassano, whom she'd known in her days of heady literary success, also perished on the scaffold.

ƎƎƎƎƎƎ PLACES TO SEE ᘃᘃᘃᘃᘃᘃ

- **THREE COMMEMORATIVE PLAQUES** – one at Largo San Martino (between the Castel Sant'Elmo and the San Martino Charterhouse) in memory of the Parthenopean Republic; another across the street from the Santa Chiara Cloister is dedicated to Eleonora while a third on Salita Sant'Anna di Palazzo (opposite pizzeria Brandi) marks the address thought to be her last residence and where she wrote her incendiary *Monitore* articles. Documentary evidence however places her apartment not far away at Via Santa Teresella degli Spagnoli, number 46.

- **CHIESA DI SANT'ANNA DI PALAZZO** - where Eleonora Fonseca Pimentel married and where her infant son is buried.

- **PALAZZO SERRA DI CASSANO ON MONTE DI DIO** - (now the Italian Institute for Philosophical Studies), where her success as a poet and lyricist gave her an entrée into the best society. When the Duke of Cassano was executed alongside Eleonora in 1799, his father shut up one of the two grand entrances to his palazzo in protest. It remains closed.

- **EXECUTION SQUARE** - now Piazza Mercato, it is a few blocks from the port. Other notables executed in Piazza Mercato include King Corradino (1268) and the popular revolutionary Masaniello (1647).

THE GAMBLING MEZZOSOPRANO: ISABELLA COLBRAN

On stage, Isabella Colbran (1785 - 1845) radiated majesty; off-stage, it was said, she had as much dignity as a milliner's assistant. A native of Madrid, she studied under Girolamo Crescenti in Paris and by the age of 20 was known throughout Europe for her velvety mezzo-soprano voice. She took her talent to Naples, a city known as the capital of European music during the 18th and 19th centuries. There the opulent Bourbon dynasty had assumed power and built the Teatro San Carlo, which quickly became the place every opera singer wanted to be, including the famous castrato Farinelli.

When Isabella Colbran arrived in Naples, she became the lover of the theatre's impresario, Domenico Barbaja. Barbaja, a coffee-shop owner from Milan with a knack for business, ran the theatre alongside a raft of gaming parlours in northern Italy – the probable cause of Colbran's lifelong gambling addiction. Barbaja commissioned Gioachino Rossini (*Barber of Seville*) to work in Naples on contract for seven years. Rossini quickly fell in love with Colbran, composing at least ten operas with her voice in mind. The threesome worked together until 1822 when Rossini and Colbran left for Bologna, where they married. Barbaja wasn't invited.

Sadly Colbran's marriage would be a failure. Rossini was 30 and his career about to take off, while Colbran was 37, her waning voice sounding the death knell of her career. While in 1824 she still played the starring role in Rossini's *Semiramide* in London, commanding the high sum of £1,500, but the critics began to pan her performances with such zeal that three years later, at the age of 42, her career was over. While Rossini continued to travel and work throughout Europe, taking on a mistress in Paris, Colbran mostly remained at her deceased father's estate in Castenaso near Bologna. Her health continued to deteriorate thanks to the gonorrhoea she contracted from her husband. She also began to sell off whatever she could of her estate to support an ever more acute gambling addiction. She died in 1845, aged 60, purportedly murmuring Rossini's name.

MEDIUM OR TRICKSTER: EUSAPIA PALLADINO

Illusionist, medium, levitator and trickster, Eusapia Palladino (1854 - 1918) lived in an epoch determined to prove the supernatural through science. To that end, all manner of scientists and writers, including Pierre and Marie Curie as well as Arthur Conan Doyle, sought out Eusapia – and paid her exorbitant fees – for the sake of finding an answer to the impassioned question of the time: Was she a fraud? Palladino was born in a mountain village near Bari. When she was orphaned at the age of 12 she was taken in by a family from her village that had transferred to Naples. The family at that time held regular séances, not at all unusual when Spiritualism was so popular. When Eusapia was invited to join these séances, objects took on a new life: tables rose up, chairs danced, glasses clinked and bells rang. Soon the family invited their friends to witness her tricks. But these gifts also tormented her - Palladino saw ghosts staring at her. She said her clothes and bed-covers would be stripped from her in the middle of the night.

Palladino married twice, the first time to a conjuror. Her second marriage was to a Neapolitan merchant whom Palladino helped in his shop; evenings were devoted to conducting séances. In 1888 Palladino first made headlines when a Professor Ercole Chiaia of Naples wrote an open letter to eminent scientist and spirit-doubter, Cesare Lombroso. Describing Palladino, he said she was:

> ...an invalid woman who belongs to the humblest class of society. She is nearly thirty years old [actually thirty-four] and very ignorant; her appearance is neither fascinating nor endowed with the power which modern criminologists call irresistible; but when she wishes, be it day or by night, she can divert a curious group for an hour or so with the most surprising phenomena.

Thus Palladino was pushed into the limelight, with respected intellectuals asking her to display her skills. She was invited to Warsaw, Vienna, Munich, Cambridge and St. Petersburg; she even displayed her skills convincingly in front of Pierre and Marie Curie in Paris. But many intellectuals also caught Palladino cheating. Whenever she did resort to tricks, her clients complained bitterly about her high fees and Palladino would blame her cheating on the pressure to perform. Her downfall came during a trip to Harvard University in 1909. There, an eminent psychologist observed her séances and found her to be a fraud. From this moment on, her international popularity waned and she fell into obscurity. Folklore has it that Palladino held her séances at a hotel in Piazza Garibaldi, but the hotel is no longer standing. She died in 1918 of unknown causes a few blocks away in an apartment on Via Benedetto Cairoli.

THE AUDACIOUS JOURNALIST: MATILDE SERAO

The Greco-Italian writer Matilde Serao (1856 - 1927) wrote twenty-nine novels and is best known for having founded the daily Neapolitan newspaper *Il Mattino*, still the most widely read daily of southern Italy. At the age of 26, Matilde left Naples to "conquer Rome". There, she wrote everything from literary criticism to gossip. It was there too that she met writer Eduardo Scarfoglio and the two were married in 1885. Their union was both romantic and professional as they established a short lived newspaper called *Corriere di Roma*. Finding themselves in serious financial difficulties, however, they took up an offer from the owner of the Neapolitan *Corriere del Mattino* who promised to pay their debts if they came to Naples and wrote for his publication. They worked for the *Corriere* for many years, until their private life went public. Eduardo began an affair with a singer and actress and two years later, his mistress became pregnant. When Eduardo refused to leave Matilde, his lover became so incensed that in 1894 she placed their daughter at Eduardo's door step and fired a pistol. While the scandal was at first suppressed, eventually the *Corriere di Napoli* broke the story. A week later, Eduardo's lover died in the hospital and Matilde began to take care of the little girl, Paulina. Although Eduardo and Matilde continued to live together, eventually Matilde couldn't take his philandering and they separated.

Her popularity as a novelist was already well assured long before this scandal when she wrote *Il Ventre di Napoli* (1884), a realistic portrayal of life in Naples, which criticised the government for its handling of the cholera epidemic and documented the appalling living conditions of the poor. Despite her own powerhouse activities, Serao was ardently opposed to giving women the right to vote. Her early fiction, including *Cuore infermo* (1881) and *Fantasia* (1883), explored her dissatisfaction with heterosexual relationships and seemed to say that more fulfilling relationships might be found between women. Matilde Serao died in 1927 of a heart attack seated at her writing desk.

THE PASSIONATE GARDENER: SUSANA WALTON

La Mortella is a garden on the island of Ischia, the result of a love affair. Look around you; you are in the presence of passion – the mutual passion of a English composer and a beautiful Argentinian woman, his for a place to inspire music, hers for ravishing and exotic flora.

Susana Gil Passo (1926 - 2010) was 22 when she met the 46 year old William Walton at a British Council press conference in Buenos Aires – he proposed immediately. Only a fortnight later she accepted and despite the doubts of her family and of Walton's friends they married within two months and moved to Italy. On Ischia the couple engaged landscape architect Russell Page to design a garden imposed upon volcanic rock – but it was to be Susana who laboured for fifty years to create La Mortella, planting, researching and interpreting the site. Sir William died in 1983; since then, a foundation in his name has promoted musical education for the young and the preservation of La Mortella, which opened to the public for the first time in 1992. Concerts are held in the hall and the Grecian-style amphitheatre and many visitors flock to see the wonders of this earthly paradise where the orchids, ferns and camellias are a living legacy of one couple's intense feeling not only for each other, but for their island home of Ischia.

La Mortella

GLAMOUR PERSONIFIED: SOPHIA LOREN

Sophia Loren was born on September 20, 1934 in Rome. When her father refused to marry Loren's aspiring actress mother, Sophia moved to the port town of Pozzuoli to live with her grandmother. That was during WWII when bombs rained down from the sky and Sophia was once struck by shrapnel in the chin. After the war, Sophia's grandmother opened a bar where Loren waited at tables until she entered a beauty contest in Naples. The judges selected the 14 year old as a finalist and she departed for Rome to begin a film career.

It was in Rome that she met Italian film producer and director, Carlo Ponti, who fell deeply in love with her and helped launch her long career. Unfortunately Carlo was married and in the Italy of the 1950's divorce was not an option, so Ponti obtained a divorce in Mexico in order to marry Loren. Denunciation from the Catholic Church followed plus arrest warrants from the Italian Government, one for Ponti for bigamy, the other for Loren for concubinage. It wasn't until the mid-60s that Ponti, his first wife and Loren became French citizens and they could resolve the legal position for good. Sophia remained faithful to short, stocky Carlo to the end of his life (in 2007) even as attractive men swarmed around her. Cary Grant and Peter Sellers were to fall deeply in love with her.

Sophia is best known for winning an Academy Award for Best Actress for her film, *Two Women*. But she never forgot her hometown, filming several movies set in Naples including: *Neapolitan Carousel* (1954), *L'Oro di Napoli* (1954), *It Started In Naples* (1960) and *Ieri, Oggi e Domani* (1963). The latter film co-starred Clark Gable and accurately portrayed the strong cultural differences between Italians and Americans. Sophia Loren continues to have an affinity for Naples, being an ardent fan of SSC Napoli. In 2007 she promised that if the soccer club won enough games to be promoted to Serie A, she would do a striptease. That year, SSC Napoli achieved this goal, but fans still ask hopefully whether Sophia will strut her stuff.

BEHIND THE MUSIC: STEFANIA RINALDI

In 2002 a young woman stepped up to the podium of the oldest Opera House in Europe, the San Carlo Theatre. A hushed silence must have fallen over the crowd as they waited for her arm to rise, the music to begin. You could have heard a pin drop as a Neapolitan woman took centre stage in the traditionally male-dominated field of orchestral conducting. Directing William Walton's *Façade* for her début performance at the San Carlo, and then a sequence of concerts dedicated to Mozart - it was a first for her city, her theatre and for her.

Just two years later, Maestra Stefania Rinaldi returned to San Carlo as director of the theatre's Children's Choir, the Coro di Voci Bianche del Teatro di San Carlo. She was one of its founders and has been its faithful director since its inception. Surrounded by her young charges, one need only look at Stefania to see her passion. In a word, she simply glows. The love and dedication she has for her music, her vocation and the children she teaches and mentors each year is plain to see. Passion breeds energy, and as Stefania explains, there is a symbiotic nature to the relationship between conductor, choir and audience. She becomes the conduit through which the energy of the music flows, feeds and grows. As a teacher, her relationship to her students is equally reciprocal.

> *I am their role model and they look up to me, but I learn just as much from them as they do from me.*

Whatever her formula for success, this phenomenon is evident at all the choir's performances which typically include: two Christmas concerts - Concerto di Natale and Aspettando... La Befana, a Mother's Day concert and several appearances a season in the theatre's programme. Part of the choir's repertoire includes Neapolitan music and in 2008 they performed live at the Rai Auditorium in *Era de Maggio*, Roberto de Simone's tribute to traditional Canzone Napoletana.

Over the past eight years, Stefania's journey with the Children's Choir has taken them all over the region, while she herself has travelled around the world. A classical pianist by training, by age 14, Stefania knew she was destined to be a conductor. A graduate of the Santa Cecilia Conservatory in Rome, she continued her studies at the National Academy of Santa Cecilia and at the Musical Academy Chigiana in Siena and has received numerous awards and accolades.

Stefania's curriculum vitae rivals that of any of her male contemporaries and the sky is the limit for this talented musician and conductor. We could easily see Stefania standing at the podium of the Metropolitan Opera House in New York, the Royal Opera House in London, La Scala in Milan or a return engagement at San Carlo. But at the same time, whatever her future glittering career, Stefania's greatest legacy will be the profound impact she has on the 120 children she guides and inspires each year. To expose children from all walks of life to this important part of their cultural heritage, imparting to them a love for the theatre, opera, classical music and Neapolitan Canzone, there really is no greater achievement than that.

THE
IMMERSION
COURSE

MUSIC, DRAMA, FOOD
WINE & SHOPPING

Cover Photo:
Porta Nolana Market

This is one
kaleidoscopic,
complex, colourful
culture.

Will you keep to the shallows, glorious though they are, or wade right in? You've checked into your accommodation, your head, still spinning from the bus or taxi ride, is full of those first exciting images of Naples' streets. What *was* that policeman gesticulating about? Don't those vegetable stalls look amazing? How many people *can* you pile onto a scooter? What is that *sensational* building up on the hill? My God, I've never been this close to a volcano before! Unpack, take a breath and begin to plan what you'd like to see and do. You may, like many, elect to pursue only those iconic sights recommended by generations of visitors. You may have limited time, in which case we can only commiserate. Whatever your experience here, it will be a memorable one, even if

Majolica Tiles, Cloister at Santa Chiara

you only have the chance to paddle in the shallows of the city. But for those who desire to dive deep into a culture and get closer to understanding its complexities, here are some ways to take the plunge.

Naples has a pulse to it, the daily life of the streets, the rhythm of the traffic, a snatch of song from the newspaper seller, the flap of wings over a quiet cloister. Music is going to be part of every visitor's day as it is of every Neapolitan's. Then there's the drama. It's a cliché, but there are few places on earth as dramatic as this city. Its views, its architecture, its art, its people are all engaged in a vast social performance and you are invited to participate. Caravaggio understood this, bringing the faces of the alleyways into high art.

Shakespeare would have loved it, if only he'd made the trip south. Then there's the food. You are about to encounter a rich culinary tradition that stays completely faithful to itself; it has taken in the influences of visiting powers and cultures in the past, but now it likes to celebrate the Neapolitan in terms of produce and presentation. And who can blame it? With mineral-enhanced fruits and vegetables like these to work with, cooks elsewhere can only weep at their deprivation. Finally, immerse yourself in real life in the many markets of Naples; buy if you can, take photos (asking *posso*, "can I?") if you can't. So much to look at, taste, smell and marvel at in this immersion course for Neapolitan life.

PASSIONE: A MUSICAL ADVENTURE IN NAPLES

Consider stringed instruments. Lutes, violins, violas, guitars, mandolins – Naples has created and played them all. (You could get the luthiers at Anema e Corde to wax lyrical on this.) There is a technique with these instruments in which alternative tunings for the strings give rise to unusual, often more beguiling effects in the pitch or timbre of the sounds. It's known as *scordatura*, 'mistuning' and Naples, in its take on life, its resilience and resourcefulness as well as in its music, has this in spades. Life lived here could never be a pedestrian one, never the average experience. The tuning of Naples' strings is exotic; the resultant music has a tone all its own.

And at the back of all this, of course, lies the beat that's essential to Neapolitan music, whether provided by folk instruments such as Pulcinella's *putipù* (friction drum), a *tammorra* (tambourine) and *nacchere* (castanets) combination or the bass and snare drum of orchestral and military music. *Battuta, battito* - onomatopoeic words for the heartbeat of the city.

Setting the metaphors aside, in purely practical terms there has always been an interplay between popular and classical music in Naples. Many classical musicians and opera singers who graced the stage of San Carlo have also played or sung

Gillian Longworth McGuire & Alessandro Zanesco at Luteria Anema e Corde

Neapolitan songs. Meanwhile more courtly or elite music in Naples of the past 400 years kept an ear to the window for melodies drifting in from the street. By the time the Piedigrotta Festival formalised *Canzone Napoletana* with a song-writing contest in 1835, opera style *bel canto* had embarked on a happy cross-fertilisation with popular airs. One Piedigrotta finalist, '*O Sole Mio*, (lyrics by poet Giovanni Capurro, music by Eduardo di Capua), took only second place in 1898, but became an international phenomenon. The song has been performed by many, many artists throughout the world. Neapolitan tenor Enrico Caruso brought '*O Sole Mio* to the New York Metropolitan Opera. Luciano Pavarotti won a Grammy Award for his rendition in 1980 and went on to sing it with artists such as Bryan Adams and Darren Hayes and his counterparts in the Three Tenors. Andrea Bocelli has done it, as has mezzo-soprano Katherine Jenkins and pop/opera cross-over trio Il Divo. Elton John played an instrumental version at his concert in Naples' Piazza del Plebiscito in 2009 that had the audience singing the words for him in a rapture of pride and emotion.

The more formal music that was heard in the San Carlo opera house, the Teatrino di Corte, "Little Court Theatre" of the Palazzo Reale or in the salons of the noble houses of the city influenced music-making elsewhere in Europe and ultimately in North America. The work of composers such as Alessandro Scarlatti, Giovanni Battista Pergolesi, Niccolò Piccinni, Domenico Cimarosa, Gioachino Rossini, Vincenzo Bellini and Gaetano Donizetti ensured Naples continued to inspire classical music-lovers around the world, especially in the 18th to early 20th centuries. Furthermore in recent decades thanks to groups such as I Turchini led by Antonio Florio, Roberto Festa's Daedalus Ensemble or Marco Beasley's Accordone, the exploration, live performance and recording of pieces from a vast archive of manuscript and printed music held in places such as the Conservatorio has been underway. This work covers a wide gamut: chamber concerti, chamber cantatas, opera and popular song. For lovers of *Canzone Napoletana*, national broadcaster Radio-RAI is building an historical archive of song in collaboration with the Campania region and the province and town council of Naples. The aim is to gather, document, digitise and make available every extant recording ever made of Neapolitan music from the pioneer days of audio reproduction to the present time. Details can be found at: radio.rai.it/canzonenapoletana.

Within the Neapolitan music scene special mention must be made of the southern Italian *tarantella* tradition, whose origins go deep into antiquity, though theories of tarantism became the subject of enquiry by writers in the 1600s citing a source from a couple of centuries earlier. According to this tradition, a person bitten by the tarantula spider may be cured **only** by several days' worth of a kind of wild but sacred dance music played on a variety of instruments including strings and drums. Today you might encounter a somewhat more light-hearted round-dance *tarantella* provided by a folk or school group on the streets of Naples, accompanied by mandolins and tambourines. However, the ability of Neapolitan couples (male/female or female/female) to break out into the beautiful stylised gestures of southern Italian folk dance can be seen whenever a crowd assembles for a *Notte* *della Tammorra* in Piazza Mercato (generally in high summer). Arms waved above shoulder level, chin tipped proudly, hips swaying, these dancers, both professional and amateur, are mesmerising to watch. Even in the *vichi* (alleyways) of the older parts of the city a line of song or a blast of music from a radio can send a Neapolitan, whether grandma or toddler, dipping and dancing across the lava flagstones. And it's a rare day in Naples when you don't hear some line from a popular song unfurl along the street from a kitchen, a workshop or a market stall. Meanwhile passionate amateurs like Alfredo Imparato continue the centuries-old tradition of the *posteggiatore*, or public singer, spending hours of his leisure time delighting passersby of all ages with his spirited renditions of classic songs, accompanied on his guitar or Neapolitan mandolin.

So touch the surface of Naples and you'll find musical energy of all kinds just primed to go, a fact that was not lost on actor/director John Turturro, (himself of Sicilian/Puglian origins), when he took up the challenge of making a film about popular music in Naples. He brought to the work an instant, visceral understanding of Naples' unique *scordatura*, its multiple roots and influences, its characteristic rhythms. For the music you find here reflects its lived experience: for centuries Neapolitans have gazed out at this most beautiful of locations with its calm blue sea while back on land there has been a revolving door of different political regimes, oppression, racial discrimination and periods of intense poverty, famine, crime and corruption. Naples' music, especially its popular musical tradition, is a product of the multiple layerings and blendings of many cultures that have by turn dominated here and been dominated. Battered by successive natural and manmade disasters - plagues, earthquakes, volcanic eruptions and the relentless bombing of the city during WWII – each time the city reeled but the unwavering spirit of Neapolitans endured. This is a spirit that brings to the music the full range of human emotion in all its contradictions and that comes from a place so deep and experiences so profound, the music literally reverberates from the depths of the Neapolitan soul. In fact *Soul* is the perfect word to use to grasp where this music is coming from; just as soul music in the US had deep roots in African-American gospel, rhythm & blues and jazz, Neapolitan popular music is grounded in a shared experience of all the tribulations and joys, deep shadows and brilliant sunshine, that life has thrown at the city.

John Turturro's 2010 film *Passione* captured and preserved this intangible piece of Neapolitan culture, presenting to the world a rich musical heritage rarely known outside Italy or indeed outside Naples. In a sense the world thinks it knows what Neapolitan music is, thanks to a century of exposure through recordings that began with artists like Enrico Caruso; southern Italian immigrants to America were both the audience for, and the means of disseminating, many of the religious, culinary and musical traditions of their much-missed homeland. But Turturro is not the only person to note that once Neapolitan music leaves its native shores, it has a tendency to sentimentalise and to shed some of its streetwise edginess and dry humour. In the 1940s song, *Dove sta Zazà?*, *Where is Zazà?*, Isiai, narrator of the story, tells how his beloved Zazà was somehow spirited away from him in the San

♪♪♪♪♪♪ THE SCORE SHEET ♪♪♪♪♪♪

- Opera, symphony concerts or ballet in the oldest opera house in Europe. teatrosancarlo.it

- Classical concerts under a Vasari ceiling at Sant'Anna dei Lombardi.

- Ensemble Vocale di Napoli & other groups. ensemblevocalenapoli.com

- The Scarlatti Association's world-class concerts at Palazzo Zevallos Stigliano and Castel Sant'Elmo (Sept - Apr). associazionescarlatti.it

- Fine music-making from the Nuova Orchestra Alessandro Scarlatti (Fall and Spring). nuovaorchestrascarlatti.it

- Seven centuries of sacred organ music (Jan - Dec). trabaci.com

- Early music at Pietà dei Turchini Foundation - Centre of Ancient Music (Oct - Jun). turchini.it

- Il Venerdi, c'è musica in Basilica! (There's music in the Basilica on Friday!) Concerts at the newly restored Basilica San Giovanni Maggiore.

- Drop in on the stringed instrument makers of Anema e Corde. p. 61

- Thrill to sunset concerts and plays in a Roman amphitheatre (Spring & Fall). suggestioniallimbrunire.org

- Takes Two to Tango Nights/Tango Festival (Sept). tamotango.it

- Find your voice with lessons in Italian/classical singing. centroitaliano.it

- Summer jazz concerts in the archaeological sites of Campi Flegrei. pozzuolijazzfestival.it

- ...or jazz atop a castle Sant'Elmo Jazz Sant'Elmo Estate (Summer).

- Naples major piano festival, Piano City Napoli (Dec). pianocitynapoli.it

Gennaro festival crowds. The band plays on (music from Parsifal) and Isiai searches desperately but cannot find her. It's obviously a disaster. He simply cannot live without her and how will she manage without him? Second verse: next year, he returns to the same place, still hoping to find her. However... if she doesn't materialise, "If I don't find her, she who is so beautiful, I'll be happy and find her sister." *Se non troverò lei, ch'è tanto bella, mm'accontenterò, 'e trová 'a sorella...* And he'll continue telling the sister how much he still loves Zazà... This encapsulates the pragmatic, darkly funny character of much Neapolitan song, conveyed as much by the choice of language as by the music. Language is essential to the authenticity of *Passione* as an account of popular music in Naples; from the first song to the last you are immersed in the cadence of the rhythmic Neapolitan language lingua napoletana, captivated by the haunting, intense, occasionally melancholy music with its deep Middle Eastern, North African and Spanish influences.

Passione opens with Mina's rendition of the Sergio Bruni classic *Carmela*. It closes with what has become the Neapolitan Anthem, Pino Daniele's tribute to his beloved city, *Napule è*. (Sadly, Pino Daniele passed away on Jan 5th, 2015.) In between, Turturro's musical vignettes interspersed with interviews and commentary, take us on a musical journey through the city. Drawing from an enormous archive of *canzoni napoletane*, Turturro selected 24 songs from the 13th century to the present to tell the Neapolitan story. The classic *'O Sole Mio* is presented as a musical montage with recordings from Sergio Bruni and a young Massimo Ranieri, ending the song with a rendition in Arabic by Tunisian M'Barka Ben Taleb. Massimo Ranieri and Lina Sastri give a dramatic, jealousy-charged rendition of *Malafemmena, Evil Woman*, one of the most popular Neapolitan songs of all time. Misia and Peppe Servillo (with Servillo's Avion Travel) perform the haunting duet, *Era De Maggio, It Was In May*, a love song written by the Neapolitan poet Salvatore Di Giacomo in 1885 and set to music by Mario Pasquale Costa.

Turturro also introduces anglophone audiences to *Tammurriata Nera*. Written in 1944 by E.A. Mario and Edoardo Nicolardi, it tells the story of a woman who gives birth to a child of colour conceived during the WWII American occupation of Naples. Performed by Peppe Barra, Max Casella and M'Barka Ben Taleb, *Tammurriata Nera* is one of the most powerful songs in the film. It is also the true life story of Neapolitan Saxophonist James Senese who performs the film's title song *Passione*, and who is himself the child of a Neapolitan mother and an African-American GI Senese never met. This song lies in the direct line of the tradition, explained by Barra in the film, where people, faced with something outside their usual experience, turn to the strong beat of the tambourine or drum to exorcise their fear. Shades of the *tarantella*...

Beat is vital to the music of Enzo Avitabile, saxophonist, conservatory-trained flautist and prolific singer-songwriter. His career has married World Music and Jazz Fusion with the sounds of Naples' own traditions and seen him collaborate with artists such as Tina Turner and James Brown. In 2012 he featured in a documentary film *Music Life*, directed by Jonathan Demme. For *Passione* Turturro filmed him playing *Faccia Gialla* with 'I Bottari', an ensemble of musicians whose trance-inducing drumming upon barrel section instruments reconnects its public with processional rhythms first heard in the 13th century. At its origins such drumming was used to chase away malign spirits and to conjure up a good growing season in springtime. This song's title means *Yellow Face* and it's a plea to San Gennaro (whose statue has a golden countenance) to liquefy the saint's blood and protect the people of Naples.

With a cast as diverse as the music, Turturro takes us on a journey to forgotten landmarks, hidden corners and through some of the most fascinating neighbourhoods in Naples. The film showcased, for example, one of Naples' poorest but most beautiful neighbourhoods, the Rione Sanità: Palazzo dello Spagnuolo is the location for Pietra Montecorvino's husky performance of *Comme Facette Mammeta, How Your Mama Made You*, while the market on Via dei Vergini was the stage for *Dove Sta Zazà?*. There are also visits to picture postcard locations such as the San Martino Charterhouse atop Vomero hill where Spakka-Neapolis 55 perform *Vesuvio* to the accompaniment of castanets and the yellow tuff rock of the Castel dell'Ovo provides the backdrop for the comical song *Don Raffaè*, performed in his inimical manner by Peppe Barra. We also share an intimate, intense interpretation by guitarist Fausto Cigliano of *Catari*, filmed beneath Caravaggio's *Seven Acts of Mercy* in Pio Monte della Misericordia church.

Outside Naples, the ancient Roman cistern of Piscina Mirabilis is the stage for the 13th-century *Canto delle lavandaie del Vomero*, sung by Fiorenza Calogero, Lorenza Tamaggio and Daniela Fiorentina. This piece became a protest song against the Aragonese domination of Naples; the washerwomen sing that they have come to collect four handkerchiefs they were promised... for handkerchiefs, read land. Out in the sunshine, Turturro himself joins performers Fiorello and Max Casella at the merrily steaming Solfatara to sing *Caravan Petrol* by the legendary Renato Carosone and Nisa (Nicola Salerno). In addition, there's a wonderfully eccentric and tearful rendition of another Carosone song, *Maruzzella* filmed mostly on the beach near Nisida, Bagnoli.

In the end *Passione* is more than a fantasy piece, more than just another tribute to a musical genre. Director John Turturro thought he was filming a straight documentary but as he and the crew went along, realised they were on 'a musical adventure.' It became an ode to Bella Napoli and a celebration of the heart, the soul, the spirit of the Neapolitan people. And, as Turturro explains, Neapolitan music embraces those most fundamental of existential themes: love, loss, exile, superstition, social protest and death. So in that sense, this is a richly human film.

WHO TO SEE

- ACCORDONE (MARCO BEASLEY): accordone.it
- ALMAMEGRETTA (RAIZ): almamegretta.it
- ENZO AVITABILE: enzoavitabile.it
- PEPPE BARRA: peppebarra.altervista.org
- MÍSIA: misia-online.com
- JAMES SENESE: jamessenese.it
- I TURCHINI (ANTONIO FLORIO): iturchini.it
- SPAKKA NEAPOLIS 55: spakka-neapolis55.it
- MASSIMO RANIERI: massimoranieri.it
- VINCENZO CAPEZZUTO: vincenzocapezzuto.com
- ENSEMBLE DAEDALUS (ROBERTO FESTA): facebook.com/pages/Daedalus-Ensemble
- PEPPE SERVILLO AND AVION TRAVEL: ondarock.it/italia/aviontravel
- M'BARCA BEN TALEB: facebook.com/bentalebofficial
- PIETRA MONTECORVINO: pietramontecorvino.com

CITY OF DRAMA: THEATRES GREAT & SMALL

Naples is a city of drama and melodrama, and not just on the streets! It's brimful of venues for theatre, music, politics and dance. Obviously, for visitors who don't speak Italian, non-spoken entertainments will be the most appealing. Your hotel or B&B host will usually be able to help you make bookings once you've done a little online research while the Napoli Unplugged website keeps abreast of every conceivable entertainment in town. Theatre lovers should also note the Napoli Theatre Festival is a twice annual event – in June and September (napoliteatrofestival.it) and for cinema-lovers the Naples Film Festival sets up stage every fall in the September/October timeframe. Here is a quick look at some of Naples' better known theatres.

TEATRO AUGUSTEO
Piazzetta Duca D'Aosta, Municipio
+39 081 414243
teatroaugusteo.it
A 1,600 seat theatre, hosting comedic and dramatic theatre productions, musicals, classical and pop music concerts and matinée programs for school children; it is home to the Carlo Buccirosso acting school.

TEATRO BELLINI
Via Conte Di Ruvo, 14, Centro Storico
+39 081 5491266
teatrobellini.it
Founded in 1864, Teatro Bellini is a 1,200 seat theatre that offers spectators a programme of plays, musicals and opera. A gorgeous theatre just steps away from the Fine Arts Academy, Teatro Bellini can be visited by day. Old playbills are on display in a small rehearsal room upstairs.

TEATRO DIANA
Via Luca Giordano, 64, Vomero
+39 081 5567527
teatrodiana.it
Many Neapolitan and national stars have trodden the boards of the Teatro Diana, from Eduardo de Filippo and Marcello Mastroianni to Luca Zingaretti (Inspector Montalbano of television fame). Drama, comedy and music, both classical and Neapolitan, find a home on the boards of this famous theatre.

TEATRO MERCADANTE
Piazza Municipio, Municipio
+39 081 5510336
teatrostabilenapoli.it
A 533 seat theatre on Piazza Municipio, the 18th-century Teatro Mercadante is part of the Teatro Stabile di Napoli. The Mercadante stages productions from the Stabile as well as major Italian works presented by directors of national and international acclaim.

TEATRO/CINEMA (DELLE) PALME
Vico Vetriera, 12, Chiaia
+39 081 4104486
teatrodellepalme.it
The theatre was built in 1925 and acquired by cinema pioneer Gustavo Cuccurullo in 1946 as part of a chain of cinemas across Italy. Major Italian and international theatre companies have continued to play there and the mix has included musical concerts (Frank Sinatra appeared there), a regular dance season as well as film.

TEATRO POLITEAMA
Via Monte di Dio, 80, Monte di Dio
+39 081 7642111
teatropoliteama.it
A 900 seat theatre which opened in 1872 and

re-opened in 1961 following a devastating fire four years earlier. Its fine acoustic means it hosts concerts and lyric opera as well as popular drama. It is managed by the Teatro Augusteo.

TEATRO SANNAZARO

Via Chiaia, 157, Chiaia
+39 081 411723
teatrosannazaro.it

Teatro Sannazaro opened the doors to its sumptuous playhouse in 1874, under the management of Don Giulio Mastrilli, Duke of Marigliano, an aristocratic note that was reflected in its clientèle. Such auspicious beginnings, alas, proved transient and by the 1930s the theatre had become a cinema showing far from respectable films. However, an enormous effort was made in the late 60s and early 70s to restore the building and revive its theatrical life; it's now a celebrated venue for popular Neapolitan shows, especially those in the café-chantant genre.

TEATRO SAN CARLO

Via San Carlo, 98, Municipio
+39 081 7972111
teatrosancarlo.it

The oldest opera house in Europe presents world-class opera, ballet and symphony concerts. The season runs from September through May, but in recent years summer performances have been added. Tickets are usually quite affordable, especially if you are willing to trek to the upper boxes. The theatre offers attractive deals to patrons under 30 and Facebook fans can get great last minute discounts.

TEATRO SAN FERDINANDO

Piazza Eduardo de Filippo, 20, Porta Capuana
+39 081 5510336
teatrostabilenapoli.it/

Reopened in 2007 after having being closed for more than 20 years, Eduardo De Fillipo bought it in 1948 after it had been almost completely destroyed by WWII air raids. Today, this 500 seat theatre is part of Teatro Stabile Napoli and is known as the "temple" of Neapolitan drama, specialising in classical and contemporary productions.

TEATRO TRIANON

Piazza Vincenzo Calenda, 9, Porta Capuana
+39 081 2258285
teatrotrianon.org

Founded in 1911, throughout much of its history Teatro Trianon has been dedicated to music, especially Neapolitan song - canzone napoletana. A 630 seat theatre, today it hosts musical performances of all kinds as well as Neapolitan comedy productions and is one of the venues played by the famous Totò.

Teatro San Carlo

EAT & DRINK NAPLES: THE CRIB NOTES VERSION

Along with the Greeks and the Spaniards, the southern Italians have their own way of eating that has come to be known as the Mediterranean Diet. Each country and region has their own take on this, but in general the emphasis is on eating whatever is in season, grown locally and brought to market with minimal processing. A plug for shopping local versus the large supermarkets should also be noted here. The Mediterranean diet is rich in fresh fruits and vegetables; rusks, grains and legumes; and nuts and seeds. The diet is more seafood and poultry and less meat and dairy; wine is consumed moderately and the principal fat is olive oil.

The key to Neapolitan cuisine is simple preparation that allows the fresh ingredients to shine. The cuisine is worthy of a tome on its own, but here are the crib notes to help you eat your way around Naples!

WHAT TO EAT

FOR STARTERS - JUST A FEW OF THE FRIED FOODS

Almost as famous as Neapolitan pizza, "Fritture Napoletane" are bite-sized fried delights made in almost every kitchen in Napoli, served as antipasti in pizzerias and restaurants and are a favourite street food sold by the *friggitorie*. Among them are: "Arancini di Riso" - deep-fried rice balls that emerge from vats of sizzling oil looking like oranges (or pears in the case of the conical ones); "Crocchè di Patate" - potato purée rolled in egg and flour and deep-fried until the potatoes and cheese melt in your mouth; "Mozzarella in Carrozza" - deep fried mozzarella triangles; and "Pasta Cresciuta" - misshapen blobs of deep-fried leavened dough seasoned with salt and often mixed with seaweed. The batter *cresce* or grows while frying and is also used to coat zucchini/courgette flowers. Dusted with sugar it is known as "Zeppole". Anything with melting mozzarella in the middle can be described as *al telefono* – on the telephone - because of the string of cheese that appears when you cut or bite it. The mother of all Neapolitan fried delectables is "Pizzette Fritte" - deep-fried pizza dough capped with a simple tomato sauce plus a little mozzarella or grated parmigiano/parmesan cheese. Pop some fresh basil on top and you have the colours of the Italian flag. Similarly, "Angioletti Fritti" - fried "angels" - are strips of pizza dough served with fresh cherry tomatoes and a bit of oregano or arugula/rocket. Topped with Nutella instead, they become a decadent dessert.

COLD PLATES

You won't find many salads for starters but you will find, almost without fail, Campania's famed *mozzarella di bufala* - mozzarella made from buffalo milk. Huge balls of it arrive surrounded by a ring of *pomodorini* - sweet cherry tomatoes - or it's sliced onto *pomodori per insalata*, one of the region's larger, greener and sourer tomatoes that make the perfect complement to the sweetness of the mozzarella when married to some fresh basil and a drizzle of olive oil. When in season and only when in season, (the melon that is), "Prosciutto e Melone" - Parma ham and melon - is a sweet and salty cold bite to start the meal. By contrast, "Insalata di Polipo" is a tangy cold salad made from octopus.

FROM THE SEA

The two main ingredients in the Neapolitan diet are seafood and pasta. And just like peanut butter and chocolate, they are a match made in heaven. Most seafood pastas start with the same basic sauce: "Aglio e Olio", garlic and olive oil; freshly chopped parsley is almost always sprinkled on top. Yet each dish yields its own particular result. Add or omit tomatoes or *peperoncino* - chilli pepper; vary the type of seafood, pasta or tomatoes or layer in several types of seafood to create a richer dish. "Spaghetti alle Vongole" - spaghetti and clams - is a year-round favourite and a tradition on Christmas Eve. Find a similar preparation without the pasta as the starter "Sauté di Vongole" or its cousin made with mussels and croutons, the "Zuppa di Cozze". For the dish "Pasta Calamarata", rings of calamari are served with calamari shaped pasta known as *pasta calamarata*, thus the seafood gives name to the pasta and the pasta gives name to the dish in a kind of culinary mutual admiration. Almost every restaurant in Naples has its own version of the medley of molluscs and crustaceans known as "Spaghetti allo Scoglio" - literally "spaghetti on the rocks".

As a *secondo* - a second course - fish is served grilled, *al forno* – baked, steamed or fried. Squeamish eaters should note that fish is often served whole, eyes and head intact and charged by the kilo; 30 or 40 Euro surprises at the point of paying the bill are not unknown... *Spigola* - sea bass - is a medium sized white fish with a succulent taste. Prepared *al forno*, it is filled with herbs and baked whole in a blanket of garlic, onions, olive oil and cherry tomatoes. During the Christmas holidays fried *capitone* - eel - and *baccalà* - cod - are perennial favourites.

Fried Calamari

SAVOURY SAUCES

A rare entry in the Neapolitan cookbook, meat sauces tend to be two for one affairs where the sauce find its way onto pasta for the *primo piatto* and the meat is the star of the *secondo*. The two favourite sauces are "Ragù Napoletano" the classic Neapolitan Sunday gravy otherwise known as *il ragù della domenica* - Sunday sauce - and the super decadent "Genovese". A Sunday pot roast with a Neapolitan flair, Genovese is a rich onion sauce flavoured with meat that is cooked slowly over the lowest of flames until the onions caramelise from crispy bites into a creamy sauce as savoury as it is sweet. "Pizzaiola" is a favourite sauce to put on top of meat, making the dish "Carne alla Pizzaiola" or meat in the style of the *pizzaiolo* - pizza maker. It's made from *pomodorini del piennolo del Vesuvio*, cherry-like tomatoes that are cultivated in the area around Vesuvius National Park and hung outside for several months to intensify their flavour. A spicy and salty sauce made from capers and olives is "Puttanesca", a dish that is said to have been named for the oldest profession in the world.

HEAVENLY CREATIONS

They will do little for your waistline and yet these classic over the top, clog your arteries kind of dishes will leave you wanting for more. The favoured meal of Carnevale, "Lasagna Napoletana" is made from three key ingredients: a good Sunday *ragù*, *le polpettine*, itty, bitty meatballs and an assortment of fresh and fabulous cheeses: ricotta, *fior di latte* or mozzarella, and grated parmigiana or pecorino - a hard ewe's milk cheese. "Timballo di Maccheroni" - from the French word *timbale*, meaning kettledrum - is a gastronomical "it" dish of the 18th and 19th-century nobility. It's a pastry-lined drum filled with a creamy mixture of pasta, meat, vegetables and cheese. Usually made from leftovers, "Frittata di Maccheroni" is a long pasta such as linguine or spaghetti combined with eggs, cheeses and *prosciutto cotto* - cooked ham, which is then fried in a pan until the outer layer of the pasta becomes golden brown. "Parmigiana di Melanzane", the Neapolitan version of eggplant/aubergine parmigiana is decidedly lighter than its North American, European and Northern Italian counterparts because it forgoes the flour, eggs and breadcrumbs.

...AND PIZZA, OF COURSE

In Naples, the birthplace of pizza, as you might imagine, pizza making is a serious business. An art, a science and a tradition, Pizza Napoletana is the pride of this city and a national treasure. It is an intangible, invaluable and indelible part of the Neapolitan culture. It is so important in fact that after years of lobbying, Pizza Napoletana won the coveted EU Trademark Status, the Traditional Speciality Guaranteed Label in February 2010. Meanwhile, pizza makers in Napoli are still lobbying to get it inscribed on UNESCO's Intangible Cultural Heritage list and they promote and protect their craft through several professional organisations. Among these are the *Associazione Pizzaiuoli Napoletani* – Association of Neapolitan Pizza Makers - and the *Associazione Verace Pizza Napoletana* (AVPN) - the True Neapolitan Pizza Association. Founded in 1984, AVPN promotes the *verace*

ꙮꙮꙮꙮꙮ PIZZA AFICIONADOS ꙮꙮꙮꙮꙮ
WILL WANT TO:

- Eat Pizza in its birthplace

- Pair their pizza with wine, beer, art and more in dozens of pizzerias throughout the city - AVPN's Le Strade del Pizza Festival (May) pizzanapoletana.org

- Choose their favourite pizzeria at Napoli Pizza Village on the Lungomare (Sept) pizzavillage.it

- Celebrate the most famous food in the world at Pizza Festival at Vulcano Buono (Jul) vulcanobuono.it

- Become a certified *pizzaiolo* pizzanapoletana.org/eng_formazione. php or Academy of Pizza academyofpizza.it/en

- Learn more about the craft at the International Pizza Museum at MAMT - Museo Arte Musica Mediterraneo Tradizioni mamt.it

Giuseppe Topo of Napoli Unplugged's Cooking with Giuseppe Series
Find all of Giuseppe's recipes at napoliunplugged.com/cooking-with-giuseppe

pizza napoletana, its affiliated pizzerias, the products related to the production of *Vera Pizza Napoletana* and the professionalisation of pizza makers in Italy and worldwide.

Today there are as many topping choices as there are pizzerias, *pizzaioli* and people. In the beginning, however, pizza started out as a very simple concoction. If you go to Da Michele, the Neapolitan pizzeria founded in 1870 and made famous in Julia Roberts' *Eat, Pray, Love,* you will have a choice between one of two pizzas: the tomato and mozzarella Margherita pizza or the true classic Neapolitan pizza, the Marinara, topped simply with tomato, garlic, oregano and extra virgin olive oil.

SWEET AND SAVOURY TREATS
At bars and pastry shops - *le pasticcerie* - around the city, you'll find both sweet and savoury treats to tempt you. Naples is best known for its "Babà al Rum" and "Sfogliatella". Babà is a cake soaked in spirits - usually rum, sometimes "Limoncello" - lemon liqueur - and sometimes filled with custard or a cream. Sfogliatella is a seashell-shaped pastry that comes in two varieties - *riccia* - the more popular puff pastry version and *frolla* - the short crust version - filled with cinnamon and vanilla-scented ricotta, a hint of candied fruit, the whole confection dusted with powdered sugar. Another Neapolitan favourite is "Tiramisù". This creamy concoction made of caffè, eggs, sugar and mascarpone cheese is, as its name says, a "pick-me-up". For breakfast, "un Cornetto" with chocolate, cream or apricot jam will keep you happy until lunch or even better, try a "Graffa Napoletana", a sugar doughnut with a kick. The *fatta in casa*, the home made version of these potato doughnuts are usually reserved for Carnevale. "Chiacchiere" - literally "chitchats" – are crunchy, fried sweet treats dusted with powdered sugar or dipped in a special chocolate sauce called "Sanguinaccio" and are another favourite during Carnevale. (You're unlikely to encounter true sanguinaccio, with its addition of freshly slaughtered pig's blood, in any restaurant or pastry shop.) Finally no Christmas table is complete without "Struffoli" - tiny deep fried dough balls bathed in a syrup of honey and citrus rinds and decorated with coloured Jordan/sugared almonds, sprinkles/hundreds and thousands and candied fruit. They are a Neapolitan Christmas delight.

On the savoury side, "Casatiello" is a *rustico* - rustic bread - filled with Neapolitan salami, cheeses and hard boiled eggs. It's eaten only at Easter while its brother "Tòrtano" - the same recipe minus the eggs - is made year round. "Panini Napoletani" are the Neapolitan version of a breakfast sandwich in which salami, cheese and sometimes hard boiled eggs are coiled up in pepper seasoned dough and baked until golden brown. The Neapolitan version of pretzels, "Taralli", are savoury twist snacks that come in a plethora of varieties, though the traditional "Sugna e Pepe" - pork lard and pepper - is ever popular.

CAFFÈ

To order a single shot espresso in Naples, "un caffè" is all that need be said. Elsewhere in Italy you should probably ask for "un espresso". In this undisputed caffè capital of the world - many believe it has to do with the water - if there are nearly 400 churches in Naples then there must be at least 4,000 cafés. Varieties of the standard "Caffè espresso" include the "Ristretto" - the same amount of coffee but about ½ the water; the "Lungo" - long, like a double - or "Caffè Macchiato" - espresso topped with a dollop of milk - usually foamed. Before 11 a.m. (at least for the men) it is acceptable to enjoy a cappuccino. Summer concoctions include: the "Granita" - espresso sweetened with a simple syrup and frozen till slushy; "Caffè Shakerato" - in its purest form, caffè, ice and a few teaspoons of sugar are shaken until the drink reaches a frothy frenzy that is poured into a Martini glass; and finally the pimped up version of a Caffè Shakerato known as "Caffè del Nonno" - "Grandad's coffee" in which espresso, sugar and cream are blended to the consistency of a mousse, usually in an electric "granita" machine and served in a glass swirled with caramel, chocolate or nut syrup, the top dusted with cocoa powder.

WINES & SPIRITS

Once a sour note in the Italian wine catalogue, Campania wines are experiencing their own renaissance thanks to some forward thinking producers such as Mastroberardino and Feudi Di San Gregorio. The region now numbers 19 DOC and 4 DOCG wines among its offerings. The Avellino region produces three of the DOCG wines: one of the reds: Taurasi, made primarily from the Aglianico grape which is said to have come here with the Greeks and the two whites, Greco di Tufo and Fiano d'Avellino. The other red, Aglianico de Taburno comes from Benevento. The local white served at most Neapolitan eateries is Falanghina, an ancient grape variety pre-dating the destruction of Pompeii and, of course, there is no shortage of Lacryma Christi from the slopes of Vesuvius. The Piedirosso varietal produces another one of the region's favourite reds and is often part of a Taurasi blend.

While *aperitivi* are common in most of Italy, Naples doesn't celebrate the tradition much beyond serving the occasional Prosecco (a respectable rival to champagne) before special meals or the consumption of the occasional Aperol Spritz or Negroni, though these are usually ordered up by tourists. In fact, since apéritif hour roughly coincides with gelato hour, you are more likely to see people licking a cone than sipping a spritz. The *digestivo*, the after dinner drink, however, reigns supreme in the south. Usually enjoyed after a large meal to aid in digestion, or so they say, the two most popular *digestivi* are "Grappa", a "pomace" brandy made from the remains of the grapes after wine making, usually for the men and, for the ladies, "Limoncello", grain alcohol infused with lemon zest and drunk ice cold.

WHERE TO EAT

Italian dining options run the gamut from small family-run eateries to high-end dining establishments. The terms used are in flux but here are your clues. A *ristorante* is in general a quality eatery with matching price tag. Food may be traditional or experimental; pizza is often an option. If pizza is truly in your sights, find a *pizzeria* – where you may also find a delicious selection of Neapolitan fried foods. Meanwhile think of a *trattoria* as Mamma's kitchen. If there is a menu, it will be handwritten and the number of tables will be small. The atmosphere is informal, the food is almost inevitably great and the bill modest. You'll also see the word *osteria*, with its historical reverberations of inns and taverns, though now that term is applied without rhyme or reason to a range of eateries. The *tavola calda* - "hot table" - is a cafeteria or fast food style place. It's not *haute cuisine*, but is good for those on a tighter budget. Finally an *enoteca* is a wine bar where food is probably restricted to nibbles, but that too is changing. *Buon appetito!*

WHERE TO
EAT

ASSOCIAZIONE
VERACE
PIZZA
NAPOLETANA

AVPN PIZZERIAS

1. 50 KALÒ DI CIRO SALVO
Piazza Sannazzaro, 201/B
tel 081 19204667
www.50kalò.it

2. ANTICA PIZZERIA DONNA REGINA
Via SS. Apostoli, 4
tel 081 4421511
www.pizzeriadonnaregina.it

3. ANTICA PIZZERIA PORT'ALBA
Via Portalba, 18
tel 081 459713
www.anticapizzeriaristoranteportalba.com

4. CAPASSO
Via Porta San Gennaro, 2/3
tel 081 456421

5. CARMNELLA
Via Cristoforo Marino, 22/23
tel 081 5537425

6. CIRO A SANTA BRIGIDA
Via Santa Brigida, 71, 73a, 74
tel 081 5524072
www.ciroasantabrigida.it

7. DON SALVATORE
Via Mergellina, 4/a-5
tel 081 681817
www.donsalvatore.it

8. ECCELLENZE CAMPANE
Via Brin, 49
tel 081 5636303
www.eccellenzecampane.it

9. GORIZIA 1962
Via Albino Albini, 18/20
(Trav. Via Cilea)
tel 081 5604642
www.pizzeriagorizia.it

10. IL FIGLIO DEL PRESIDENTE
Via Duomo, 181/183
tel 081 0330913
www.ilfigliodelpresidente.it

11. IL SALOTTO ARCADIA
Via Nicolardi, 5
Parco Arcadia
tel 081 7430300

12. LA FIGLIA DEL PRESIDENTE
Via Grande Archivio, 23/24
tel 081 286738
www.lafigliadelpresidente.it

13. LA TAVERNA DI BACCO SASÀ PIZZA MIA
Via Sementini, 28
tel 081 5466119
www.sasapizzamia.it

14. L'ARTE DELLA PIZZA
Via Santa Maria della Libera, 5
tel 081 2411907

15. LOMBARDI A FORIA
Via Foria, 12
tel 347 7921400
www.pizzerialombardi.it

16. MAMMINA
Via Partenope, 15
tel 081 2400001
www.mammina.eu

17. MA TU VULIVE A' PIZZA
Via Santa Maria La Nova, 46
tel 081 5514490

18. MAESTRI PIZZAIOLI
Via Cassano, 75
tel 081 7382835
www.maestripizzaioli.it

19. MATTOZZI A PIAZZA CARITÀ
Piazza Carità, 2
tel 081 5524322
www.ristorantemattozzi.it

20. MONDO PIZZA 2004
Via Egiziaca a Pizzofalcone 99/100
tel 081 0322495
www.mondopizzanapoli.com

21. O' CALAMARO
Viale Campi Flegrei, 30/A
tel 081 5704387
www.ocalamaro.it

22. PIZZERIA LA NOTIZIA
Via M. da Caravaggio, 94/A
tel 349 2886327
www.pizzaconsulting.it

23. PIZZAZZÀ
Viale dei Pini, 25
tel 081 7418243
www.pizzazzanapoli.com

24. PIZZERIA AL 22
Via Pignasecca, 22
tel 081 5522726
www.pizzeriaal22.it

25. PIZZERIA DA ATTILIO
Via Pignasecca, 17
tel 081 5520479

26. PIZZERIA ERRICO
Via Luigia Sanfelice, 8
tel 081 0124555
www.safado.it

27. PIZZERIA OLIVA DA CONCETTINA AI TRE SANTI
Via Arena alla Sanità, 7 bis
tel 081 290037
www.pizzeriaoliva.it

28. PIZZERIA VESI
Via Bellini, 23/24
tel 081 5442859
www.vesi.it

29. SALVATORE ALLA RIVIERA
Via Riviera di Chiaia, 91
tel 081 680490
www.salvatoreallariviera.it

30. SOLO PIZZA DI G. GENOVESI
Via Manzoni, 26/i
tel 081 7146634
www.solopizzaviamanzoni.it

31. SORBILLO
Via Tribunali, 31/32
tel 081 446643
www.sorbillo.it

32. TRATTORIA CAPRESE
Via Luca Giordano, 25
tel 081 5587584
www.trattoriacaprese.it

33. UMBERTO
Via Alabardieri, 30/31
tel 081 418555
www.umberto.it

34. VESI
Via S. Biagio dei Librai, 115
tel 081 5511035
www.vesi.it

ASSOCIAZIONE
VERACE
PIZZA
NAPOLETANA

OTHER FAVOURITES FOR PIZZA, FRIED FOODS & QUICK BITES

(I) DECUMANI ANTICA PIZZERIA
Via Tribunali, 58, Centro Storico
+39 081 557 1309

(LA) FOCACCIA
Vico Belledonne a Chiaia, 31, Chiaia
+39 081 412277

(DI) MATTEO ANTICA PIZZERIA E FRIGGITORIA
Via dei Tribunali, 94, Centro Storico
+39 081 455262
salvatoredimatteo.com

(DA) MICHELE PIZZERIA
Via Cesare Serasale, 1, Porta Capuana
+39 081 5539204
damichele.net

FRIGGITORIA VOMERO
Via Domenico Cimarosa, 44, Vomero
+39 081 5783130

PIZZA FRITTE
Via Giuseppe Simonelli, 58, Municipio
+39 334 3695502

(IL) PIZZAIOLO DEL PRESIDENTE
Via Tribunali, 120/121, Centro Storico
+39 081 210903
ilpizzaiolodelpresidente.it

ROSSOPOMODORO
Via Partenope, 11, Lungomare
+39 081 7646012
partenope.rossopomodoro.com

STARITA A MATERDEI
Via Materdei, 27-28, Capodimonte & the Sanità
pizzeriastarita.it
+39 081 5441485

DINNERS WITH A VIEW

(AL) CASTELLO RISTORANTE HOTEL CONTINENTAL
Via Partenope, 38/44, Lungomare
+39 081 2452068
royalgroup.it/royalcontinental

('A) FENESTELLA
Calata Ponticello, 23, Marechiaro
+39 081 7690020
afenestella.it

REGINELLA RISTORANTE
Via Posillipo, 45A, Posillipo
+39 081 5754020
ristorantereginella.com

RENZO E LUCIA
Via Tito Angelini, 33, Vomero
+39 081 19171022
renzoelucianapoli.it

FINE DINING

AMICI MIEI
Via Monte di Dio, 77/78, Monte di Dio, Chiaia
+39 081 7644981
ristoranteamicimiei.com

CARUSO ROOF GARDEN AT THE GRAND HOTEL VESUVIO
Via Partenope, 45, Lungomare
+39 081 7640044
vesuvio.it/il-lusso/ristorazione

(IL) COMANDANTE RISTORANTE HOTEL ROMEO
1 MICHELIN STAR
Via Cristoforo Colombo, 45, Municipio
+39 081 0175001
romeohotel.it/hotel/naples/en/Il-Comandante

WHERE TO EAT

CRU DO RÈ
Piazza Vittoria, 11/12, Lungomare
+39 81 764 5295
crudore.it

L'EUROPEO DI MATTOZZI - AVPN
Via Marchese Campodisola 4-8, near Piazza Bovio
+39 081 5521323
mattozzieuropeo.com

MIMI ALLA FERROVIA RISTORANTE
Via Alfonso D'Aragona, 19/21, Porta Capuana
+39 081 5538525
mimiallaferrovia.it

NAPOLI MIA
Riviera di Chiaia, 269, Chiaia
+39 081 5522266
ristorantenapolimia.it

PALAZZO PETRUCCI
1 MICHELIN STAR
Piazza San Domenico Maggiore, Centro Storico
+39 081 5524068
palazzopetrucci.it

(AL) POETA RISTORANTE
Piazza Salvatore Di Giacomo, 135, Posillipo
+39 081 5756936
ristorantelapoetanapoli.com

TERRAZZA CALABRITTO
Piazza Vittoria, 1, Chiaia
+39 081 2405188
terrazzacalabritto.it

UMBERTO RISTORANTE - AVPN
Via Alabardieri, 30/31, Chiaia
+39 081 418555
umberto.it

CASUAL FARE

ANTICA LATTERIA
Vico II Alabardieri, 30/32, Chiaia
+39 081 0128775
anticalatteria.it

(DA) ANTONIO
Via Depretis, 143, Municipio
+39 081 5510138

(LA) CANTINA DI VIA SAPIENZA
Via Sapienza, 40, Centro Storico
+39 081 459078
cantinadiviasapienza.it

DONNA TERESA OSTERIA
Via Michele Kerbaker, 58, Vomero
+39 081 5567070

MUU MUUZZARELLA LOUNGE
Vico II Alabardieri, 7, Chiaia
+39 081 405370
muumuuzzarellalounge.it

(DA) NENNELLA TRATTORIA
Vico Lungo Teatro Nuovo, 105, Municipio
+39 081 414338

DELL'OCA TRATTORIA
Via Santa Teresa A Chiaia, 11, Chiaia
+39 081 414865
trattoriadelloca.it

TANDEM
Via G. Paladino, 51, Centro Storico
+39 081 19002468
ristorantetandemragu.it

(DA) TONINO ANTICA OSTERIA
Via Santa Teresa a Chiaia, 47, Chiaia
+39 081 421533

(LE) ZENDRAGLIE TRIPPERIA & TRATTORIA
Via Pignasecca, 14, Municipio

+39 081 5511993
lezendraglie.it/en

CAFFÈ AND SWEET TREATS

ANHELO CAFFÈ BISTRO EMPORIO
Via Bisignano, 3, Chiaia
+39 081 402432
anhelonapoli.it

(F.LLI) ATTANASIO
Vico Ferrovia, 3, near the Central Train Station
+39 081 285675
sfogliatelleattanasio.it

BAR BRASILIANO
Galleria Umberto I, 78, Municipio
+39 081 413497

BILANCIONE
Via Posillipo, 238, Posillipo
+39 081 7691923

CAFFÈ MEXICO
Piazza Dante, Piazza Garibaldi and other locations around the city

CARRATURO
Via Casanova, 97, Porta Capuana
+39 081 5545364

CASA INFANTE
Via Toledo, Via Chiaia and other locations around the city
casainfante.it

CHALET CIRO
Via Mergellina, 31, Lungomare
+39 081 6699928
chaletciro.it

FANTASIA GELATI
Via Toledo, Via Chiaia and other locations around the city

+39 081 5511212
fantasiagelati.it

GAY-ODIN
Centro Storico, Chiaia and other locations around the city
gay-odin.it

GRAN CAFFÈ GAMBRINUS
Via Chiaia, 1/2, Municipio
+39 081 417582
grancaffegambrinus.com/en

GRAN CAFFÈ LA CAFFETTIERA
Piazza dei Martiri, 26, Chiaia
+39 081 7644243
grancaffelacaffettiera.com

MOCCIA
Via San Pasquale, 21-23, Chiaia
+39 081 411348

PATISSERIE S. CAPPARELLI
Via dei Tribunali, 325, Centro Storico
+39 081 454310

PINTAURO
Via Toledo, 275
+39 081 417339

SCATURCHIO
Piazza San Domenico Maggiore, 19, Centro Storico
San Carlo Theatre, Municipio
+39 081 5517031
scaturchio.it

(LA) SFOGLIATELLA MARY
Via Toledo, 66 inside Galleria Umberto I, Municipio
+39 081 402218

TARALLIFICIO LEOPOLDO
Chiaia, Vomero and other locations around the city
leopoldo.it

Pastiera

〰〰〰〰〰 ATMOSPHERIC APÉRITIFS 〰〰〰〰〰〰

• Mix wine and jazz 25 metres below ground in an ancient Greco-Roman cistern. p. 304

• Sip rooftop drinks in Bidder's Bar at Grand Hotel Parker's. grandhotelparkers.it/ita/hotel_ristorante_napoli.htm

• Sample a seaside spritz at Bar Partenope on the Lungomare.

• Release those champagne bubbles at the Beluga Skybar, Hotel Romeo. romeohotel.it/hotel/naples/en/Beluga-Skybar

• Educate your palate... Italian wine tasting in a medieval castle (May – Jun). vitignoitalia.it

• Fine tune your taste... Sommelier certifications from the Italian Association of Wine Sommeliers. aisnapoli.it/corsi-sommelier-napoli/

• Indulge yourself... the ultimate wine pairings with art, fashion, jewellery and design (May - Jun). wineandthecity.it

• Wine crawl through Chiaia's charming alleys. p. 162

• Eavesdrop on the spirited conversations at Piazza Bellini. p. 62

SHOP DAILY, SHOP LOCAL: NAPLES – A CITY OF MARKETS

A city's markets are the gateways to its soul. Or, if you will, veritable smorgasbords of local culture, customs and traditions. While street markets are a thing of the past in many other cities, by contrast Naples, with nearly 60 permanent markets (most are in the open-air) scattered across its neighbourhoods, is THE quintessential market city. And even as supermarkets slowly encroach on deeply rooted traditions, shopping at a local market is still a way of life.

Shopping in Naples' markets is an experience not to be missed! They are often crowded, usually chaotic and always animated. From food to fashion and everything in between, no matter what you seek or where, you'll definitely go home with more than you bargained for. With so many places to choose from the only question is where to start. The brave at heart should head to Naples' two biggest markets, Poggioreale on the eastern end of the city or Fuorigrotta on the west. For the toe-dippers there are many small neighbourhood markets like La Toretta and Chiaia that won't leave you frazzled. If you're looking for high end clothes and shoes, check out Posillipo. And for the best seafood in town head to Porta Nolana. Finally, don't forget that dozens of lively, colourful *mercati* and *mercatini* (small markets) pepper the region of Campania and a little exploring in places like Pozzuoli, Caserta and Monteruscello will reward the intrepid traveller.

WEEKEND ANTIQUES & COLLECTIBLES BY THE SEA: NAPLES' ANTIQUES MARKET

Weekends were made for strolling and what better place to stroll than an antiques market - the Fiera Antiquaria Napoletana? Whether you're buying or browsing, the market's eclectic assortment of antiques and collectibles will keep you occupied for hours and make for a great weekend jaunt. Set in one of the prettiest parts of the city, the market runs along the Villa Comunale Park. Open selected Sat and Sun throughout the year 08.00 – 14.00 on Viale Dohrn in Chiaia.

FOOD AND FASHION: THE CHIAIA MARKETS

If you live in Chiaia or are staying there, these two *mercatini* are a godsend. Fruit and vegetable stands rule at the daily open air market along Via Achille Torelli just off Via San Pasquale in Chiaia. At the east end of the market find the lone seafood stand spilling out of a local *pescheria* - a fishmonger's store. Along Via Vittorio Imbriani are some thirty stands selling mainly seasonal clothes, shoes, fabrics and accessories. Here, as in all the markets, if you're trying on shoes, the sellers are grateful if you keep the shoes on the pieces of cardboard provided, so as not to scuff the soles. Cars creep by slowly (you hope) 2 inches behind you as you shop so don't step backwards into the road without looking! Both markets are open daily 07.00 – 15.00.

SOLAR-POWERED SHOPPING: THE FUORIGROTTA MARKET

Known as La Canzanella, this market serves the everyday needs of the residents of the western end of the city. This is the product of an ambitious redevelopment project completed in 2007, when Fuorigrotta's fading market was moved into a brand new complex complete with an immaculate covered building that houses 218 of the market's 320 stalls and a covered parking area whose roof supplies solar power. It's clean, well organised and believe it or not, you'll even find toilets there. But don't let its pristine façade fool you. This market boasts some of the best prices, best quality and best range of goods – i.e. it sells everything - in the city. Open daily 07.00 – 19.30 on Via Metastasio in Fuorigrotta.

SHOP LIKE A LOCAL: THE PIGNASECCA

A favourite of locals, students and anyone on a tight budget, the Pignasecca is a wallet-friendly, bustling street market that offers a great selection of fresh seafood

Fuorigrotta Market

and produce, groceries and just about everything else imaginable. Open daily 07.00 – 15.00 on Via Pignasecca and Piazza Pignasecca.

SHOE ALLEY: THE POGGIOREALE MARKET

If you're looking for great bargains on shoes (and everything else for that matter) and have nerves of steel, head to Naples' largest open air market - Il Mercatino delle Scarpe. Jam-packed and frenetic, this market is not for the faint at heart. With some 550 vendors offering the best deals in the city, it can get so crowded you'll feel like a salmon swimming upstream. Open Fri, Sun & Mon 07.00 – 15.00 at Via Marino di Caramanico, north of the Poggioreale Prison.

NAPLES' BEST SEAFOOD MARKET: PORTA NOLANA

In the shadow of the two towers that once stood guard over the ancient port entrance to the city, you'll find Naples' best seafood market - Porta Nolana. If you don't mind crowds, chaos and confusion, this market is a must-visit. Of course, seafood isn't the only game in town. Fresh fruits and vegetables, meats and cheeses, breads and desserts and grocery items round out the market's offerings. Open daily 07.00 – 15.00 at Via Cesare Carmignano near the Circumvesuviana Train Station.

Remember - sea-fresh fish are also available at Rotonda Diaz and Pozzuoli harbour.

UNDER THE UMBRELLA PINES: POSILLIPO MARKET

It seems only fitting that the most picturesque neighbourhood in Naples also hosts the city's most elegant market. Posillipo market originated in 1984 in Piazza Salvatore di Giacomo but eventually found its home at Parco Virgiliano a Posillipo. Today, 140 stalls stretch along the entrance to the park, under the natural umbrella of the massive pines that line both sides of the promenade. From Armani suits to bathing suits, you'll find a seasonal assortment of clothes for every occasion and in every style; shoes, boots and handbags galore; cosmetics and jewellery and a wide assortment of household items and fabric. Open Thurs 09.00 – 14.00 on Viale Virgilio in Posillipo.

BEST DAILY SHOPPING: RIONE SANITÀ

Close by the Cavour Metro station Mercatino Rionale dei Vergini - the Rione Sanità daily market - is a bargain hunter's paradise and a convenience lover's dream. Here you'll find fresh produce aplenty, whether seafood, meat, fruit or vegetables as well as stuff to clean, to decorate or to eat in your flat. Add clothes, shoes and handbags galore. Open daily 07.00 – 15.00 on Via Vergini, Via Mario Pagano and Via Sanità.

ONE-STOP SHOPPING IN MERGELLINA: LA TORRETTA MARKET

Located in the Mergellina district, just a few blocks west of the American Embassy, La Toretta is one-stop shopping at its best. One of Naples' few covered markets, you'll find the convenience of everything in one place without the big market crowds or the supermarket feel. In this excellent combination of permanent market stalls and shops, fresh ingredients abound inside and out and you'll find everything you need for a romantic dinner for two or a dinner party for twenty. There's also an *enoteca* for your wine, a bread store, a chocolatier and a fresh pasta store. Open Mon - Sat 07.30 – 19.30; some stalls are open on Sundays at Via Giordano Bruno and Via Ferdinando Galiani in Mergellina.

CHRISTMAS ALLEY: VIA SAN GREGORIO ARMENO

Affectionately known as Christmas Alley by English speakers, Via San Gregorio Armeno is the tiny alley in Naples' Centro Storico world famous for the shops and artisan workshops that make and sell Naples' foremost artisan craft - the *presepe*. Open year round; hours vary by shop.

OLD AND NEW: THE VOMERO MARKETS

A great start to any day in the Vomero is a stroll through its market streets. Though they are often lumped together, Vomero has two major markets: the historic food market known as Il Mercatino di Antignano (a reference to the ancient Roman road known as Via Antignano that traversed Vomero hill) and the market that sells everything else: clothes, shoes, handbags, household goods and more. It's one of the oldest markets in the city and is open daily 07.00 – 15.00 along Via Annella di Massimo to Piazza degli Artisti, one of the oldest districts of the Vomero. The "other" market, known simply as the Vomero market picks up at Via Casale de Bustis Marcello and runs to Piazza Medaglie d'Oro and is open daily 07.00 – 19.30. To shop food then fashion, take M1 to the Quattro Giornate station and head north-east. For fashion then food, take the M1 to the Medaglie d'Oro station and head south-west.

THE BACK STORY

The Napoli Unplugged Guide to Naples – four women united by a common passion have created an extraordinary tribute to the city they love.

Barbara Zaragoza moved to Naples for her husband's work and for three years she set off, kids in tow, to explore Naples and beyond, recording her adventures in her blog, *The Espresso Break*. Soon after returning to the U.S., those blog pages became the guidebook, *The Espresso Break: Tours and Nooks of Naples, Italy and Beyond*. Barbara enlisted Penny Ewles-Bergeron, a writer and artist living in the heart of Naples at the time to edit *The Espresso Break*.

Around the same time, Bonnie Alberts was busy creating *Napoli Unplugged*, a website that has become the English language voice of Naples and a true labour of love as, day by day, she presents her adoptive city to the world. She and Penny met through the website and became fast friends, bonding over their shared fascination with the city and serial plates of pasta genovese (research). The trio's current venture brings together content from Barbara's book and blog and Bonnie's website along with a substantial quantity of new material written by Bonnie and Penny, who also served as editor-in-chief. Erin Romano, a graphics designer who lives in Positano, completes this quartet of women who share a passion for Naples. The layout and design of the book is owed entirely to Erin's creative vision.

The book is illustrated by a blend of Bonnie's photographs enlivened with ink and watercolour paintings by urban sketchers Lorenzo Dotti and Simonetta Capecchi. Rome-based *plein air* painter Kelly Medford was commissioned to paint four new views of Naples in oil and these feature in the book, one of them providing the beautiful cover illustration and she is the brush behind the maps in Rambles Through Naples. Rome blogger, tweeter, beach girl and author of the *Amalfi Coast Travel Essentials* iPhone app, Gillian Longworth McGuire added her expertise to the Seaside Delights: The Bay of Naples & The Amalfi Coast. Finally, Holly Willmott, an English teacher living in Naples and whose mastery of the Italian language rivals that of her native tongue, was relentless in tracking down every last detail in the "Plan Your Visit" sections and navigating the various Italian bureaucracies in hot pursuit of photo permissions. And as the Napoli Unplugged News and Events Co-ordinator, Holly kept the website humming while Bonnie was otherwise consumed with the book.

MEET THE TEAM

BONNIE ALBERTS

After a long (and unrewarding) career in the high-tech industry, Bonnie went back to school and earned her degree in Historic Preservation. Six months later she found herself living in Naples where she immediately put her training to use. Her curiosity and love of the story took her all over the city and Campania and she recorded everything she took in with a camera and a pen. That work became the basis of *Napoli Unplugged* and the rest, as they say, is history. Today, Bonnie is busy working on the next books in this series, *the Napoli Unplugged Guide to the Bay and the Amalfi Coast* and the *Napoli Unplugged Guide to Campania*. Meanwhile it's business as usual on the website; those updates won't write themselves!

BARBARA ZARAGOZA

Barbara Zaragoza is a freelance writer whose prose embraces history, local cuisine, myth, archaeology, politics and more. While living in Naples she penned the *Espresso Break* blog and went on to write *The Espresso Break: Tours and Nooks of Naples, Italy and Beyond*. Since moving back to California, Barbara has continued to be a freelance writer of many books, articles and websites.

PENNY EWLES-BERGERON

Writer and artist Penny Ewles-Bergeron is the English half of an Anglo-American couple who met through an advert in satirical magazine *Private Eye*. Their love affair with Italy began with a honeymoon in San Gimignano. For seven joyful years they enjoyed a wildly different part of the country, living in the very heart of Naples. Though they now reside in England, Penny's passion for the city continues to find daily expression on social media, as her numerous Twitter followers can attest. She was delighted when Barbara Zaragoza invited her to edit *The Espresso Break* and returns to her favourite subject as editor and contributor to the Napoli Unplugged Guide to Naples.

ERIN ROMANO

Growing up in a number of foreign countries, Erin Romano had wanderlust from an early age. Travelling and exploring were like food and water, and thanks to her career as a graphic designer, she was able to continue working as she roamed. She eventually found herself in Florence, Italy studying Italian and immersing herself in the culture. A couple of years later, she met her now-husband while traveling in the South. They currently live on the Amalfi Coast with their son.

MILLE GRAZIE

Steve & Tom; Robert, Nadia, Sofia & Mimi; Jim & Phoebe; Pasquale & Giovanni - our husbands and amazing children for their love, support and encouragement.
Ann Pizzorusso, Napoli Unplugged's resident geologist, creator of the website's *EarthScape Naples* series, and author of *Tweeting Da Vinci* for her expertise, wise council, unwavering support and enduring friendship.
Michael McOsker, a classics scholar who lived in Naples while studying the Papyrus Scrolls at the National Library. Michael wrote about the scrolls in the Municipio section and made major contributions to the Vesuvius Excavations section.
The Noi Boys, who have been huge supporters of Napoli Unplugged over the years - Rick Breco, Massimo Topo and especially Giuseppe Topo, the Napoli Unplugged resident chef and star of the "Cooking with Giuseppe" series.
GB Bernadini for his kind permission to republish material from Penny and Barbara that previously appeared on the Italian Notebook website. Also for his continued wonderful work in presenting Italy to an anglophone audience in daily notes.
Tricia Reynolds and the American International Women's Club, Naples, a constant source of information and inspiration. The AIWC represents decades of experience and lived history of the city, something to be celebrated and treasured.
Michelle Sterry, whose Facebook messages led us to a number of the lesser known curiosities around the city.

Our thanks are also due to all those who supported and encouraged our endeavours: Adrian Bedford, Deborah Bernardi, Cristian Bonetto, Tina Carignani, Giorgio Cossu, Françoise Clechet, Riccardo Dalisi, Rossana Di Poce, Massimo di Porzio, Carmen De Rosa, Elisabetta De Rosa and the entire staff at Centro Italiano, Ferrante di Somma, Maria Giovanna di Somma, Brandy Falconer, Francesco Filippini, Diego and Annie Forquet, Michelangelo Iossa, Maria Irace, Joshua John Lawrence, Carlo Leggiere, Marinella Lista, Magda Marasco, Teresa Massa, Gabriel and Oana Moldovan, the Pellino family - Carlo, Claudia, Massimo, Sonia and Salvatore, Cynthia and Renato Penna, Dario Pennino, Giuseppe and Rosa Perone, Salvatore Pica, Wendy L. Price, Gennaro Reder, Douglas W. Sanford, Gabriella Sannino, Kathy Sherak, Miscenka Solima, Mario Squillace, Pietro Treccagnoli, Francesco Vecchione.

Final thanks are due to the many Neapolitans who work in cultural heritage sites, often under severe budgetary constraints and over long hours to preserve the artefacts of the city and answer the many questions posed by visitors. We've lost count of the number of times they have gone the extra mile to share their knowledge or to show us something extraordinary – a view, a painting, a single rose with a heavenly scent. These ambassadors of Naples are too many to name individually but we are grateful to them for such warm-heartedness.

THE FINE PRINT

Cover Design by Erin Sloan and Kelly Medford
Creative Cartography by Kelly Medford
Sketches by Kelly Medford, Lorenzo Dotti and Simonetta Capecchi

Publishing Information

ISBN: 978-0-9908051-0-6

First edition published March 2015 by
Partenope Press
411 Walnut Street #7120
Green Cove Springs, FL 32043-3443
www.partenopepress.com
info@partenopepress.com

Printed in South Korea by WeSP for Four Colour Print Group, Louisville, Kentucky

Updates and Errors
The authors and publisher have taken all care and precautions preparing this guide, however, we make no warranty about the accuracy or completeness of its content and accept no responsibility for any loss, injury, or inconvenience sustained by any traveller as a result of information or advice contained in this guide.

IMAGES

Many of the images in this guide are available for licensing from napoliunplugged.com

All images © Napoli Unplugged Images except the following:

Associazione Tunnel Borbonico, Bourbon Tunnel, p. 298
Associazione Verace Pizza Napoletana (AVPN), AVPN Pizza Map, p. 350 - 353
Capecchi, Simonetta, Urban Sketcher
• Palazzo Donn'Anna, p. 310 - 311
• Santa Maria Francesca delle Cinque Piaghe, p. 323
Dotti, Lorenzo, Urban Sketcher
• Antro della Sibilla, Acropoli di Cuma, 2009, p. 204 - 205
• Castel dell'Ovo from Santa Lucia, 2008, p. 132

- 133
• Castel Sant'Elmo, 2008, p. 174 - 175
• Piazza San Gaetano, 2009, p. 54 - 55
• Pompeii Amphitheatre, 2009, p. 226 - 227
• San Martino Charterhouse, 2007, p. 170 - 171
Ewles-Bergeron, Penny, Paestum Wildflowers, 2006, p. 285
Fondazione Mondragone, Elena Aldobrandini Textile and Costume Museum, p. 183
Heidesheimer, S. & Co., Il Vesuvio, postcard ca.1905, p. 234
Medford, Kelly, Artist, Creative Cartography, 2014
• Centro Storico, p. 52 - 53
• Capodimonte & the Sanità, p. 108 - 109
• Chiaia, p. 148 - 149
• Lungomare, p. 130 - 131
• Municipio & the City Centre, p. 26 - 27
• Porta Capuana, p. 82 - 83
• Vomero Hill, p. 168 - 169
Medford, Kelly , Artist, Plein Air Paintings, 2014
• The Bay of Naples, Front Cover
• Lungomare, p. 197
• Panorama of Monte di Dio, Back Cover
• Via Chiaia, p. 155
Napoli Sotterranea, Napoli Sotterranea, p. 294
Ragozino, Ettore, L'eruzione del Vesuvio (Aprile 1906), postcard c.1910, p. 263
Romano, Luciano for Teatro San Carlo, Teatro San Carlo, p. 46
Sherak, Kathy, Alfredo Imparato in Piazza San Gaetano, 2013, p. 65

Our sincerest gratitude to the following organisations who:

Provided images for use in this guide:

Associazione Tunnel Borbonico
Associazione Verace Pizza Napoletana (AVPN)
Fondazione Mondragone
Napoli Sotterranea
Teatro San Carlo

Authorised the use of our images in this guide:

Catacombe di Napoli
Comune di Napoli (Fontanelle Cemetery)
Fondo Edifici di Culto
Gaetano Filangieri Municipal Museum
Soprintendenza Speciale per i Beni Archeologici di Napoli
Soprintendenza Speciale per i Beni Archeologici di Pompei, Ercolano e Stabia
Soprintendenza Per i Beni Archeologici di Salerno, Avellino, Benevento e Caserta
Vulcano Solfatara srl

THEMATIC INDEX

PANORAMIC VIEWS

PARKS & NATURE